idc Institute for Diversity Certification™

The Institute for Diversity Certification would like to thank the following contributors:

Delmar Lee, PhD, CDE;

Ann Bargains, PhD, CDP;

Dr. Deidra Dennie, CDE; and

Karla Rodgers, PHR, SHRM-CP, CDP

All rights reserved. No part of this book may be reproduced by any mechanical, photographic, or electronic process, or in the form of a phonographic recording; nor may it be stored in a retrievable system, transmitted, or otherwise be copied for public or private use- other than for "fair use" as brief quotations embodied in articles and reviews- without prior written permission from The Society for Diversity Inc.

Copyright © 2018 by The Society for Diversity Inc. (an Indiana Corporation), DBA Institute for Diversity Certification, Registration Number: TX 8-450-560, effective April 11, 2017

Institute for Diversity Certification (IDC) is a Registered Trademark by the United States of America US Patent and Trademark Office, Reg. No: 5,226,655, Registered June 20, 2017, Int. Cl.: 41

Certified Diversity Professional (CDP) is a Registered Trademark by the United States of America US Patent and Trademark Office, Reg. No: 5,208,283, Registered May 23, 2017, Int. Cl.:41

CERTIFIED DIVERSITY PROFESSIONAL (CDP)® EXAM STUDY GUIDE

Table of Contents

The Role of a Diversity Practitioner 3

The Business Case for Diversity & Inclusion 26

EEO Laws in the US and Abroad 49

Harassment Around the World 94

Diversity Recruiting & Retention 120

Reinventing Diversity Training 137

Handling Difficult Conversations 167

Employee Resource Groups & Diversity Councils 184

Empowering Women in the Workplace 198

Disability & Special Needs Accommodations 215

Generational Intelligence 241

Designing Programs for Veterans 259

Immigrant Groups in the Workplace 275

Navigating Through Religion & Belief Systems 302

LGBTQ+ Inclusion 326

Measuring the Impact of Diversity & Inclusion 346

CDP Answer Key

References

THE ROLE OF A DIVERSITY PRACTITIONER

> *The field of Diversity and Inclusion is constantly changing. As key strategists, Diversity Practitioners must not only be prepared for revolutionary Inclusion, they must also be adept in leading change. Hence, the role of the Diversity Practitioner is not for the fearful, neither is it for the novice. It is a position of power, courage, and accountability for a visionary strategist who is willing to breathe new life into ordinary business practices and intolerant work environments.*

OVERALL OBJECTIVES AND COMPETENCIES

The purpose of this competency is to empower practitioners to assemble the foundational components of a successful Diversity and Inclusion effort by creating a strategic plan and developing standard operating procedures. Diversity and Inclusion leaders must also be competent in effectively communicating the role of a Diversity Practitioner.

BACKGROUND AND CONTEXT

Although modern-day Diversity and Inclusion efforts are global, the field has roots in American history. During the 1960s and 1970s, the U.S. took its first steps toward promoting diversity in the workplace. In 1961, President John F. Kennedy established the President's Committee on Equal Employment Opportunity, the goal of which was to end discrimination in employment by the government and its contractors. The Civil Rights Act of 1964 went further, prohibiting discrimination in any federal program or activity.

The following year President Lyndon B. Johnson went further still with an executive order to promote equal employment opportunities through "a positive, continuing program in each department and agency". This was a turning point for the Civil Rights Act because it moved from prohibiting consideration of "race, creed, color, or national origin" to acting on the principle that fairness required more than a commitment to impartial treatment. In 1971, the Nixon Administration took this one step further in a revised order requiring contractors to develop an affirmative action program with goals and timetables. Nevertheless, legal mandates had little effect on attitudes, behaviors, or subtle discrimination.

While organizational human resource efforts improved, the behavior of individual employees within organizations often did not improve. Moreover, employers found that simply hiring a more diverse workforce did not bring some of the benefits expected. In fact, evidence suggested that management would have to take a more sustained and committed approach in order to realize the benefits of diversity. This remedial approach gave way, during the 1980s, under the recognition that diversity should not only be legislated or mandated, but also valued as a business attribute.

Training, at the time, focused on employee attitudes, as businesses and government agencies tried to raise awareness of, and increase employee sensitivity to, diversity issues.

From the mid-1980s to the late 1990s, the role of Diversity Officer, Director, or Manager lacked positive connotations in the business world and offered no career path. It was often an obscure role far down in the HR organization or otherwise occupied some anomalous and essentially powerless position on the organizational chart. Some employers put individuals into the diversity role who had no previous experience, people whose careers were in decline, or someone who happened to be a visible minority with a passion for diversity. The same type of person was placed into an Affirmative Action or Equal Employment Opportunity (EEO) role. Diversity strategies were not tied to business results and diversity professionals were not expected to be strategic business partners or demonstrate strong business acumen.

Table 1 documents the evolution of the field and demonstrates how the skills of Diversity and Inclusion leaders must adjust to the changing nature of the work.

TABLE 1: THE EVOLUTION OF WORKFORCE DIVERSITY

Model	Ideology	Focus	Driver	Benefits	Foundation
Affirmative Action	Remedial	Equal opportunity	Laws	Targeted groups	Assimilation model
Valuing Diversity	Idealistic	Appreciation of differences	Ethics	All employees	Diversity model
Managing Diversity	Practical	Building skills and changing policies	Corporate strategy	The organization and all employees	Synergy model
High Performance	Inclusive	Growth, continual change, and tangible impact	Globalization and demographics	The organization, all employees, shareholders, vendors, and other partners	Integrated business model

FROM AFFIRMATIVE ACTION TO CHANGE AGENT

The focal point of diversity work has shifted from counting people of color or women, towards creating a space that is inclusive of everyone. Some African Americans in the field of diversity believe that including everyone "waters down" the purpose of creating diversity programs in the first place. While true in some ways, in other ways, this philosophy neglects the intent of Affirmative Action—which is the origin of Diversity and Inclusion programs. The intent of Affirmative Action was to create a level playing field for all, not empowering some, while disenfranchising others. This merely reverses unfairness and inequity.

Today, diversity is no longer an issue of equity in hiring practices; it is a modern-day strategy for success. Deloitte University Press recently updated its *Global Human Capital Trends Report*, which illustrates why D&I efforts should shift. In 2015, culture, leadership, learning, and development were at the top of the list (Figure 2). By 2017, global leaders' priorities shifted to preparing for the organization of the future, as well as addressing careers and learning (Figure 3). Hence, D&I leaders must also be flexible enough to flow with shifting priorities.

Figure 2. Talent trends: Global importance vs. readiness

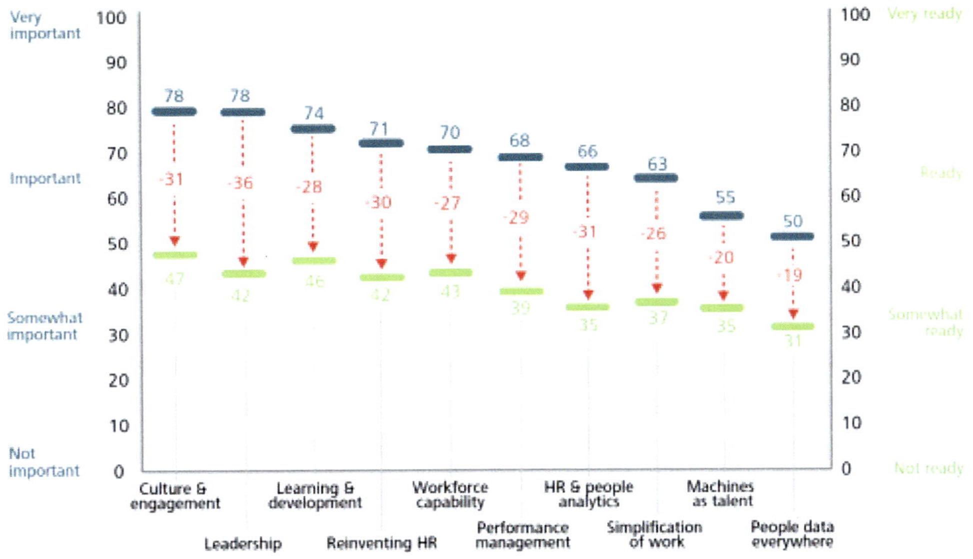

Figure 3. The 2017 trends by importance

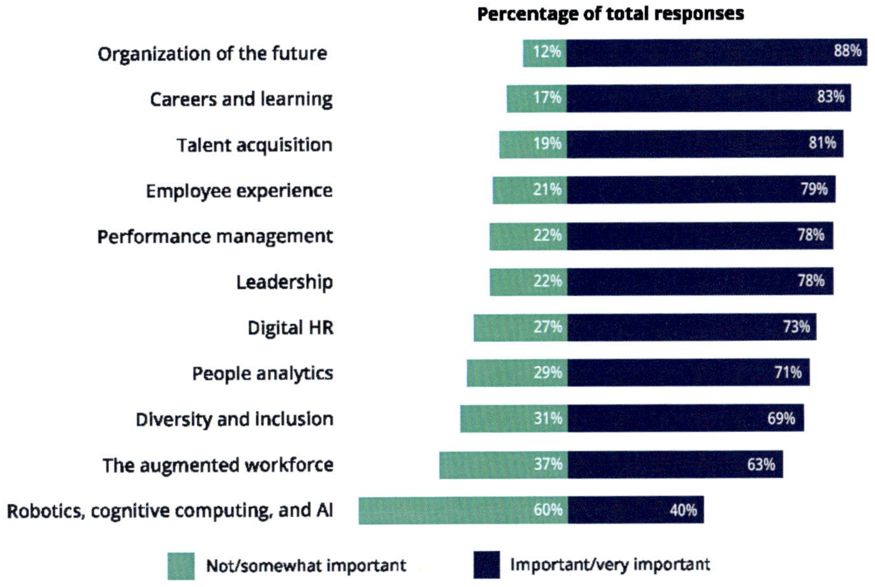

Trend	Not/somewhat important	Important/very important
Organization of the future	12%	88%
Careers and learning	17%	83%
Talent acquisition	19%	81%
Employee experience	21%	79%
Performance management	22%	78%
Leadership	22%	78%
Digital HR	27%	73%
People analytics	29%	71%
Diversity and inclusion	31%	69%
The augmented workforce	37%	63%
Robotics, cognitive computing, and AI	60%	40%

Note: Ratings for "The augmented workforce" and "Robotics, cognitive computing, and AI" both relate to the broader trend on "The future of work" discussed in this report.

Deloitte University Press | dupress.deloitte.com

Around the world, senior level leaders are very concerned about issues connected to Diversity and Inclusion (D&I). However, many do not understand that culture, innovation, engagement, relationships, operational excellence and leadership are inextricably tied to an organizations equity and inclusion practices.

In 2016, BCG and the Technical University of Munich conducted a study of diversity managers, human resource executives, and managing partners at 171 German, Swiss and Austrian companies. The empirical analysis found a clear relationship between the diversity on a company's management team and the revenues they generated from innovative products and services. Among the key findings:

- The positive relationship between diversity and innovation is statistically significant, with higher levels of diversity netting more revenue from new products and services.

- The innovation boost isn't limited to a single type of diversity, such as gender. Innovation can be driven from multiple dimensions of diversity.

- Management diversity has a positive effect on complex companies and/or larger organizations.

- Having a high percentage of diversity within the lower ranks of an organization doesn't account for anything if the diversity is not reflected in management.

- At companies with diverse management teams, openness to ideas/contributions from lower level employees and nurturing an environment where diverse perspectives are valued, are key traits in fostering innovation.

Figure 4 illustrates the results of the study.

Figure 4

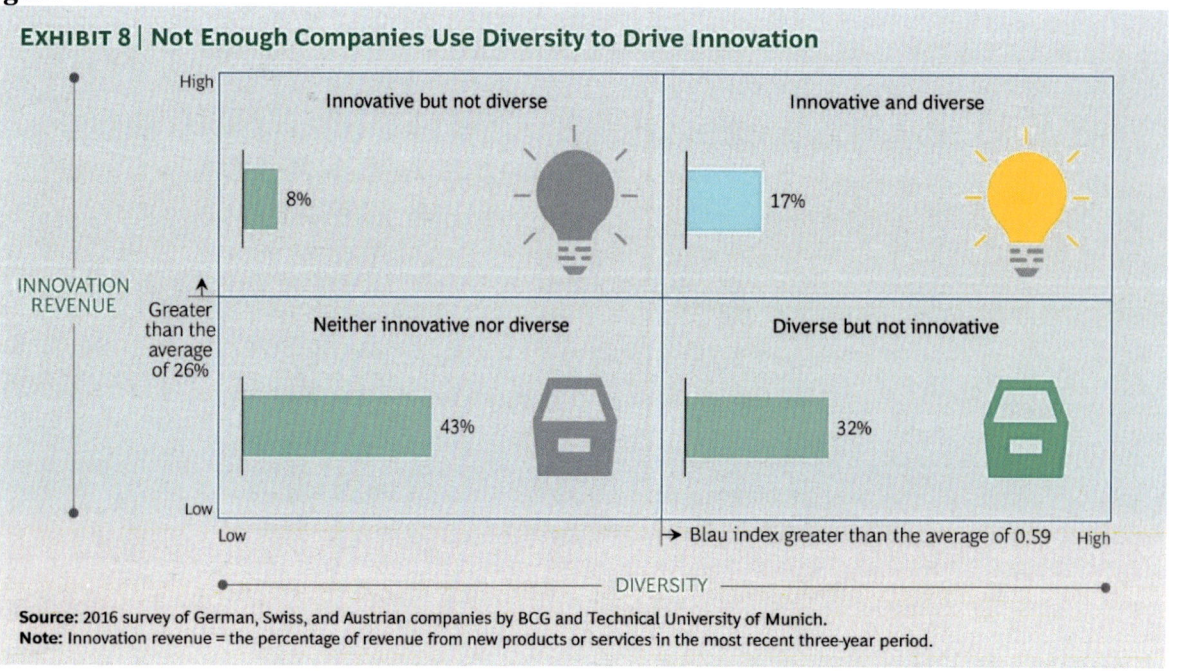

EXHIBIT 8 | Not Enough Companies Use Diversity to Drive Innovation

INNOVATION REVENUE (High / Greater than the average of 26% / Low)

- Innovative but not diverse: 8%
- Innovative and diverse: 17%
- Neither innovative nor diverse: 43%
- Diverse but not innovative: 32%

DIVERSITY (Low → Blau index greater than the average of 0.59 → High)

Source: 2016 survey of German, Swiss, and Austrian companies by BCG and Technical University of Munich.
Note: Innovation revenue = the percentage of revenue from new products or services in the most recent three-year period.

Similar studies have been verified by Gallup, McKinsey & Company, Catalyst, Credit Suisse, and many other organizations in recent years. However, if the data is there to support the inclusion of different groups, why are so many companies struggling with the creation, and presence, of a diversity practitioner position? Part of the reason is grounded in the fact that senior managers still equate Diversity and Inclusion work with Affirmative Action. As long as managers liken the purpose of D&I with counting how many women or people of color are visible in the organization, the position is relegated to an outdated workplace model of limited effectiveness. (Refer to Table 1)

As you think about D&I's purpose, it is easy to see why Diversity and Inclusion must advance its focus beyond equity in hiring. In fact, because of globalization, shifting demographics, and changing competition, Diversity and Inclusion will be a key element in how organizations do business better.

Globalization is the process of interaction and integration amongst the people, companies, and governments of different nations. It is an ongoing global convergence driven by international trade and investment and aided by information technology. This process influences the environment, culture, political systems, economic development, and human physical well-being of societies around the world. Globalization, in effect, expands the context in which organizations function. It creates an opportunity to disseminate information, glean best practices, or compete for larger market share. Globalization is also one of the key reasons why diversity is not going away. *Think about it like this:* it is improbable that a *multi-billion*-dollar, *multi-national* company would dial back its efforts so that it can generate hundreds of thousands of dollars in one country.

Demographics are statistical characteristics of a population. Demographics, or demographic data, are selected population characteristics used in government, marketing, opinion research, or other statistical analyses. Commonly examined demographics include gender, age, ethnicity, knowledge of languages, disabilities, home ownership, employment status, and geographic location. Demographic trends describe the historical changes in a population over time (for example, the average age of a population may increase or decrease over time). Within an organization or field, customers, students, patients or constituents may also change over time. Thus, diversity practitioners must learn to understand and master demographic data and trends in their industry; provide insights about different demographic groups; as well as explain why customer preferences, expectations and priorities matter to an organization. All countries keep track of their demographics through a census. Most countries conduct census every 10 years, and nations are finding that demographics are changing at a rapid pace around the world.

Finally, the nature of competition is changing. In the past, an organization's competitors were fairly linear. Today, the cross-sectoral nature of competition makes the idea of industry domination complex. This means that organizations must re-think how and where they will play, as well as reimagine the strategy for culture, innovation, engagement, relationships, operational excellence, and leadership.

Once again, as competition evolves, the nature of diversity work must evolve as well. The current integrated business model (see Table 1) incorporates Diversity and Inclusion into all aspects of the organizational strategy. Therefore, diversity practitioners can no longer merely serve as diversity awareness trainers and coordinators for multicultural celebrations; they must act as front-line strategists. Diversity practitioners must lead organizations to understand that these dynamics have evolved the role of diversity practitioner from its earlier incarnations in equal opportunity and compliance officers to that of a change agent. In this demanding new role, the diversity practitioner must be able to help guide the company through a cultural transformation to harness the business value of Diversity and Inclusion as a core competency of the organization.

The Future of the Position
As more organizations seize global opportunities, the position of the Diversity Practitioner will become increasingly important. Diversity will be useful for every type of entity including:

- *For-profit, nonprofit, government and educational institutions*
- *Domestic and international organizations*
- *Companies in every stage of development including start-up, growth, mature, and declining*

The most successful organizations will understand how to leverage the power of the Office of Diversity for information, cost containment, innovation, branding, outreach, relationship management, etc.

Ideally, the Diversity Practitioner will report to a Chief Diversity Officer, who will report directly to the President. However, in many organizations, Diversity Practitioners report to the Senior Vice President of Human Resources, and on some occasions, directly to the President. In other cases, the Diversity Practitioner may be a Consultant, Diversity Champion, Diversity Council, or Resource Group Member. There are a number of different reporting structures that may exist; however, as a whole, Diversity and Inclusion is not the sole domain of Human Resources or Talent Management.

OVERVIEW OF COMPETENCIES

Within the Diversity and Inclusion space is the concept of a "toolbox", which is a set of programs or functions used to accelerate change. Traditionally, some professionals in the field have led with training or recruiting tools. However, it is necessary for D&I leaders to expand their toolbox to encompass: coaching, mentoring, updating policies, communicating, listening, planning, sponsoring, researching, assessing/analyzing, managing, piloting, comparing, introducing or fine-tuning work-life programs, measuring, and more. Ideally, an effective intervention will combine multiple tools to drive effectiveness at various stages of the organization's development.

The foundation of the Office of Diversity and Inclusion is change. The word *change* is a verb that means to replace one thing for another or to become different. Change in business often denotes that a company must engage in a process in which they alter their organization for a structured purpose. Rather than making changes for the sake of change, organizations must have a plan for change that improves current processes or maximizes profit. Change management can involve defining new business values or behaviors, generating an agreement to better meet the needs of customers or stakeholders involved in the business, or transitioning the company's organizational structure to improve operations.

Unfortunately, not every change process leads to expected results, especially in the field of Diversity and Inclusion. There are two issues that can derail or complicate Diversity and Inclusion efforts. First, the dynamics of the external environment place many organizations in a state of continuous change. A perpetually changing environment can present challenges for diversity practitioners who must reach goals, while the organization is constantly focused on resolving short-term needs.

Second, the change process takes time and a lot of work. It is easy for Diversity and Inclusion Practitioners to focus on the activities that are visible to employees and senior management (i.e., training and events) but neglect the substantive business aspects (i.e., planning and evaluation). Other factors that can influence failure in the Office of Diversity include: unexpected changes in ownership (e.g., a merger or acquisition), a lack of leadership commitment, resistance from mid-level management, and an overly passive Diversity Officer. The implications of failed change initiatives go beyond missed objectives. More important is the negative symbolism and skepticism that may develop for future change projects; these can be viewed as "another fancy idea from management".

However, it is possible for diversity practitioners to minimize the potential for failure-- even in environments that are far from perfect. In addition to being highly competent, a diversity practitioner can utilize differing levels of change skills to accomplish organizational goals.

Figure 5 illustrates the various levels.

FIGURE 5: LEVELS OF CHANGE LEADERSHIP SKILLS
Source: "Are You a Change Leader?" By Jim Canterucci

Level I	- Accepts the need for change; communicates and defends the need for change throughout the organization; creates an open and receptive environment - Develops small change initiatives with clear direction
Level II	- Defines and initiates change; identifies leverage points for change in processes and work habits - Executes change projects at the local level
Level III	- Leads change; translates the vision of the organization into the context of a specific change initiative and brings this message to the entire organization; redirects approaches in the face of new opportunities - Transformation of a central vision into change initiatives and organization-wide communication
Level IV	- Manages complex change; understands the cultural dynamics of the current state of an organization, creates a strategic practical course, balancing the current reality with the need for rapid adoption of the desired future reality - Generates change with a high degree of transformation
Level V	- Champions change, challenges the status quo by comparing it to an ideal or a vision of change; causes crisis in order to support dramatic actions and change efforts; transforms the organization - Able to revolutionize organizations

A Change Agent is an individual or a group who takes responsibility for changing the existing pattern of behavior of a person or social system. This person must be able to support the implementation of a new idea and bring it into fruition. This movement and involvement of people requires a high degree of Emotional Intelligence (EI), which refers to the ability to perceive, control, and evaluate emotions—both of self and of others. Emotional intelligence entails understanding that the role of Change Agent may not be popular because the agent's responsibility is to affect change, not to gain popularity. Concurrently, Change Agents must possess the ability to communicate, understand, and consider the opinions and doubts of others. This refers to self-awareness, and it will alleviate the tensions and mistakes caused by blind spots.

In addition to being a Change Agent, the Diversity Practitioner must possess other competencies and skills in order to achieve maximum effectiveness. These competencies and skills are:

Strategic
1. Ability to set clearly defined and realistic goals in a strategic diversity plan.
2. Knack for linking Diversity and Inclusion tenets to business objectives.
3. Capacity to demonstrate the financial impact of Diversity and Inclusion.
4. Foresight to prepare for the workforce and marketplace of the future.

Knowledge of Diversity Issues
1. Excellent command of diversity issues within, and outside of, your organization.
2. Understanding of the laws, international landscape, and employee policies.
3. Knowledge of the cultural climate, different demographic groups, and business case for diversity at your organization.
4. Adept in illustrating how diverse dimensions overlap, as well as describing how equity or Inclusion issues intersect with traditional business functions such as management, communication, etc.

Politically Savvy
1. Astute at navigating the political environment; responds well to politically charged or politically sensitive issues, such as race and religion.
2. Aware of top management perceptions, changes in key personnel, market conditions, and the way in which these things impact Diversity and Inclusion goals.
3. Ability to present win-win solutions when contentious circumstances arise, as well as to build consensus, accrue buy-in, and work through competing interests.

Champion for Diversity
1. Personal enthusiasm in expressing Diversity and Inclusion plans and ideas.
2. Adept at stimulating motivation and commitment in others.
3. Tolerant of ambiguity—able to function comfortably, patiently and effectively in an uncertain environment.

Collaborator
1. Skilled in influencing and gaining commitment from potential skeptics and resisters for project plans and ideas.
2. Ability to work successfully with others to ensure Diversity and Inclusion is a priority.
3. Proficient in mindfulness, empathy, compassion, and emotional intelligence.

Diversity & Inclusion Consultant
1. Challenge the status quo and present innovative solutions to common workplace issues.
2. Serve as an example of excellence-- going above and beyond expectations.

3. Adaptable to different audiences and exhibiting passion and patience—understanding that change does not happen overnight.
4. Resourceful and responsive to issues and requests.

Excellent Communicator
1. Succinctly describes the role of the Office of Diversity, as well as summarizes the organization's Diversity and Inclusion accomplishments in an annual report.
2. Effectively transmits to colleagues and subordinates the need for changes in Diversity and Inclusion goals or in individual tasks and responsibilities.
3. Strong interpersonal skills across the board, including listening, collecting appropriate information, identifying the concerns of others, and managing meetings.

Results-Oriented
1. Accountable for, desirous of, and committed to achieving significant results, although not singularly responsible.
2. Detail oriented, and skilled, in tracking projects and programs from start to finish.
3. Focused on measurable outcomes and tangible organizational benefits.
4. Proficient in managing multiple tasks and functional employees for maximum results.

Many individuals still view the role of Diversity Practitioner as an "unnecessary waste" of resources. Nevertheless, the Diversity Practitioner's role is not to debate with these individuals. Instead, the Practitioner's role should be to help them understand the business advantages of Diversity and Inclusion. Remember, Diversity and Inclusion is not just about changing people at work; first and foremost, we want to change organizations.

THE ROLE OF THE STRATEGIC DIVERSITY PLANNER

Strategic diversity planning is an ongoing process that maps, controls, and evaluates an organization's Diversity and Inclusion efforts.

In today's highly competitive business environment, event planning or budget-oriented planning methods are insufficient for an organization's Diversity and Inclusion efforts to survive and prosper. An organization must engage in a strategic diversity planning process that explores critical questions such as:

- What is the vision for our organization's Diversity and Inclusion efforts?
- What is our philosophy? What are our ethical concerns, social responsibilities, and values?
- What did our customers/students/constituents look like 20 years ago? What did our customers/students/constituents look like 10 years ago?
- Describe the demographic make-up of your current customers/students/constituents.
- What new demographics can we tap into to increase our market share in 5-10 years? Why?
- How will our market change in the next 5-10 years? What trends are occurring in our industry?

- What key competencies should employees possess? How do we measure the gap between current and required skills? Who do we need to hire to meet the future needs of our market?
- What role will our Board of Directors play? How can we increase diversity on the Board or otherwise engage the Board in leading Diversity and Inclusion?
- How can we find highly qualified and diverse talent to meet our customers'/students'/constituents' projected needs?
- How can we best reach, or communicate with, our current and prospective customers/students/constituents? Employees? Volunteers?
- What role will employee resource groups play in our organization's growth and development? What role will the Corporate Diversity Council play?
- What value do we want suppliers to bring to our organization? How can diverse suppliers advance our corporate goals?
- How can we best link our diversity plan to our organization's strategic goals?

Effective strategy formulation skills are highly prized in corporate leaders. The ability to develop operational business strategies and take those business strategies from plan to action (or to rethink them on short notice) sets true leaders apart from their peers. Forward-looking strategy formulation can make the difference between a profitable organization and one that stagnates.

To begin a successful process, review your current plan. If you do not have a plan, here is how to get started:

Step 1: Conduct a Diversity Climate Analysis or Cultural Audit

You can find out what employees need, as well as determine what they really think about inclusion, by conducting a Diversity Climate Analysis. This assessment is important because it will help you to properly diagnose the organization's issues. It can be done via focus group, anonymous survey, or through e-mail feedback. Get creative to ensure that everyone is involved. If a random sampling is selected, make sure the selected group represents a broad spectrum of individuals throughout your organization.

Examples of questions that you could ask include:

- Have you witnessed behavior or heard comments that were discriminatory or biased (such as jokes, non-inclusive language, double standards, exclusion in meetings, harassment, etc.)?
- Are you comfortable working with individuals from different ethnicities? Different economic statuses? Different languages?
- Are you satisfied with your job?
- What is the perception of management?
- How would you rate communication and collaboration within the organization?
- What hinders or contributes to your sense of productivity? Creativity? Risk taking?
- Do you feel you have the tools and resources to perform your job effectively? Does your manager properly support you?
- What type of training should be required?

Once the employee's needs are determined, develop a plan that addresses professional development concerns, as well as justifies the need for ongoing diversity interventions.

Step 2: Conduct a SWOT Analysis

A SWOT Analysis is a strategic planning method used to evaluate the **S**trengths, **W**eaknesses, **O**pportunities, and **T**hreats involved in your diversity initiatives.

FIGURE 6: SWOT ANALYSIS

Strengths
Attributes of the organization that are helpful

Weaknesses
Attributes of the organization that can be harmful

Opportunities
External conditions that can be helpful

Threats
External conditions that could do damage

In conducting a SWOT analysis, ask these questions and generate as many ideas as possible to develop strategies:

- How can we use and capitalize on each strength?
- How can we improve each weakness?
- How can we exploit and benefit from each opportunity?
- How can we mitigate each threat?

An example of a SWOT Analysis follows:

FIGURE 7: SAMPLE SWOT ANALYSIS

Strengths	Weaknesses	Opportunities	Threats
• Reputation in marketplace	• No formal diversity plan	• Well established position in the market	• Weak Economy
• High Employee Satisfaction	• No streamlined D&I policies across business units	• Diverse employee groups	• Competition for Talent

Step 3: Develop the Details of The Plan

Define diversity, describe the mission, and select three or more organizational objectives that the Diversity and Inclusion plan support. Next, outline the plan. For example:

- *Goal A: To* develop and execute a comprehensive Multicultural Communications Campaign
- *Strategy:* Through multi-media forms, promote diversity as a core value for the organization
- *Objective 1:* Determine which departments/business units would benefit most from multicultural publications and/or a global perspective.
- *Objective 2:* Translate the website(s) and certain materials to different languages.
- *Objective 3:* Develop a targeted communications campaign for our top 3 diverse market segments.
- *Partners:* Marketing and communications, Office of Diversity, Employee Resource Groups
- *Measures:* Changes to materials, quantity of publications produced, and responses to communications materials

Step 4: Design a Strategy for Evaluation

What is an effective way to determine if you are succeeding? It is difficult to measure the impact of Diversity and Inclusion without evaluating how you performed on your plan. The best way to find out if the plan is succeeding is to conduct an annual evaluation. This requires tracking all supporting data throughout the year and focusing on concrete results.

Use a logic model to assess the efforts of the plan. A **logic model** is a general framework for describing work within an organization (Refer to Figure 8).

FIGURE 8: SAMPLE 'GROUP ACTION LOGIC MODEL'

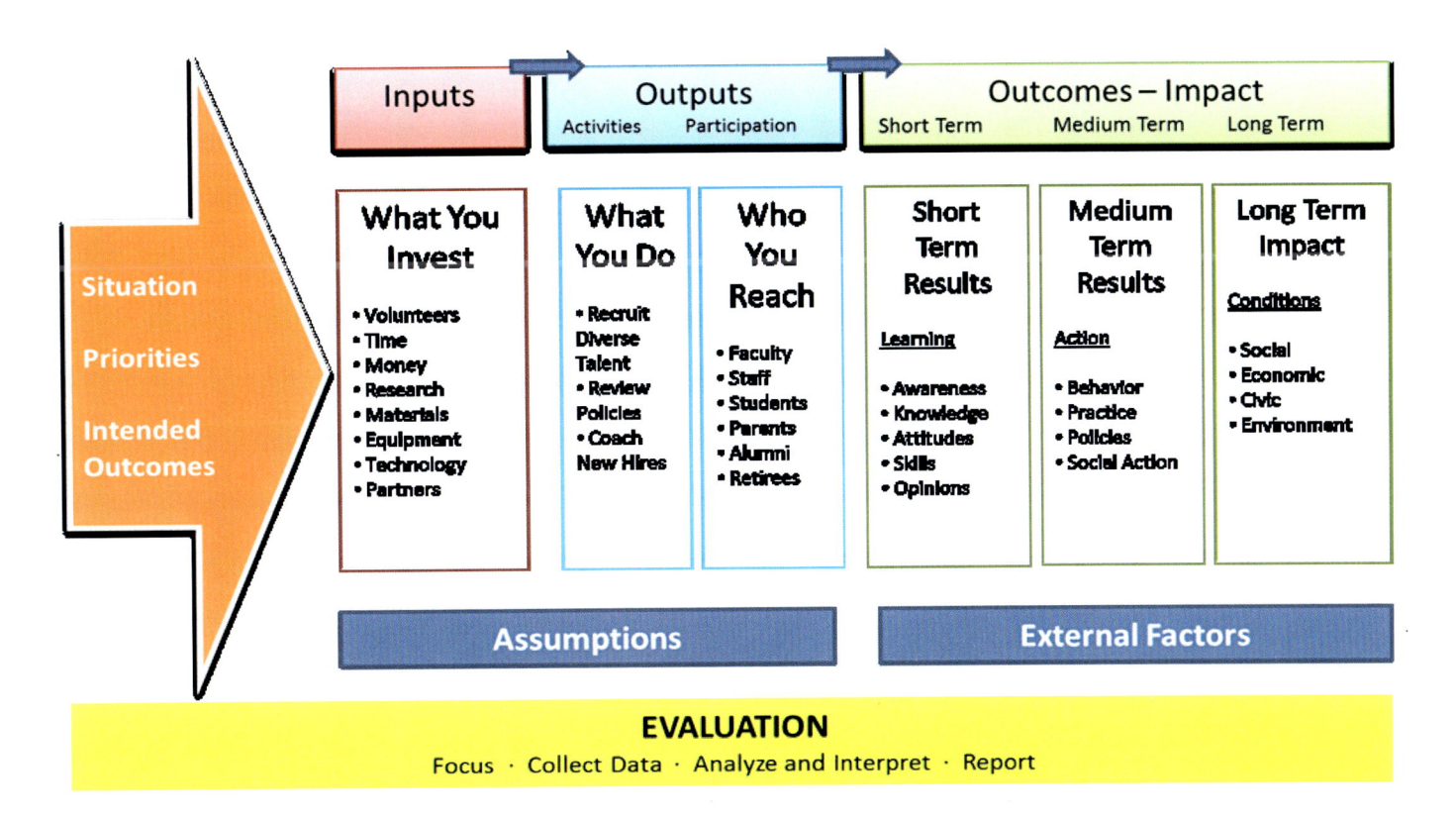

Inputs

Outputs
Activities · Participation

Outcomes – Impact
Short Term · Medium Term · Long Term

Situation · Priorities · Intended Outcomes

What You Invest
- Volunteers
- Time
- Money
- Research
- Materials
- Equipment
- Technology
- Partners

What You Do
- Recruit Diverse Talent
- Review Policies
- Coach New Hires

Who You Reach
- Faculty
- Staff
- Students
- Parents
- Alumni
- Retirees

Short Term Results
Learning
- Awareness
- Knowledge
- Attitudes
- Skills
- Opinions

Medium Term Results
Action
- Behavior
- Practice
- Policies
- Social Action

Long Term Impact
Conditions
- Social
- Economic
- Civic
- Environment

Assumptions | **External Factors**

EVALUATION
Focus · Collect Data · Analyze and Interpret · Report

Source: UW Extension, 2003, Program Development & Evaluation

In its simplest form, the logic model analyzes work into four categories or steps: inputs, activities, outputs, and outcomes. These represent the logical flow from:

1. **Inputs** (resources such as money, employees, and equipment) to
2. Work **activities**, programs or processes, to
3. The immediate **outputs** of the work that are delivered to clients/students, to
4. **Outcomes** or results that are the long-term consequences of delivering outputs.

By describing work in this method, diversity professionals have an easier way to define their work and measure it. Performance measures can be drawn from any of the steps. One of the key insights of the logic model is the importance of measuring final outcomes or results. Through this process, it is possible to avoid wasting time and money (inputs) "spinning the wheels" on work activities or producing outputs without achieving desired outcomes. Keep in mind that these outcomes (impacts, long-term results) are the only justification for doing the work in the first place.

The **Group Logic Model** is used to help sort through initiatives or design a tool specifically for the task. At the very minimum, make sure the diversity plan evaluation:

- Describes All Activities
- Compares Goals to Actual Accomplishments

- Lists Group Participants & Partners
- Details Budget Items & Expenditures
- Explains Challenges & Resolutions (if any)

The key focus is on results and being able to justify the existence of your diversity program as well as any budget allocations.

Finally, diversity initiatives should be evaluated annually, and it should be in writing. To bolster the success of goals, review your diversity plan quarterly or semi-annually. Conducting a quarterly or semi-annual review facilitates any adjustments needed to meet or exceed the diversity goals by the year's end.

THE ROLE OF THE FINANCIAL MANAGER

In business, Financial Management can be defined as:

The management of an organization's finances in order to achieve financial objectives

Using a commercial business as the most common organizational structure, the key objectives of financial management would be to:

- Create wealth for the business
- Generate cash
- Provide an adequate return on investment bearing in mind the risks that the business is taking, and the resources invested

There are three key elements to the process of financial management:

(1) Financial Planning- Management needs to ensure that enough funding is available at the right time to meet the needs of the business. In the Office of Diversity, the Diversity Practitioner may be responsible for managing a budget, and for creating a financial plan each year to utilize the funds in that budget.

(2) Financial Control- Financial control is a critically important activity to help the organization ensure that it is meeting its objectives. In the Office of Diversity and Inclusion, financial control addresses questions such as:

- Are assets being used efficiently?
- Are we meeting or exceeding planned expenses?
- Does the Office of Diversity and Inclusion act in the best interest of stakeholders (i.e., saving money or making money) and in accordance with business goals?

(3) Financial Decision-Making- The key aspects of financial decision-making relate to investment, financing, and dividends. For instance, in the Office of Diversity and Inclusion, a diversity practitioner may have limited sponsorship dollars, therefore he or she must make the best decision on whom to sponsor. This will depend on the amount of the investment, other sponsors involved, and the return on investment.

In the Office of Diversity and Inclusion (ODI), the budget can be very large, relatively small, or anything in between. If the budget is small, do not compare your funding to that of other departments and complain. Instead, figure out creative ways to achieve your goals based on the limited funds available. If the ODI lacks formal staffing, request volunteers for a Diversity Council and assign specific tasks to satisfy the work normally performed by an ODI staff. From another perspective, if the Marketing Department has a larger budget, there may be an opportunity for a collaborative effort that would allow the funds assigned for the Marketing department to be shared with the Office of Diversity and Inclusion. The key point is to be creative in your efforts to finance Diversity and Inclusion and seek partners whenever possible.

Figure 9 shows a common budget:

FIGURE 9: SAMPLE OFFICE OF DIVERSITY BUDGET

Compliance & Human Capital $200,000 - $1 million	Corporate Communications $120,000 to $3 million	Supplier Diversity $100,000 to $750,000	Measurement / ROI $25,000 to $500,000
• D&I Staff • Recruiting • Training • Travel • Expos & Conferences • College relations • Employee Resource Groups & Diversity Councils • Meeting resources • External Legal & Consultant fees	• Event sponsorships • Internal communication vehicles • Publications • Intranet • External communication vehicles • Advertising • Web site • Public relations	• Advertising in media targeted toward diverse suppliers • Supplier-database development and software • Organizational memberships to foster supplier Diversity • Sponsorship of other events that attract diverse suppliers • Supplier-training programs	• Research, surveys, and application of various metrics to measure the effectiveness of diversity efforts • Consultant fees

Whether the work is with a for-profit, nonprofit, government agency, or educational institution, the diversity practitioner must have an in-depth understanding of how the organization generates revenue. Additionally, you must think through how to help the organization save money, make more money or achieve organizational goals, using the integrated business model. Keep in mind, while **you** are passionate about equity and inclusion, your senior level executives are concerned with the financial implications of your work. Therefore, the numbers **must** make sense.

It is possible to create many allies within any organization if there is a shared focus on the "traditional" revenue generating units. For example, if the diversity practitioner is working on a college campus, it would be a good idea to partner with the alumni relations office. Assist the office in creating a plan for retaining and cultivating diverse students and/or help create a customized campaign to secure contributions from diverse alumni. Through this type of assistance, departmental myths such as "All other groups give generously except for _____", can be dispelled. In fact, diverse individuals find many ways to support other people and charitable efforts. Certainly, your organization can figure out how to better target diverse groups, and the Office of Diversity and Inclusion can help!

Figure 10 illustrates potential financial opportunities:

FIGURE 10: POTENTIAL FINANCIAL OPPORTUNITIES

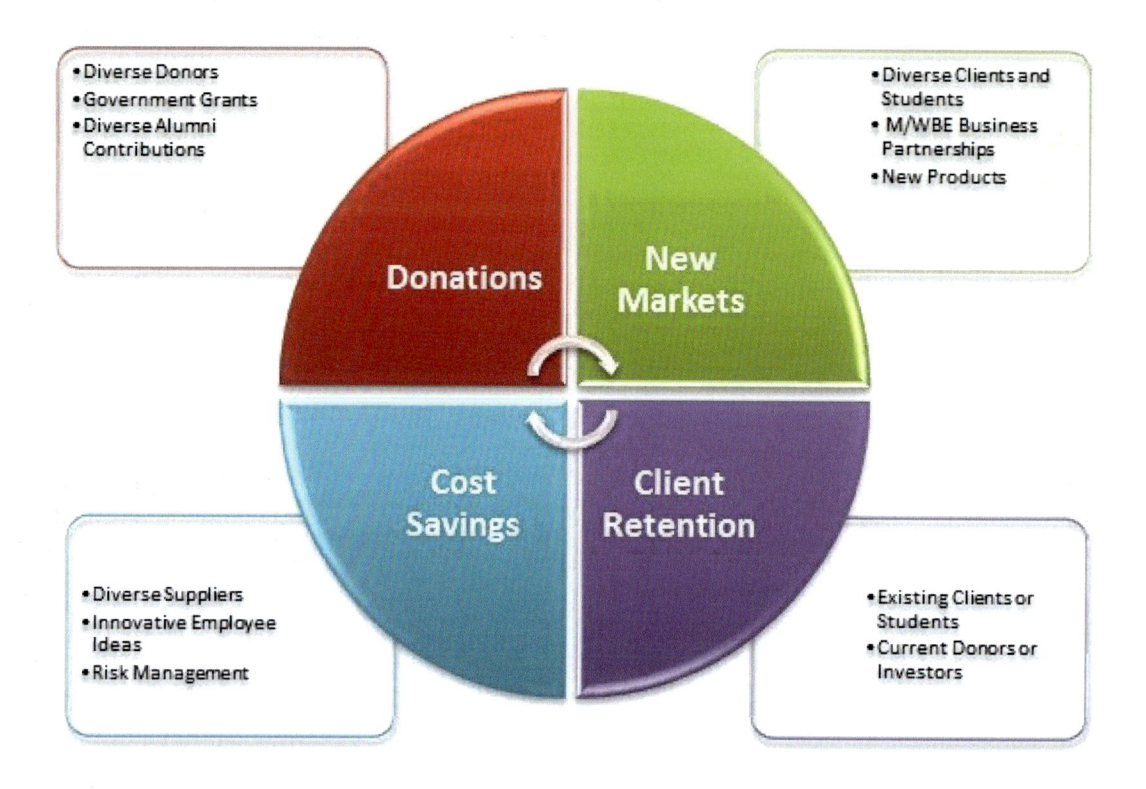

- Diverse Donors
- Government Grants
- Diverse Alumni Contributions

- Diverse Clients and Students
- M/WBE Business Partnerships
- New Products

Donations | **New Markets**
Cost Savings | **Client Retention**

- Diverse Suppliers
- Innovative Employee Ideas
- Risk Management

- Existing Clients or Students
- Current Donors or Investors

THE ROLE OF THE SUCCESSION PLANNER

Very few Offices of Diversity have a succession plan in place in the event of an unforeseen termination. Nevertheless, the succession plan is one of the most important tools in the Office of Diversity. It identifies candidates to replace planned and unplanned losses of key leaders. Without a succession plan, the future continuity and performance of the Office of Diversity is at risk.

Following are some practical ideas on how to get more impact from the organization's succession planning efforts.

1. **Assess your need.**
   Your succession plan should go beyond the traditional description of the position and delve deeply into both the competencies and experiences required for the next Diversity Officer, Director, Manager, or Coordinator. This document can then be translated into a dashboard for grading succession candidates in an objective manner.

2. **Ask critical questions.**
   First, is there an emergency candidate who can temporarily takeover if the Director of Diversity or Chief Diversity Officer were to leave tomorrow? Who, within the organization, has the skill set to be successful in the Office of Diversity? This candidate is usually a member of the Diversity Council, Employee Resource Group, Human Resources, or Legal department. Next, has the organization developed a team strong enough to allow for the smooth transition of a new Diversity and Inclusion leader? Finally, is a seasoned executive in place who is willing to coach and mentor a new diversity leader? The answers to these questions will help you to develop the proper infrastructure for the Office of Equity, Diversity and Inclusion.

3. **Change the name of the process from Succession Planning to Succession Development.**
   Plans do not develop anyone—only development *experiences* develop people. Many employers put more effort and attention into the planning process than they do into the development process. Succession planning processes have lots of to-do's—forms, charts, meetings, due dates, and checklists. They sometimes create a false sense that the planning process is an end, rather than a precursor to real development. Hence, the focus and end result should be developing the person and not the plan.

4. **Measure outcomes, not process.**
   This change of emphasis is important for several reasons. First, executives' pay attention to what gets measured and what is rewarded. If leadership development is not enough of a priority for the company to establish goals and track progress against those goals, it will be difficult to make any succession planning process work. Second, the act of engaging with senior executives to establish these goals will build support for succession planning and ownership of leadership development. Third, these results will help guide future efforts and mid-course corrections.

   An organization could also establish metrics for succession development in the Office of Diversity. One such metric might include goals (e.g., the percent of vacancies that are filled with an internal promotion vs. an external hire, or the percent of promotions that come from the high-potential pool). Too often, we find companies measure only the percent of managers that had completed succession plans in place.

5. **Keep it simple.**
   Sometimes companies add excessively complex assessment criteria to the succession planning process in an effort to improve the quality of the assessment. Some of these criteria are challenging for experts to assess, thus, even more challenging for the average Diversity Manager. Since the planning process is only a precursor to focus on the development of the plan, it does not have to be perfect. More sophisticated assessments can be built into the development process and administered by a competent coach.

6. **On-board the successor.**
   The most neglected step when it comes to succession planning is preparing for what happens *after* naming the successor. Making succession a sink-or-swim shock is simply too risky to endure. There is no such thing as a "ready now" candidate. Anyone named as a successor has learning to do and mistakes to make. Mistakes are not catastrophic; they are simply learning opportunities to help the successor understand how to do things better.

Additionally, part of the succession-planning process must be to take advantage of the time between the announcement and the acceptance of the top job so that the leadership can address as many needs as possible. Crucial support must be provided—a good team, wise and accessible mentors, executive coaching, and a feedback-rich environment—to create a setting in which the new diversity leader can be the most effective.

Throughout this process, it is important to identify the tasks that the successor should accomplish in the first year. Oftentimes, successors in the Office of Diversity are left to figure this out on their own. Unfortunately, because few people outside of the office actually know what a Diversity Practitioner does, they cannot provide much assistance. However, this is where well-documented processes and reports provide an advantage. Additionally, this is where guidance can be offered through Standard Operating Procedures (SOP).

Standard Operating Procedures are used in industries such as food services and manufacturing to ensure excellence and consistency. Essentially, the SOP is a detailed explanation of how a procedure is to be executed. An effective SOP communicates the responsibilities that are to be performed in the Office of Diversity (i.e., which tasks are a priority, what materials are necessary, where the tasks take place, who performs the tasks, and how to evaluate the outcomes, etc.). The details in a SOP standardize the processes and provide step-by-step instructions so that anyone in your organization can perform certain D&I tasks in a consistent manner.

A standard operating procedure can also be applied to the strategic diversity planning process if one is necessary for the Office of Diversity or supporting plans must be developed for other entities (e.g., divisions, schools, employee resource groups, or countries of operation). Additionally, a SOP can be created for job descriptions, employee training, recruiting and interviewing, corrective action and discipline, performance reviews, coaching, mentoring, policy creation/revisions, and exit interviews. The SOP can apply to anything that needs a systematic approach or that must be duplicated in the future. The objective is to create best practices for the organization and the Office of Diversity.

Step-by-step written procedures can increase employee accountability and improve the chances of success in the Office of D&I. The SOP document serves as an instructional resource that allows the successor to act with minimum directions, reassurance, or guidance. Communicating procedures that are clearly understood, and easy to replicate, will ensure the organization continually provides high quality Diversity and Inclusion interventions.

Critical to the success of Standard Operating Procedures is creating a system for periodic review. Care must be taken to design a review that prevents the SOP from becoming outdated, without making frequent changes to the document. Incorporate as much feedback as possible in the SOP review process. Additionally, make sure the revision date is included on the SOP so that everyone knows that this is the most recent policy.

A MULTI-FACETED ROLE

Essentially, the role of Diversity Practitioner is multifaceted. Whether an employee, Diversity Council Member, Employee Resource Group Member, Diversity Champion, or Consultant, the Diversity and Inclusion practitioner may perform a variety of necessary tasks including:

- Providing an acceptable definition of diversity
- Developing the Strategic Diversity Plan
- Overseeing staff
- Coordinating Diversity Council and/or Employee Resource Group efforts
- Managing compliance and other legal risks
- Designing and executing diversity interventions
- Leading the diversity change process
- Fostering inclusive work environments or an inclusive Board of Directors
- Financial planning
- Succession planning
- Overseeing all aspects of equity, Diversity and Inclusion
- Evaluating and reporting accomplishments

The most effective Diversity Practitioners will create an "elevator pitch" that succinctly describes their role within the organization. This pitch may be as simple as:

"My role as _____ (insert your title) is to help the organization leverage differences in an effort to outperform competitors and exceed client/student/patient expectations."

OR

"As the _____ (insert your title), I create opportunities for our organization to better meet the changing needs of our students/clients/patients with appropriate staff and programming interventions."

OR

"I help the organization meet the global demands of business and address the challenges that come along with changing demographics, differing points of view, and workplace fairness."

Finally, the Diversity Practitioner is responsible for ensuring that the organization does not experience diversity fatigue. This workplace epidemic concerns one or more of the following questions: Are we there yet? Why haven't we accomplished more? Where do we go from here?

Diversity fatigue is best described as a sentiment of disinterest and even dislike of diversity activities that are taking place at an organization. Diversity fatigue should not be confused with the general resistance to change. Diversity fatigue occurs after the launch of a diversity initiative at a company, followed by months or years of diversity programming. When diversity takes too long to reach goals, people get tired. Additionally, when diversity is positioned as an "add-on" for an organization, there will always be fatigue. Keep in mind that these employees consider diversity to be something that is not central to their work, an added burden or a nuisance.

Over the last decade, more and more companies have launched diversity programs and incorporated key concepts of diversity management into their organizations. These efforts were initiated with a great deal of enthusiasm that quality work would be accomplished. What organizations are discovering after years, or in some cases, decades, is diversity fatigue in the workplace. Key indicators of the phenomena include the fact that diversity programs are not well-attended, senior leaders are not as engaged, and employees are not supportive.

The idea of diversity fatigue is not new. As Time magazine columnist Po Bronson said in a May 2006 column on diversity fatigue, "It's clear that people are tired of walking on eggshells, afraid to offend those with different beliefs, ideas, and lifestyles. It has grown exhausting, and they want their lives back. The idea of diversity seems to have worn out its welcome. It is now like a house guest who has stayed too long." While the concept is deep-rooted, the fact that it has been echoed in the nationalist movement and anti-immigration sentiments during the 2016 U.S. election is unusual. While there are many reasons for diversity fatigue, here are eight that encompass many of the issues:

1. Lack of senior executive endorsement, involvement, and accountability
2. Lack of a progressive diversity strategy
3. Diversity interventions are not connected to the business case
4. Activities are sporadic
5. A lack of metrics to regularly evaluate effectiveness
6. Lack of communication
7. An exaggerated focus on primary dimensions of diversity (e.g., race, ethnicity, gender, etc.)
8. No one else is responsible for Diversity and Inclusion efforts except the Office of D&I

Diversity practitioners must lead the organization through diversity fatigue with a progressive Diversity and Inclusion plan. The strategy should become more proactive and complex over time. Do not start with a complex plan or a big planning committee and make little to no progress. Ensure that your effort is manageable and attainable. Set smaller goals, work with smaller groups, and require smaller amounts of funding for initial interventions. Upon demonstrating success, you can grow and expand your efforts.

Second, connect the dots. Ensure the Diversity and Inclusion strategy is linked to organizational goals, engagement, productivity, innovation, and retention. Next, take the necessary steps to ensure that Diversity and Inclusion makes a bottom-line impact. There should be cost savings or some kind of contribution to revenue generation as a result of your Diversity and Inclusion interventions.

Keep in mind, stand-alone diversity interventions rarely work. D&I efforts must be integrated within an organization's management and systems. A systemic framework for how D&I work is conducted should go beyond isolated initiatives and individual behaviors. It includes the interconnected elements in the system, such as the organizational strategy, corporate architecture, people, processes, and rewards. These elements operate together to form a system that informs how things function properly in an organization. When misaligned, any component can be significantly impacted by another component pulling in a different direction. When cohesively coordinated, the components work together in a mutually reinforcing and self-sustaining way. This systems lens is useful in identifying all the components that need to be simultaneously realigned to improve D&I outcomes for a broader, more sustainable impact.

As a diversity practitioner, be responsible for helping the organization to leverage its differences to maximize potential growth, competitive positioning, and compliance. The most effective practitioner will understand the role, and tactically go beyond superficial expectations toward innovation, inclusion, interdependence, and excellence.

References:

Lorenzo, R. et al (April 26, 2017). The Mix That Matters. Retrieved from:
https://www.bcg.com/publications/2017/people-organization-leadership-talent-innovation-through-Diversity-mix-that-matters.aspx

Bronson, P. and Merryman, A (May 31, 2006). Are Americans Suffering Diversity Fatigue? Retrieved from:
http://content.time.com/time/nation/article/0,8599,1199702,00.html

Sample Test Questions:
THE ROLE OF A DIVERSITY PRACTITIONER

1. This concept often denotes that a company must engage in a process in which they alter their organization for a structured purpose.
   A. Leadership development
   B. Organizational change
   C. Cultural competency

2. The modern-day role of a Diversity Practitioner is:
   A. Influenced by affirmative action and political correctness
   B. An important part of the overall business strategy
   C. Legally required for employers with 100 or more workers

3. Related to Diversity and Inclusion, which is **NOT** a significant emphasis today?
   A. Awareness training and multicultural celebrations
   B. Strategic business planning and growth
   C. Recruiting and retaining the best talent

4. Which is a key driver behind diversity in today's high performing organizations?
   A. The threat of lawsuits
   B. Chief Executive Officers
   C. Globalization

5. In the evolution of workforce diversity, the "Managing Diversity" model has _____ as its foundation.
   A. Diversity
   B. Assimilation
   C. Synergy

6. It is easy for D&I Practitioners to focus on the activities that are visible to senior management but neglect substantive, business aspects such as:
   A. Training and events
   B. Compliance and lawsuits
   C. Planning and evaluation

7. This is a process for identifying and developing internal people with the potential to fill key leadership positions in the company:
   A. Executive Sponsorship
   B. Succession Planning
   C. Strategic Planning

CDP EXAM STUDY GUIDE © 2018-2020

Sample Test Questions:
THE ROLE OF A DIVERSITY PRACTITIONER (cont'd)

8. Strategic diversity planning is an ongoing process that:
    A. Coordinates a schedule for regular Diversity and Inclusion activities
    B. Serves as an internal report of the organization's goals and initiatives
    C. Maps, controls, and evaluates an organization's Diversity and Inclusion efforts

9. The Group Action Logic Model describes inputs, outputs, activities, and:
    A. Investments
    B. Outcomes
    C. Assumptions

10. The key focus of your diversity evaluation effort is:
    A. Results
    B. Support
    C. Inclusion

11. All of the following are key elements to the process of financial management EXCEPT:
    A. Financial planning
    B. Financial control
    C. Financial know-how

12. The best way to determine if your Diversity and Inclusion efforts are succeeding is to conduct:
    A. An employee survey
    B. An exit interview
    C. An annual evaluation

13. _____ are the statistical characteristics of a population.
    A. Cultural data
    B. Demographics
    C. Populism

14. Standard Operating Procedures can systematize processes to ensure leadership continuity in the Office of Diversity.
    A. True
    B. False

THE BUSINESS CASE FOR DIVERSITY & INCLUSION

> *The business case for Diversity and Inclusion theorizes that an organization which employs a diverse workforce is better able to understand marketplace demographics, is more proactive in managing costs, identifying opportunities, and is poised to thrive in a global economy—in comparison to an employer that has a limited range of employee demographics.*

OVERALL OBJECTIVES AND COMPETENCIES

The purpose of this competency is to help practitioners use traditional business principles to justify the case for maximizing Diversity and Inclusion efforts. Practitioners must demonstrate competence in writing a compelling business case that provides information and/or gains support for equity and inclusive excellence.

BACKGROUND AND CONTEXT

A business case for Diversity and Inclusion (D&I) is a reasoned proposal to educate executives and convince them to take action. The business case must pertain to business. Yes, you work for a nonprofit organization, school, or government agency, but senior executives at these places of business are just as concerned about finance as leaders at for-profit corporations. That is why your business case must speak the language of senior leadership in any industry. **Most organizations operate based on the "bottom line".** In general, a business case for diversity defines:

- How much money an organization will make by valuing Diversity and Inclusion,
- How much an organization will save through comprehensive Diversity and Inclusion interventions, and/or
- How Diversity and Inclusion will contribute to the achievement of organizational goals.

Personal opinions are valued, but they do not hold a lot of authority in this area. High-level executives, board members, and other stakeholders often evaluate the business case from a reasoned (i.e., financial) perspective.

The most obvious reason for putting together a business case for diversity is to justify the resources and capital investment necessary to bring cultural competence and inclusion to fruition. However, this implies that the business case for diversity is simply a financial document. While all business cases should include financial justification, it should not be the only purpose of the document. Diversity recognizes that each employee is unique and can contribute to an organization in different ways by virtue of their individual experiences, backgrounds, and ideas. While appreciating diversity may be an intrinsic individual value held by many employees, the business case outlines how diversity adds value in an organizational context. It describes the reasons why an organization feels that it is important to make diversity an explicit effort with specific actions and activities. It is about leveraging the organization's most strategic competitive resource—its human capital.

Nevertheless, here is why a dissertation about race or gender does not work for a business case: race-based diversity initiatives result in a zero-sum ratio in some minds. This is where someone must lose (us) in order for another to gain (them). It presents a divisive approach to establishing a culture where differences are valued. Accordingly, diversity will be viewed as a program for "African Americans, others, or the less qualified", and not viewed as a business imperative. This will certainly derail your business proposal to change the organizational culture. Therefore, we want to establish the initial links to business goals and its benefits, as well as validate our credentials and expertise in business.

The business case for diversity states the opportunity and the importance of maximizing the potential of human capital. It highlights the significance of enhancing accessibility for any individual to use his or her abilities to perform the organization's mission and enables all employees to be recognized for their contributions. The business case outlines why employees need to be engaged and how this engagement can be fully utilized in order for the organization to meet its commitments. Additionally, the business case delineates projected demographic changes and its effect on current and future market shares; constituent services and fundraising for nonprofits; student enrollment and retention for educational institutions; or taxpayer and constituent services for government agencies.

The business case for diversity is one place where all relevant facts are documented and linked together into a cohesive story. The case tells people about the what, when, where, how, and why diversity is advantageous for business.

For example:

- Why does the organization need diversity, equity, or cultural competence (issues & opportunities)?
- How will cultural competence and inclusion solve the issues or opportunities facing the organization (benefits)?
- What will happen if Diversity and Inclusion becomes an insignificant factor at the organization (the 'do nothing' scenario)?
- How much time, treasury and talent will be needed to deliver the solution and realize the benefits?

The business case for diversity stems from a progression of workplace Diversity and Inclusion models. Since the 1960s, various models have advanced the field of diversity, ranging from the **Compliance Model** (where organizations strived to satisfy Affirmative Action requirements and goals) to the **Social Justice Model** (where tokenism prevailed because it was the right thing to do) to the **Diversity Model** (where all elements of diversity management connect and align with different approaches and tools in a strategic and synergistic way).

Today, there is a push for the **Inclusive Business Model**, where different communities are included in a company's value chain on the demand side as clients and consumers, and/or on the supply side as producers, entrepreneurs, or employers in a sustainable way. The concept was first formalized in an early United Nations report called *Creating Value for All: Strategies for Doing Business with the Poor (2008),* published by the Growing Inclusive Markets Initiative and guided by an international Advisory Board.

Inclusive business models build bridges between organizations and diverse groups for mutual benefit. The organizational benefits go beyond immediate profits and higher incomes. For business, they include driving innovations, building markets, and strengthening supply chains. For traditionally disadvantaged groups, they include access to essential goods and services, higher productivity, sustainable earnings, and greater empowerment.

Inclusive business is not corporate philanthropy or corporate social responsibility, which have inherent limitations of scope, impact, and budget. Rather, it is the search for sustainable business models that "do well by doing good" and are part of the companies' core business activities.

Hence, this model indicates the need to distinguish between different terms in the field of diversity. Sometimes D&I professionals use the words diversity, inclusion, and cultural competence interchangeably; however, they are distinctly different terms. Diversity refers to a broad mix of people. It can consist of primary dimensions (things you can see), secondary dimensions (things you can change), organizational dimensions (things that you do), and personality.

More concisely, we are all diverse. However, governments around the world establish protections for certain primary characteristics because they may result in under-representation, discrimination, or exclusion from resources and opportunities. From a business perspective, the term diversity, in its broadest sense, refers to all of the different characteristics that make each of us unique. Diversity can be defined in various ways, but in this study guide, we will define **diversity** as, the mosaic of people who bring a variety of backgrounds, styles, perspectives, values, and beliefs as assets to the groups and organizations with which they interact. Describing diversity as an asset implies something of value or worth.

Outside of economics, value-added refers to the extra features of an item of interest that go beyond standard expectations and offer something more, while adding little or nothing to its cost. Value-added features provide competitive advantages to organizations. The entire value-in-diversity notion rests on the assumption that outside of greater representation, workforce diversity adds different types of knowledge, skills, and abilities. This increases an organization's ability to:

- Reduce risks associated with lawsuits and negative publicity
- Decrease costs associated with lower productivity and turnover
- Innovate products and services
- Save money with diverse suppliers
- Demonstrate higher returns for investors
- Improve customer/student satisfaction
- Capitalize on greater sales (or grants, conventions, visitors to a city, tuition, etc.)
- Gain an edge over competitors
- Strategically prepare for the future

A schematic of diversity is illustrated in Figure 1: The Diversity Wheel

FIGURE 1: THE DIVERSITY WHEEL

Source: Lee Gardenswartz and Anita Rowe, *Diverse Teams at Work*. Burr Ridge, Ill.: Irwin Professional Publishing, 1994. Internal dimensions and external dimensions are adapted from Marilyn Loden and Judy B. Rosener, *Workforce America!* Homewood, Ill.: Business One Irwin, 1991.

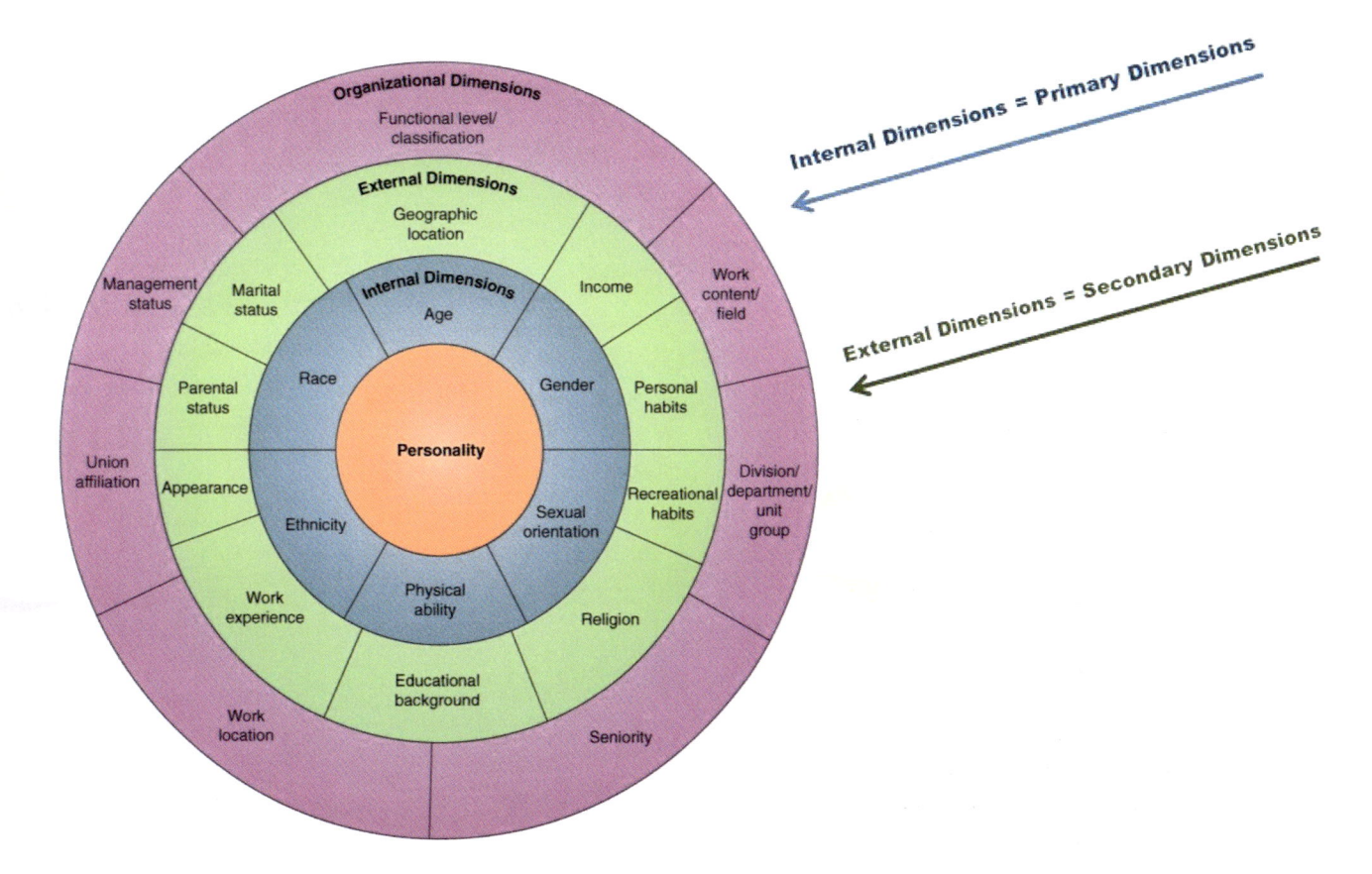

Inclusion describes the way that an organization configures opportunity, interaction, communication, and decision-making to utilize the potential of its diversity. Inclusion makes diversity work and leverages the resources that it brings. In other words, diversity pertains to people, while inclusion concerns the organization.

Cultural competence, on the other hand, refers to an ability to interact effectively with people of different cultures, particularly in the context of organizations where employees work with persons from different cultural and/or ethnic backgrounds. Cultural competence comprises four components: (a) Awareness of one's own cultural worldview, (b) Attitude towards cultural differences, (c) Knowledge of different cultural practices and worldviews, and (d) Cross-cultural skills. Developing cultural competence results in an ability to understand, communicate, and effectively interact with people across cultures. Thus, in lieu of politically correct environments, D&I leaders should strive for culturally competent workplaces and campuses.

In a workplace, diversity refers to all of the different people who work for an employer. Culturally competent managers are skilled in engaging diverse groups in the workplace and enabling them to be more productive. Inclusion is what makes each unique individual feel as if they are a part of the group and can be a deciding factor in whether they stay with or are retained by your organization. Distinguishing between these terms will facilitate a better understanding of your business case.
It is also important to develop a systematic approach to the business case to ensure key steps are not overlooked, pitfalls are avoided, and executive-level support is secured.

Figure 2 illustrates a methodology for developing the business case for diversity

FIGURE 2: ELEMENTS OF THE BUSINESS CASE FOR DIVERSITY

Ideally, your business case is accepted, and you will be able to proceed with your vision. However, there are times when your business case is not well received.

Figure 3 exemplifies the various stages of the business case and where your proposal can stall.

FIGURE 3. BUSINESS CASE GUIDANCE

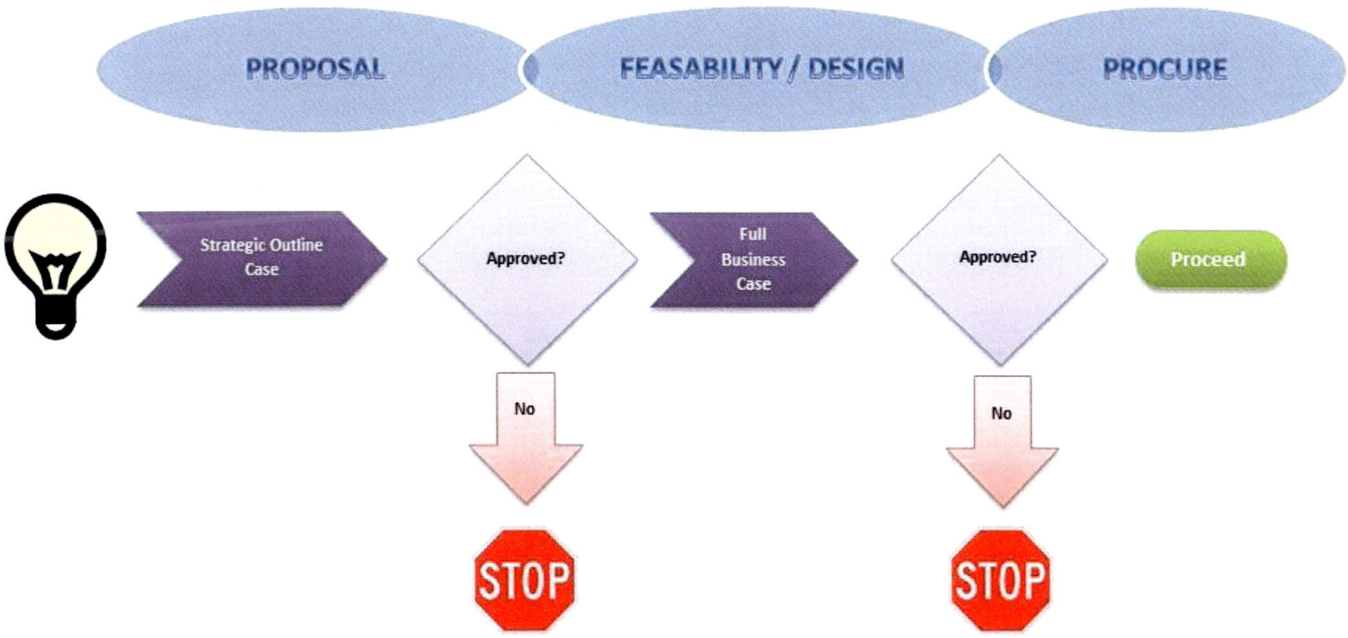

THE BENNETT SCALE

The best way to overcome objections is to prepare well and ensure that your business case addresses organizational concerns. While you are preparing your methodology, you should also consider the fact that some executives, board members, and other stakeholders will have varying degrees of maturity in diversity. If you do not have the support of a Chief Executive, you may have to prepare your business case based on individual reactions to Diversity and Inclusion tenets.

Dr. Milton Bennett, co-founder of the Intercultural Communication Institute and director of the Intercultural Development Research Institute, created the Bennett Scale, also called the Developmental Model of Intercultural Sensitivity (DMIS). This framework describes the different ways people can react to cultural differences and the degree to which they have adapted to them. In this framework, there is an emphasis on education versus training. According to Dr. Bennett, training changes skills, but education changes mindsets.

DMIS uses six stages to scale the level of cultural adaptation, where it should be the goal to reach the highest stage. The first three stages are ethnocentric, as one sees his own culture as central to reality. Moving up the scale, the individual develops a more ethnorelative point of view, meaning that one's own culture is experienced in the context of other cultures.

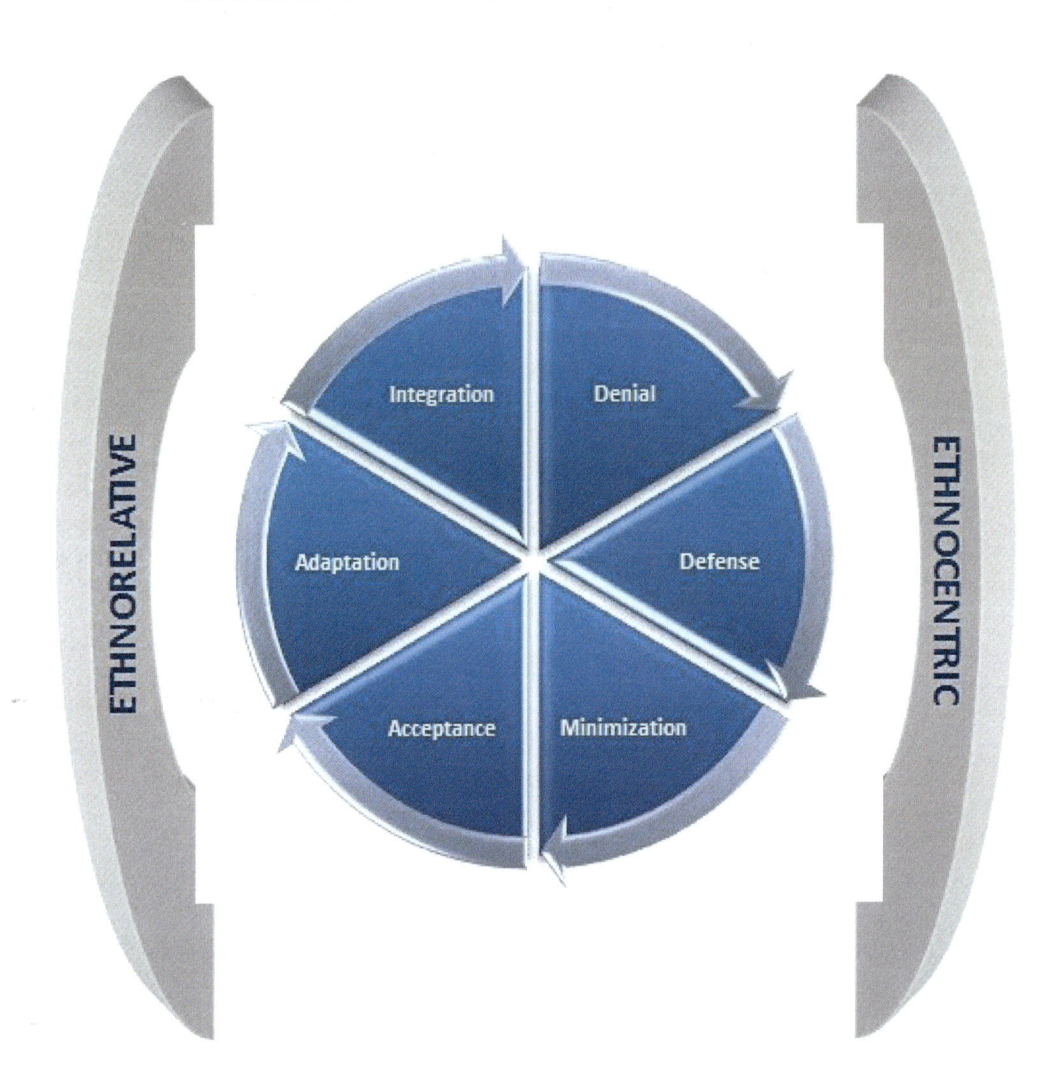

FIGURE 4: THE SIX STAGES OF DMIS

The ethnocentric stages of the Bennett scale are:

- **Denial**
    - The inability to construe cultural difference. Indicated by benign stereotyping (well-intended, but ignorant or naive observations) and superficial statements of tolerance.

    - May sometimes be accompanied by the attribution of deficiency to intelligence or to culturally deviant behavior; tendency to dehumanize outsiders

    - Developmental task: To recognize the existence of cultural differences

    - The process of changing a mind in denial:
        - ✓ Illustrate ideas and arouse curiosity with user-friendly activities, such as self-directed research, panel discussions, and films
        - ✓ Embed differences in non-threatening contexts

- ✓ Promote an inclusive, non-blaming climate
- ✓ Address anxieties in existing categories, but limit time
- ✓ Build on what they already know

- **Defense**
  - The recognition of cultural difference coupled with negative evaluations of most variations from the native culture-- the greater the difference, the more negative the evaluation. Characterized by dualistic thinking (us/them) and frequently accompanied by overt negative stereotyping. Evolutionary view of cultural development with the native culture at the acme. A tendency towards social/cultural proselytizing of "underdeveloped" cultures.

  - *Developmental task:* Mitigate polarization by emphasizing "common humanity"

  - The process of changing a mind in defense:
    - ✓ Avoid cultural contrasts
    - ✓ Provide reassurance and information about similarities, including shared needs and goals between different groups
    - ✓ Allow structured opportunities to share concerns
    - ✓ Focus curiosity on the culture of their own group
    - ✓ Promote cooperative activities by stressing conflict mediation and team building

- **Minimization**
  - Recognition and acceptance of superficial cultural differences, such as eating customs, etc., while holding that all human beings are essentially the same.

  - Emphasis on the similarity of people and commonality of basic values

  - Tendency to define the basis of commonality in ethnocentric terms (i.e., since everyone is essentially like us, "just be yourself")

  - *Developmental task:* Develop cultural self-awareness

  - The process of changing a mind that minimizes:
    - ✓ Avoid excessive stress on cultural contrasts; focus instead on self-awareness
    - ✓ Expand curiosity about their own culture to other cultures, in relation to privilege, justice, advertising and the media
    - ✓ Facilitate structured activities with ethnorelative resource persons
    - ✓ Coordinate opportunities for difference-seeking

The **ethnorelative stages** of the Bennett Scale are:

- **Acceptance**
  - Recognition, appreciation, and acceptance of cultural differences in behavior and values; cultural relativity.

- The beginning of an ability to interpret phenomena within the proper context; categories of difference are consciously elaborated

- *Developmental task:* Refine analysis of cultural contrasts

- The process of changing a mind that is accepting:

    - ✓ Build on enthusiasm for "difference-seeking" to promote examination of more profound contrasts
    - ✓ Provide guided experiential learning opportunities
    - ✓ Make cultural difference the focus while deepening cultural self-awareness
    - ✓ Prepare individuals for cultural frame-of-reference shifting by distinguishing issues of cultural relativity from ethical or moral relativity

- **Adaptation to Difference**
    - The development of communication skills that enable intercultural communication

    - Effective use of empathy, or frame of reference shifting, to understand and be understood across cultural boundaries

    - *Developmental task:* Develop frame of reference shifting skills

    - The process of changing a mind that is adaptive:

        - ✓ Facilitate opportunities for individuals to practice behavior in known cultures
        - ✓ Use trained ethnorelative cultural informants in less structured activities (small groups, case studies, etc.)
        - ✓ Prepare individuals to learn autonomously (use research strategies, etc.)

- **Integration**
    - The internalization of bicultural or multicultural frames of reference

    - Maintaining a definition of identity that is marginal to any particular culture. Seeing one's self as in process

    - *Developmental task*: Resolve the multicultural identity

    - The process of changing a mind that is integrated:

        - ✓ Create opportunities for peer group interaction
        - ✓ Provide options for individuals to serve as resource persons
        - ✓ Model constructive marginality
        - ✓ Encourage commitments and boundary setting
        - ✓ Discuss strategies for cultural identity construction

OBJECTIONS TO THE BUSINESS CASE

Understanding objections will help you to anticipate adversity, as well as enable you to prepare a concrete business imperative for critics. The following excerpt provides a sketch of what you may encounter in the workplace.

AN EXCERPT FROM
"Diversity's Business Case Doesn't Add Up"
By Fay Hansen · Workforce · April 2003, p. 28-32

The multibillion-dollar diversity industry is thriving in corporate America. But before you spend another dime on your diversity program, carefully consider this conclusion reached by Thomas A. Kochan, one of the most respected human resources management scholars in the country: "The diversity industry is built on sand," he declares. "The business case rhetoric for diversity is simply naive and overdone. There are no strong positive or negative effects of gender or racial diversity on business performance."

Kochan, a professor of management at MIT's Sloan School of Management, bases his conclusions on a recently completed five-year study of the impact of diversity on business results. The investigation involved a detailed examination of large firms with well-deserved reputations for their long-standing commitment to building a diverse workforce and managing diversity effectively. It builds on a growing body of research that raises painful questions for companies that pour money into diversity programs, and for the diversity industry that supplies them with a dazzling array of diversity products.

At a time when charges of racial harassment are way up, and racial discrimination class-action lawsuits are enjoying a renaissance, diversity programs are flourishing.

Organizations are appointing diversity officers, and hiring diversity consultants, coaches, and trainers. They adopt diversity scorecards, benchmarks, and best practices, and send executives to diversity conferences and leadership academies. However, despite the astonishing number of products and services—ranging from the worthy to the banal—one item is in very short supply: hard metrics for measuring performance results or the return on diversity spending.

For years, the industry has claimed that diversity programs yield higher performance and greater productivity; however, the evidence offered is largely anecdotal or based on limited data collected through questionable methods. The link to the bottom line, an entrenched part of diversity rhetoric, remains largely undocumented. Of the 20 large corporations with well-established diversity programs that Kochan initially contacted for his study, none had ever conducted a systematic examination of the effects of their diversity efforts on bottom-line performance measures.

The diversity industry and its corporate clients continue to promote diversity programs as a "strategic imperative" that boosts performance by unleashing the creative power of diverse groups. But according to Kochan, "Diversity has been promoted on the basis of a very weak construction of the business case and on the grounds of social justice, but to be successful, programs must be built on scientific evidence". Without this evidence, especially in the context of budget constraints forced by the economic downturn, diversity programs may come under the same scrutiny routinely turned on most business functions.

Some believe that an industry shakeout is on the horizon. "Five or 10 years from now, there are only going to be a few serious practitioners left—those who have demonstrated the ability to help organizations with measurable results," he says.

"There are estimates that companies spend $8 billion on diversity training annually," he adds. Kochan's study also presents findings that have dramatic implications for the kind of diversity training that must be provided to achieve performance improvements. Training programs aimed at "valuing diversity" and addressing subtle forms of discrimination and exclusion do not lead to long-term changes in behaviors, the study notes. Instead, group members and leaders must be trained to deal with group process issues, with a focus on communicating and problem solving in diverse teams.

Michael C. Hyter, president and CEO of J. Howard & Associates/Global Novations, a large diversity consultancy in Boston, says the diversity industry includes "all types of people who profess to be experts in this area". Accordingly, diversity consultants are chasing what he estimates to be $400 to $600 million annually in consulting fees alone. Yet, human resources executives often don't demand documented results from outside consultants or in-house diversity staff because "it's easier to create activities and get credit for doing something than it is to create metrics and measures and hold people accountable," he says.

Some companies measure diversity results with recruitment, promotion, or turnover rates; few look beyond simple headcounts to measure the full financial or performance impact of their programs. The difficulty of creating valid measures is part of the problem. "There is a connection between diversity and financial success, but typical profit-and-loss systems don't capture the benefits that diversity creates," says Laura Liswood, senior adviser to Goldman Sachs on diversity issues and a senior scholar at the University of Maryland's Academy of Leadership. "A lot of the benefits are not quantifiable, but it's also true that we have not devoted the same level of resources to attempt to quantify diversity results."

The business case for diversity that dominates industry claims and corporate goals, focuses on three related objectives: to allow organizations to tap talent pools and incorporate new ideas and perspectives from employees of different backgrounds; to expand market share; and to ensure legal compliance.

Several studies, including Kochan's, have found that companies generally are more successful in managing diversity with respect to gender issues than racial and ethnic issues. The empirical studies indicate that racial and ethnic diversity may have a negative impact on business performance unless specific forms of analysis, training, and monitoring are in place. If left unattended or mismanaged, diversity is likely to produce miscommunication, unresolved conflict, higher turnover, and lower performance.

Diversity practitioners must learn to address backlash head-on. Delaying a response causes negativity to fester and spread. Keep in mind, many critics of Diversity and Inclusion efforts have axes to grind, and their observations may be replete with methodological flaws and logical fallacies. Nevertheless, some criticism may be valid.

An excellent strategy to distinguish between valid criticism and pure backlash is to engage in a conversation about the facts and the corresponding organizational data within the proper context. Also, highlight the contributions of different groups while applying what you know about the antagonist's cultural competence. If none of this works, use another framework.

MULTI-DIMENSIONAL VS. UNI-DIMENSIONAL FRAMEWORKS

The broadest definition of diversity today centers around our differences. Proponents endorse the idea that a diverse work force allows for greater utilization of different perspectives, skills, ideas, and innovations.

To advance this idea even further, Andres Tapia, Senior Partner at Korn/Ferry International, and Mary-Frances Winters, President of The Winters Group, espouse the concept of transitioning from a uni-dimensional to a multi-dimensional framework in diversity leadership. This framework assumes that no single dimension of diversity takes place in isolation.

What does this mean? There are still many people who define diversity as a program for minorities, women, or some other singular identity, consisting of external descriptors or primary dimensions (see Figure 5).

FIGURE 5: UNI-DIMENSIONAL FRAMEWORK

- Race
- Ethnicity
- Age
- Sexual Orientation/Gender Identity
- Gender
- Physical Qualities

Instead, it may be more helpful to enable senior leadership and critics to define diversity from a multidimensional perspective.

Figure 6 provides a simplistic example of how this framework might look in your organization:

FIGURE 6: MULTIDIMENSIONAL FRAMEWORK

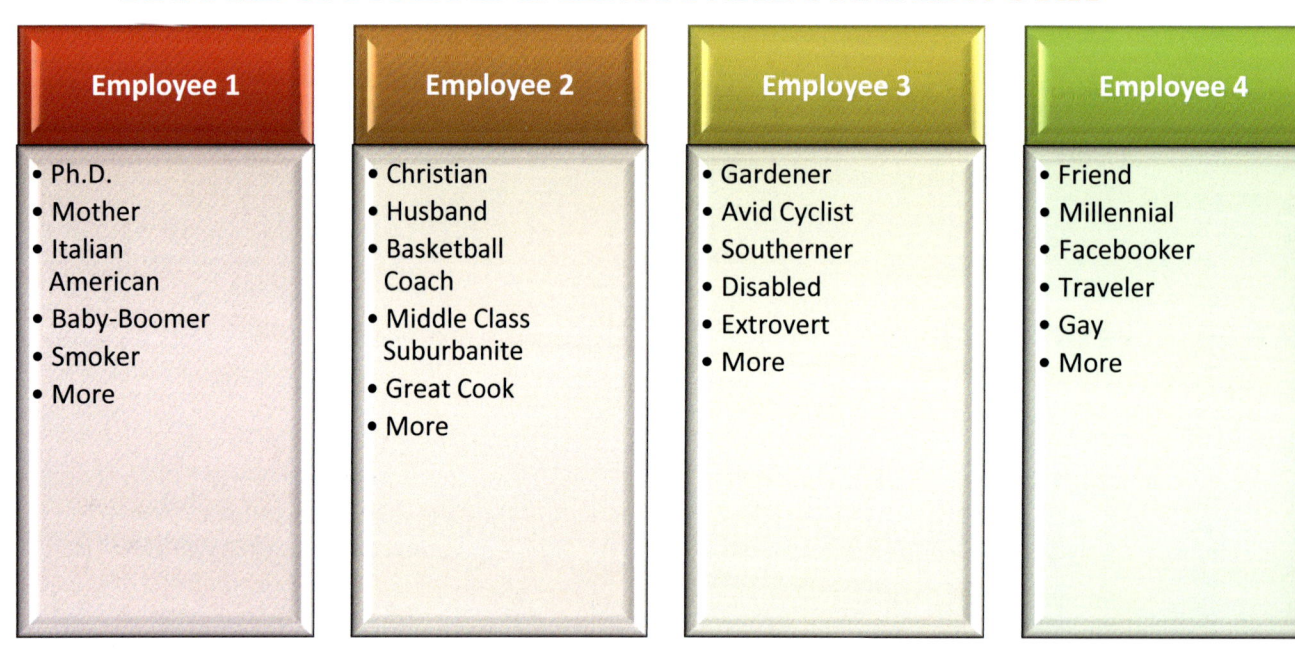

Employee 1	Employee 2	Employee 3	Employee 4
• Ph.D. • Mother • Italian American • Baby-Boomer • Smoker • More	• Christian • Husband • Basketball Coach • Middle Class Suburbanite • Great Cook • More	• Gardener • Avid Cyclist • Southerner • Disabled • Extrovert • More	• Friend • Millennial • Facebooker • Traveler • Gay • More

This type of framework moves beyond external observations of groups toward multiple levels of human existence. A key assumption in this approach is that people cannot be understood or managed independent of complex determinants for human behavior (Ashford & Winston, 2009). It also assumes that the one-dimensional identifier may not be the dimension that the employee values most.

HOW TO CONSTRUCT A BUSINESS CASE

Upon understanding the possible reactions, and developing the framework for Diversity and Inclusion, you are now ready to construct your business case.

Figure 7 illustrates the steps to writing a business case.

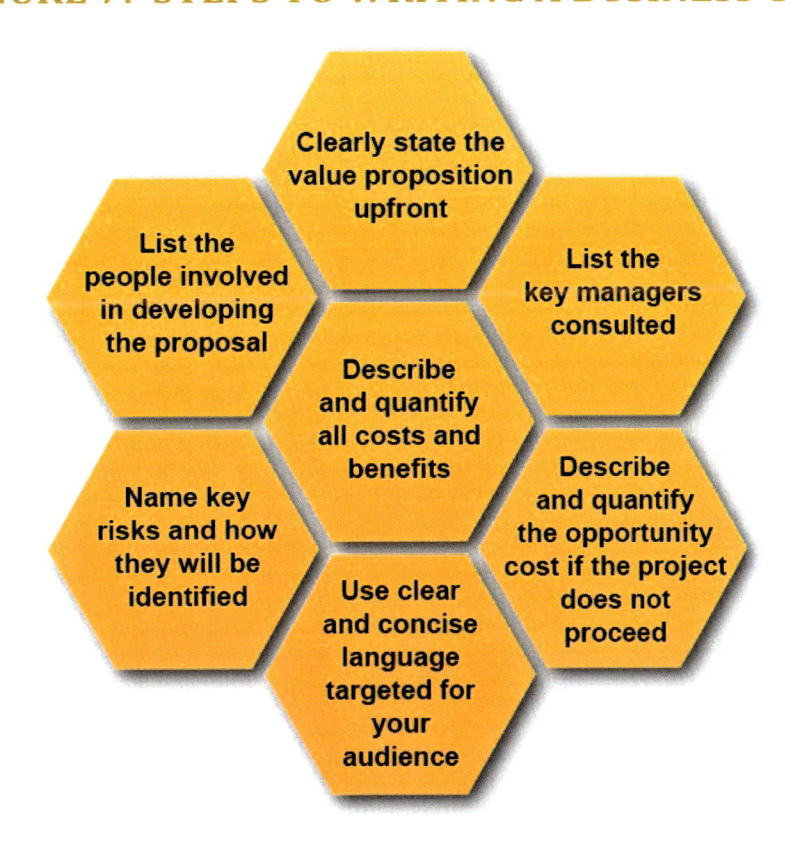

FIGURE 7: STEPS TO WRITING A BUSINESS CASE

- Clearly state the value proposition upfront
- List the people involved in developing the proposal
- List the key managers consulted
- Describe and quantify all costs and benefits
- Name key risks and how they will be identified
- Describe and quantify the opportunity cost if the project does not proceed
- Use clear and concise language targeted for your audience

Your business case for diversity should be succinct and easy-to-understand. The following are tips to develop your business case:

- **Title**
Everyone expects the title to briefly identify the case. An example of a good title would be: "The Business Case for Diversity and Inclusion."

- **Purpose**
Generally, increased global competition supports the business case for diversity. Nevertheless, good statements include these objectives—business objectives, financial objectives, functional objectives, or operational objectives. It is important to note that your business case should not include the moral imperative or societal goals.

    The purpose will be designed to invoke action such as:

    o Developing a formal diversity plan
    o Conducting a diversity climate analysis, or cultural audit
    o Providing diversity training by business unit, or management level
    o Recruiting, promoting, and retaining diverse talent
    o Preparing for a merger or acquisition, where two corporate cultures will mesh
    o Establishing Employee Resource Groups, or a Diversity Council

- Expanding operations internationally, nationally, or regionally, where the organization must understand customer's cultural nuances in the new market
- Building a supplier diversity program
- Creating multicultural curriculum or a multicultural marketing strategy
- Designing a generational diversity or multi-cultural communications campaign
- Pursuing socially responsible investors
- Any combination of these, or other Diversity and Inclusion objectives

The purpose should also align with the organization's strategic goals. Additionally, a short narrative description should identify the subject, scope, method of analysis, and major results.

- **Introduction**
Position the case by telling the audience about the background, history, context, or record of accomplishment. Again, do not use this as an opportunity to talk about slavery, ethnic cleansing, homophobia, or some other global issue-- stay focused on the business task.

Remind the audience about the problems, or business needs, such as lowering operating costs, improving customer satisfaction, developing professional skills, recruiting skilled human capital, and increasing capacity, production, or efficiency. Include other external factors such as competition or compliance with governmental regulations, as well as internal factors like policies or management directives. Briefly, describe alternatives.

- **Assumptions & Methods**
What will it take for the business case to accomplish its purpose? Set the audience's expectations properly with a formal and diplomatic disclaimer, but at the same time, base your projections in terms of financial metrics. These metrics may include, but are not limited to:

    - Return on Investment (ROI)
    - Cost per employee, client/student, or transaction
    - Legal costs and fines resulting from lawsuits
    - Lost client/student or market share
    - Other specific metrics

Include general assumptions pertaining to demographics, future trends, or competition. Equal Employment Opportunity (EEO) metrics and focus group data are popular sources to use in support of the case for diversity; however, the one of the most effective metrics to use to measure diversity's return on investment is organizational culture.

On the surface, organizational culture appears to be a soft metric. However, when you breakdown various aspects of organizational culture, you will find many opportunities for hard data. For example, cultural metrics may reflect inequities in the treatment of diverse employees, which correlates with disparities in the provision of services for diverse patients, students, constituents, or patrons. Alternatively, it may reflect lax discipline policies which results in unprofessional workplace conduct such as harassment and incivility. On the other hand, it may reflect gaps in employee skills that translate into lost customers or students.

Using metrics pertaining to organizational culture will secure and maintain the attention of senior level executives more than EEO or focus group data. Nevertheless, EEO and focus group data can be helpful in providing background information.

- **Scope & Boundaries**
Scope is the range of coverage encompassed by the business case along several dimensions. Boundaries define the scope of the business case more precisely; providing rules for which data belongs in the business case as well as guidelines for which data should be omitted. One dimension that always needs bounding is time. Other dimensions are geography/location, organization, function, and technology.

- **Scenarios**
Business cases are built to answer questions such as: Will the return justify the investment? What will this action do for our business performance? How will a Diversity and Inclusion strategy solve problems?

Such questions can only be answered if the business case is logically designed to address them. The term **scenario** refers to a story showing one way that events may unfold. Scenarios are designed to make the business case clear and tangible. Use concrete details to illustrate marketing opportunities in the Hispanic community, or to describe the costs of brick-and-mortar buildings in making the case for flexible work-life programs.

The best thing about scenarios is that you can compare what you are proposing with the current trajectory or a "do nothing" scenario. Comparing scenarios is an effective way to paint the picture for change.

- **Cost Model**
"Cost" refers to the expenditures of an organization. Financial impacts in each scenario that affect the business case should include costs—cost savings, avoided costs, continuing costs, and increased costs. For example, a Diversity and Inclusion strategy may reduce turnover costs.

The cost associated with turnover can be calculated using the formula in Figure 8.

FIGURE 8: TURNOVER CALCULATION

Annual salary x the number of employees who terminated in the last year = X

X (0.30% in benefits*) = Y

X + Y = Z

Z x 0.25% = Annual Turnover Cost

$30,000 annual salary x 12 diverse employees terminating = $360,000

$360,000 x 0.30 in benefits = $108,000

$360,000 + $108,000 = $468,000

$468,000 x 0.25% = $117,000 Annual Turnover Cost

30% in benefits represents the industry average

It may be convenient for a business to focus on a department that has high turnover with its diverse staff. However, the costs associated with operations, acquisitions (including new customers, investors, students, or donors), growth, and change may also be calculated.

When evaluating the cost, assess the price of NOT implementing a Diversity and Inclusion strategy. For instance, an organization may increase its share of a new market that is not diverse. Temporarily, it may appear to compensate for neglecting diverse markets. But over the long term, the cost of not implementing a diversity strategy may exponentially multiply with an increase in the global buying power of underrepresented populations. A great example of this phenomenon occurred recently in the retail sector-- where dozens of retailers are now struggling with bankruptcy because they ignored diverse markets. Thus, the short-term gain in new markets will not recover the cost of forgoing a Diversity and Inclusion program now.

- **Benefits**
  Although business is more than costs and savings, finances drive the business case. The following are objectives and contributions that may belong in the business case:

    o *Multicultural sales and marketing objectives*
        - ✓ To increase sales revenue
        - ✓ To improve market share

    o *Financial/business performance objectives*
        - ✓ To increase cash flow, margins or profits
        - ✓ To improve earnings per share

    o *Operational/functional objectives*
        - ✓ To shorten new product development time
        - ✓ To increase order-processing capacity

    o *Product/service objectives*
        - ✓ To improve customer/student/constituent satisfaction
        - ✓ To update the product line or curriculum

    o *Image enhancement objectives*
        - ✓ To be recognized as a leading product/service provider
        - ✓ To be known as a leader in social, educational or environmental issues

    o *Internal objectives*
        - ✓ To improve employee morale / job satisfaction by eliminating harassment, discrimination and incivility
        - ✓ To provide a challenging career path for employees

    o *Other business objectives*
        - ✓ To establish strategic alliances
        - ✓ To become a "total solution" provider

When the business case for diversity is presented via these objectives, the impact may be immediately recognized and measured in financial terms. Additionally, presenting the business case in this manner will avoid disagreements about "soft benefits."

Take supplier diversity for example. While supplier diversity provides economic benefits to the organization and the community by making bidding on contracts feasible for all vendors (the soft benefit), diverse suppliers can also provide significant ***cost savings*** on products and services in comparison to traditional vendors (hard, or tangible, benefits). Supplier diversity can also indirectly contribute to employment growth in underrepresented communities when small businesses hire new workers to fulfil contracts. Together with cost savings, these are just a few of the areas that supplier diversity can directly support a number of key organizational objectives.

- **Results**
Accordingly, there may be financial results and non-financial results. Nevertheless, if you assign no financial value to a real impact, it contributes nothing to the financial analysis. In this case, you run the risk of contributing to the bottom line but not receiving credit for doing so.

Financial results should be recorded as improvements to cash flow and compared to other scenarios. For example, your LGBTQ Employee Resource Group may invite other LGBTQ associations to your organization for a meeting to discuss strategic business opportunities. The result may be that your organization is selected as an exclusive partner by one of the associations. This partnership results in a 15% increase in new customers, new students, or new donors. A comparison could be made to equate the advantages of pursuing this business model over traditional methods, such as cold calls or direct mail.

When non-financial results are large enough to matter, and when they clearly influence a business objective, follow these three rules:

1. Be sure the impact is recorded. Describe it immediately after your financial benefits.
2. Make the impact tangible. Describe it in ways that can be observed or verified.
3. Compare the impact directly to the financial results, but in non-financial terms. Then illustrate non-financial results with a simple chart, graph, or picture (see Figure 9).

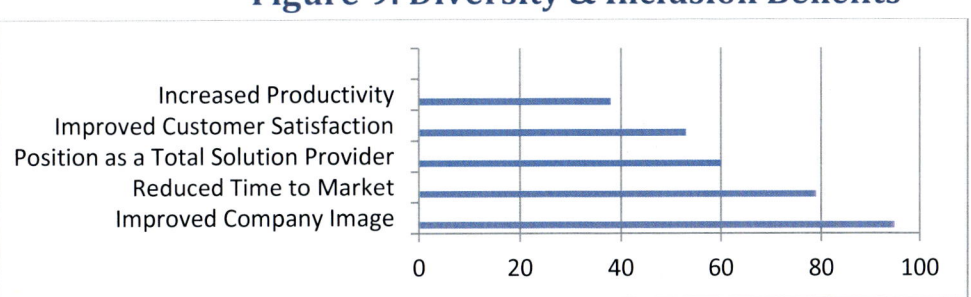

Figure 9: Diversity & Inclusion Benefits

SAMPLE BUSINESS CASE FOR DIVERSITY

Chubb developed one of the best business cases for diversity. The company offers its clients more than 170 commercial insurance products, which are innovative, comprehensive, and tailored to individual customer needs. In addition, Chubb provides an array of property and casualty insurance products for individuals and families with fine homes and possessions. Their customers include many of the most affluent families in the world, CEOs of Fortune 500 companies, and art collectors.

Fortune 500 Chubb has a worldwide network of offices in 54 countries staffed by 30,000 employees. After their merger with ACE Limited, the Chubb Corporation reported $37 billion in revenues in 2014 to become the world's largest publicly traded property and casualty insurer.

As stated throughout this competency, when organizations are particularly large and complex, the fundamental need for a Diversity and Inclusion strategy grows more profound.

Figure 10 encapsulates Chubb's business case for diversity:

FIGURE 10: THE BUSINESS CASE FOR DIVERSITY
THE CHUBB GROUP

Those who perceive diversity as exclusively a moral imperative or societal goal are missing the larger point. Workforce diversity needs to be viewed as a competitive advantage and a business opportunity. That's why Chubb makes diversity a business priority and strives to achieve a fully inclusive diverse workforce.

Defining Diversity
Diversity is about recognizing, respecting and valuing differences based on ethnicity, gender, color, age, race, religion, disability, national origin and sexual orientation. It also includes an infinite range of individual unique characteristics and experiences, such as communication style, career path, life experience, educational background, geographic location, income level, marital status, military experience, parental status and other variables that influence personal perspectives.

These life experiences and personal perspectives make us react and think differently, approach challenges and solve problems differently, make suggestions and decisions differently, and see different opportunities. Diversity, then, is also about diversity of thought. In addition, superior business performance requires tapping into these unique perspectives.

Diverse Workforce
As our U.S. and global customer base becomes steadily more diverse, significant portions of Chubb's future growth must come from tapping into these diverse markets. If we are to form lasting business relationships with our customers and become a true global leader in the industry, we must understand our customers' diverse cultures and decisional processes, not merely their languages.

> To do so, we must begin with a diverse workplace. It is well proven that diverse, heterogeneous teams promote creativity, innovation and product development. Only by fully embracing diversity and maximizing the well-being and contributions of our people can we fully maximize the strength and competitiveness of our company. We must encourage individuals to reach their full potential, in pursuit of organizational objectives, without anyone being advantaged or disadvantaged by our differences.
>
> **Demographics**
> Once a largely homogeneous group, the faces of customers, claimants, producers, employees and suppliers have been transformed into a dynamic mix of people comprised of various races, cultures and backgrounds. In 2008, "minorities" were roughly one-third of the U.S. Population; by 2042, "minorities" will be the majority.
>
> Clearly, the U.S. population—and the worlds—is changing dramatically. Forward-looking companies that recognize and understand the implications of these demographic shifts accordingly alter their customer focus, employee base and business practices to better manage the needs of current and future customers and employees.
>
> **Buying Power**
> To disregard the data on changing demographics, is to disregard the substantial growth in the buying power of diverse markets. Not only are these diverse minority groups increasing as a percentage of the U.S. population, but so too is the buying power they wield.
>
> From 1990 to 2007, minority market share and purchasing power doubled and in some cases tripled. In 2012, that buying power increased another 30%. This economic power is not limited to minorities. Gay and lesbian consumers will control a 6.4% market share, or $835 billion. The present and future monetary power of diverse markets is more apparent each year.
>
> **Business Imperative**
> In order for Chubb to remain competitive for talent and for customers, it is imperative that we attract and value diverse talent and enable that talent to attract and value diverse customers.

This model can be followed when developing a business case for diversity for any organization. The data and objectives can be tailored based on whether your organization is a for-profit, nonprofit, government agency, or an educational institution.

Sample Test Questions:
THE BUSINESS CASE FOR DIVERSITY & INCLUSION

1. The ethnorelative stage of the Bennett Scale includes:
   A. Defense
   B. Minimization
   C. Adaptation

2. The business case for Diversity and Inclusion is a:
   A. Summary of corporate grievances
   B. Reasoned proposal for change
   C. Detailed description of EEO data

3. The framework that assumes no single dimension of diversity takes place in isolation is:
   A. Uni-dimensional
   B. Bi-dimensional
   C. Multi-dimensional

4. The primary purpose of the business case for diversity is to:
   A. Invoke action
   B. Educate employees
   C. Eliminate bias

5. The following metric is a popular method for communicating the business case, but it is generally considered an ineffective metric by senior executives:
   A. Return on Investment
   B. Legal costs and fines
   C. Internal EEO data

6. Scope can be defined as:
   A. The range of coverage encompassed by the business case along several dimensions
   B. The rules for which data belongs in the business case, and which do not
   C. The instrument that you use to create your Diversity and Inclusion vision

Sample Test Questions:

THE BUSINESS CASE FOR DIVERSITY & INCLUSION (cont'd)

7. Any reference to the "organizational dimensions" of diversity pertains to:
   A. Things you can see
   B. Things you can change
   C. Things that you do

8. General assumptions about the diversity business case should include all of the following EXCEPT:
   A. Future trends
   B. Training goals
   C. Competition

9. For some people, ethnicity-based diversity initiatives result in:
   A. A zero-sum ratio
   B. Reverse discrimination
   C. Lower standards

10. Financial results in the Business Case should be recorded as improvements to cash flow and:
    A. Compared to other scenarios
    B. Described after non-financial results
    C. Be detailed in chart form

11. Diversity allows an organization to leverage its most strategic competitive resource, which is:
    A. An Innovative Product
    B. The Organizational Culture
    C. Its Human Capital

12. An example of a uni-dimensional framework is gender.
    A. True
    B. False

Sample Test Questions:
THE BUSINESS CASE FOR DIVERSITY & INCLUSION (cont'd)

13. If properly distinguishing between the terms: Inclusion pertains to people, while diversity concerns the organization.
    A. True
    B. False

14. Scenarios are designed to make the business case clear and tangible.
    A. True
    B. False

15. Financial justification is the only purpose of the business case for Diversity and Inclusion.
    A. True
    B. False

EEO LAWS IN THE U.S. & ABROAD

> *Preventing discrimination claims and lawsuits, as well as ensuring compliance, is a major role of the Diversity Officer and Practitioner. Accordingly, it requires commitment, diplomacy, leadership, teamwork, and persistence to effect change in long-standing practices and policies that ultimately lead to complaints. It entails educating front-line supervisors, managers and organizational leaders about their duties and responsibilities under the law.*

OVERALL OBJECTIVES AND COMPETENCIES

The purpose of this competency is to ensure that human resource officers and diversity practitioners can educate, compare and consult with supervisors about the basic tenets of global legislation that prohibits employment discrimination. Within the strategic and risk management functions of D&I, this competency necessitates empowering and delegating responsibility for addressing a wide range of unprofessional and/or illegal behavior to the supervisor.

OVERVIEW

The U.S. Equal Employment Opportunity Commission (EEOC) enforces Federal laws prohibiting employment discrimination. These laws protect employees, former employees, and job applicants against employment discrimination when it involves:

- Unfair treatment because of a person's race, color, religion, sex (including pregnancy, gender identity, and sexual orientation), national origin, age (40 or older), disability, or genetic information.
- Harassment by managers, co-workers, or others in the workplace, because of a person's race, color, religion, sex (including pregnancy, gender identity, and sexual orientation), national origin, age (40 or older), disability, or genetic information.
- Denial of a reasonable workplace accommodation that the employee needs because of religious beliefs or a disability.
- Retaliation because the employee complained about job discrimination, participated in a job discrimination investigation or lawsuit, or is associated with an employee that has filed a complaint of discrimination.

An employee or job applicant who believes that he or she has been discriminated against at work can file a "Charge of Discrimination." All the laws enforced by EEOC, except for the Equal Pay Act, require employees and applicants to file the Charge of Discrimination with the EEOC before they can file a job discrimination lawsuit against their employer. Employees of Federal government agencies must file with the agency where the alleged discriminatory action occurred. In addition, there are strict time limits for filing a charge.

The fact that the EEOC has taken a charge does not mean that discrimination has occurred or that the EEOC has found that the claim has merit. The charging party has alleged that an employer has discriminated against him or her, and it is the EEOC's job to investigate the matter to determine whether there is reasonable cause to believe that discrimination has occurred. Complaints of discrimination filed by Federal government employees against their employer are investigated by the respective Federal government agency before the complaint goes to the EEOC.

Other Requirements

EEOC regulations require that employers keep all personnel or employment records for one year. If an employee is involuntarily terminated, his/her personnel records must be retained for one year from the date of termination. If a charge has been filed, employers have additional recordkeeping obligations.

Employers are required to post notices describing the Federal laws prohibiting job discrimination based on a person's race, color, religion, sex (including pregnancy, gender identity, and sexual orientation), national origin, age (40 or older), disability or genetic information.

Additionally, some employers are required to submit the EEO-1 Report, a government form requiring many employers to provide a count of their employees by job category and by ethnicity, race and gender. The EEO-1 Report is submitted to both the EEOC and the Department of Labor. It must be filed annually by September 30th by (1) all employers with 100 or more employees; or (2) all federal government contractors and first-tier subcontractors with 50 or more employees **and** a contract amounting to $50,000 or more.

Coverage

Not all employers are covered by the laws that the EEOC enforces, and not all employees are protected. This can vary depending on the type of employer, the number of employees it has, and the type of discrimination alleged.

If an employer has the required number of employees, a person is protected by the anti-discrimination laws if he or she is:

- *An employee*
- *A job applicant*
- *A former employee*
- *An applicant or participant in a training or apprenticeship program*

Figuring out whether or not a person is an employee of an organization can be complicated, since people who are not employed by the employer, such as independent contractors, are not covered by the anti-discrimination laws.

EQUAL EMPLOYMENT OPPORTUNITY LAWS

While Diversity and Inclusion practitioners may be familiar with U.S. Equal Employment Opportunity (EEO) laws, it is imperative that front line supervisors, managers, and even some human resource professionals, know the laws as well. These laws include:

- **THE AGE DISCRIMINATION IN EMPLOYMENT ACT (ADEA)**
  The Age Discrimination in Employment Act of 1967 (ADEA) protects individuals who are 40 years of age or older from employment discrimination based on age. The ADEA's protections apply to both employees and job applicants. Under the ADEA, it is unlawful to discriminate against a person because of his/her age with respect to any term, condition, or privilege of employment, including hiring, firing, promotion, layoff, compensation, benefits, job assignments, and training.

  The ADEA only forbids age discrimination against people who are age 40 or older. It does not protect workers under the age of 40, although some states do have laws that protect younger workers from age discrimination. It is not illegal for an employer or other covered entity to favor an older worker over a younger one, even if both workers are age 40 or older. Additionally, discrimination can occur when the victim and the person who committed the discriminatory action are both over 40.

  It is also unlawful to retaliate against an individual for opposing employment practices that discriminate based on age or for filing an age discrimination charge, testifying, or participating in any way in an investigation, proceeding, or litigation under the ADEA.

  Employees have 180 calendar days from the day that the discrimination took place to file a charge with the EEOC. The 180 calendar-day filing deadline is extended to 300 calendar days if a state or local agency enforces a law that prohibits employment discrimination on the same basis. The ADEA applies to employers with 20 or more employees, including state and local governments. It also applies to employment agencies and labor organizations, as well as to the federal government. ADEA protections include:

  - Apprenticeship Programs
    It is generally unlawful for apprenticeship programs, including joint labor-management apprenticeship programs, to discriminate because of an individual's age. Age limitations in apprenticeship programs are valid only if they fall within certain specific exceptions under the ADEA or if the EEOC grants a specific exemption.

  - Job Notices and Advertisements
    The ADEA generally makes it unlawful to include age preferences, limitations, or specifications in job notices or advertisements. A job notice, or advertisement may specify an age limit only in the rare circumstances where age is shown to be a "bona fide occupational qualification" (BFOQ) reasonably necessary to the normal operation of the business.

- Pre-Employment Inquiries
  The ADEA does not specifically prohibit an employer from asking an applicant's age or date of birth. However, because such inquiries may deter older workers from applying for employment or may otherwise indicate possible intent to discriminate based on age, requests for age information will be closely scrutinized to make sure that the inquiry was made for a lawful purpose, rather than for a purpose prohibited by the ADEA. If the information is needed for a lawful purpose, it can be obtained after the employee is hired.

- Benefits
  The Older Workers Benefit Protection Act of 1990 (OWBPA) amended the ADEA to specifically prohibit employers from denying benefits to older employees. Congress recognized that the cost of providing certain benefits to older workers is greater than the cost of providing those same benefits to younger workers, and that those greater costs might create a disincentive to hire older workers. Therefore, in limited circumstances, an employer may be permitted to reduce benefits based on age, if the cost of providing the reduced benefits to older workers is not less than the cost of providing benefits to younger workers.

Employers are permitted to coordinate retiree health benefit plans with eligibility for Medicare or a comparable state-sponsored health benefit.

- Waivers of ADEA Rights
  An employer may ask an employee to waive his/her rights or claims under the ADEA. Such waivers are common in settling ADEA discrimination claims in relation to an exit incentive or other employment termination program. However, the ADEA sets out specific minimum standards that must be met for a waiver to be considered valid. Among other requirements, a valid ADEA waiver must:

    ✓ Be in writing and be understandable;
    ✓ Specifically refer to ADEA rights or claims;
    ✓ Not waive rights or claims that may arise in the future;
    ✓ Be in exchange for valuable consideration in addition to anything of value to which the individual is already entitled;
    ✓ Advise the individual in writing to consult an attorney before signing the waiver; and
    ✓ Provide the individual at least 21 days to consider the agreement and at least seven days to revoke the agreement after signing it.

If an employer requests an ADEA waiver relating to an exit incentive or other employment termination program, the minimum requirements for a valid waiver are more extensive.

- **THE AMERICANS WITH DISABILITIES ACT (ADA)**
  Title I of the Americans with Disabilities Act of 1990 prohibits private employers, state and local governments, employment agencies and labor unions from discriminating against qualified individuals with disabilities in job application procedures, hiring, firing, advancement, compensation, job training, and other terms, conditions, and privileges of employment. The ADA covers employers with 15 or more employees, including state and local governments, employment agencies and labor organizations.

In 2008, the ADA was amended to provide further protections. The Act retains the ADA's basic definition of "disability" as an impairment that substantially limits one or more major life activities, a record of such an impairment, or being regarded as having such an impairment. However, it changes the way that these statutory terms should be interpreted in several ways. Most significantly, the Act:

- Directs EEOC to revise that portion of its regulations defining the phrase "substantially limits";
- Expands the definition of "major life activities" by including two non-exhaustive lists:

    1) The first list includes many activities that the EEOC has recognized (e.g., walking) as well as activities that EEOC has not specifically recognized (e.g., reading, bending, and communicating);

    2) The second list includes major bodily functions (e.g., "functions of the immune system, normal cell growth, digestive, bowel, bladder, neurological, brain, respiratory, circulatory, endocrine, and reproductive functions").

- States that mitigating measures other than "ordinary eyeglasses or contact lenses" shall not be considered in assessing whether an individual has a disability;
- Clarifies that an impairment that is episodic or in remission is a disability if it would substantially limit a major life activity when active;
- Changes the definition of "regarded as" so that it no longer requires a showing that the employer perceived the individual to be substantially limited in a major life activity, and instead says that an applicant or employee is "regarded as" disabled if he or she is subject to an action prohibited by the ADA (e.g., failure to hire or termination) based on an impairment that is not transitory and minor;
- Provides that individuals covered only under the "regarded as" prong are not entitled to a reasonable accommodation.

Not everyone with a medical condition is protected by the law. To be protected, a person must be qualified for the job and have a disability as defined by the law. A person can show that he or she has a disability in one of three ways:

1) A person may be disabled if he or she has a physical or mental condition that substantially limits a major life activity (such as walking, talking, seeing, hearing, or learning).

2) A person may be disabled if he or she has a history of a disability (such as cancer that is in remission).

3) A person may be disabled if he is believed to have a physical or mental impairment that is not transitory (lasting or expected to last six months or less) and minor (even if he does not have such an impairment).

A qualified employee or applicant with a disability is an individual who, with or without reasonable accommodations, can perform the essential functions of the job in question. Reasonable accommodation may include, but is not limited to:

- Making existing facilities used by employees readily accessible to and usable by persons with disabilities.
- Job restructuring, modifying work schedules, or reassignment to a vacant position.
- Acquiring or modifying equipment or devices; adjusting or modifying examinations, training materials, or policies; and providing qualified readers or interpreters.

An employer or other covered entity is required to make a reasonable accommodation to the known disability of a qualified applicant or employee if it would not impose an "undue hardship" on the operation of the employer's business. **Reasonable Accommodations** are adjustments or modifications provided by an employer to enable people with disabilities to enjoy equal employment opportunities. Accommodations vary depending on the needs of the individual applicant or employee. Not all people with disabilities (or even all people with the same disability) will require the same accommodation.
For example:

- A deaf applicant may need a sign language interpreter during the job interview.
- An employee with diabetes may need regularly-scheduled breaks during the workday to eat properly and monitor blood sugar and insulin levels.
- A blind employee may need someone to read information posted on a bulletin board.
- An employee with cancer may need leave to have radiation or chemotherapy treatments.

An employer does not have to provide a reasonable accommodation if it imposes an "undue hardship." **Undue Hardship** is defined as an action requiring significant difficulty or expense when considering factors such as an employer's size, financial resources, and the nature and structure of its operation. An employer is not required to lower quality or production standards to make an accommodation; nor is an employer obligated to provide personal use items such as glasses or hearing aids.

An employer generally does not have to provide a reasonable accommodation unless an individual with a disability has made a request for one. If an employer believes that a medical condition is causing a performance or conduct problem, the employer may ask the employee how to solve the problem and whether the employee needs a reasonable accommodation. Once a reasonable accommodation is requested, the employer and the individual should engage in an interactive process to determine the individual's needs and to identify the appropriate reasonable accommodation. Where more than one accommodation would work, the employer may choose the one that is less costly or that is easier to provide. In some cases, medical documentation may be required and recommendations for what may be considered as a reasonable accommodation by the attending physician or medical provider. The employer makes the ultimate decision regarding which reasonable accommodation will be provided.

Title I of the ADA also covers:

- Medical Examinations and Inquiries
  Employers may not ask job applicants about the existence, nature, or severity of a disability. Applicants may be asked about their ability to perform specific job functions but not the types of doctors, frequency of visits, or required medications for their disability. A job offer may be conditioned on the results of a medical examination, but only if the examination is required for all entering employees in similar jobs. Medical examinations of employees must be job related and consistent with the employer's business needs.

- Confidential Medical Records
  The basic rule is that, with limited exceptions, employers must keep any medical information they learn about an applicant or employee confidential. Information can be confidential even if it contains no medical diagnosis or treatment course and even if it is not generated by a health care professional. For example, an employee's request for a reasonable accommodation would be considered medical information subject to the ADA's confidentiality requirements.

- Drug and Alcohol Abuse
  Employees and applicants currently engaging in the illegal use of drugs are not covered by the ADA when an employer acts based on such use. Tests for illegal drugs are not subject to the ADA's restrictions on medical examinations. Employers may hold illegal drug users and alcoholics to the same performance standards as other employees.

It is also unlawful to retaliate against an individual for opposing employment practices that discriminate based on a disability or for filing a discrimination charge, testifying, or participating in any way in an investigation, proceeding, or litigation under the ADA.

- **THE EQUAL PAY ACT AND COMPENSATION DISCRIMINATION**
  The Equal Pay Act requires that men and women are given equal pay for equal work in the same establishment. The jobs need not be identical, but they must be substantially equal. It is job content, not job title, that determines whether jobs are substantially equal. Specifically, the EPA provides that employers may not pay unequal wages to men and women who perform jobs that require substantially equal skill, effort, and responsibility, and that are performed under similar working conditions within the same establishment.

  Each of these factors is summarized below:

  - Skill
    Measured by factors such as the experience, ability, education, and training required to perform the job. The issue is what skills are required for the job, not what skills the individual employees may have. For example, two bookkeeping jobs could be considered equal under the EPA even if one of the job holders has a master's degree in physics, since that degree would not be required for the job.

  - Effort
    The amount of physical or mental exertion needed to perform the job. For example, suppose that men and women work side by side on a line assembling machine parts. The person at the end of the line must also lift the assembled product as he or she completes the work and places it on a board. That job requires more effort than the other assembly line jobs if the

extra effort of lifting the assembled product off the line is substantial and is a regular part of the job. As a result, it would not be a violation to pay that person more, regardless of whether the job is held by a man or a woman.

- Responsibility
  The degree of accountability required in performing the job. For example, a salesperson who is delegated the duty of determining whether to accept customers' personal checks has more responsibility than other salespeople. On the other hand, a minor difference in responsibility, such as turning out the lights at the end of the day, would not justify a pay differential.

- Working Conditions
  This encompasses two factors: (1) physical surroundings like temperature, fumes, and ventilation; and (2) hazards.

- Establishment
  The prohibition against compensation discrimination under the EPA applies only to jobs within an establishment. An establishment is a distinct physical place of business rather than an entire business or enterprise consisting of several places of business. In some circumstances, physically separate places of business may be treated as one establishment. For example, administrative unit hires employees, sets their compensation, and assigns them to separate work locations; the separate work sites can be considered part of one establishment.

  The law against compensation discrimination includes all payments made to or on behalf of employees as remuneration for employment. All forms of compensation are covered, including salary, overtime pay, bonuses, stock options, profit sharing and bonus plans, life insurance, vacation and holiday pay, cleaning or gasoline allowances, hotel accommodations, reimbursement for travel expenses, and benefits.

  Pay differentials are permitted when they are based on seniority, merit, quantity or quality of production, or a factor other than sex. These are known as "affirmative defenses" and it is the employer's burden to prove that they apply. In correcting a pay differential, no employee's pay may be reduced. Instead, the compensation of the lower paid employee(s) must be increased.

  The EPA was amended by the Lilly Ledbetter Fair Pay Act (the "Act"). On January 29, 2009, President Obama signed the first piece of legislation of his Administration: the Lilly Ledbetter Fair Pay Act of 2009. This law overturned the Supreme Court's decision in Ledbetter v. Goodyear Tire & Rubber Co., Inc. (2007), which severely restricted the time for filing complaints of employment discrimination concerning compensation.

  The Act states the EEOC's longstanding position that each paycheck that contains discriminatory compensation is a separate violation regardless of when the discrimination began.

People challenging a wide variety of practices that resulted in discriminatory compensation can benefit from the passage of this Act. These practices may include employer decisions about base pay or wages, job classifications, career ladder or other noncompetitive promotion denials, tenure denials, and failure to respond to requests for raises.

For example, some states have begun to supplement Federal laws with legislation outlawing pay history questions. According to HRDIVE, "The laws are aimed at ending the cycle of pay discrimination and some go further than merely banning pay history questions. A few also prohibit an employer from relying on an applicant's pay history to set compensation if discovered or volunteered; others prohibit an employer from taking disciplinary action against employees who discuss pay with coworkers." Therefore, as a best practice, employers are encouraged to pay employees based on the job experience and work that will be performed, or according to the salary range appropriated in the job description.

- **THE GENETIC INFORMATION NONDISCRIMINATION ACT (GINA)**
  The Genetic Information Nondiscrimination Act (GINA) became law on May 21, 2008. Title I of GINA amends portions of the Employee Retirement Income Security Act (ERISA), the Public Health Service Act, and the Internal Revenue Code to address the use of genetic information in health insurance. Title II prohibits the use of genetic information in employment; restricts employers and other entities covered by Title II from requesting, requiring, or purchasing genetic information; and strictly limits the disclosure of genetic information. Laws in 34 states also prohibit employment discrimination based on genetic information.

  Effective 2009, GINA makes it illegal to discriminate against employees or applicants because of genetic information. Genetic information includes data about an individual's genetic tests and the genetic tests of an individual's family members, as well as information about any disease, disorder or condition of an individual's family members (i.e., an individual's family medical history). The law also makes it illegal to retaliate against a person because the person complained about discrimination, filed a charge of discrimination, or participated in an employment discrimination investigation or lawsuit.

  GINA was enacted, in large part, because of developments in the field of genetics, the decoding of the human genome, and advances in the field of genomic medicine. Genetic tests now exist that can determine whether individuals are at risk for specific diseases or disorders. As the number of genetic tests increases, so do the concerns of individuals fearing negative employment actions because of their genetic information. Congress enacted GINA to address these concerns by prohibiting discrimination based on genetic information and restricting the acquisition and disclosure of such information.

  Title II of GINA prohibits the use of genetic information in making decisions related to any terms, conditions, or privileges of employment (e.g., hiring, firing, and opportunities for advancement); restricts employers and other entities covered by Title II from requesting, requiring, or purchasing genetic information, with limited exceptions; generally requires covered entities to keep any genetic information they have about applicants or employees confidential; and prohibits retaliation.

  The final rule clarifies that a "request" for genetic information includes actions such as conducting an Internet search on an individual in a way that is likely to result in a covered entity obtaining genetic information; actively listening to third-party conversations, or searching an individual's personal effects for the purpose of obtaining genetic information; and making requests for information about an individual's current health status in a way that is likely to result in a covered entity obtaining genetic information.

The statute and the final rule state that "genetic information" includes:

- Information about an individual's genetic tests;
- Information about the genetic tests of a family member;
- Family medical history;
- Requests for and receipt of genetic services by an individual or a family member; and
- Genetic information about a fetus carried by an individual or family member or of an embryo legally held by the individual or family member using assisted reproductive technology.

There are six narrowly-defined situations where genetic information can be acquired:

1) When the information is acquired inadvertently;
2) As part of health or genetic services (including a wellness program) that a covered entity provides on a voluntary basis;
3) In the form of family medical history to comply with the certification requirements of the Family and Medical Leave Act, state or local leave laws, or certain employer leave policies;
4) From sources that are commercially and publicly available, such as newspapers, books, magazines, and even electronic sources;
5) As part of genetic monitoring that is either required by law or provided on a voluntary basis; and
6) By employers who conduct DNA testing for law enforcement purposes as a forensic lab, or for human remains identification.

- **NATIONAL ORIGIN DISCRIMINATION**
  Whether an employee or job applicant's ancestry is Mexican, Ukrainian, Filipino, Middle Eastern, Native American, or any other nationality, he or she is entitled to the same employment opportunities as anyone else. EEOC enforces the federal prohibition against national origin discrimination in employment under Title VII of the Civil Rights Act of 1964, which covers employers with 15 or more workers.

  Under the law, no one can be denied equal employment opportunity because of birthplace, ancestry, culture, linguistic characteristics common to a specific ethnic group, or accent. National origin discrimination also involves treating people (applicants or employees) unfavorably because they are from another country or part of the world, because of ethnicity or accent, or because they **appear** to be of a certain ethnic background. Equal employment opportunity cannot be denied because of marriage or association with persons of a national origin group; membership or association with specific ethnic groups; attendance or participation in schools, churches, temples or mosques generally associated with a national origin group; or a surname associated with a national origin group.

  Discrimination can occur when the victim and the person who inflicted the discrimination are the same national origin.

Title VII prohibits any employment decision based on national origin, including but not limited to actions such as recruiting, hiring, disciplining, and firing. Title VII also prohibits offensive conduct, such as ethnic slurs, that creates a hostile work environment based on national origin. Employers are required to take appropriate steps to prevent and correct unlawful harassment. Likewise, employees are responsible for reporting harassment at an early stage to prevent its escalation.

Furthermore, the law addresses the following:

- Accent Discrimination
    An employer may not base a decision on an employee's foreign accent unless the accent materially interferes with job performance.

- English Fluency
    A fluency requirement is only permissible if it is required for the effective performance of the position for which it is imposed.

- English-Only Rules
    English-only rules must be adopted for nondiscriminatory reasons. An English-only rule may be used if it is needed to promote the safe or efficient operation of the employer's business.

- Coverage of Foreign Nationals
    Title VII and the other antidiscrimination laws prohibit discrimination against individuals employed in the United States, regardless of citizenship. However, relief may be limited if an individual does not have work authorization. The Immigration Reform and Control Act of 1986 (IRCA) requires employers to prove all employees hired after November 6, 1986 are legally authorized to work in the United States. IRCA also prohibits discrimination based on national origin or citizenship.

- **SEX-BASED DISCRIMINATION**
  Sex discrimination involves treating someone (an applicant or employee) unfavorably because of that person's sex. Discrimination against an individual because of gender identity (including transgender status) or because of sexual orientation is also a violation of Title VII. Additionally, sex discrimination includes protections for caregivers.

  Sex discrimination can involve treating someone less favorably because of his or her connection with an organization or group that is generally associated with people of a certain sex. An employment policy or practice that applies to everyone, regardless of sex, can be illegal if it has a negative impact on the employment of people of a certain sex and is not job-related or necessary to the operation of the business.

- **SEXUAL ORIENTATION AND GENDER IDENTITY DISCRIMINATION**
  Sexual orientation means one's emotional or physical attraction to the same and/or opposite sex. Gender identity means one's inner sense of one's own gender, which may or may not match the sex assigned at birth. Different people choose to express their gender identity differently. For some, gender may be expressed through, for example: dress, grooming,

mannerisms, speech patterns, and social interactions. Gender expression usually ranges between masculine and feminine, and some transgender people express their gender consistent with how they identify internally, rather than in accordance with the sex they were assigned at birth.

It is the policy of the Federal Government to provide equal employment opportunity to all individuals. Executive Order 11478, as amended, expressly prohibits discrimination based on sexual orientation and gender identity within executive branch civilian employment. It also prohibits discrimination based on race, color, religion, sex, national origin, disability, parental status, and age. The Executive Order states that this non-discrimination policy "must be an integral part of every aspect of personnel policy and practice in the employment, development, advancement, and treatment of civilian employees of the Federal Government, to the extent permitted by law."

There are a number of administrative and legal protections available to workers who believe they have been discriminated against because of their sexual orientation or gender identity, including Title VII of the Civil Rights Act of 1964; Civil Service Reform Act of 1978; and/or other procedures.

Title VII's prohibition on sex discrimination protects persons who have been discriminated against based on sexual orientation and gender identity. Further, civil service laws prohibit certain employment decisions or personnel actions when the decisions or actions are based on conduct that does not adversely affect job performance, including sexual orientation and gender identity. In addition, individual agencies and unions may establish procedures to resolve disputes, including complaints of discrimination based on sexual orientation and gender identity.

This resource guide provides basic and general information about these various procedures and the circumstances under which applicants and employees may be able to take a particular course of action. Under some circumstances, more than one procedure may be available, and the choice of one procedure may preclude the use of others.

Most of the available avenues require employees to raise the allegations within a specific time frame from the date that the alleged discrimination occurred. The remedies available may also differ depending on the course of action that is chosen.

- **PREGNANCY DISCRIMINATION**
  The Pregnancy Discrimination Act amended Title VII of the Civil Rights Act of 1964, and covers employers with 15 or more employees, including state and local governments. Title VII also applies to employment agencies and labor organizations, as well as to the federal government. In passing the PDA, Congress intended to prohibit discrimination based on "the whole range of matters concerning the childbearing process."

  Women who are pregnant or affected by pregnancy-related conditions must be treated in the same manner as other applicants or employees with similar abilities or limitations.

  Title VII's pregnancy-related protections cover women based on a current pregnancy; past pregnancy; potential or intended pregnancy; and any medical conditions related to pregnancy or childbirth. It also includes:

- Hiring
  An employer cannot refuse to hire a pregnant woman because of her pregnancy, because of a pregnancy-related condition, or because of the prejudices of co-workers, clients, or customers.

- Pregnancy & Maternity Leave
  An employer may not single out pregnancy-related conditions for special procedures to determine an employee's ability to work. However, if an employer requires its employees to submit a doctor's statement concerning their inability to work before granting leave or paying sick benefits, the employer may require employees affected by pregnancy-related conditions to submit such statements.

If an employee is temporarily unable to perform her job because of her pregnancy, the employer must treat her the same as any other temporarily disabled employee. For example, if the employer allows temporarily disabled employees to modify tasks, perform alternative assignments, or take disability leave or leave without pay, the employer also must allow an employee who is temporarily disabled because of pregnancy to do the same.

Pregnant employees must be permitted to work if they are able to perform their jobs. If an employee has been absent from work because of a pregnancy-related condition and recovers, her employer may not require her to remain on leave until the baby's birth.

- Break Time for Nursing Mothers
  Employers are required to provide "reasonable break time for an employee to express breast milk for her nursing child for one (1) year after the child's birth each time such employee has a need to express the milk." Employers are also required to provide "a place, other than a bathroom, that is shielded from view and free from intrusion from coworkers and the public, which may be used by an employee to express breast milk."

- Health Insurance
  Any health insurance provided by an employer must cover expenses for pregnancy-related conditions on the same basis as costs for other medical conditions. An employer need not provide health insurance for expenses arising from abortion, except where the life of the mother is endangered. Pregnancy-related expenses should be reimbursed exactly as those incurred for other medical conditions, whether payment is on a fixed basis or based on a percentage of reasonable-and-customary-charges.

  The amounts payable by the insurance provider can be limited only to the same extent as amounts payable for other conditions. No additional, increased, or larger deductible can be imposed.

  Employers must also provide the same level of health benefits for spouses of male employees as they do for spouses of female employees.

- Fringe Benefits
  Pregnancy-related benefits cannot be limited to married employees. In an all-female workforce or job classification, benefits must be provided for pregnancy-related conditions if benefits are provided for other medical conditions.

If an employer provides any benefits to workers on leave, the employer must provide the same benefits for those on leave for pregnancy-related conditions.

Employees on leave because of pregnancy-related conditions must be treated the same as other temporarily disabled employees for accrual and crediting of seniority, vacation calculations, pay increases, and temporary disability benefits.

It is also unlawful to retaliate against an individual for opposing employment practices that discriminate based on pregnancy or for filing a discrimination charge, testifying, or participating in any way in an investigation, proceeding, or litigation under Title VII.

- **RACE/COLOR DISCRIMINATION**
With all the advances that most Americans believe the country has made pertaining to discrimination, bias, prejudice, and stereotypes, racial discrimination is still one of the top issues for employers and employees throughout the U.S. In 2017, 33.9% of EEOC charges involved race discrimination-- which surpassed every other claim type except retaliation. Additionally, the unemployment rate for people of color is disproportionately higher than the unemployment rates for Caucasians. While discrimination may not be overtly blamed for *all* employment inequities, **it is** covertly responsible for many adverse employment outcomes for people of color.

    Title VII of the Civil Rights Act of 1964 protects individuals against employment discrimination based on race and color as well as national origin, sex, or religion.

    It is unlawful to discriminate against any employee or applicant for employment because of race or color in regard to hiring, termination, promotion, compensation, job training, or any other term, condition, or privilege of employment. Title VII also prohibits employment decisions based on stereotypes and assumptions about abilities, traits, or the performance of individuals of certain racial groups.

    Title VII prohibits both intentional discrimination and neutral job policies that are not job related and that disproportionately impacts minorities.

    Equal employment opportunity cannot be denied because of marriage to or association with an individual of a different race; membership in or association with ethnic-based organizations or groups; attendance or participation in schools or places of worship generally associated with certain minority groups; or other cultural practices or characteristics often linked to race or ethnicity, such as cultural dress or manner of speech, as long as the cultural practice or characteristic does not materially interfere with the ability to perform job duties.

    o Race-Related Characteristics and Conditions
    Discrimination based on an immutable characteristic associated with race, such as skin color, hair texture, or certain facial features violates Title VII, even though not all members of the race share the same characteristics.

    Title VII also prohibits discrimination because of a condition which predominantly affects one race unless the practice is job related and consistent with business necessity.

For example, since sickle cell anemia predominantly occurs in African-Americans, a policy which excludes individuals with sickle cell anemia is discriminatory unless the policy is job related and consistent with business necessity. Similarly, a "no-beard" employment policy may discriminate against African-American men who have a predisposition to pseudo folliculitis barbae (severe shaving bumps) unless the policy is job-related and consistent with business necessity.

- Color Discrimination
  Even though race and color clearly overlap, they are not synonymous. Color discrimination can occur between persons of different races or ethnicities, or between persons of the same race or ethnicity. Although Title VII does not define "color," the courts and the Commission read "color" to have its commonly understood meaning – pigmentation, complexion, skin shade, or tone. Thus, color discrimination occurs when a person is discriminated against based on the lightness, darkness, or other color characteristic of the person. Title VII prohibits race/color discrimination against all persons, including Caucasians.

  Although a plaintiff may prove a claim of discrimination through direct or circumstantial evidence, some courts take the position that if a Caucasian person relies on circumstantial evidence to establish a reverse discrimination claim, he or she must meet a heightened standard of proof. The Commission, in contrast, applies the same standard of proof to all race discrimination claims, regardless of the victim's race or the type of evidence used. In either case, the ultimate burden of persuasion always remains with the plaintiff.

Title VII's protections include:

- Recruiting, Hiring, and Advancement
  Job requirements must be uniformly and consistently applied to persons of all races and colors. Where a job requirement is applied consistently, if it is not important for job performance or business needs, the requirement may be found unlawful if it excludes persons of a certain racial group or color significantly more than others.

  Examples of potentially unlawful practices include: (1) soliciting applications only from sources in which all or most potential workers are of the same race or color; (2) requiring applicants to have a certain educational background that is not important for job performance or business needs; (3) testing applicants for knowledge, skills or abilities that are not important for job performance or business needs.

  Employers may legitimately need information about their employees or applicants race for affirmative action purposes and/or to track applicant flow. One way to obtain racial information and simultaneously guard against discriminatory selection is for employers to use separate forms or otherwise keep the information about an applicant's race separate from the application. In that way, the employer can capture the information it needs but ensure that it is not used in the selection decision.

Unless the information is for a legitimate purpose, pre-employment questions about race can suggest that race will be used as a basis for making selection decisions. If the information is used in the selection decision and members of particular racial groups are excluded from employment, the inquiries can constitute evidence of discrimination.

- Segregation and Classification of Employees
Title VII is violated where minority employees are segregated by physically isolating them from other employees or from customer contact. Title VII also prohibits assigning primarily minorities to predominantly minority establishments or geographic areas. It is also illegal to exclude minorities from certain positions or to group or categorize employees or jobs so that certain jobs are generally held by minorities. Title VII does not permit racially motivated decisions driven by business concerns – for example, concerns about the effect on employee relations, or the negative reaction of clients or customers. Race or color as a bona fide occupational qualification is prohibited under Title VII.

Coding applications/resumes to designate an applicant's race, by either an employer or employment agency, constitutes evidence of discrimination where minorities are excluded from employment or from certain positions. Such discriminatory coding includes the use of facially benign code terms that implicate race, for example, by area codes where many racial minorities may or are presumed to live.

- **RELIGIOUS DISCRIMINATION**
Title VII of the Civil Rights Act of 1964 prohibits employers from discriminating against individuals because of their religion in hiring, firing, and other terms and conditions of employment. The Act also requires an employer or other covered entity to reasonably accommodate the religious practices of an employee or prospective employee, unless to do so would create an undue hardship on the employer. A reasonable religious accommodation is any adjustment to the work environment that will allow the employee to practice his/her religion. Flexible scheduling, voluntary substitutions or swaps, job reassignments and lateral transfers are examples of accommodating an employee's religious beliefs.

Employers generally should not schedule examinations or other selection activities in conflict with a religious practice, inquire about an applicant's future availability at certain times, maintain a restrictive dress code, or refuse to allow observance of a Sabbath or religious holiday, unless the employer can show that doing so would cause an undue hardship.
An employer can claim undue hardship when asked to accommodate an applicant's or employee's religious practices if allowing such practices requires more than ordinary administrative costs, diminishes efficiency in other jobs, infringes on other employees' job rights or benefits, impairs workplace safety, causes co-workers to carry the accommodated employee's share of potentially hazardous or burdensome work, or if the proposed accommodation conflicts with another law or regulation. Undue hardship also may be shown if the request for an accommodation violates the terms of a collective bargaining agreement or job rights established through a seniority system.

An employee whose religious practices prohibit payment of union dues to a labor organization cannot be required to pay the dues but may pay an equal sum to a charitable organization.

- **LEGAL 101**
  The courts are going to dissect discrimination claims according to the facts. Therefore, evidence may fall into one of the following case categories: *disparate treatment, disparate impact*, and *prima facie.*

    o **In a disparate treatment case**, the employee is claiming that the employer treated her differently than other employees who were in a similar situation. For example, both Jane and Paul skip work one day; the employer fires Jane but does not fire Paul. If the *reason* is because Jane is female, then this is disparate treatment because of sex, which would violate Title VII. If the *real reason* is because Jane had a worse attendance record, then it could be disparate treatment because of differences in attendance, and therefore lawful.

    o **In a disparate impact case**, the claim is that the employer has a practice that has a much bigger impact on one group than on another. For example, the employer won't hire janitors unless they are high school graduates. This might have a much bigger impact on blacks than on whites.

    o A **"prima facie case"** is what an employee must prove in a discrimination case in order to require an employer to explain itself in court. It is that minimum set of facts that a plaintiff has to include in a court complaint and be prepared to actually prove it. There are three basic ways to make a prima facie case.

        1) When the employer has a **"facial" policy** of unlawful discrimination. For example, the employer has stated a policy that it will hire only females to be food servers. This is an extremely rare situation because employers have become more sophisticated.

        2) Where there is **"direct evidence"** or what a lawyer might call a 'smoking gun'. For example, the employer says to an applicant "I'm not going to hire you because you're not white." Again, this is rare, but sometimes it happens. It's amazing how often an employee can prove that an employer said something like "Let's get rid of all the old employees" or "We've already hired one Mexican and that's enough."

        3) When there is **"circumstantial evidence."** Tons of cases fall into this category, and things can get a bit complicated.

  The US Supreme Court made a landmark decision in a case in which a man claimed he wasn't hired because he was black. The Court said this is what he had to show:

    ✓ He was a member of a protected class (in this case, he was black).
    ✓ He applied for the job, and the job was open.
    ✓ He had the minimum qualifications for the job.
    ✓ He was not hired.
    ✓ The job remained open, or a person of another race was hired for it.

  That framework became the model for all other circumstantial evidence discrimination claims: race, sex, religion, national origin, age, disability, etc. It also became the framework for cases involving not just failure to hire, but also discharge, demotion, transfer, suspension, and other adverse employment decisions.

Of course, for each specific case the elements of proof might need to be adjusted to fit the different situation. For example, in a discharge case, the employee might have to prove that she was meeting the employer's reasonable expectations. In a case claiming discharge because of age, the employee might have to prove that someone significantly younger was kept on the job.

Notice that the Supreme Court made it somewhat easy for a plaintiff to make out a prima facie case; however, that doesn't necessarily mean the employee will prevail in his/her complaint or charge. It only means that the employer must now put forth evidence that the individual was fired (or not hired, etc.) for a "legitimate non-discriminatory reason."

- **RETALIATION**
  A new leader has emerged among claims as retaliation has become the most frequently asserted claim by individuals in EEOC charges. In fact, 48.8% of all charges filed with the EEOC in 2017 included a claim of retaliation. In the Federal sector, retaliation is the most frequently alleged basis of discrimination and the most common discrimination finding in federal sector cases.

  Regardless of whether discrimination is proven, it is relatively easier to demonstrate that retaliation has occurred in this world of layoffs, position eliminations, and other common workplace changes.

  According to the EEOC, an employer or other covered entity may not fire, demote, harass or otherwise "retaliate" against an individual for filing a charge of discrimination, participating in a discrimination proceeding, or otherwise opposing discrimination. The same laws that prohibit discrimination based on race, color, sex, religion, national origin, age, and disability, as well as wage differences between men and women performing substantially equal work, also prohibit retaliation against individuals who oppose unlawful discrimination or participate in an employment discrimination proceeding.

  In addition to the protections against retaliation that are included in all the laws enforced by EEOC, the ADA also protects individuals from coercion, intimidation, threat, harassment, or interference in the exercise of their own rights or their encouragement of someone else's exercise of rights granted by the ADA.

  There are three main terms that are used to describe retaliation. Retaliation occurs when an employer, employment agency, or labor organization takes an **adverse action** against a **covered individual** because he or she engaged in a **protected activity**. Following is a detailed explanation of each term:

  o *Adverse Action*
    An adverse action is an action taken to try to keep someone from opposing a discriminatory practice, or from participating in an employment discrimination proceeding. Examples of adverse actions include:

    - ✓ Employment actions such as termination, refusal to hire, and denial of promotion;
    - ✓ Other actions affecting employment such as threats, unjustified negative evaluations, unjustified negative references, or increased surveillance; and
    - ✓ Any other action such as an assault, or unfounded civil or criminal charges that are likely to deter reasonable people from pursuing their rights.

Adverse actions do not include petty slights and annoyances, such as stray negative comments in an otherwise positive or neutral evaluation, "snubbing" a colleague, or negative comments that are justified by an employee's poor work performance or history.

Even if the prior protected activity alleged wrongdoing by a different employer, retaliatory adverse actions are unlawful. For example, it is unlawful for a worker's current employer to retaliate against him for pursuing an EEO charge against a former employer.

Of course, employees are not excused from continuing to perform their jobs or follow their company's legitimate workplace rules just because they have filed a complaint with the EEOC or opposed discrimination.

- Covered Individuals
  Covered individuals are people who have opposed unlawful practices, participated in proceedings, or requested accommodations related to employment discrimination based on race, color, sex, religion, national origin, age, or disability.

  Individuals who have a close association with someone who has engaged in such protected activity also are covered individuals. For example, it is illegal to terminate an employee because his/her spouse participated in employment discrimination litigation.

  Individuals who have brought attention to violations of law other than employment discrimination are NOT covered individuals for purposes of anti-discrimination retaliation laws. For example, "whistleblowers" who raise ethical, financial, or other concerns unrelated to employment discrimination are not protected by the EEOC enforced laws.

- Protected Activity
  The EEO laws prohibit punishing job applicants or employees for asserting their rights to be free from employment discrimination including harassment. Asserting these EEO rights is called "protected activity," and it can take many forms. Protected activity includes:

  - *Opposition to a practice believed to be unlawful discrimination*
    Opposition is informing an employer that you believe that he/she is engaging in prohibited discrimination. Opposition is protected from retaliation as long as it is based on a reasonable, good-faith belief that the complained of practice violates anti-discrimination law; and the manner of the opposition is reasonable.

    Examples of protected opposition include:

    - ✓ Complaining to anyone about alleged discrimination against oneself or others;
    - ✓ Threatening to file a charge of discrimination;
    - ✓ Picketing in opposition to discrimination; or
    - ✓ Refusing to obey an order reasonably believed to be discriminatory.

Examples of activities that are NOT considered "protected opposition" include:

- ✓ Actions that interfere with job performance to render the employee ineffective; or
- ✓ Unlawful activities such as acts or threats of violence.

- *Participation in an employment discrimination proceeding*
  Participating in a complaint process is protected from retaliation under all circumstances. Other acts to oppose discrimination are protected as long as the employee was acting on a reasonable belief that something in the workplace may violate EEO laws, even if he or she did not use legal terminology to describe it.

  Engaging in EEO activity, however, does not shield an employee from all discipline or discharge. Employers are free to discipline or terminate workers if motivated by *non-retaliatory and non-discriminatory* reasons that would otherwise result in such consequences. However, an employer is not allowed to do anything in response to EEO activity that would discourage someone from resisting or complaining about future discrimination.

  Participation means taking part in an employment discrimination proceeding. Participation is a protected activity even if the proceeding involved claims that ultimately were found to have no merit or basis.

  Examples of participation include:

  - ✓ Filing a charge of employment discrimination;
  - ✓ Cooperating with an internal investigation of alleged discriminatory practices; or
  - ✓ Serving as a witness in an EEO investigation or litigation.

  A protected activity can also include requesting a reasonable accommodation based on religion or disability.

PROHIBITED EMPLOYMENT POLICIES & PRACTICES

The laws enforced by EEOC prohibit an employer or other covered entity from using neutral employment policies and practices that have a disproportionately negative effect on applicants or employees of a race, color, religion, sex (including pregnancy, gender identity, and sexual orientation), national origin, age, or disability, if the polices or practices at issue are not job-related and necessary to the operation of the business. Therefore, it's important to periodically review company policies to ensure that they are in compliance and reflect EEOC's most recent guidance.

- Job Advertisements
  It is illegal for an employer to publish a job advertisement that shows a preference for or discourages someone from applying for a job because of his or her race, color, religion, sex (including pregnancy, gender identity, and sexual orientation), national origin, age (40 or older), disability, or genetic information.

For example, a help-wanted ad that specifically seeks "females" or "recent college graduates" may discourage men or people over 40 from applying and may violate the law. Alternatively, an online advertisement that seeks workers "without gaps in employment history" may discriminate against caregivers or disabled individuals.

- Recruitment
  It is illegal for an employer to recruit new employees in a way that discriminates against them because of their race, color, religion, sex (including pregnancy, gender identity, and sexual orientation), national origin, age (40 or older), disability or genetic information. For example, an employer's reliance on word-of-mouth recruitment by its mostly Hispanic work force may violate the law if the result is that almost all new hires are Hispanic.

- Application & Hiring
  It is illegal for an employer to discriminate against a job applicant because of, or base hiring decisions on stereotypes and assumptions about, a person's race, color, religion, sex, national origin, age (40 or older), disability or genetic information. For example, an employer may not refuse to give employment applications to people of a certain race.

  If an employer requires job applicants to take a test, the test must be necessary and related to the job and the employer may not exclude people of a particular race, color, religion, sex, national origin, or individuals with disabilities. In addition, the employer may not use a test that excludes applicants age 40 or older if the test is not based on a reasonable factor other than age.

- Job Referrals
  It is illegal for an employer, employment agency or union to consider a person's race, color, religion, sex, national origin, age (40 or older), disability, or genetic information when making decisions about job referrals.

- Pre-Employment Inquiries
  As a general rule, the information obtained and requested through the pre-employment process should be limited to information that is essential for determining if a person is qualified for the job. Information regarding race, sex, national origin, age, and religion are irrelevant in such determinations.

  Employers are explicitly prohibited from making pre-employment inquiries about disabilities. Although state and federal equal employment opportunity laws do not clearly forbid employers from making pre-employment inquiries that relate to, or disproportionately screen out members based on race, color, sex, national origin, religion, or age, such inquiries may be used as evidence of an employer's intent to discriminate unless the questions asked can be justified by some business purpose.

  Therefore, inquiries about organizations, clubs, societies, and lodges of which an applicant may be a member or any other questions, which may indicate the applicant's race, sex, national origin, disability status, age, religion, color or ancestry if answered, should generally be avoided.

  Similarly, employers should not ask for a photograph of an applicant. If needed for identification purposes, a photograph may be obtained after an offer of employment is made and accepted.

- In general, it is assumed that pre-employment requests for information will form the basis for hiring decisions. Therefore, employers should not request information that discloses or tends to disclose an applicant's race unless it has a legitimate business need for such information. If an employer legitimately needs information about its employees' or applicants' race for affirmative action purposes and/or to track applicant flow, it may obtain the necessary information and simultaneously guard against discriminatory selection by using a mechanism, such as a "tear-off" sheet. This allows the employer to separate the race-related information from the data used to determine if a person is qualified for the job.

- Height and weight requirements tend to disproportionately limit the employment opportunities of some protected groups and unless the employer can demonstrate how the need is related to the job, it may be viewed as illegal under federal law. A number of states and localities have laws specifically prohibiting discrimination on the basis of height and weight unless based on actual job requirements.

- Inquiry into an applicant's current or past assets, liabilities, or credit rating, including bankruptcy or garnishment, refusal or cancellation of bonding, car ownership, rental or ownership of a house, length of residence at an address, charge accounts, furniture ownership, or bank accounts generally should be avoided because they tend to adversely impact minorities and females more. Exceptions exist if the employer can show that such information is essential to the job in question.

- Questions about an applicant's religious affiliation or beliefs [unless the religion is a bona fide occupational qualification (BFOQ), are generally viewed as non-job-related and problematic under federal law.

Religious corporations, associations, educational institutions, or societies are exempt from the federal laws that EEOC enforces when it comes to the employment of individuals based on their religion. In other words, an employer whose purpose and character is primarily religious is permitted to lean towards hiring persons of the same religion. This exception relieves religious organizations only from the ban on employment discrimination based on religion. It does not exempt such organizations from employing individuals due to their race, gender, national origin, disability, color, and/or age. Other employers should avoid questions about an applicant's religious affiliation, such as place of worship, days of worship, and religious holidays and should not ask for references from religious leaders, e.g., minister, rabbi, priest, imam, or pastor.

- Questions about marital status, family size, and ages of children are frequently used to discriminate against women and may violate Title VII if it is used to deny or limit employment opportunities.

It is clearly discriminatory to ask such questions only of women and not men (or vice-versa). Even if asked of both men and women, such questions may be evidence of intent to discriminate against women with children.

Generally, employers should not use non-job-related questions involving marital status, number and/or ages of children or dependents, or names of spouses or children of the applicant. Such inquiries may be asked after an employment offer has been made and accepted if needed for insurance or other legitimate business purposes.

- The ADA places restrictions on employers when it comes to asking job applicants to answer medical questions, take a medical exam, or identify a disability.

An employer may not ask a job applicant if he or she has a disability (or about the nature of an obvious disability). An employer also may not ask a job applicant to answer medical questions or take a medical exam before making a job offer. An employer may ask a job applicant whether they can perform the job and how they would perform the job. The law allows an employer to condition a job offer on the applicant answering certain medical questions or successfully passing a medical exam, but only if all new employees in the same job have to answer the questions or take the exam.

Once a person is hired and has started work, an employer generally can only ask medical questions or require a medical exam if the employer needs medical documentation to support an employee's request for an accommodation or if the employer has reason to believe an employee would not be able to perform a job successfully or safely because of a medical condition.

The law also requires that employers keep all medical records and other confidential information in separate medical files.

- There is no federal law that clearly prohibits an employer from asking about arrest and conviction records. However, using such records as an absolute measure to prevent an individual from being hired could limit the employment opportunities of some protected groups and thus cannot be used in this way.

Since an arrest alone does not necessarily mean that an applicant has committed a crime, the employer should not assume that the applicant committed the offense. Instead, the employer should allow him or her the opportunity to explain the circumstances of the arrest(s) and should make a reasonable effort to determine whether the explanation is reliable.

Even if the employer believes that the applicant did engage in the conduct for which he or she was arrested, that information should prevent him or her from employment only to the extent that it is evident that the applicant cannot be trusted to perform the duties of the position when:

- ✓ considering the nature of the job,
- ✓ the nature and seriousness of the offense,
- ✓ and the length of time since it occurred.

This is also true for a conviction.

Several state laws limit the use of arrest and conviction records by prospective employers. These range from laws and rules prohibiting the employer from asking the applicant any questions about arrest records to those restricting the employer's use of conviction data in making an employment decision.

- Employers should not ask whether or not a job applicant is a United States citizen before making an offer of employment. The Immigration Reform and Control Act (IRCA) makes it illegal for employers to discriminate with respect to hiring, firing, or recruitment or referral for a fee, based on an individual's citizenship or immigration status. For example, the law prohibits employers from hiring only U.S. citizens or lawful permanent residents unless required to do so by law, regulation or government contract; it also prohibits employers from preferring to hire temporary visa holders or undocumented workers over qualified U.S. citizens or other protected individuals, such as refugees or individuals granted asylum.

IRCA requires employers to verify the identity and employment eligibility of all employees hired after November 6, 1986, by completing the Employment Eligibility Verification (I-9) Form, and reviewing documents showing the employee's identity and employment authorization.

The law prohibits employers from rejecting valid documents or insisting on additional documents beyond what is legally required for employment eligibility verification (or the Department of Homeland Security (DHS) Form I-9), based on an employee's citizenship status or national origin. For example, an employer cannot require only individuals the employer perceives as "foreign" to verify their employment eligibility or produce specific documents, such as Permanent Resident ("green") cards or Employment Authorization Documents. It is up to the employee to choose which of the permitted documents to show for employment eligibility verification. As long as the document appears reasonably genuine on its face, and relates to the employee, it should be accepted.

- Job Assignments & Promotions
  It is illegal for an employer to make decisions about job assignments and promotions based on an employee's race, color, religion, sex, national origin, age (40 or older), disability, or genetic information, or stereotypes or assumptions about these characteristics. For example, an employer may not give preference to employees of a certain race when making shift assignments and may not segregate employees of a particular national origin from other employees or from customers.

- Pay and Benefits
  It is illegal for an employer to discriminate against an employee in the payment of wages or employee benefits on the basis of race, color, religion, sex, national origin, age (40 or older), disability or genetic information. Employee benefits include sick and vacation leave, insurance, access to overtime as well as overtime pay, and retirement programs. For example, an employer may not pay Hispanic workers less than African-American workers because of their national origin, and men and women in the same workplace must be given equal pay for equal work.

- Employment References
  It is illegal for an employer to give a negative or false employment reference (or refuse to give a reference) because of a person's race, color, religion, sex, national origin, age (40 or older), disability, or genetic information.

- Reasonable Accommodations & Religion
  The law requires an employer to reasonably accommodate an employee's religious beliefs or practices, unless doing so would cause difficulty or expense for the employer. This means an employer may have to make reasonable adjustments at work that will allow the employee to

practice his or her religion, such as allowing an employee to voluntarily swap shifts with a co-worker so that he or she can attend religious services.

- Training & Apprenticeship Programs
  It is illegal for a training or apprenticeship program to discriminate on the basis of race, color, religion, sex (including pregnancy), national origin, age (40 or older), disability, or genetic information. For example, an employer may not deny training opportunities to African-American employees because of their race.

  In some situations, an employer may be allowed to set age limits for participation in an apprenticeship program.

- Terms & Conditions of Employment
  The law makes it illegal for an employer to make any employment decision because of a person's race, color, religion, sex, national origin, age (40 or older), disability, or genetic information. This means an employer may not discriminate when it comes to such things as hiring, firing, promotions, and pay. It also means an employer may not discriminate, for example, when granting breaks, approving leave, assigning work stations, or setting any other term or condition of employment -- however small.

- Dress Code
  In general, an employer may establish a dress code which applies to all employees or workers within certain job categories. However, there are a few possible exceptions.

  While an employer may require all workers to follow a uniform dress code even if the dress code conflicts with some workers' ethnic beliefs or practices, a dress code must not treat some employees less favorably because of their national origin. For example, a dress code that prohibits certain kinds of ethnic dress, such as traditional African or East Indian attire, but otherwise permits casual dress would treat some employees less favorably because of their national origin.

  Moreover, if the dress code conflicts with an employee's religious practices and the employee requests an accommodation, the employer must modify the dress code or permit an exception to the dress code unless doing so would result in an undue hardship.

  Similarly, if an employee requests an accommodation to the dress code because of his/her disability, the employer must modify the dress code or permit an exception to the dress code, unless doing so would result in undue hardship.

- Discipline & Discharge
  An employer may not consider a person's race, color, religion, sex, national origin, age (40 or older), disability, or genetic information when making decisions about discipline or discharge. For example, if two employees commit a similar offense, an employer may not discipline them differently because of their race, color, religion, sex, national origin, age (40 or older), disability, or genetic information.

  When deciding which employees will be laid off, an employer may not choose the oldest workers because of their age. Employers also may not discriminate when deciding which workers to recall after a layoff.

- Constructive Discharge/Forced to Resign
  Discriminatory practices under the laws enforced by EEOC also include constructive discharge or forcing an employee to resign by making the work environment so intolerable a reasonable person would not be able to stay.

WORKPLACE LAWS NOT ENFORCED BY THE EEOC

Each federal government agency may have laws that prohibit discrimination, but these laws are not under the purview of the EEOC. The following laws, prohibiting discrimination or regulating workplace issues, are not enforced by the EEOC:

The Civil Service Reform Act of 1978 (CSRA)
This law makes it illegal to discriminate against a federal employee or job applicant on the basis of race, color, national origin, religion, sex, age, or disability. The CSRA also prohibits discrimination on the basis of certain other factors that don't adversely affect employee performance, such as marital status, political association, and sexual orientation. The CSRA makes it illegal to fire, demote, or otherwise "retaliate" against a federal employee or job applicant for whistle-blowing or for exercising the right to file a complaint, grievance, or an appeal. The Office of Special Counsel (OSC) and the Merit Systems Protection Board (MSPB) enforce the CSRA.

The Immigration Reform and Control Act of 1986 (IRCA)
This law makes it illegal for certain employers to fire or refuse to hire a person on the basis of that person's national origin or citizenship. This law also makes it illegal for an employer to request employment verification only from people of a certain national origin or only from people who appear to be from a foreign country. An employer who has citizenship requirements or gives preference to U.S. citizens also may violate IRCA.

Executive Order 11246
This law makes it illegal for federal contractors and certain subcontractors to discriminate on the basis of race, color, religion, sex, or national origin. It also requires federal contractors and subcontractors to take steps to ensure equal employment opportunity in the workplace.

Title VI of the Civil Rights Act of 1964
This law makes it illegal to discriminate on the basis of race, color, or national origin in programs and activities receiving federal financial assistance.

Title II of the Americans With Disabilities Act (ADA)
This law makes it illegal to discriminate against people with disabilities in all programs, activities, and services offered by state and local government agencies. This includes public transportation services and physical access to state and local government buildings.

Title III of the ADA
This law prohibits disability discrimination by private entities that provide services to the public (also known as "public accommodations"). Public accommodations include, for example, restaurants, hotels, movie theaters, stores, doctors' offices, parks, and schools. The law applies to buildings, programs, and services. Under the law, public accommodations may have to provide "auxiliary aids and services" such as sign language interpreters, assistive listening devices, or large print materials, unless doing so would cause significant difficulty or expense.

Title IX of the Education Amendments of 1972
This law protects people from discrimination based on sex in education programs and activities that receive federal financial assistance. Title IX regulation describes the conduct that violates the law. Examples of the types of discrimination that are covered under Title IX include sexual harassment, the failure to provide equal opportunity in athletics, and discrimination based on pregnancy. Within the context of Title IX, we often hear of the 3-pronged test, which articles three (3) ways in which Title IX compliance can be achieved. Because Title IX only addresses public and private schools that receive federal funding, several states have enacted similar laws to prohibit discrimination based on sex regardless of whether the school receives federal funding. The U.S. Department of Education's Office for Civil Rights enforces Title IX.

The Family and Medical Leave Act (FMLA)
This law requires certain employers to grant up to 12 weeks of leave during a 12-month period to eligible employees who need time off because of a "serious health condition" that they or someone in their family is experiencing. FMLA leave can sometimes overlap with Title VII requirements concerning leave for pregnancy and pregnancy-related conditions, and ADA and Rehabilitation Act requirements concerning leave as an accommodation for an employee with a disability. The U.S. Department of Labor Wage and Hour Division enforces FMLA.

The Occupational Safety and Health Act of 1970 (OSHA)
This law sets out safety requirements for workplaces. The Occupational Safety and Health Administration works with states to investigate and enforce OSHA requirements.

Section 503 of the Rehabilitation Act
This law prohibits certain federal contractors and subcontractors from discriminating against qualified employees and job applicants with disabilities. Section 503 also requires contractors to take affirmative steps to hire and promote qualified people with disabilities. Some provisions of Section 503 mirror those found in the ADA and Section 501 of the Rehabilitation Act.

Section 504 of the Rehabilitation Act
This law prohibits disability discrimination in programs and activities that receive federal financial assistance. This includes discrimination against qualified applicants and employees with disabilities, as well as discrimination in the services and activities provided by federal agencies to the public. The non-discrimination provisions of Section 504 are similar to those found in Title I of the ADA, covering employment discrimination, and Title II of the ADA, covering the programs, activities, and services offered by state and local governments.

Section 508 of the Rehabilitation Act
This law requires federal agencies to ensure that electronic and information technology used by the government can be accessed and used by people with disabilities. The U.S. Access Board oversees this law.

The Social Security Act
This law provides Social Security Disability Insurance (SSDI) to certain individuals with severe disabilities who can no longer work. The Social Security Administration's definition of "disability" is different from the ADA definition of disability. For this reason, whether or not a person is eligible to receive disability benefits does not determine coverage under the ADA.

The Fair Labor Standards Act
This law regulates workplace practices related to minimum wage, overtime pay, and child labor.

National Labor Relations Act
This law protects workers who wish to form, join or support unions; those who are already represented by unions; and individuals who join together as a group (two or more employees) without a union seeking to modify their wages or working conditions.

Section 1981 of the Civil Rights Act of 1866
This law protects the equal right of all persons within the jurisdiction of the United States to make and enforce contracts without respect to race. This includes all contractual aspects of the employment relationship, such as hiring, discharge, and the terms and conditions of employment. The Supreme Court has held that the statute also prohibits retaliation against persons who complain about race discrimination prohibited by the statute. This law is enforced by individuals, not a federal agency.

Workers Compensation
Every state (and the federal government) has a worker's compensation law. It provides compensation for on-the-job injuries and illnesses. Some workers' compensation programs also require employers to provide job modifications or alternative assignments, which also may be a reasonable accommodation under the ADA. If an employee's occupational injury is covered under both Workers Compensation and the ADA (or Rehabilitation Act), the employee may be entitled to a job modification or reassignment under both laws.

Diversity practitioners must keep current on EEO laws and the changing legislation that impacts these laws. They must be aware of EEOC guidance to employers, as well as stay abreast of why legislators adjust the laws from time to time.

INTERNATIONAL CONSIDERATIONS FOR DIVERSITY AND INCLUSION

Affirmative action or positive discrimination (known as employment equity in Canada, reservation in India, and positive action in the UK) is the policy of providing special opportunities for, and favoring members of, one group over another, when those being favored are perceived as a disadvantaged group who suffer from discrimination within a culture.

The nature of positive discrimination policies varies from region to region. Some countries, such as India, use a quota system, whereby a certain percentage of jobs or school vacancies must be set aside for members of a certain group. In some other regions, specific quotas do not exist; instead, members of minorities are given preference in selection processes.

Human Resource and Diversity and Inclusion (D&I) executives must be aware of the intricate laws, customs, business activity, and employment levels in the countries where their organizations operate. It is difficult to know everything about foreign countries, but it is helpful to have general knowledge through research before embarking on a major D&I effort. For example, before offering an employee resource group for the LGBTQ+ community in a Middle-Eastern or African country, it would be helpful to know if the territory has laws prohibiting same-sex relationships. The following pages provide an overview of Diversity and Inclusion in international workplaces.

CANADA

The Constitution of Canada is the supreme law in Canada; the country's constitution is an amalgamation of codified acts and uncodified traditions and conventions. Canada is one of the oldest constitutional democracies in the world. The constitution outlines Canada's system of government, as well as the civil rights of all Canadian citizens and those residing in Canada. While the Canadian Charter of Rights and Freedoms was adopted in 1982, it was not until 1985 that the main provisions regarding equality rights (Section 15) came into effect. The delay was meant to give the federal and provincial governments an opportunity to review pre-existing statutes and strike potentially unconstitutional inequalities.

The Canadian Charter of Rights and Freedoms (Section 15) states, "Every individual is equal before and under the law and has the right to the equal protection and equal benefit of the law without discrimination and, in particular, without discrimination based on race, national or ethnic origin, color, religion, sex, sexual orientation, gender identify, age, mental or physical disability." In general terms, the purpose of Section 15(1) is to prevent the violation of essential human dignity and freedom through the imposition of disadvantage, stereotyping, or political or social prejudice, and to promote a society in which all persons enjoy equal recognition at law as human beings or as members of Canadian society, equally capable and equally deserving of concern, respect and consideration.

Canada's legislation ensures that the country is well-prepared for the future. Figure 1 illustrates the nation's projected population growth and how it will be primarily driven by migration.

FIGURE 1. IN CANADA

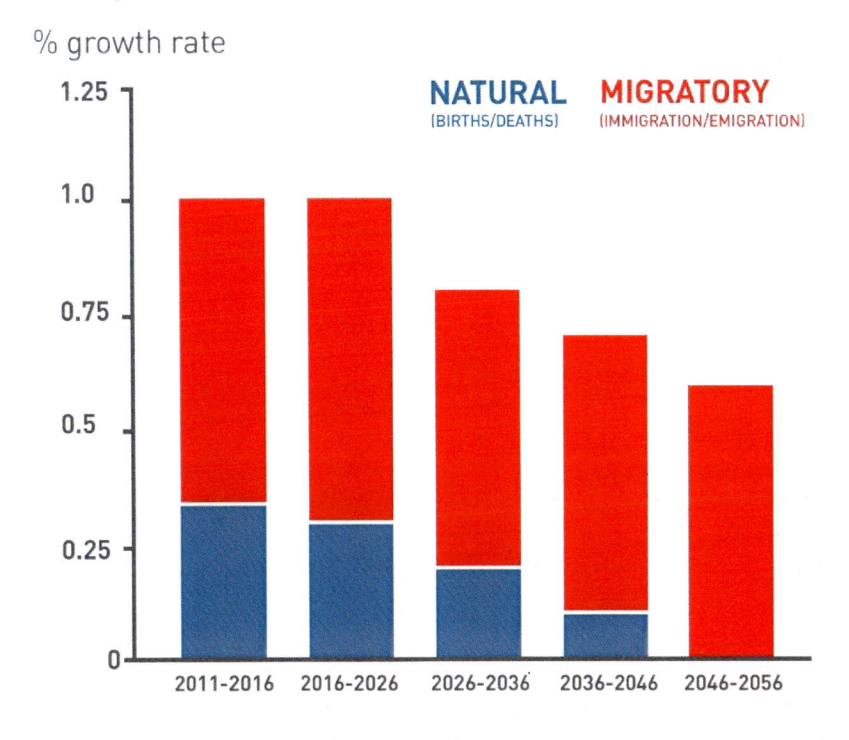

Projected population growth

% growth rate

Years	Natural (Births/Deaths)	Migratory (Immigration/Emigration)
2011-2016	~0.35	~1.0
2016-2026	~0.30	~1.0
2026-2036	~0.20	~0.80
2036-2046	~0.10	~0.70
2046-2056	~0	~0.60

CBC NEWS   Source: Statistics Canada/Census 2016

In fact, the diversity of Canada's population is expected to increase significantly in the next two decades, especially in the large metropolitan cities. Statistics Canada projects that visible minorities are expected to account for 63 percent of the population in Toronto, 59 percent of Vancouver and 31 percent of Montreal. Statistics Canada also estimates that by 2031, between 25 to 28 percent of the population will be foreign-born and 29 to 32 percent of the population will belong to a visible minority group.

Nevertheless, diversity in Canada extends beyond race and ethnicity, but spans language, gender, religious affiliations, sexual orientation, abilities and economic status. One area where diversity is often discussed is in the labor market. Canadian employers have taken strides to ensure their organizations are representative of the diverse Canadian population. Canada's *Best Diversity Employers* competition has been held for the past seven years and recognizes employers across the country who have developed exceptional workplace Diversity and Inclusion programs towards five major groups of employees: women, members of visible minorities, persons with disabilities, aboriginal peoples, and lesbian, gay, bisexual and transgendered/transsexual individuals.

The Charter of Human Rights and Freedoms (French: Charte des droits et libertés de la personne) is a statutory bill of rights and human rights passed by the National Assembly of Quebec on June 27, 1975. This charter was amended in 1977 to prohibit discrimination based on sexual orientation. Thus, the province of Quebec became the first jurisdiction to prohibit sexual orientation discrimination in the private and public sectors. In 2005, Canada became the fourth country in the world to legalize same-sex marriage nationwide with the enactment of the Civil Marriage Act. Today, sexual orientation discrimination is explicitly prohibited in the human rights acts of all jurisdictions in Canada.

In 2016, gender identity or expression was added to the Quebec Charter. Sexual orientation is not defined in any human rights act, but is widely interpreted as meaning heterosexuality, homosexuality, and bisexuality. It does not include transsexuality or transgender people. The Federal Court of Canada has stated that sexual orientation "is a precise legal concept that deals specifically with an individual's preference in terms of gender" in sexual relationships and is not vague or overly broad. The Ontario Human Rights Commission has adopted the following definition, "Sexual orientation is more than simply a 'status' that an individual possesses; it is an immutable personal characteristic that forms part of an individual's core identity. Sexual orientation encompasses the range of human sexuality from gay and lesbian to bisexual and heterosexual orientations." All human rights laws in Canada also explicitly prohibit discrimination based on disability, which has been interpreted to include AIDS, ARC, being HIV positive, and having membership in a high-risk group for HIV infection.

Since June 2017, the Canadian Human Rights Act, equal opportunity and/or anti-discrimination legislation in Canada prohibit discrimination against gender identity or expression. In addition, several human rights commissions consider sex discrimination to include discrimination based on gender identity at the federal level and in New Brunswick. The Ontario Human Rights Commission defines gender identity as follows: Gender identity is linked to an individual's intrinsic sense of self and, particularly the sense of being male or female. Gender identity may or may not conform to a person's birth assigned sex. The personal characteristics that are associated with gender identity include self-image, physical and biological appearance, expression, behavior and conduct, as they relate to gender. Individuals whose birth-assigned sex does not conform to their gender identity include transsexuals, transgenderist, intersexed persons, and cross-dressers. A person's gender identity is fundamentally different from, and not determinative of, their sexual orientation.

EUROPEAN UNION

The European Union (EU) is an economic and political union of 28-member states (as of December 2017) which are located primarily in Europe. The EU has developed an internal single market through a standardized system of laws that apply in all member states. EU policies aim to ensure the free movement of people, goods, services, and capital; enact universal legislation; and maintain common policies.

A referendum on the U.K.'s membership in the European Union was held in June 2016, following years of campaigning by eurosceptics. This phenomenon is known as "Brexit" and was driven by efforts to slow down or reverse globalization and multiculturalism (via immigration). In fact, the U.K.'s financial markets were negatively impacted since the announcement of Brexit, and there was a sharp increase in hate crime reports. According to CNN, U.K. police said that compared to the same period in 2015, hate crime reports rose by 42% in the last two weeks of June 2016 following the aftermath of the Brexit decision.

FIGURE 2: EUROPEAN UNION MEMBER COUNTRIES

In European law, six "grounds" of discrimination in the labor market and in the workplace are recognized, including gender, age, ethnicity and race, disability, religion and belief, and sexual orientation. This protection has been included within the legal frameworks of all EU Member States at the national level.

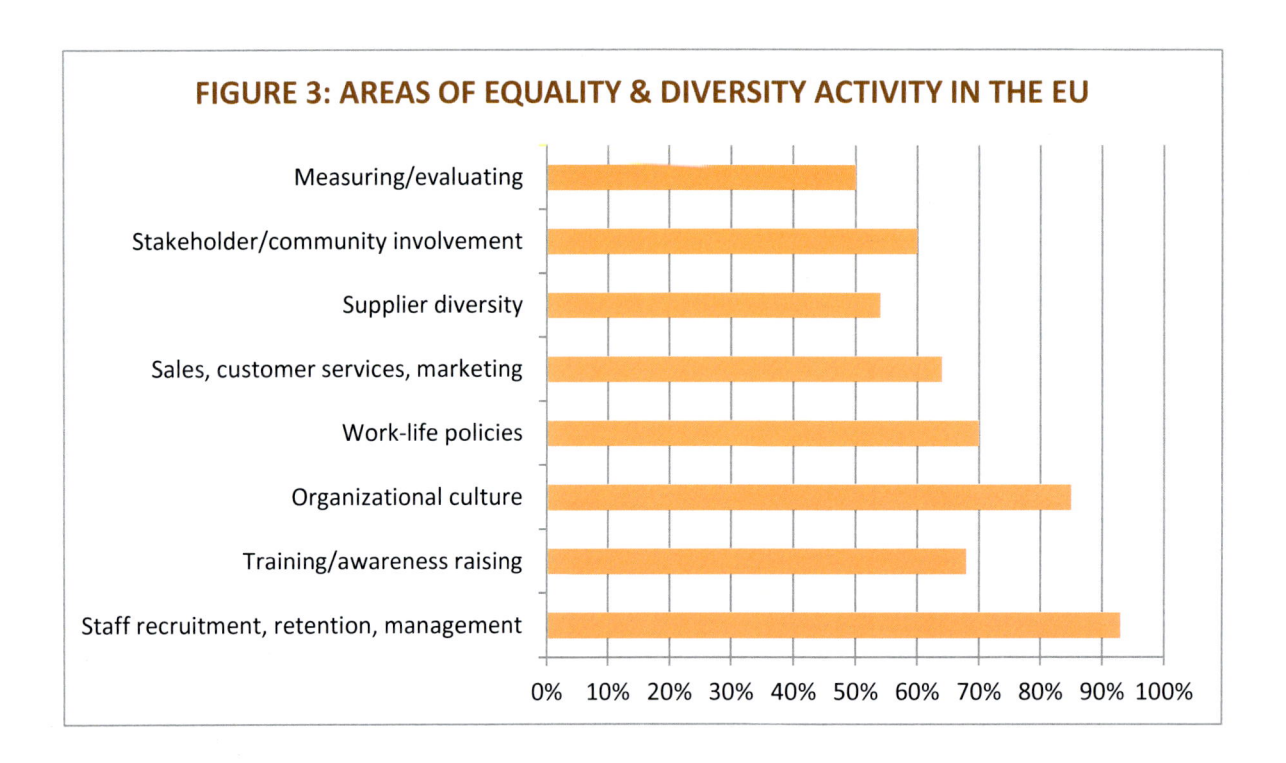

FIGURE 3: AREAS OF EQUALITY & DIVERSITY ACTIVITY IN THE EU

Area	Percentage
Measuring/evaluating	~50%
Stakeholder/community involvement	~60%
Supplier diversity	~55%
Sales, customer services, marketing	~65%
Work-life policies	~70%
Organizational culture	~85%
Training/awareness raising	~68%
Staff recruitment, retention, management	~93%

The European Community Programme for Employment and Social Solidarity conducted a survey of more than 330 companies with the European Business Test Panel (EBTP) in 2005 and 2008 on the subject of diversity management. The survey found that companies suggested that the most important issue they faced when addressing workplace Equality and Diversity (E&D) in practice was leadership commitment (39 percent). Following this were, second, discriminatory attitudes and behaviors amongst staff (28 percent) and third, lack of information and awareness (26 percent). Financial limitations, time constraints, and difficulties measuring the impact of E&D policies were considered the least important challenges.

Figure 3 illustrates where most Equality and Diversity efforts are concentrated in the EU. Given that the majority of EBTP companies are at the beginning of their diversity journey – combined with the fact that very few companies set and measure targets – it is not surprising that the benefits they perceive are still rather restricted (see Figure 4). Almost two-thirds of EBTP companies suggested that E&D policies had made a positive impact upon their business-- almost one-third claimed that they could not tell how E&D efforts affected the organization.

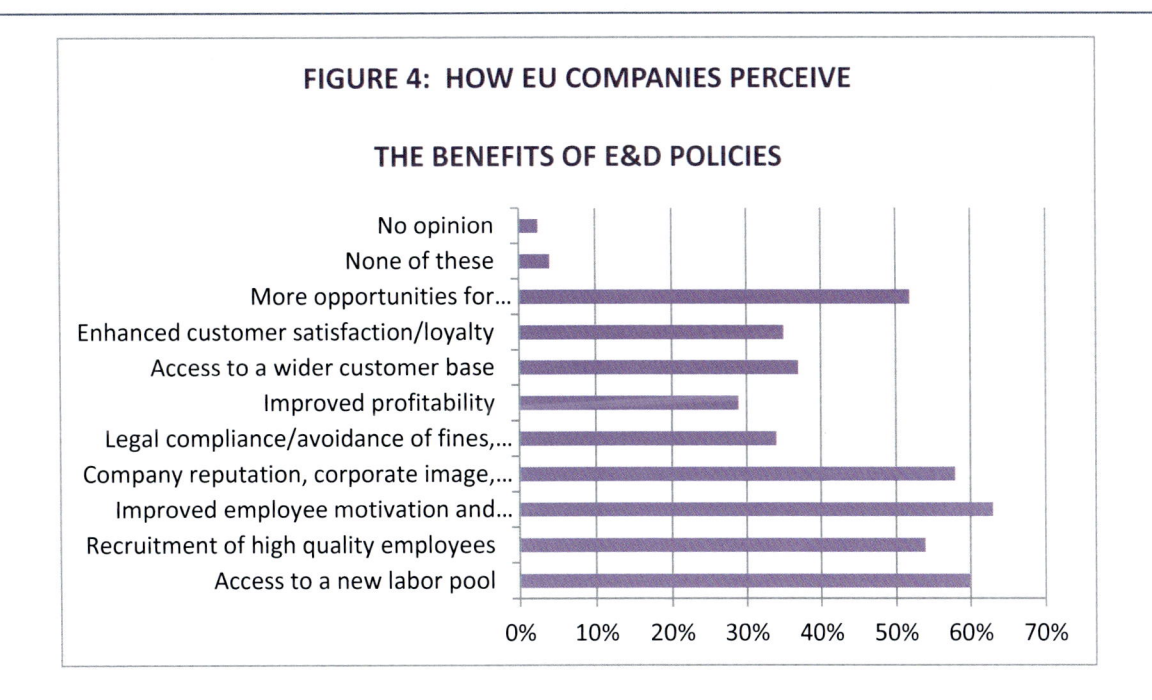

FIGURE 4: HOW EU COMPANIES PERCEIVE THE BENEFITS OF E&D POLICIES

FRANCE

As home to the largest Islamic community in Europe, France and its approach to immigration are likely to define the ongoing debate about successful Diversity and Inclusion measures. There is a lot at stake as several terrorist attacks in 2015 have come to overshadow France's integration efforts.

Since the mid-19th century, French immigration policy has had two aims: (1) to meet the needs of the labor market by introducing migrant workers, and (2) to compensate French demographic deficits by favoring the permanent installation of foreign families while ensuring their integration into the national body.

FIGURE 5: MAP OF FRANCE

On the labor market front, the deepening of French colonial relations in the 19th and early 20th centuries laid the groundwork for steady movements of people between France and its colonies. While early information on the foreign population dates back to France's first census in 1851, the initial attempts to codify and regulate immigration to France began in the post-World War II era.

The devastation of two world wars and low birthrates thereafter had left France with a limited national labor pool. The country saw a partial answer to its dwindling workforce in the recruitment of foreign labor, initially from Belgium and Germany as well as from Poland, Russia, Italy, and Spain.

Immigration to France increased during the wars of liberation and decolonization in the 1950s and 1960s. For France, the impact was felt acutely in the free and unregulated entries of immigrants from Algeria.

This was particularly true in the period leading up to and following Algerian independence from France in 1962 with the signing of the Evian Agreement.

The late 1960s and early 1970s ushered in a period of tremendous social change. The maturing of the baby boom generation and the entrance of large numbers of women into the labor force limited the need for foreign workers. Economically, the oil price shock of 1973 further hamstrung economic performance, and led to an extended period of high unemployment.

In July 1974, the French government followed the lead of other European counterparts and officially ended its labor migration programs. The legislation also included provisions for sanctions affecting employers who hired illegal immigrants, a French policy innovation originally developed in the 1930s. Nonetheless, immigration continued and diversified over the following decades.

Since then, immigrant integration issues and social reversals suffered by politicians on both the left and right have had an impact on French immigration policies. In 1993, the conservative government's interior minister, Charles Pasqua, put forth the goal of "zero immigration," later qualified to mean zero *illegal* immigration.

The so-called Pasqua Laws prohibited foreign graduates from accepting in-country employment, increased the waiting period for family reunification from one to two years, and denied residence permits to foreign spouses who had been in France illegally prior to marrying. The legislation also enhanced the powers of police to deport foreigners and eliminated opportunities to appeal asylum rejections. The election of a conservative president in 1995 continued the course of limiting immigration channels.

After more than a decade of public debate and sharp media criticism, in February 2004 France adopted a law banning the wearing of ostentatious religious symbols in public schools. That controversial decision, one of many recommendations by a 19-member commission established by President Jacques Chirac, has highlighted the complexity of managing diversity in the context of France's strongly secular traditions.

The country's diversity issues had already reached the boiling point when riots broke out in October 2005 in the Paris suburb of Clichy-sous-Bois.

The 2005 riots in Paris forced the French government to declare a state of emergency for three months. The riots broke out in neighborhoods where the population was mainly comprised of immigrants from former French colonies in Northern and Central Africa, and unemployment was high among the younger generations.

When President Nicolas Sarkozy took office in May 2007, he promised to bring relief to the unemployed and disaffected youth. Sarkozy immediately shook up the French political elite by appointing Rachida Dati, of Moroccan descent, as justice minister; Rama Yade, of Senegalese origin, as Secretary for Human Rights; and Fadela Amara of Algerian origin, as State Secretary in Charge of City Politics.

Sarkozy continued to shake up the political scene when he created the new government post of diversity and equality commissioner in 2008 and appointed Yazid Sabeg, who was well known in the country for his efforts in promoting diversity and workplace rights.

When Yazid Sabeg, France's newly appointed Commissioner for Diversity and Equality, stated that his country was heading toward an apartheid system and possible social warfare, diversity experts from around the globe applauded his candor. While many of these experts agree that France faces some serious diversity challenges, the extent and effect of these challenges are up for debate.

In January 2011, France implemented a gender quota law for supervisory boards (or Boards of Directors). The law became legally binding in 2017. The quota applies to companies that have more than 500 employees and that generate at least €50 million ($69 million) in annual sales. If a supervisory board doesn't meet the 40% gender quota, its decisions are valid, but the board election is invalidated, and members aren't paid for attending the meetings. This will hurt the advisory boards that resist installing female members, but it doesn't penalize the companies.

Other EU member countries applaud and seek to duplicate France's efforts toward gender equality. According to Fortune, France's share of female directors has surged from 8% in 2006 to 35% in 2015.

In April 2011, France's law banning the burqa and other Islamic face coverings in public places went into effect. The ban pertains to the burqa, a full-body covering that includes a mesh over the face, and the niqab, a full-face veil that leaves an opening only for the eyes. The hijab, which covers the hair and neck but not the face, and the chador, which covers the body but not the face, apparently are not banned by the law.

The law imposes a fine of 150 Euros ($190). The person breaking the law can be asked to carry out public service duty as part of the punishment or as an alternative to the fine. Penalties for forcing a person to wear a burqa are also part of the law. The government has called this coercion "a new form of enslavement that the republic cannot accept on its soil."

French people backed the ban by a margin of more than four to one, the Pew Global Attitudes Project found in a survey. Clear majorities also backed burqa bans in Germany, Britain and Spain, while two out of three Americans opposed it, the survey found.

CHINA
With a population surpassing 1,300,000,000, China is the most populous nation on earth. Add on a history of nearly 5,000 years, in which the borders expanded and contracted many times, and massive migrations between points in the vast region, the cultural diversity of China is inevitably great. Although ethnic diversity is not always apparent to many foreign visitors who limit their stays to Shanghai, Guangzhou, Shenzhen, or Beijing, any trip between geographical regions – and especially to the border areas -- will give a different picture.

China is, by far, the most diverse country in East Asia. Ethnicity in the People's Republic of China is understood in terms of a group's common history, language, area of inhabitation, customs, and livelihood (criteria borrowed from the former Soviet Union). While there are more than 50 different ethnic groups, the Han Chinese represents the largest ethnic group. Nevertheless, members of each ethnic group are all citizens and equal under the law.

One of the greatest demographic challenges facing China is the aging population. The Wall Street Journal cites United Nations data that estimates "the number of Chinese people over the age of 65 will jump 85% to 243 million by 2030."

The Chinese government has responded to this population issue with legislation that alters its 30-year policy allowing couples to have one-child. As of January 1, 2016, China allows couples to have two-children—but many fear this step is too little, too late. Some couples are already opting out of having a second child because the cost of living is too high in cities such as Beijing and Shanghai.

For Chinese workers who migrate to America, there are many challenges to overcome. The main differences between American and Chinese workforces revolve around authority and individualism. In China, people accept differences in authority or inequality, more willingly, and therefore have more hierarchical tendencies. In a country such as the U.S., people tend to be more egalitarian.

FIGURE 6: CHINA VS. U.S. AUTHORITY

Authority in China tends to feature:	Authority in the U.S. tends to feature:
Hierarchical tendencies	Egalitarian tendencies
Top-down communication	Side-by-side communication
One-way communication	Two-way communication
Infrequent feedback	Frequent feedback

Traditionally, foreign-born Chinese employees have found it difficult to question the boss, offer up ideas, take the initiative or disagree with people in authority at a company. However, in American companies, empowerment is expected. American employers encourage workers to speak their minds and offer alternative ideas. Thus, an HR or D&I practitioner must be ready to educate an organization's management team about the intricacies in empowering a foreign-born Chinese workforce versus those Chinese employees that were raised with, or acclimated to, U.S. customs.

The U.S. is more individualistic than any other country in the world, while the Chinese culture promotes group orientation. Figure 6 compares the cultural orientation of the two nations.

FIGURE 7: CULTURAL ORIENTATION

Group Orientation: China	Individualism: U.S.
Relationships are emphasized	Tasks are emphasized
Indirect communication	Direct communication
High context	High content
Conflict avoidance	Conflict acceptance

Americans tend to focus on accomplishing the task at hand, which can be facilitated by a low-context communication style (i.e., "get to the point"). This drive to get things done causes Americans to be more aggressive and direct; sometimes this approach supersedes relationships.

What an American says (direct communication) often matters less to the Chinese than how it is said (context-based or indirect communication). The Chinese will send and receive messages based as much on the indirect context of the message--which includes their relationship to the messenger-- as on the actual, direct content of the message itself.

For Chinese, how you say things is critical. In the West, what you say is more important. Without a doubt, your single greatest challenge will be helping your American managers learn how to solicit and receive feedback from Chinese workers. You also must prepare your colleagues for other cultural obstacles. For example, having to account for Asian concerns--such as saving face and preserving relationships--can be a major source of frustration for Western employers.

JAPAN

Although Japan is nearly racially homogeneous, the country has a long history and culture that excludes certain groups of people from equally participating in the workforce.

It is imperative to understand the history and culture of Japan from a workplace-standpoint. Right now, Japan is lagging behind other developed nations in its diversity practices. They also lag behind other Asian countries. As a result, Japanese businesses and leaders are starting to have conversations around diversity. They understand that to effectively compete in today's international arena, Japan must fully utilize all of its available talent.

One very apparent and critical issue that Japan faces is the representation of women in the workforce. Japan has a long history of men being the bread-winners and women staying home and raising the family. When you look at the United States and Japan in comparison, Japan is just now having the same conversations that the U.S. had in the 1960s and 1970s in regard to women's rights in the workplace.

FIGURE 8: MAP OF JAPAN

In a culture that is dominantly male seniority-based, women are on the bottom rung. And there are two underlying factors that have perpetuated this culture:

1. Women are so programmed as to the appropriateness of their roles as homemakers that they do not attempt to break into corporate work environments and;

2. Working women get little to no support from their spouses in raising the kids and taking care of the home so they shirk additional responsibilities or promotions at work because they simply do not have the time or energy.

The organizational culture in Japan, as it stands now, does not support working women; but current and projected demographics have begun to force cultural change upon Japanese lawmakers and businesses. In 2006, Japan's Baby Boomers started to turn 60 and began to retire, much like the crisis the rest of the world currently faces.

In 2007, more people died in Japan than were born, and the average number of children that couples had dropped significantly, partly due to the overwhelming responsibility that women had in working and raising kids. Thus, with a huge labor shortage in the workforce, the Japanese are turning their focus on women.

The Financial Post reports that "The scale of Japan's problem can be seen in its vacant buildings. Every year, 400 to 500 schools are shut down due to a lack of children. More and more homes, too, are being vacated, especially outside the largest cities. The Japan Center for International Exchange predicts that 20 per cent of the country's houses will be empty by 2025 at the current rate."

In Japan, valuing women in the workforce may be the lesser of two evils, compared to valuing foreigners. In the past, Japan has hesitantly embraced immigrants and refugees. In fact, the Japan Times reported that, "Out of the 7,533 people who applied for refugee status in 2014, or appealed earlier refusals, only 11 were approved." Hence, there are many sectors of Japanese society that strive to preserve a mono-cultural, homogeneous population. Yet, depopulation may not allow for a comfortable choice. The Financial Post adds, "Japan, with 128 million people, sought to let in 200,000 immigrants in 2016. By comparison, Canada, with 35 million people, sought to let in 300,000 immigrants."

Japan has been plagued by corporate scandal and corruption in recent years. The business model (male, seniority-based) that has served them well since World War II started to crack because there was no accountability. Since Japan wants to stay ahead in the global economy, it has to begin working through its diversity challenges. Continuing down the path of inequality will only weaken the country economically and weaken their ability to hold their culture together.

Tradition is the primary reason why Japanese women are willing to serve as subordinates to men. One of the most popular Japanese sayings was *ryosai kebo*, which means "good wife, wise mother". This subservient role can be traced to the widely accepted and revered teachings of Hayashi Razan, who developed a Confucian school of thought that emphasized superiority and inferiority in certain relationships. According to this school of thought, the relationship between husband and wife relied upon a woman fully devoting herself to the needs and success of her husband.

The dearth of Japanese women in managerial roles goes well beyond the challenge of balancing work and home life -- an issue that confronts female corporate ladder-climbers around the globe. In Japan, professional women face a set of socially complex issues -- from overt sexism to deep-seated attitudes about the division of labor -- problems that are not easily reversed.

Japan's government -- responding to mounting international criticism about the paucity of women's career opportunities -- has made moves to improve the situation. In 1986, the country passed a law barring sex discrimination in the workplace. But real progress has been limited.

Japan's prime minister selected five women for his Cabinet in 2014, sending the strongest message yet about his determination to change deep-seated views on gender, as well as revive the economy by getting women on board as workers and leaders. Additionally, in 2015, Japanese lawmakers passed legislation that would require large companies to publicly set goals for hiring and promoting women to managerial roles. Nevertheless, other nations are proactively making similar advancements; the World Economic Forum ranked Japan 114 out of 144 countries in the 2017 Global Gender Gap Report, which measures global economic participation and opportunity.

SOUTH AFRICA
Africa is the world's second-largest and second most-populous continent, after Asia. The Republic of South Africa is a country in southern Africa. While many people are familiar with the country's legally mandated apartheid system, South Africa has a rich history of diverse cultures, ethnicities, and languages. In fact, *eleven* official languages are recognized in the constitution.

About 79.5% of the South African population is of black African ancestry. South Africa also contains the largest communities of European, Asian, and racially mixed ancestry in Africa.

FIGURE 9: MAP OF SOUTH AFRICA

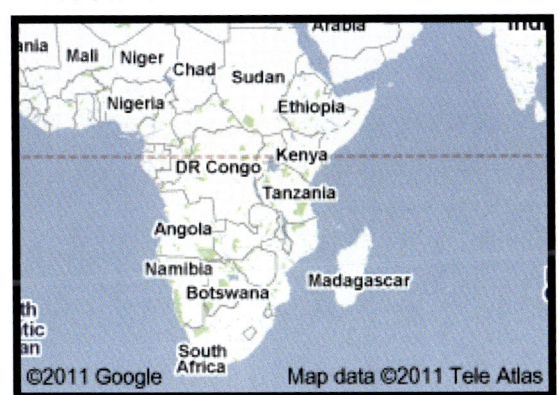

Unemployment in the nation is high for people of color though. According to Statistics South Africa, the unemployment rate was 27.7% in the first quarter of 2017, which is down from an all-time high of 31.2% in 2003. Diversity efforts were driven in the 80's, and early 90's primarily by the need to begin to adapt to the realities of a shrinking talent pool and revised legislation 'outlawing' discriminatory HR practices based on color and gender.

Equal employment opportunity practices and subsequent valuing diversity efforts focused on a subset of the population, requiring employers to increase the presence of underrepresented groups in their workforce.

The scope of diversity work expanded dramatically from 1994 onwards with the promulgation of the South Africa Constitution Act, and from 1998 onwards with the passing of the Employment Equity Act. Employers have been forced (by law) to accelerate the hiring of a more diverse workforce and to remove the barriers to employment progress for previously disadvantaged groups.

While heeding the law is mandatory, this "extra effort," which focuses on diversity training and interpersonal learning, is still perhaps viewed as an optional luxury frequently not tied to the business, and often not as effective as the legislation intended. While there are a few success stories, there were many cases in which training participants either did not know why they were there or were not able to apply what they had learned back on the job because their corporate culture did not reinforce components of the diversity education they received.

Some organizations are undoubtedly beginning to take a more comprehensive view of diversity issues, not simply completing diversity training, then "checking the box" as if the work was done but rather looking at how the issue of diversity impacts their ability to achieve their mission and enhance the bottom-line.

To further complicate matters, diversity consultants in South Africa are often poorly versed in the requirements of the law and the business case. They view training as a magic bullet for changing behavior and they often do not grasp the scope of human capital issues and challenges that need to be dealt with in order to leverage individual behavioral change, or organizational cultural change. Most often, internal and external consultants are also unwilling to deal with the underlying power and value orientation that prevents a company from effectively managing diversity.

Finally, many South African organizations continue to focus on short-term survival in this challenging economy, failing to see diversity as a critical priority. Creating and managing a diverse workforce is perceived as one more thing imposed on business by government. Thus, diversity is treated as programmatic rather than integral to the business' success. Further, with South Africa's participation in the annual Brazil, Russia, India, China, and South Africa (BRICS) Summit, diversity is recognized as a growth initiative and economic development priority.

MEXICO

To attract more foreign investment, many Latin American countries and regions have eliminated trade barriers; reduced or removed duties and importation requirements; executed free trade agreements; reduced licensing requirements; unified currency as in the European Union; modernized obsolete labor laws; created incentive programs to encourage relocation of companies into their territories; provided appropriate intellectual property protection laws; and supplied security for investors, their capital, and their imported assets.

Nevertheless, workers in countries like Mexico face discrimination in a number of ways. Cultural differences pertain to things such as language and religion. For example, there are important variations spoken among the regions of Spain and throughout Spanish-speaking America. Also, due to their deep faith in Catholicism, there are a number of days when Mexican employees may not show up to work due to Catholic holidays, even without notice or permission.

In many of the factories along the Mexico-United States border, for example, women face massive amounts of sexual discrimination. Despite the fact that Mexico has criminalized pregnancy testing when hiring women, females are still forced to take pregnancy tests. Also, in the same factories, women (and sometimes men) are forced to sign three-month employment contracts, even though such contracts are outlawed by the Mexican government.

In Mexico, some workers are discriminated against through wages. Once again, women face the brunt of such discrimination. In general, women in Mexico—like women in the United States—tend to be paid notably less for doing the exact same or comparable work as men. This finding has been substantiated through an extensive amount of sociological and government research.

Mexico's Federal Labor Law Reform of 2012 protects workers from various forms of discrimination including when female workers are fired or never hired for being pregnant; LGBTQ+ workers are retaliated against for their sexual orientation or gender identity; and men and women are sexually harassed in the workplace.

While Mexico is notorious for its discrimination against women, age discrimination is most common accordingly to human rights groups. Mexican authorities admit they are lax in enforcing laws against age discrimination. Hence in Mexico, blatant age discrimination is not only tolerated but expected for people over age 35.

According to the Yucatan Times, "The country's median age is 24, compared with 35 in the USA, and 58.8 million of Mexico's 103 million people are under age 30. That leaves a glut of young people looking for work. And because many Mexican youth live with their parents until marriage, they're willing to work for much less than older, married employees."

The first article of Mexico's 1917 constitution reads "all discrimination motivated by ethnic or national origin, gender, age, disabilities, social condition, health conditions, religion, opinions, preferences, marital status or anything else that threatens human dignity or degrades the rights and liberties of people." Additionally, Mexico's Law to Prohibit and Eliminate Discrimination outlaws age-based hiring practices but does not specify a punishment. Consequently, both Mexican and multi-national employers discriminate against older Mexican workers, which results in higher than average levels of poverty amongst senior populations. The National Survey of Discrimination in Mexico (ENDM in Spanish) reveals "61.8 % of the elderly people in Mexico are supported economically by their relatives". This explains why the Bank of Mexico reported that emigrants sent more than *$26 billion* in remittances to Mexico in 2017.

REDUCING DISCRIMINATION THROUGH ANONYMOUS APPLICATIONS

Finding gainful employment can be difficult for anyone these days, but a recent study in Germany concluded that candidates with foreign-sounding names, older job seekers or women with small children have a much harder time finding work. While it may seem anathema in many other Western countries, Germany has a standard practice for potential employees to submit a photo and disclose their gender, age, home address, marital status and other sensitive information like nationality on their applications.

In a recently completed report, researchers at the Institute for the Study of Labor (IZA) randomly assigned foreign and German-sounding names to applications for an internship. The candidates all had the same or similar qualifications, but the researchers found that applicants with names that sounded German had a 14 percent greater chance of landing an interview.

Thus, in a German pilot project, sensitive personal information was removed before the application was processed by a personnel department. Decisions on whether to grant a job interview were supposed to be based exclusively on qualifications -- at least that was the aim. Applications were only matched with a name and a face after a decision was made over whether or not to interview the person.

French cosmetics giant L'Oréal has employees from 36 countries working in its German division. The company says the creativity spawned by its diverse teams makes it easier for the multinational firm to create global products for customers who vary widely in tastes from country to country. "Diversity is an absolute priority for L'Oréal," said Oliver Sonntag, Head of Human Resources for Europe. "To further promote this diversity, we want our personnel (managers) to avoid making any subconscious decisions during the selection of applicants. Our workers have already been given sensitivity training on the issue, but we still want to develop further in this area, and that is why we are participating in the pilot project."

Others in the business world are split over the potential effectiveness of anonymous applications. Smaller companies say that the process will create additional burdens that they cannot afford. Others argue that anonymous resumes will not stop the problem of discrimination, they will merely serve to delay it to the interview stage.

Advocates for the new initiative remain undeterred and point to similar trials in Sweden or France, where President Nicolas Sarkozy promoted an anonymous application program that 50 companies participated in.

In addition to Germany and France, Anonymous Applications have been used in Canada, the U.K., Belgium, Finland, the Netherlands, Norway, Switzerland, and Sweden. According to SHRM, there are two common processes that are used:

> 1) Employers have online applications that use a software that could hide certain information—such as name, age or gender—during the initial screening stage.

2) Employers that use traditional paper or e-mail applications simply instruct the applicants to submit two versions of their resume—one anonymous, one conventional—or to put their personal information on the last page.

Several multi-national employers in America have also begun to explore the concept of Anonymous Applications to reduce discrimination against applicants. Within the next decade or so, it will be interesting to see if there will be a global standard for reducing discrimination in diversity recruiting when this initiative is tied to other interventions.

Understanding and complying with Equal Employment Opportunity laws is a critical component of utilizing Diversity and Inclusion to save money and achieve organizational goals. Nevertheless, front-line supervisors, managers and human resource professionals must play in integral part in reducing the risks that are ever-present in the workplace.

References:

HRDIVE [online], "Salary History Bans: A running list of states and localities that have outlawed pay history questions", February 15, 2018. Retrieved from: https://www.hrdive.com/news/salary-history-ban-states-list/516662/

U.S. Equal Employment Opportunity Commission (online), "Charge Statistics: FY1997 to FY2017". Retrieved from: https://www.eeoc.gov/eeoc/statistics/enforcement/charges.cfm

Government of Canada (online), "Canadian Charter of Rights and Freedoms". Retrieved from: http://laws-lois.justice.gc.ca/eng/Const/page-15.html

European Commission, "Progress in Action: The European Community Programme for Employment and Social Solidarity 2007-2013", August 2011. Luxembourg: Publications Office of the European Union

Zillman, Clair. "The EU Is Taking a Drastic Step to Put More Women on Corporate Boards". Fortune, November 20, 2017. Retrieved from: http://fortune.com/2017/11/20/women-on-boards-eu-gender-quota/

Shmuel, John. "Japan in transition: Economic realities mean Japan must confront its reluctance to accept immigrants". Financial Post, August 17, 2016. Retrieved from: http://business.financialpost.com/news/economy/japan-in-transition-why-japan-needs-to-open-its-doors-to-more-than-just-foreign-trade

World Economic Forum. "The Global Gender Gap Report", 2017

Jaramillo, Krishna. "Why Remittances From U.S. to Mexico Set a New Record?" Latin American Post, January 10, 2018. Retrieved from: https://www.latinamericanpost.com/index.php/macroeconomy-2/19057-why-remittances-from-us-to-mexico-set-new-record

Sample Test Questions:
EEO LAWS IN THE U.S. & ABROAD

1. Globally, _____ is the policy of providing special opportunities for one group over another, when those being favored are perceived as disadvantaged.
    A. Positive discrimination
    B. Equal opportunity
    C. Legal remediation

2. Disparate Treatment is illegal even if the reason for the employment action is based on factors other than those protected under Title VII.
    A. True
    B. False

3. The Equal Employment Opportunity Commission (EEOC) is responsible for enforcing this law:
    A. The Family and Medical Leave Act
    B. The Immigration Reform and Control Act
    C. Genetic Information Nondiscrimination Act

4. EEO-1 data would NOT be required from:
    A. A nonprofit organization with 150 employees
    B. A company with 55 workers and a $75,000 federal government contract
    C. A first-tier subcontractor with 90 employees and a $25,000 contract

5. The Age Discrimination in Employment Act provides protection for workers:
    A. Over age 40
    B. Over age 65
    C. Under age 40

6. The Equal Pay Act does allow for variations IF:
    A. The compensation is based on seniority or merit
    B. Less mental or physical exertion is required
    C. An employee was paid less on his/her last job

7. National origin discrimination applies to individuals who are:
    A. Employees or job applicants from any nationality
    B. Migrant workers, seasonal employees or expatriates only
    C. Hired to work for foreign employers in the U.S.

Sample Test Questions:

EEO LAWS IN THE U.S. & ABROAD (cont'd)

8. In addition to Title VII, which law prohibits discrimination based on national origin or citizenship?
    A. National Labor Relations Act
    B. Immigration Reform and Control Act
    C. The Social Security Act

9. A corporate dress code may need to be modified to accommodate:
    A. Religious practices
    B. Customer preferences
    C. Industry best practices

10. The difference between race and color discrimination is that color:
    A. Applies only to African Americans
    B. Is not defined by Title VII
    C. Does not imply lightness or darkness

11. The three main terms used to describe retaliation are:
    A. Adverse action, covered individuals, and protected activity
    B. Discrimination, harassment, and supervisor
    C. Termination, denial and refusal

12. The Ontario Human Rights Commission defines _____ as "linked to an individual's intrinsic sense of self and, particularly, the sense of being male or female".
    A. Sexual orientation
    B. Gender expression
    C. Gender identity

13. China's newest legislation is designed to offset one of the greatest demographic challenges facing the country, which is:
    A. An increase in immigration
    B. The gender composition
    C. The aging population

Sample Test Questions:

EEO LAWS IN THE U.S. & ABROAD (cont'd)

14. Compensating for demographic deficits by favoring the permanent installation of foreign families is one prong of France's:
    A. Immigration policy
    B. Refugee strategy
    C. Migration legislation

15. Many European employers are researching ways to eliminate irrelevant ethnic or personal information from being used in hiring decisions by testing:
    A. Enhanced job descriptions
    B. Virtual interviews
    C. Anonymous applications

HARASSMENT AROUND THE WORLD

> *While harassment is not as pervasive as it once was, it is still quite prevalent in today's workplace. There exists an opportunity for Diversity and Inclusion professionals to assist the organization with developing proactive policies and practices to prevent incidents of harassment, as well as to build an organizational climate that ensures a workplace free of harassment of any kind.*

OVERALL OBJECTIVES AND COMPETENCIES

Mastering this competency will allow Diversity and Inclusion practitioners to advise managers and employees about strategies to prevent and correct harassment in the workplace. Diversity and Inclusion professionals will also learn techniques for investigating and following-up with complaints in order to reduce organizational liability in unlawful situations.

BACKGROUND AND CONTEXT

Harassment of women over their choice of religious attire has spread dramatically in recent years, according to a new study from the Pew Research Center. In 2012, women were intimidated for wearing religious dress such as Muslim headscarves in 32 percent of countries in 2012, up from 25 percent in 2011 and 7 percent of countries in 2007.

Pew's data shows that there tends to be more harassment of women over wearing religious dress in countries where government regulates the practice—more than a quarter of the countries on earth; however, the report is careful to note that it cannot show a causal connection between regulation and harassment. In recent years, bans on women wearing the veil have been a growing trend globally, particularly in European countries such as France and Belgium. In 2016, France extended its bans by prohibiting Burkini's (full-body swimwear used by some Muslim women) on beaches. After several terrorist attacks in Europe, Muslim women on French beaches were fined, and on some occasions, stripped of the swimwear throughout the nation. France's highest administrative court eventually overturned the ban, but the decision was quite controversial.

Harassment covers a wide range of offensive behavior, and it affects both men and women. It is commonly understood as "behavior intended to disturb or upset", and it is characteristically repetitive. In the legal sense, it is intentional behavior that is found threatening, intimidating, or offensive.

Around the world, harassment appears in many different forms. The recent increase in complaints can be attributed to better awareness and education pertaining to what constitutes harassment. Nevertheless, governments, employers, and communities alike have struggled to prevent or stop it.

The legal backdrop for harassment in the U.S. spans nearly 50 years. In 1964, the United States Congress passed Title VII of the Civil Rights Act, which prohibited discrimination at work based on race, color, religion, national origin, and sex. This later became the legal basis for early harassment law. The practice of developing workplace guidelines prohibiting harassment was pioneered in 1969, when the U.S. Department of Defense drafted a Human Goals Charter, establishing a policy of equal respect for both sexes.

In *Meritor Savings Bank v. Vinson (1986),* the U.S. Supreme Court recognized certain forms of sexual harassment as a violation of Title VII of the Civil Rights Act of 1964 and established the standards for analyzing whether conduct was unlawful and when an employer would be liable. In a more recent measure to prevent harassment, former President George W. Bush signed a law in 2008, which prohibited the transmission of annoying messages over the Internet (*i.e.,* spamming) without disclosing the sender's true identity.

Other abusive behaviors that fall under the purview of harassment include:

- **Bullying**
  Bullying is harassment that can occur on the playground, at school, in the workplace, or at any other site. Bullying is usually physically, and psychologically harassing behavior perpetrated against an individual, by one or more persons. In recent years, bullying in the workplace and in schools has come to light as being much more serious and widespread than previously thought.

  For teachers in particular, addressing bullying in the classroom is a challenge. According to the Student and Youth Travel Association (SYTA), "bullying is not a new concept, but with rampant use of the internet and social media among teenagers, bullying has adopted new tactics."

- **Psychological Harassment**
  Psychological harassment is humiliating, intimidating, or abusive behavior that is often difficult to detect leaving no evidence other than the victim's reports or complaints. It has the effect of lowering a person's self-esteem or causing torment. Psychological harassment can take the form of verbal comments, engineered episodes of intimidation, aggressive actions, or repeated gestures. This category can be perpetuated by individuals or groups.

  Another subtype of psychological harassment is Community Based Harassment — group stalking of an individual using repeated distractions that the individual is sensitized to, such as clicking an ink pen or using social media.

- **Racial Harassment**
  Racial harassment involves targeting an individual because of his/her race or ethnicity. The harassment may include words, deeds, and actions that are specifically designed to make the target feel degraded due to their race or ethnicity. Racial harassment will be discussed in greater detail later in this guide.

- **Religious Harassment**
  Verbal, psychological, or physical harassment is used against targets because they choose to practice a specific religion. Religious harassment can also include forced and involuntary conversions.

- **Sexual Harassment**
  Sexual harassment involves unwanted and unwelcome words, deeds, actions, gestures, symbols, or behaviors of a sexual nature that has the effect of creating a hostile, intimidating, or offensive environment. Gender and sexual orientation harassment are included in this grouping. Youth, who use the terms "gay" or "homo" as an insult, fall into this category as well. The main focus of groups working against sexual harassment is protection for women, but protection for men has come to light in recent years. Sexual harassment will be discussed in detail later in this guide.

- **National Origin Harassment**
  It is unlawful to harass a person because of his or her national origin. Harassment can include, for example, offensive or derogatory remarks about a person's national origin, accent, or ethnicity. National Origin Harassment may also include harassment based on:

  - ✓ *Affiliation*: Harassing or otherwise discriminating against a person because he/she is affiliated with a religious or ethnic group. For example, harassing an individual because she practices Islam, or paying an employee less because she is Middle Eastern.

  - ✓ *Physical or cultural traits and clothing:* Harassing or otherwise discriminating against an individual because of his/her physical, cultural, or linguistic characteristics, such as accent or dress associated with a particular religion, ethnicity, or country of origin. For example, harassing a woman wearing a body covering and/or headscarf, or not hiring a man with a dark complexion and an accent because he is believed to be Middle Eastern.

  - ✓ *Perception:* Harassing or otherwise discriminating against an individual because of the perception or belief that he/she is a member of a particular racial, ethnic, or religious group whether or not that perception is correct. For example, failing to hire a Latino person because the hiring official believed that he was from Pakistan, or harassing a Sikh man wearing a turban because the harasser thought he was Muslim.

  - ✓ *Association:* Harassing or otherwise discriminating against an individual because of his/her association with a person or organization of a particular religion or ethnicity. For example, harassing an employee whose husband is from Afghanistan, or refusing to promote an employee because he attends a Mosque.

- **Stalking**
  Stalking is the unauthorized following and surveillance of an individual, to the extent that the person's privacy is unacceptably intruded upon, and the victim fears for his/her safety.

- **Mobbing**
  Violence committed directly or indirectly by a loosely affiliated or organized group of individuals to punish or even execute a person for some alleged offense without a lawful trial is known as mobbing. The "alleged offense" can range from a serious crime like murder to the simple expression of undesired ethnic, cultural, or religious attitudes. The issue of the victim's actual guilt or innocence is often irrelevant to the mob, since the mob usually relies on contentions that are unverifiable, unsubstantiated, or completely fabricated. In recent years, mobbing is a phenomenon that has been evolved. In particular, youth around the world orchestrate "flash mobs" via social media to rally around a cause, protest, or raise awareness.

Some organizations even specialize in helping to coordinate large groups of viral and spontaneous assemblers. Flash mobs have also been used to engage in mayhem such as fight at malls during the holidays, attack police officers, or commit robberies.

- **Hazing**
  Hazing is the process of persecuting, harassing, or torturing individuals in a deliberate, calculated, and planned manner as part of an induction into a group. Because hazing tends to take place as a part of a group's initiation rituals, the targeted individual is typically a subordinate or outsider. For example, a fraternity pledge, a new employee, or a first-year military cadet. Hazing is illegal in many instances.

  Lately, hazing has garnered much more attention after the 2011 death of a band member at Florida A&M University and after hazing was exposed in many high school athletic departments at small and large districts around the U.S.

- **Police Harassment**
  Unfair treatment conducted by law officials, including but not limited to excessive force, profiling, threats, coercion, and racial, ethnic, religious, gender/sexual, age, or other forms of discrimination is known as police harassment.

- **Cyberstalking**
  Cyberstalking has become more prevalent due to the integration of work and personal lives, and the increased use of the Internet. It is the use of electronic tools such as email, social networks, or text messaging to harass or abuse a person or persons. It can also include particularly intense and/or coordinated incidents of trolling, especially when they occur repeatedly, and specifically target a single person or group.

- **Electronic Harassment**
  Electronic harassment is the invisible (to the unaided eye) use of electronic weapons or social media to harass or abuse a person or persons. This category includes using tools such as "Fake News", paid actors who create viral videos, or posting other damaging information or pictures.

Although laws do not prohibit simple teasing, offhand comments, or isolated incidents that are not very serious, harassment is illegal when it is so frequent or severe that it creates a hostile or offensive work environment or when it results in an adverse employment decision (such as the victim being fired or demoted). The harasser can be the victim's supervisor, a supervisor in another area, a co-worker, or someone who is not an employee of the employer, such as a client or customer.

Situations are more likely to be defined as harassment when people *know* that the intention of a negative behavior is to cause harm (intent); the recipient of the behavior *believes* that the purpose of the behavior is to cause harm (perceived intent); and the behavior has negative consequences (consequences). According to a study conducted by University of New Brunswick researchers, the number of times the behavior occurs (repetition) does not appear to influence the definition of harassment, but it does demonstrate a pattern of harassment that can be used to establish liability in the courts. Thus, to establish a viable claim of harassment in the U.S., a complainant must show that:

1) He/she belongs to a statutorily protected class;
2) He/she was subjected to unwelcome verbal or physical conduct involving the protected class;
3) The harassment complained of was based on the statutorily protected class;
4) The harassment had the purpose or effect of unreasonably interfering with his/her work performance and/or creating an intimidating, hostile, or offensive work environment; and
5) There is a basis for imputing liability to the employer. Where a complaint does not challenge an organization's action or inaction regarding a specific term, condition, or privilege of employment, a claim of harassment is actionable only if, the harassment was sufficiently severe or pervasive to alter the conditions of the complainant's employment.

An employer is more likely to be sued over harassment issues in America, as compared to other countries around the world. Nevertheless, legal protections for American citizens extend to employers abroad when hiring Americans to work in different countries. Therefore, it is wise to adopt best practices to correct and prevent harassment from occurring.

HARASSMENT OR MICRO-INEQUITY?

It is difficult to provide a universal definition of harassment that is accepted everywhere mainly because the term is used in common English, and the legal term varies by jurisdiction globally. The ambiguity begins with the fact that some forms of harassment are, or seem to be, unconscious, small, ephemeral, and non-actionable. Many of these actions can be considered micro-inequities, which is possible to confuse harassment. Both harassment and "micro-inequity" can be ambiguous in nature; however, they should be distinguished in form and substance.

Micro-inequity refers to the ways in which individuals are "either singled out, or overlooked, ignored, or otherwise discounted" based on an unchangeable characteristic such as race or gender. A micro-inequity generally takes the form of a gesture, different kind of treatment, or what some may consider petty actions. It is suggested that the perceptions that cause the manifestation of micro-inequities are deeply rooted and unconscious. The cumulative effect of micro-inequities can impair a person's performance in the workplace or classroom, damage self-esteem, and may eventually lead to that person's withdrawal from the situation.

Mary Rowe, PhD, of MIT in 1973, coined the terms micro-inequities and micro-affirmations. She wrote yearly articles about the importance of micro-behavior. The articles were originally named the "Saturn's Rings Phenomenon" because the planet Saturn is surrounded by rings, which obscure the planet, but are made just of tiny bits of ice and sand. Dr. Rowe defined micro-inequities as "apparently small events which are often ephemeral and hard-to-prove, events which are covert, often unintentional, and frequently unrecognized by the perpetrator. These micro-behaviors occur wherever people are perceived to be 'different' ".

A micro-affirmation, according to Rowe, is the reverse phenomenon. Micro-affirmations are subtle or apparently small acknowledgements of a person's value and accomplishments. They may take the shape of public recognition of the person, "opening a door," referring positively to the work of a person, commending someone on the spot, or making a happy introduction. Apparently "small" affirmations form the basis of successful mentoring, successful partnerships, and of most caring relationships. They may lead to greater self-esteem and improved performance.

In addition to micro-inequities, there is also the concept of "micro-inequality". An inequality implies that there is some comparison being made. For example, if one's boss does not listen attentively to a diverse individual, that in and of itself is not a micro-inequality. However, if one's boss listens attentively to all of the other team members, but not to the diverse individual, that might be considered a micro-inequality.

An inequity by contrast is simply something (that may be perceived to be) unfair or unjust under the circumstances. Thus, a micro-inequity may occur with only one person on the scene, if that person is treated in an unfair or unjust manner. Of course, it is possible and even likely that many micro-inequities support or lead to an unequal environment for people of a given group, but the two concepts are different.

Another term that is confused with harassment is microaggression. According to BuzzFeed, "The term "microaggression" was used by Columbia professor Derald Sue to refer to 'brief and commonplace daily verbal, behavioral, or environmental indignities, whether intentional or unintentional, that communicate hostile, derogatory, or negative racial slights and insults toward people of color.' Sue borrowed the term from psychiatrist Dr. Chester Pierce who coined the term in the '70s."

Examples of microaggressions include:

- "What are you?"
- "You don't look like a doctor."
- "You speak well for an immigrant."
- "You're not like the other blacks."
- "Where are you from?"
- Which is normally followed up with, "No, where are you *really* from?"
- "You don't speak Spanish?"

Although microaggressions may be offensive to people of color, they may not rise to the occasion of racial harassment.

RACIAL HARASSMENT

According to the EEOC, the most prevalent form of harassment in the U.S. is racial harassment. Harassment on the basis of race and/or color violates Title VII. Ethnic slurs, racial "jokes," offensive or derogatory comments, or other verbal or physical conduct based on an individual's race/color constitutes unlawful harassment if the conduct creates an intimidating, hostile, or offensive working environment, or interferes with the individual's work performance.

Examples of harassing conduct include: offensive jokes, slurs, epithets or name calling, physical assaults or threats, intimidation, ridicule or mockery, insults or put-downs, offensive objects or pictures, and interference with work performance. An employer may be held liable for the harassing conduct of supervisors, coworkers, or non-employees (such as customers or business associates) over whom the employer has control.

An isolated incident would not normally create a hostile work environment, unless it is extremely serious or egregious (e.g., a racially motivated physical assault or a credible threat of one, or use of a derogatory term such as the N-word, etc.). On the other hand, an incident of harassment that is not severe by itself may create a hostile environment when frequently repeated.

> **EXAMPLE**
>
> A day after a racially charged dispute with a white coworker, an African American employee finds a hangman's noose hanging above his locker, reminiscent of those historically used for racially motivated lynchings. Given the violently threatening racial nature of this symbol and the context, this incident would be severe enough to constitute harassment.

The most important step for an employer in preventing harassment is clearly communicating to employees that harassment based on race will not be tolerated and that employees who violate the prohibition against harassment will be disciplined. Other important steps include adopting effective and clearly communicated policies and procedures for addressing complaints of racial harassment, and training managers on how to identify and respond effectively to harassment. By encouraging employees and managers to report harassing conduct at an early stage, employers generally will be able to prevent the conduct from escalating to the point that violates Title VII.

> **EXAMPLE**
>
> An African American librarian presents an idea to his supervisor to create a section devoted to African American authors and history, similar to those in major bookstore chains. The supervisor rejects the idea, stating that he does not want to create a "ghetto corner" in the library. This statement alone, while racially offensive, does not constitute severe or pervasive racial harassment in the absence of additional incidents.

An employer is liable for harassment by a supervisor if the employer failed to take reasonable care to prevent and promptly correct the harassment or if the harassment resulted in a tangible job action (termination, demotion, less pay, etc.). An employer is liable for harassment by co-workers or non-employees if it knew or should have known of the harassment and failed to take prompt corrective action.

Racial harassment is wrong because:

- It identifies a person's racial or ethnic background as a negative rather than a positive characteristic;
- It makes the victim feel powerless;
- It insults and degrades;
- It creates a climate that often leads to mistrust among workers.

Racial or ethnic jokes have a history. They originated in times when a race or group of people were socially under attack and lacked the power to respond effectively. These jokes, whether intended or not, are reminders of that history. Racial or ethnic jokes can:

- Endanger a worker's job performance through stress;
- Create an environment where more serious forms of discrimination and abuse can take place.

SEXUAL HARASSMENT

Another form of harassment, perhaps the most widely known form, is *sexual harassment*. In many countries around the world, sexual harassment is the number one form of harassment. There are some who assert that recent trends towards revealing clothing, television, and sexting have created a more sexualized environment, in which actions are unfairly labeled harassment. To others, this line of reasoning perpetuates a "blame the victim" mentality.

In America, sexual harassment is a type of discrimination that violates Title VII of the Civil Rights Act of 1964. Title VII applies to employers with 15 or more employees, including state and local governments, employment agencies, and labor organizations.

Around the world, sexual harassment has evolved and generated various legislative actions such as:

- *In India, the case of Vishakha and others vs. State of Rajasthan in 1997 has been credited with establishing sexual harassment as illegal.*

- *In Israel, the 1988 Equal Employment Opportunity Law made it a crime for an employer to retaliate against an employee who had rejected sexual advances; but it wasn't until 1998 that the Israeli Sexual Harassment Law made such behavior illegal.*

- *In May 2002, the European Union Council and Parliament amended a 1976 Council Directive on the equal treatment of men and women in employment to prohibit sexual harassment in the workplace, naming it a form of sex discrimination and violation of dignity. This Directive required all Member States of the European Union to adopt laws on sexual harassment, or amend existing laws to comply with the Directive by October 2005.*

- *In 2005, China added new provisions to the Law on Women's Rights Protection to include sexual harassment. In 2006, "The Shanghai Supplement" was drafted to help further define sexual harassment in China.*

Beginning in the 1980s, several high profile cases brought sexual harassment to the forefront in the workplace. As the number of high-profile complaints increased, the average profile of victims changed. This resulted in more laws being created in order to set new precedents and protect individuals against sexual predators. Following are examples of sensational cases:

1. **Bill Clinton and Monica Lewinsky:** Perhaps the most famous presidential scandal in U.S. history is Bill Clinton's affair with White House intern Monica Lewinsky. People all over the world watched as Clinton's presidency took a backseat to Ken Starr's interest in whether or not Clinton had "sexual relations with that woman". Eventually, he became the second U.S. president to face an impeachment trial.

2. **Anita Hill v. Clarence Thomas:** Conservative Clarence Thomas was nominated to the U.S. Supreme Court in 1991 by President George H.W. Bush, an action that "was instantly controversial" among the National Association for the Advancement of Colored People (NAACP), which "feared that Thomas's conservative stance on issues such as affirmative action would reverse the civil rights gains that Justice [Thurgood] Marshall had fought so hard to achieve." Women's groups also feared that Thomas would enact anti-abortion legislation. All groups were ultimately shocked, however, when Clarence Thomas was accused of sexual harassment by a University of Oklahoma law professor named Anita Hill, who had once worked for him at the Equal Employment Opportunity Commission. Despite the allegations and investigation, Thomas was narrowly elected to the U.S. Supreme Court, and Hill was criticized for "character assassination".

3. **Oncale v. Sundowner Offshore Services:** This groundbreaking case concerned a male oil-rig worker who spent periods of time on an oil platform in the Gulf of Mexico. According to the case, Joseph Oncale was sodomized, threatened, and humiliated by members of his crew. He reported the incidents, but no action was taken against the offenders, and Oncale "eventually quit — asking that his pink slip reflect that he 'voluntarily left due to sexual harassment and verbal abuse.' " Oncale filed a sexual-harassment suit against his crew, but the District Court of Eastern Louisiana held that as a male, Oncale was not protected in the 1964 legislation that prohibits sexual harassment. After the decision was appealed to the U.S. Supreme Court, however, it was reversed by a ruling that declared sexual harassment also "applied to harassment in the workplace between members of the same sex."

4. **Dov Charney v. American Apparel Inc. Employees:** Dov Charney, the founder and former CEO of popular clothing chain American Apparel, is known in the fashion industry and beyond as an "unconventional, sexed-up boss", according to The New York Times. However, he could only get away with sleeping with employees and showing up to meetings naked for so long. At least five (5) American Apparel employees filed suit against Charney for sexually harassing them at work by giving them sex toys, making derogatory comments and more. Many have negated the employees' claims, maintaining that the office culture at American Apparel is uniquely lax and that the company's marketing strategies—designed to attract young sexy buyers—naturally leak into the workplace. The board terminated Dov Charney in 2014 after another sexual harassment claim.

5. **DSK:** Dominique Strauss-Kahn was considered the sixth most influential Jewish person in the world by the Jerusalem Post in 2010; but by 2011, he became a global symbol of political disgrace after international allegations of sexual harassment surfaced. Strauss-Kahn became the Managing Director of the International Monetary Fund (IMF) in 2007 and he was the leading Presidential candidate in France, but while on a business trip in New York, he was accused of sexually assaulting a maid at Hotel Sofitel. After a lengthy investigation, all charges in New York were dropped but other sexual assault allegations were made by different women in France, as well as in Washington, DC.

6. **#ReleaseMarte:** Marte Deborah Dalelv, a Norwegian interior designer, was on a work trip to Dubai in 2013 when she reported to police that she had been raped by a colleague at the hotel where she was staying. She was then detained and charged with having unlawful sex, making a false statement, and illegal consumption of alcohol. A court sentenced her to 16 months in prison, prompting outrage in Norway. Eventually she was released, but charges against the alleged perpetrator were also dropped. Her employer, Al Mana Interiors, terminated both Dalelv and the Sudanese man she accused -- who is married with three children-- for "drinking alcohol at a staff conference that resulted in trouble with the police".

7. **#MeToo:** The MeToo movement spread virally in October 2017 as a hashtag used on social media to help demonstrate the widespread prevalence of sexual assault and harassment, especially in the workplace. It followed soon after the public revelations of sexual misconduct allegations against Harvey Weinstein. The phrase, long used by social activist Tarana Burke to help survivors realize they are not alone, was popularized by actress Alyssa Milano when she encouraged women to tweet it to "give people a sense of the magnitude of the problem". Since then, the phrase has been posted online millions of times, often with an accompanying personal story of sexual harassment or assault. Dozens of celebrities were suspended, fired or disciplined for sexual misconduct in the workplace in the months following the #MeToo movement.

Unwelcome sexual advances, requests for sexual favors, and other verbal or physical conduct of a sexual nature constitute sexual harassment when this conduct explicitly or implicitly affects an individual's employment, unreasonably interferes with an individual's work performance, or creates an intimidating, hostile, or offensive work environment.

Sexual harassment can occur in a variety of circumstances, including but not limited to the following:

- The victim as well as the harasser may be a woman or a man. The victim does not have to be of the opposite sex.
- The harasser can be the victim's supervisor, an agent of the employer, a supervisor in another area, a co-worker, or a non-employee.
- The victim does not have to be the person harassed but could be anyone affected by the offensive conduct.
- Unlawful sexual harassment may occur without economic injury to, or discharge of, the victim.
- The harasser's conduct must be unwelcome.

Accordingly, there are different degrees of sexual harassment. The less physically threatening forms of sexually harassing behaviors are also the most commonly reported. These include:

- Sexual jokes
- Sexual comments
- Sexual questions
- Sexual teasing
- Inappropriate sexual advances
- Requests for sex

Sometimes sexual harassment takes the form of words that are directed at specific genders, such as:

- Calling a woman "doll", "babe", or "honey"
- Using sexist phrases, like "dumb blondes"
- Asserting that "women cry more"
- Asking male workers to "think above the belt buckles today"
- Announcing that "women can't manage" or "employees won't work for a woman"
- Claiming that "some jobs are for women only"
- Suggesting that women should be "barefoot and pregnant"

A harasser's physical conduct may also contribute to a sexually harassing environment. Although most of these examples alone may not constitute harassment, a combination of these actions with intent or perceived intent, may indicate that an employee is a harasser. Examples of sexually harassing conduct without words include:

- Looking a person up and down (elevator eyes)
- Staring at someone
- Cornering a person or blocking a person's path
- Following the person
- Giving personal gifts
- Hanging around a person
- Intentionally standing too close to or brushing against a person
- Looking up a skirt or down a blouse
- Pulling a person onto one's lap
- Displaying sexist or sexual calendars
- Writing sexist or sexual graffiti
- Massaging or touching a person's clothing, hair or body
- Hugging, kissing, patting or stroking
- Touching or rubbing oneself sexually around another person
- Making facial expressions such as winking, throwing kisses, or licking lips
- Making sexual gestures with hands or through body movements
- Making "catcalls", whistling suggestively or engaging in lip smacking

Some harassment may include physical and verbal sexual advances toward one or more victims. Examples of these are:

- Turning discussions to sexual topics
- Telling sexually explicit or suggestive jokes or stories
- Asking about sexual fantasies, experiences, preferences, or history
- Making sexual comments or innuendos
- Telling lies or spreading rumors about a person's sex life
- Making sexual comments about a person's clothing, anatomy or looks
- Asking personal questions about social or sexual life
- Repeatedly asking a person out who is not interested
- Making harassing phone calls or e-mails

Harassment outside of the workplace may also be illegal if there is a link with the workplace. For example, if a supervisor harasses an employee while driving the employee to a meeting.

U.S. law recognizes two types of sexual harassment:

1. The first falls under the category of *quid pro quo*, or one thing in exchange for another. A person in authority demanding sexual favors of a subordinate as a condition of getting or keeping a job or benefit is an example of quid pro quo sexual harassment. Allegations of such incidents account for only 5 percent of sexual harassment complaints filed with the EEOC in recent years.

> **EXAMPLE**
>
> A young woman worked for an equipment rental company as a forklift manager. For two years, the president of the company repeatedly asked her and other women workers to reach into the front pocket of his pants to retrieve coins. He also threw items to the ground in front of them and asked them to bend over in front of him and pick the items up. He frequently made sexual comments when referring to the women's clothing. He also told the young forklift manager: "you're a woman, what do you know," and "you're a dumb ass woman," and "we need a man as the rental manager". He also told her in front of other employees and a client, that they should go to a motel to negotiate her raise. *(Harris v. Forklift Sys., Inc., 510 U.S. 17 (1993).)*

2. The second type occurs when verbal and/or physical conduct creates an intimidating or offensive atmosphere. The behavior in question must be shown to be not only sexual, but also severe and pervasive, offensive and unwelcome—with the last criterion being a subjective consideration on the part of the person on the receiving end.

> **EXAMPLE**
>
> A transgender woman who worked at a fast food chain in North Carolina, was repeatedly subjected to offensive comments about her gender identity and appearance. Managers and assistant mangers demanded that the employee, who identifies and presents as a woman, to behave and groom in ways that are stereotypically male since the employee was born male. Although the employee reported the comments on at least two occasions, the harassment continued. Shortly after the employee's complaints, she was fired in retaliation. *(U.S. Equal Employment Opportunity Commission v. Bojangles Restaurants, Inc., Civil Action No. 5:16-cv-00654-BO)*

Although it is incorrect to think that someone offended by certain behavior must confront the perpetrator in order to mount a viable complaint, it is helpful for the victim to inform the harasser directly that the conduct is unwelcome and must stop.

When investigating allegations of sexual harassment, EEOC looks at the circumstances, such as the nature of the sexual advances, and the context in which the alleged incidents occurred. A determination on the allegations is made from the facts on a case-by-case basis.

While there are few bright lines in the area of sexual harassment, most cases can be determined by asking: *Is it physical? Is it severe? Is it intended to be hurtful or disrespectful? How does the person respond to the behavior or conduct?* The Supreme Court has recently made clear that unless the conduct is physically invasive (like grabbing a breast), a victim must usually show a pattern of harassing behavior in order to demonstrate a legal claim for sexual harassment. This is because the anti-discrimination laws are not a "general civility code". Teasing, general comments, or isolated instances of sexual conduct will not usually rise to the level of a legal case of sexual harassment. In addition, flirting or isolated joking is not usually considered sufficient to constitute sexual harassment.

EXAMPLE

It was not sexual harassment but just "the ordinary tribulations of the workplace" where, over a period of six to seven months, a supervisor asked the plaintiff to lunch several times, told her she looked "very beautiful" and put his hand on her knee one time. *(Gupta v. Florida Board of Regents, 212 F.3d 571 (11th Cir. 2000).)*

Prevention is the best tool to eliminate sexual harassment in the workplace. Prevention is most effective when workers understand appropriate workplace behaviors and the consequences for illegal actions. Employers have a responsibility, in some cases, a legal obligation, to provide sexual harassment training to their employees, establish an effective complaint or grievance process, and take immediate and appropriate action when an employee complains of harassment.

High levels of sexual harassment exist when there is a low number of one particular gender in the workplace. The more nontraditional the job, the more likely sexual harassment will occur. For example, a male nurse, teacher, or administrative assistant may attract male and female harassers. Similarly, a female accountant, auto-mechanic, engineer, or police officer may attract harassers as well. When women enter fields considered "nontraditional for women" and achieve success, those men who believe the stereotype that males are superior, feel threatened by the entry of females. It is an accurate statement, then, that sexual harassment is more about power than about sex, and it is the abuse of power that is the key to understanding why sexual harassment occurs.

If the woman becomes frustrated enough, she may begin to make mistakes, "get sick," be absent from work, or fail to carry out the job, leaving the harasser with the satisfaction of thinking that "women just cannot make it in a man's world". Nevertheless, victims of all forms of harassment may respond in the same manner—whether harassment is racial, sexual, age, religious, or disability-related.

SEXUAL HARASSMENT OUTSIDE OF THE U.S.

If you are a woman living in Cairo, chances are you have been sexually harassed. It happens on the streets, on crowded buses, in the workplace, in schools, and even in a doctor's office. According to a 2008 survey of 1,010 women conducted by the Egyptian Center for Women's Rights, 98 percent of foreign women and 83 percent of Egyptian women have been sexually harassed. After releasing these dismal figures in 2008, the Egyptian Center for Women's Rights prepared a follow-up report in 2014 upon which, "For the first time in June 2014, Egypt ratified a law criminalizing sexual harassment as an amendment to the Egyptian legal code, punishing those found guilty of sexual harassment by imprisonment and/ or a fine with stricter penalties with multiple perpetrators, repeated crime and authoritative figures. The law imposes stricter penalties on those who use their authority in settings of family, work or education to commit sexual harassment. Violators will face a jail sentence of two to five years in jail and a fine."

Right now, two of the major hubs for organized action against street harassment are Egypt and India—countries where some of the most notorious street sexual assaults against women have occurred in recent years. In Egypt, a group called HarassMap tracks, in real time, reports of street harassment that women can make anonymously using mobile technology. HarassMap, in Arabic and English, also provides links for assistance and education. In 2012, Egypt toughened laws against street sexual harassment, including groping and catcalls, but in general, "they are not enforced," HarassMap says, while often, the victim who reports harassment is blamed.

It sounds almost playful, but "Eve teasing" is a daily torment for many women in South Asia, who are now trying to call 'time-out' on what they see as a bland euphemism for sustained sexual harassment. Widely used for decades by the media and police in India and Bangladesh, and to a lesser extent in Nepal and Pakistan, "Eve-teasing" is a catch-all term that encompasses anything from lewd comments to assault. As a reference to the biblical Eve, women activists argue that it carries an additional offensive inference—one where the "temptress" is complicit in her own downfall.

Following a spate of suicides by victims of sexual harassment, activists in Bangladesh successfully petitioned the High Court, which ruled in January 2011 that the term Eve-teasing belittled the seriousness of the behavior it described. According to a local rights group, from January to November 2010, twenty-six (26) women and one father of a bullied girl committed suicide in Bangladesh, and ten (10) men and two (2) women were murdered after protesting against sexual harassment.

Estimates differ on when the phrase "Eve-teasing" came into common usage, although it appears in newspaper articles dating back to the 1950s and 60s. There are suggestions that it was appropriated by the media in order to avoid the word "sexual" which might offend sensibilities in culturally conservative countries. Even though today's Indian newspapers are laced with sexual references, the usage has persisted—often in headlines to stories which, on closer inspection, detail cases of women being slapped, groped, and having their clothes torn off.

As a result, activists say, the common perception of an Eve-teasing incident is often one of young men having some innocent fun at women's expense. A recent survey of 1,000 teenage boys in Mumbai, by the International Centre for Research on Women (ICRW), showed that the overwhelming majority viewed the practice of Eve-teasing as harmless and inoffensive.

There have long been complaints that police in countries like India and Bangladesh are dismissive of sexual harassment as a serious crime and many argue that this mentality is reinforced by the idea that victims are only being "teased." Many incidents go unreported, activists say, because women believe they will simply be courting ridicule and even further harassment.

India engaged in a national-debate on combating violence against women after a 23-year-old student was gang-raped aboard a bus in New Delhi in 2012—a crime that prompted mass protests and spurred legislative overhaul. Still, attacks on women continued to dominate headlines, tarnishing India's image abroad.

In November 2013, a few months after an American woman was gang-raped in a popular hill town in northern India, Nancy Powell, the U.S. ambassador to India, said fear of rape had deterred American students from planning trips to the country. Canada, Ireland, New Zealand, and Australia also warned women of the risks involved in traveling alone to India.

The U.K. first issued a travel advisory in March 2013, after a British woman jumped out of a hotel balcony in the northern city of Agra, home to the Taj Mahal, to escape an alleged assault. That advisory asked women to "respect local dress codes and customs and avoid isolated areas, including beaches, when alone at any time of day".

The U.K. revised its advisory for British travelers to India after a Danish tourist was allegedly gang-raped and robbed in New Delhi in January 2014. "Reported cases of sexual assault against women and young girls are increasing; recent sexual attacks against female visitors in tourist areas and cities show that foreign women are also at risk," the advisory, published on the website of the U.K. government, read. "Women travelers should exercise caution when traveling in India even if they are travelling in a group," it added.

In a bid to contain damage, Indian officials have enhanced security at popular tourist destinations and spearheaded gender-sensitization programs, among other initiatives. Travelers assert that these actions are unlikely to dispel fear, at least in the near future.

Human Resource Executive Online recently released a new survey conducted by the Centre for Transforming India on sexual harassment in the Information Technology (IT) / Business Process Outsourcing (BPO) workplace. The results of the 2010-2011 survey are eye opening regarding occurrences inside India's IT sector through the eyes of women:

- Eighty-Eight percent of the 600 women surveyed at different levels reported experiencing sexual harassment.
- Ninety-One percent said they failed to report the problem because of fear.
- Seventy-Two percent of incidents reported were carried out by superiors harassing subordinates.
- Forty-Seven percent indicated there was no clear path on how to report the incident to superiors.
- Eighty-Two percent of the incidents reported occurred outside of the office.

Human Resource and Diversity Executives who are charged with leading a global brand for their firms needs to know and embrace this information. For the purposes of ensuring a safe work environment and for Inclusion, Human Resource and Diversity Leaders:

1. *Need to know that US sexual harassment programs will not be effective in India. Changes are required.*
2. *Must understand that India's hierarchy presents difficulties when employees report offenses.*
3. *Can create a strong brand in India by leading the way with effective policies around sexual harassment that build trust for women employed by the organization.*

Sexual Harassment in Europe
Within European jurisdictions, there is a degree of uniformity in laws concerning sexual harassment on account of European Union (EU) legislation. The issue was first addressed in a concerted way at the EU level in 1991, with the adoption of a Recommendation on the dignity of women and men at work and a Code of Practice on measures to combat sexual harassment. The current EU definition of sexual harassment set out in the 2006 Equal Treatment Directive (2006/54/EC) affirms that harassment exists: "where any form of unwanted verbal, non-verbal or physical conduct of a sexual nature occurs, with the purpose or effect of violating the dignity of a person, in particular when creating an intimidating, hostile, degrading, humiliating or offensive environment". While EU regulation has led to some measure of consistency in member states' laws dealing with sexual harassment, there are significant differences of emphasis and approach. Some of the key differences are:

- In the U.K., the definition of harassment specifically covers unwanted conduct "of a sexual nature", which is prohibited if it has the purpose or effect of violating a person's dignity or creating an intimidating, hostile, degrading, humiliating or offensive environment. It is also harassment if the harasser treats the victim less favorably because of the victim's rejection of or submission to this conduct. Employers in the UK are liable for acts of sexual harassment committed by their employees, even if these were not authorized or known about. An employer has a defense in this situation if it can show that it has taken all reasonable steps to prevent the harassment from occurring.

- Italy defines sexual harassment as a form of discrimination and, in particular, as unwanted conduct of a sexual nature expressed in any way which violates or is intended to violate the dignity of an employee or which creates an intimidating, hostile, degrading, humiliating or offensive working environment. Even if the employer is not itself the perpetrator of the harassment, it could still be liable on account of the general obligation to ensure the health and safety of all employees.

- Sexual harassment is a criminal offence in France. It is defined by the fact of repeatedly imposing behaviors or discussions with a sexual connotation on a person that either: offends the individual's human dignity because of degrading or humiliating characteristics; or creates an intimidating, hostile or offensive situation for that person.

- In Denmark, employers are required to take action when they become aware that an employee is alleging sexual harassment, but, there are no specific legal obligations in relation to an investigative procedure to be followed. According to the Danish Working Environment Authority, it is advisable for the employer to talk with the alleged harasser as well as the alleged victim to determine the facts. As it may be difficult for the employer to be objective, it is also advisable for it to involve a third-party adviser in these matters. Most large companies have implemented a sexual harassment policy that provides guidelines on information regarding the type of behavior which will not be tolerated, specifying that sexual harassment is prohibited and laying down clear directions on how and where employees can file a report. However, it is not common for companies offer training courses for their managers to prevent sexual harassment.

- In Belgium, Companies need to take measures to prevent sexual harassment. Such measures must be based on a risk analysis and will differ from one business to another, taking into account factors such as the activities, the context and whether it is a large or small organization.

Employers also need to implement internal procedures to enable employees who have been sexually harassed to contact a neutral and objective person of trust and/or a specialized prevention counsellor (usually someone who is external to the company and a certified psychologist). Employees who use these internal procedures are protected against dismissal. Finally, employers should provide psychological assistance and support to victims.

PREVENTING HARASSMENT

All employers have a responsibility to prevent harassment of any kind in the workplace. As mentioned earlier, the best way to prevent harassment is through strong policies and procedures and through education and training programs. An employer who is serious about preventing harassment in the workplace will sensitize all of its employees to the issues surrounding harassment. Many employers are in fact adopting zero tolerance policies, which strictly prohibit certain comments or acts.

Employers are required to have a harassment policy that clearly explains to all employees that harassment will not be tolerated by any employee, supervisor, coworker, customer, contractor, or anyone else who conducts business with the organization. Strong policies encourage victims to report harassment promptly before it affects the entire workplace.

The policy should require any employee to report the conduct that he or she believes is sexually harassing to one or more designated individuals who can take action on the complaint. The policy should:

- Clearly define sexual harassment
- Include specific examples of unlawful behavior
- Make clear that the behavior need not be directed at any particular person
- Provide for confidentiality for those who report or assist in the investigation of harassment

Additionally, employers must also keep detailed records of the reports, investigation, and outcome of harassment cases. The policy should include the fact that records could be made available on the same need-to-know basis. Furthermore, the policy should also:

- Guarantee that there will be no retaliation against the victim or any person who reported the harassment
- Provide information on what legal remedies are available, such as filing a complaint with the state or federal anti-discrimination agency
- State that the employer is committed to making a prompt, thorough and impartial investigation of the complaint
- Provide that the victim will get notice of the results
- Tell violators that they will be subject to disciplinary action and what the potential sanctions are
- Include follow-up procedures to ensure subsequent acts of harassment or retaliation are not occurring

Employers also have a responsibility to provide training for all workers on its harassment policies and procedures. Managers and supervisory personnel will often be given additional training to help them recognize their responsibilities to the workers they supervise. Some states even have mandatory harassment training for supervisors every 2-5 years.

In June 2016, EEOC held a public meeting where the latest Task Force report and recommendations on workplace harassment were released. The report notes that while more research is needed in this area, workplace harassment too often goes unreported, as "roughly three out of four individuals who experienced harassment never even talked to a supervisor, manager, or union representative about the harassing conduct." The report also acknowledged that training must change. In fact, "much of the training done over the last 30 years has not worked as a prevention tool-- it's been too focused on simply avoiding legal liability". The translation is that the law is for lawbreakers, and some people may think that because they are not breaking "the law", policies governing harassment do not apply to them. Nevertheless, training should address some of these "fuzzy" areas. Following are examples:

- When and how will a consensual relationship cross the line?
- Jen hugs some of her male co-workers, but how should she handle the guys that she doesn't feel comfortable hugging?
- Bob normally tells jokes about all sorts of things-- although a few of his jokes may not be appropriate for the workplace. Are Bob's jokes really offensive if everyone always laughs?
- Tom often misses deadlines and some people in XYX department give him a gentle nudge right before a due date. He complains that they are harassing him. Should a supervisor step in?
- Everyone sees Gail, who is a Senior Vice President, engaging in unprofessional behavior. How can someone report Gail without jeopardizing their job or their ability to get a promotion?
- Nigel regularly makes outbursts in the classroom about political issues. If another student tells him to be quiet, he attacks them verbally. The teacher has sent Nigel to the Office, moved his seat, and called his parents. At what point should the teacher simply ignore Nigel?
- Everyone knows that you can always count on Tina for the juicy office scoop. There's no harm in a little workplace gossip, is there? Even if 1 or 2 people are (deservedly) frequent targets?

Providing employee education in bystander interventions, workplace civility and making harassment complaints are all crucial skills that workers can use. In addition to training, an employer may evaluate whether its policies and procedures are helpful to employees. The evaluation used by an employer may include surveys, questionnaires, and/or employee focus groups. Should an employee have a concern, this may be an appropriate time to provide input.

Employees Will Respond Differently
How a person handles any crisis depends on his or her personality and the circumstances of the crisis. Most harassers will continue to harass, and unless they quit or are transferred, the harasser is unlikely to stop. There are several strategies that can help to end this obnoxious abuse of power. Choosing the strategy that is best for the victim depends on the severity of the harassment and on his/her personality or circumstance.

When faced with harassment, most workers:

- Ignore it
- Deny it
- Avoid the harasser or the environment
- Support or enable it

Some are able to confront the harasser. Others will join in the joking or sexual banter in order to feel like they have some control over the situation. Finally, and rarely, victims may threaten to report a complaint or file a grievance. So, what is the best strategy to stop sexual harassment? The most effective way to end harassment is to tell the harasser to stop his/her conduct. Employees can also try to gain the support of their friends in the workplace to put pressure on the harasser to stop his/her conduct or ask their employer to set up a workplace harassment training program. For example, in Bystander training, participants can learn different intervention techniques to interrupt harassing behavior.

Additionally, if the employee is not at risk of harm, he or she could say something like:

- "Your conduct is not acceptable."
- "You are not funny."
- "Your conduct / behavior is hurtful."
- "It is not a joke."
- "It is degrading."
- "Stop it!"

Employees must say it firmly and with conviction. It is important to note that it can be helpful under the law if the victim lets the harasser know that his/her conduct is "unwelcome".

It may be that the harasser is a beginner or just totally insensitive. It is also possible that the harasser does not even realize that the behavior is offensive. Nevertheless, clear words will put the harasser on notice that his/her jokes, comments, conduct, or innuendo are simply not appropriate.

The employee handbook or harassment policy should signify who to make complaints to, how to file them, and what to expect after reporting an incident of harassment. The company policy should also provide for the length of time within which a report may be filed and when the employer's conclusions will be made. Normally, a report is filed:

- Orally
- In writing
- In person
- By hotline
- Anonymously

Employers are required to promptly investigate whether a complaint is valid and, if so, what the appropriate remedies should be. Employers may also investigate when there is no formal complaint. Ideally, supervisors will discover different help-seeking behaviors and signs of harassment in training, as well as learn about steps that they can take to intervene in harassing situations, as well as prevent or stop further harassment.

To ensure that every complaint is taken seriously, ensure that employees do not use the term "harassment" lightly or in jest. Harassment is illegal in many countries, and it is important for supervisors to ascertain the seriousness of reports. Additionally, the rationale for conducting an investigation should not reflect television crime shows which state, "proof beyond a reasonable doubt." In the U.S., there merely needs to be a preponderance of evidence, which is a 51% chance that harassment occurred.

If the complaint is against a higher-up (e.g., CEO), renowned media personality, or a "rainmaker", institute a policy where the Board of Directors can get involved to address the harassment. The Board can form a committee or a working group to investigate the charges and take action.

After a complaint is filed, and while it is being investigated, the employer has a duty to protect the victim and to prevent continued harassment or retaliation for reporting. Interim measures allow the employer to temporarily correct the situation. For example, a victim can request a:

- Transfer
- Shift change
- New seat assignment
- Increased supervision or monitoring

It is important to note that the victim has to request the action, versus employment decisions being made **for** the employee that may have an adverse impact on work/life integration, job satisfaction, or productivity. Such adverse decisions could be perceived as retaliation against the victim.

After an investigation, the employer's conclusion may be:

- No substantive evidence of harassment
- Restoration of leave taken because of the harassment
- Deletion of negative evaluations in the employee's personnel file that arose from harassment
- Reinstatement
- Apology by the harasser
- Monitoring treatment of the employee to ensure that she or he is not subjected to retaliation by the harasser or others in the workplace because of the complaint
- Correction of any other harm caused by the harassment (e.g., compensation for losses)
- Discipline

If discipline is required, the harassment policy should specify exactly what the discipline would be. Usually, employers will have a progressive disciplinary policy depending on the severity of the violation. For example, a reprimand may be instituted for a first-time offender and relatively minor case, but the procedure might include that immediate dismissal will result from more severe conduct or repeated offenses even if of a less severe nature. The following sanctions may also apply to a harassment discipline policy:

- Oral or written warning or reprimand
- Transfer, suspension, reassignment, demotion or discharge
- Reduction of wages
- Training or counseling for the harasser
- Monitoring of the harasser to ensure that harassment stops

As a best practice, employers should proactively communicate with the victim, as well as follow-up to determine whether the harassment has indeed stopped. Understand, however, that the victim may still be upset and that every victim will respond differently. Nevertheless, taking extra precautions will be invaluable in restoring the employee relationship with the organization.

EMPLOYER LIABILITY FOR HARASSMENT BY SUPERVISORS

Title VII of the Civil Rights Act of 1964 prohibits harassment of an employee based on race, color, sex, religion, or national origin. The Age Discrimination in Employment Act of 1967 (ADEA) prohibits harassment of employees who are age 40 or older, the Americans with Disabilities Act of 1990 (ADA) prohibits harassment based on disability, and the Genetic Information Nondiscrimination Act of 2008 (GINA) prohibits harassment of an employee based on genetic information. All of the anti-discrimination statutes enforced by the EEOC prohibit retaliation for complaining of harassment or participating in complaint proceedings.

The Supreme Court issued two major decisions in June 1998 that explained when employers would be held legally responsible for unlawful harassment by supervisors. The EEOC's Guidance on Employer Liability for Harassment by Supervisors examines those decisions and provides practical guidance regarding the duty of employers to prevent and correct harassment and the duty of employees to avoid harassment by using their employers' complaint procedures.

- ✓ *When does harassment violate federal law?*
    - o Harassment violates federal law in the U.S. if it involves discriminatory treatment based on race, color, sex, religion, national origin, age, disability, genetic information, or because the employee opposed job discrimination or participated in an investigation or a complaint proceeding under the EEO statutes. Federal law does not prohibit simple teasing, offhand comments, or isolated incidents that are not extremely serious. The conduct must be sufficiently frequent or severe to create a hostile work environment or result in a "tangible employment action", such as hiring, firing, promotion, or demotion.

- ✓ *When is an employer legally responsible for harassment by a supervisor?*
    - o An employer is always responsible for harassment by a supervisor that culminated in a tangible employment action. If the harassment did not lead to a tangible employment action, the employer is liable unless it proves that: 1) it exercised reasonable care to prevent and promptly correct any harassment; *and* 2) the employee unreasonably failed to complain to management or to avoid harm otherwise.

- ✓ *Who qualifies as a "supervisor" for purposes of employer liability?*
    - o An individual qualifies as an employee's "supervisor" if the individual has the authority to recommend tangible employment decisions affecting the employee *or* if the individual has the authority to direct the employee's daily work activities.

- ✓ *What is a "tangible employment action"?*
    - o A "tangible employment action" means a significant change in employment status. Examples include hiring, firing, promotion, demotion, undesirable reassignment, a

decision causing a significant change in benefits, compensation, and work assignment.

- ✓ *How might harassment culminate into a tangible employment action?*
  - o This might occur if a supervisor fires or demotes a subordinate because she rejects his sexual demands or promotes her because she submits to his sexual demands.

- ✓ *What should employers do to prevent and correct harassment?*
  - o An employer's anti-harassment policy should make clear that the employer would not tolerate harassment based on race, sex, religion, national origin, age, disability, or genetic information, or harassment based on opposition to discrimination or participation in complaint proceedings. The policy should also state that the employer would not tolerate retaliation against anyone who complains of harassment or who participates in an investigation. Employers should distribute the policy to all employees, as well as establish a procedure for making complaints. In most cases, the policy and procedure should be in writing and made available to all employees.
  - o Small businesses may be able to discharge their responsibility to prevent and correct harassment through less formal means. For example, if a business is sufficiently small that the owner maintains regular contact with all employees, the owner can tell the employees at staff meetings that harassment is prohibited, that employees should report such conduct promptly, and that a complaint can be brought "straight to the top." If the business conducts a prompt, thorough, and impartial investigation of any complaint that arises and undertakes swift and appropriate corrective action, it will have fulfilled its responsibility to "effectively prevent and correct harassment".

- ✓ *What are important elements of a complaint procedure?*
  - o The employer should encourage employees to report harassment to management before it becomes severe or pervasive. The employer should designate more than one individual to take complaints and should ensure that these individuals are in accessible locations. The employer also should instruct all of its supervisors to report complaints of harassment to appropriate officials. The employer should assure employees that it would protect the confidentiality of complainants to the extent possible.

- ✓ *Is a complaint procedure adequate if employees are instructed to report harassment to their immediate supervisors?*
  - o No, because the supervisor may be the one committing harassment or may not be impartial. It is advisable for an employer to designate at least one official outside an employee's chain of command to take complaints, to assure that the complaint will be handled impartially.

- ✓ *How should an employer investigate a harassment complaint?*
  - o An employer should conduct a prompt, thorough, and impartial investigation. The alleged harasser should not have any direct or indirect control over the investigation.

- The investigator should interview the employee who complained of harassment, the alleged harasser, and others who could reasonably be expected to have relevant information. The EEOC Guidance provides examples of specific questions that may be appropriate to ask.

- Before completing the investigation, the employer should take steps to make sure that harassment does not continue. If the parties have to be separated, then the separation should not burden the employee who has complained of harassment. An involuntary transfer of the complainant could constitute unlawful retaliation. Other examples of interim measures are making scheduling changes to avoid contact between the parties or placing the alleged harasser on non-disciplinary leave with pay pending the conclusion of the investigation.

✓ *Are there other measures that employers should take to prevent and correct harassment?*
- An employer should correct harassment that is clearly unwelcome regardless of whether a complaint is filed. For example, if there is graffiti in the workplace containing racial or sexual epithets, management should not wait for a complaint before erasing it.

- An employer should ensure that its supervisors and managers understand their responsibilities under the organization's anti-harassment policy and complaint procedures.

- An employer should screen applicants for supervisory jobs to see if they have a history of engaging in harassment. If so, and the employer hires such a candidate, it must take steps to monitor actions taken by that individual in order to prevent harassment.

- An employer should keep records of harassment complaints and check those records when a complaint of harassment is made to reveal any patterns of harassment by the same individuals.

An employer should also set up programs that create a fair and respectful workplace. Examples might include the following:

- *Organize a gender-focused caucus to review issues as they arise and regularly brainstorm about new ways to improve working conditions.*
- *Review with managers how work is assigned and encourage supervisors to consider department needs and opportunities for growth when assigning new tasks.*
- *Hold regular trainings for both managers and staff that include gender issues, guidelines for professional behavior, and sexual harassment.*
- *Plan on bringing in outside consultants to help analyze what else can be done.*
- *Implement a mediation or conflict resolution program.*
- *Require communication classes.*
- *Create outreach & diversity recruitment programs.*
- *Develop leadership & mentorship programs (especially any that assist women in traditionally male-dominated environments).*

- ✓ *Is an employer legally responsible for its supervisors' harassment if the employee failed to use the employer's complaint procedure?*
    - No, unless the harassment resulted in a tangible employment action or unless it was reasonable for the employee not to complain to management. An employee's failure to complain would be reasonable, for example, if he or she had a legitimate fear of retaliation. The employer must prove that the employee acted unreasonably.

- ✓ *If an employee complains to management about harassment, should he or she wait for management to complete the investigation before filing a charge with EEOC?*

It may make sense to wait to see if management corrects the harassment before filing a charge. However, if management does not act promptly to investigate the complaint and undertake corrective action, then it may be appropriate to file a charge. The deadline for filing an EEOC charge is either 180 or 300 days after the last date of alleged harassment, depending on the state in which the allegation arises. **This deadline is *not* extended because of an employer's internal investigation of the complaint.**

References:

Breeden, Aurelien and Blaise, Lilia. "Court Overturns Burkini Ban in French Town". The New York Times - Europe, August 26, 2016. Retrieved from: https://www.nytimes.com/2016/08/27/world/europe/france-burkini-ban.html

Westrate, Cassie. "What's a Teacher to Do? Addressing and Preventing Cyberbullying in the Classroom". Student & Youth Travel Association, October 18, 2017. Retrieved from: https://syta.org/whats-a-teacher-to-do-addressing-and-preventing-cyberbullying-in-the-classroom/

U.S. Equal Employment Opportunity Commission (online), "Policy Guidance Documents Related to Sexual Harassment". Retrieved from: https://www.eeoc.gov/laws/types/sexual_harassment_guidance.cfm

Ward, James. "The Life and Death of the Flash Mob". August 23, 2017, A Blog by James Ward. Retrieved from: https://iamjamesward.com/2017/08/23/the-life-and-death-of-the-flash-mob/

Rowe, Ph.D., Mary. "Barriers to Equality: the Power of Subtle Discrimination". The Employee Responsibilities and Rights Journal, June 1990 (Vol. 3, No. 2, pp. 153-163)

Rowe, Ph.D., Mary. "Micro-Affirmations and Micro-inequities. "The Journal of the International Ombudsman Association", March 2008 (Volume 1, Number 1)

Nigatu, Heben. "21 Microaggressions You Hear on a Daily Basis". Buzzfeed, December 9, 2013. Retrieved from: https://www.buzzfeed.com/hnigatu/racial-microaggressions-you-hear-on-a-daily-basis?utm_term=.gvzOKzK4g#.abkj040Gz

The Egyptian Center for Women's Rights. "2014: The Year of Unfulfilled Promises for Women." Women's Status Report 2014 Summary

U.S. Equal Employment Opportunity Commission, "EEOC Select Task Force on the Study of Harassment in the Workplace". June 20, 2016. Available at: https://www.eeoc.gov/eeoc/task_force/harassment/index.cfm

Sample Test Questions:
HARASSMENT AROUND THE WORLD

1. **The difference between harassment and a micro-inequity is that a micro-inequity is often:**
   A. More severe than harassment
   B. Outside of the workplace
   C. Unintentional and unconscious

2. **Sexual harassment law in the U.S. allows for:**
   A. Frequent teasing
   B. Isolated incidents
   C. Severe conduct

3. **Harassment is a form of employment discrimination that can violate this EEOC enforced law:**
   A. The Immigration Reform and Control Act
   B. The Family & Medical Leave Act (FMLA)
   C. The Americans with Disabilities Act of 1990 (ADA)

4. **Sexual harassment prevention is NOT effective when:**
   A. Workers understand appropriate workplace behaviors
   B. Complaints can only be filed with direct supervisors
   C. There are clear harassment policies and grievance processes

5. **The key to understanding why sexual harassment occurs is knowing that:**
   A. Harassment affects men as much as women
   B. Harassment is only illegal in the U.S.
   C. Harassment is an abuse of power

6. **The most prevalent form of harassment in the U.S. is:**
   A. Sexual harassment
   B. Racial harassment
   C. Religious harassment

7. **In India, sexual harassment is called:**
   A. Feminine complaints
   B. Gender bashing
   C. Eve teasing

Sample Test Questions:
HARASSMENT AROUND THE WORLD (cont'd)

8. In order for harassment to violate U.S. laws, it must be frequent or severe to create a hostile work environment, or:
   A. Be directed at a female subordinate
   B. Result in a tangible employment action
   C. Lead to workplace violence or injury

9. For purposes of employer liability, an individual qualifies as a "supervisor" if:
   A. The individual had previous management experience
   B. The individual works in the department of human resources
   C. The individual can recommend tangible employment decisions

10. An effective harassment prevention program can rely on verbal policies.
    A. True
    B. False

11. High levels of sexual harassment exist when there is a low number of one particular gender in the workplace.
    A. True
    B. False

12. The employer is *automatically* liable for harassment by a supervisor that results in a negative employment action such as termination, failure to promote, and loss of wages.
    A. True
    B. False

13. A complaint procedure is adequate if employees are instructed to report harassment to their immediate supervisors.
    A. True
    B. False

DIVERSITY RECRUITING & RETENTION

> *The ability of an organization to commit to hiring a diverse workforce is challenging for many reasons. First, technological advancements are driving employers to drastically cut back the number of full time positions. Second, decision makers within the organization might not be committed to hiring a diverse workforce. Third, the organization itself may not have systems in place to include, engage, and retain a diverse workforce-- which affects future recruiting.*

OVERALL OBJECTIVES AND COMPETENCIES

The purpose of this competency is to coordinate best practices and innovative techniques to recruit, onboard, develop, include, engage and retain diverse workers. As a result, employers will be better positioned for future demographic changes by implementing a strong diversity recruiting and retention policy now.

BACKGROUND AND CONTEXT

Diversity recruiting can be defined as "the process of broadening the candidate pool for purposes of hiring the **best** qualified candidate for the job". Contrary to popular opinion, diversity recruiting doesn't necessarily mean that an underrepresented individual will be hired for the job; it simply indicates that a wide pool of candidates has been seriously considered for a position. This task requires a different set of skills and knowledge, and it involves more than hiring for the sake of representation. In other words, the diversity recruiting process is both deliberate and strategic.

Leadership should be fully committed to the process and demonstrative of the support needed for diversifying the employee base. If an organization recruits diverse individuals simply to meet a self-imposed or an external quota, the efforts will fail. For one, employment quotas are not legal in the U.S.; and second, hiring is a contractual arrangement between employer and employee based on the need for a worker's skills. Both have a stake in the success of the hire; therefore, the hiring process should reflect high standards and professionalism.

The United States population is already diverse, so it's no longer a question of when the workforce will change; it already has. There has been a huge increase in women, people of color, and immigrants in the workforce over the last 25 years. For local, national, and international organizations, diversity is not just a "good idea", it is a business imperative if an organization depends on the support of people (i.e., customers, students, patients, constituents, etc.) for survival.

People want to be served by organizations who value them, as well as by individuals who understand their expectations and cultural preferences. If not, they will choose to go elsewhere.

Yet, before asking *how* to recruit diverse employees, organizations should identify their own diversity recruiting objectives, perceived obstacles, and work environment. To rephrase, much more hinges on this process than getting diverse people in the door; an employer may also have to consider the onboarding process, as well as the environment for inclusion, engagement and retention.

Consider the search process as the first step in diversity recruiting. How well the company matches the person to the position will determine the individual's success in the position. Successful searches begin with an engaged search committee or hiring panel, with members who are trained, dedicated, and experienced individuals. Search teams succeed when they build highly qualified, diverse applicant pools and these pools lead to the potential for outstanding hires which, in turn are natural recruitment vehicles for subsequent hiring.

DIVERSITY RECRUITING CONSIDERATIONS AND CHALLENGES

Why is recruiting diverse candidates different from recruiting all other candidates? This is a critical question that must be answered by any organization that seeks to diversify its employee base.

Since 2016, the conversation and the atmosphere for diversity recruiting has subtly become more hostile. Therefore, it is important to ensure that the process of recruiting diverse individuals is viewed as valuable and effective. Diversity recruiting is not a simplistic process whereby an organization finds a diverse candidate and hires them. Diverse candidates expect that their knowledge, skills and abilities will be evaluated free from discrimination, sexism, ageism, or other biases. Furthermore, once on the job, they do not want to be treated as if they are a "token", an Affirmative Action candidate, or "less qualified".

Traditionally, diversity recruiting fails for many reasons, some of which may be accredited to the organization having:

- A bad reputation for mistreating diverse talent
- Unclear goals (e.g., we only have 5 women; let's hire 2 more to meet our quota goal)
- A simplistic strategy (e.g., don't worry about turnover right now)
- A weak Business Case (e.g., this isn't a priority because "it's hiring for the less qualified")
- No innovation in tools and strategies (e.g., we use the same tools that we've always used)
- Weak recruiters who focus only on the active candidate pool (e.g., "they're not out there")
- Stereotypical biases (e.g., the candidate is cast aside due to a foreign or ethnic name, urban address, or sexual orientation)
- Not enough emphasis on orientation, engagement and retention-- prior to recruiting

Diversity recruiting **is** different, and it has changed the nature of hiring. The following blog clarifies some of the modern-day challenges that organizations face with this issue.

Challenges in Recruiting & Hiring Diverse Employees
By Lila Kelly

To remain competitive in today's market, it is important to make an effort to attract, hire, and retain qualified diverse employees. Unfortunately, organizations sometimes lose qualified job applicants in the process. This can happen because of two reasons. One, the applicant's potential for the job is underestimated, and the applicant is screened out. Perhaps this is due to prejudice, cultural misunderstandings, or just a lack of interviewing skills on the part of the interviewer. Or two, the applicant decides the organization is not a good place for them to work, and the applicant screens the employer out.

An Asian-American marketing manager spoke of a challenge organizations have in recruiting people of color, especially in professional level positions. She said, "When you look at more highly educated minorities, these people have a lot of choices—professional choices about where they want to go that makes them feel comfortable." As a consultant, I have worked with hiring managers in organizations where they have had to learn to sell the organization to qualified job applicants. This was new for them, compared to just letting the applicants sell themselves, as they had always done in the past. Interviewers need to be skilled both at assessing the applicant's true potential for the job and at selling the job to the applicant.

Diverse applicants have talked about how the interviewers they meet reflect the whole organization. One person said, "In one interview, I would answer a question, and the interviewer would correct my thinking. It became an argument as opposed to a conversation. This did not sound like a very team-oriented, nurturing or developing environment, and not a place I would like to be." Perhaps the applicant misunderstood the interviewer's approach, or perhaps the interviewer lacked an understanding of different cultures and communication styles, which interfered with his ability to assess the applicant's true potential for the job. As society becomes more diverse, interviewers need to learn more about the cultural backgrounds of the people they interview.

In another situation, an African American woman who is an HR employment representative said that the supervisor who interviewed her and the people she met in the HR department were very nice. However, when introduced to the individual who administered the employment tests, it was another story. She stated, "It was like she was sure that I would not understand the test and wouldn't do well. She said, 'I'm going to give you a chance to read these, but when I come back, I will give you a little bit more time than we normally do.' When she came back she felt it was necessary for her to explain what I had just read. It was that kind of thing that really ticked me off and gave me a negative feeling about that organization." Luckily this applicant was not lost. She started working there, discussed the experience with her supervisor, and the organization acted to correct the problem. It is important that all employees who meet job applicants have a respectful and welcoming manner.

Job applicants also notice things in the work environment. When a Middle Eastern man in restaurant management arrived for an interview, he saw pictures in the receptionist area of *Employees of the Month*. Two pictured were African American and some were female. This made him feel better about the organization. He said, "Psychologically it made me feel more comfortable going into the interview, not as nervous. I didn't think there would be prejudice in the interview."

> Seeing diversity in an organization is important to some applicants, but not to all. To help applicants get a feel for the environment, include a tour and introductions to other employees. The more the applicant knows about the job and the environment beforehand, the better the match will be. Practices such as these can also affect the retention of employees in the future.
>
> As the merging of cultures continues into the 21st century, cross-cultural competencies are increasingly important for interviewers, and organizations need to think through and strategically plan their recruiting and selection practices.
>
> *Lila Kelly has over 20 years of experience in the area of diversity in employment interviewing, structuring the recruitment and selection process, diversity in the workplace, career-transition skills, recruiting, and HR management. Lila Kelly Associates is an independent consulting firm established in 1992.*

These issues perplex some who long for the organizational make-up to change but, understand that it's hard to figure out where to begin making adjustments. The first place to start is to ensure that your organization is inclusive. You can have diversity, but not inclusion. Diversity denotes the spectrum of human similarities and differences, while Inclusion describes the way your organization configures opportunity, interaction, communication and decision making to utilize the potential of its diversity. Diversity is a noun because it entails a multiplicity of people who think differently and possess unique worldviews, whereas Inclusion is an action verb that illustrates how the organization works. In order to evaluate an organization's readiness for Diversity AND Inclusion, one must:

Analyze Diversity Recruiting: It's important to take a look at the organization itself to understand its relationship with diversity. This means evaluating where diversity exists within your organization—are people of color and women primarily populating lower level positions with little to no authority? Do you have diverse employees or students, but lack diverse doctors, agents, tenure track professors, franchisees, contractors, Board members, or other stakeholders? Are hiring managers and other decision makers encouraged to be more inclusive in candidate selection? You must also take a closer look at the organization's policies, procedures, hiring strategies, orientation, training, performance appraisal system, goals, mission and values. Do these structures support or inhibit diversity?

Communicate the Definition & Mission of Diversity: There are still people who associate "Diversity" with Affirmative Action, quotas, and hiring unqualified individuals. This attitude or belief displays itself through subtle resistance to hiring diverse candidates as possibly being unable to fit into the organization. Therefore, it's important to frequently communicate your organization's definition of diversity and assure interviewers and hiring managers that 'Diversity' does not imply lower standards.

Seek Diversity Champions: Senior leadership needs to talk about diversity in a public setting. Employees need to hear from the top that diversity is important. And, when leadership positions are open, hiring managers must do their part to seek out diverse candidates. Also, special attention must be paid to "Diversity Champions"-- those who get it and want to do something about it. These are the folks who can act as catalysts to get others excited about diversity.

Institutionalize Diversity: It's one thing to talk about diversity. It's quite another thing to have a systematic approach for embracing it. Diversity must be a keynote topic during orientation and throughout training. The more people hear about diversity, the more opportunities they will have to look at what it means to them and their department or program. For some hiring managers, this implies being more open when hearing a person with an accent. Instead of shutting the person off, it instead implies keeping an open mind and working to discover the individual's unique strengths.

Move Diversity Forward: All organizations seek to improve in some way. By embracing diversity, an organization can significantly enrich itself by gaining new perspectives and insights. The key is to look at diversity as a way to grow the organization and take it to the next level. The more positive outcomes that are achieved with diversity, the more diversity gets branded as a positive employee experience. The "diversity experience" will begin to take on a life of its own with proper maintenance and dedication. Also, think of ways to illustrate the value of diversity within your organization. For example, compare the sales results of successful sales teams that have diverse team members against those that are homogeneous in makeup. Identify equity gaps in student learning by course and design interventions to address these gaps.

Branch Out: Organizations often put their public affairs and/or marketing departments in charge of social responsibility projects. This is another way for organizations to learn about a community's diverse assets. Not only could organizations contribute to their communities, but they can also team up with diverse individuals, who might one day become an employee, student, client, volunteer, vendor or board member.

SOURCING DIVERSE CANDIDATES

Placing ads in mainstream newspapers do not necessarily attract diverse hires. However, there are a plethora of target media outlets that could provide an array of candidates. For example, in large cities there are newspapers that cater to women, older individuals, people of different faiths, Blacks, Hispanics, Asians, Native Americans, LGBTQ+ individuals, Veterans, people with disabilities, and more. It would be helpful to conduct a Google search of local media outlets that specialize in diverse populations.

A 2014 Pew Research Report found that, "about eight-in-ten Latino, black and white adults who are online use at least one of five social media sites – Facebook, Instagram, Pinterest, LinkedIn and Twitter." Reviewing online job boards, LinkedIn, and other social media outlets is one way to source excellent candidates. Nevertheless, SHRM warns that "companies [should] generally avoid requesting photos and videos attached to resumes and application forms. Social media sites present employers with information such as race, ethnicity and approximate age. They might include information about religion, marital status, disabilities, political affiliations and other personal interests." Hence, do not use information that could substantiate a lawsuit.

Posting positions with industry specific or professional associations is another great source. There are a whole host of organizations that employers can tap into such as the: National Black MBA Association, Urban League Young Professionals, UnidosUS, National Association of Asian American Professionals, and more. LatPro and Catalyst Career Group host nationwide job fairs. Some groups utilize professional job boards such as: Diversity.com, DiversityNetwork.com, and Indeed.com.

Also, the Human Rights Campaign (HRC) has a listing of LGBTQ+ professional and student associations, and the National Organization on Disability (NOD) has a wealth of virtual resources for employees and employers alike.

Another potential avenue is to poach talented employees from competitors or tap the networks of your organization's employees. The United States Postal Service and FedEx both use their own employees to help them recruit new workers-- as word of mouth attracts diverse candidate pool.

Most higher education institutions have a vested interest in getting their graduates hired. Contacting the career services department of Hispanic Serving Institutions (HSI's), Historically Black Colleges and Universities (HBCU's), or other institutions will provide an easy way to have recruiters outside the organization working on your behalf. Many of these institutions host or attend career fairs and job expositions to showcase the talent of their students as well. Additionally, recruiters may contact the Diversity Officer at a few mainstream institutions to find out which career fairs they will host or attend.

Professional conferences are another outlet to consider for recruitment. As employees attend or present at regional and local conferences, recruiters should participate as well. Many conferences have vendors that offer products and services to the organization; a recruitment booth with available and upcoming positions at the company gives your organization an opportunity to showcase the best aspects of working for an industry leader.

Finally, consider billboards in high traffic areas; gospel or Latino radio; National Pan-Hellenic Council fraternities and sororities; individuals who volunteer at nonprofit organizations who serve diverse segments of the population; or houses of worship, where the job announcement can be placed in the weekly bulletin at no cost.

Sourcing in personnel management work refers to the identification and uncovering of candidates (also known as talent or human capital) through proactive recruiting techniques. Sourcing for candidates refers to proactively identifying people who are either: a) not actively looking for job opportunities (passive candidates); or b) candidates who are actively searching for job opportunities (active candidates). Some corporate recruiters or individuals within the Office of Diversity specialize in sourcing diverse candidates for inclusion in a broader pool. Methods for sourcing a broader pool of diverse candidates include searching for specific keywords found on resumes, sourcing from affinity groups and researching other communities. The key is to develop a source where you can find highly qualified diverse candidates, and then eliminate the barriers that keeps these individuals from getting hired or from terminating shortly after hire.

Expanding the candidate pool requires engaging a variety of different sources and employing unique strategies. Again, in previous decades, employers could afford to sit back and wait until employees found them. In this generation, employers must utilize a collection of different techniques to find talented workers. Once the organization sets up a viable system, the process becomes more organic; nevertheless, putting in the extra effort to initiate expanding the candidate pool can be viewed as atypical. Yet, the organizations who do not put in the extra effort will experience a dire skills and talent shortage within the next 5-10 years.

THE FINALIST POOL

According to the Harvard Business Review, "Despite the ever-growing business case for diversity, roughly 85% of board members and executives are white men. This doesn't mean that companies haven't tried to change. Many have started investing hundreds of millions of dollars on diversity initiatives each year. But the biggest challenge seems to be figuring out how to overcome unconscious biases that get in the way of these well-intentioned programs."

FIGURE 1. IMPROVE THE CHANCES OF HIRING DIVERSE CANDIDATES

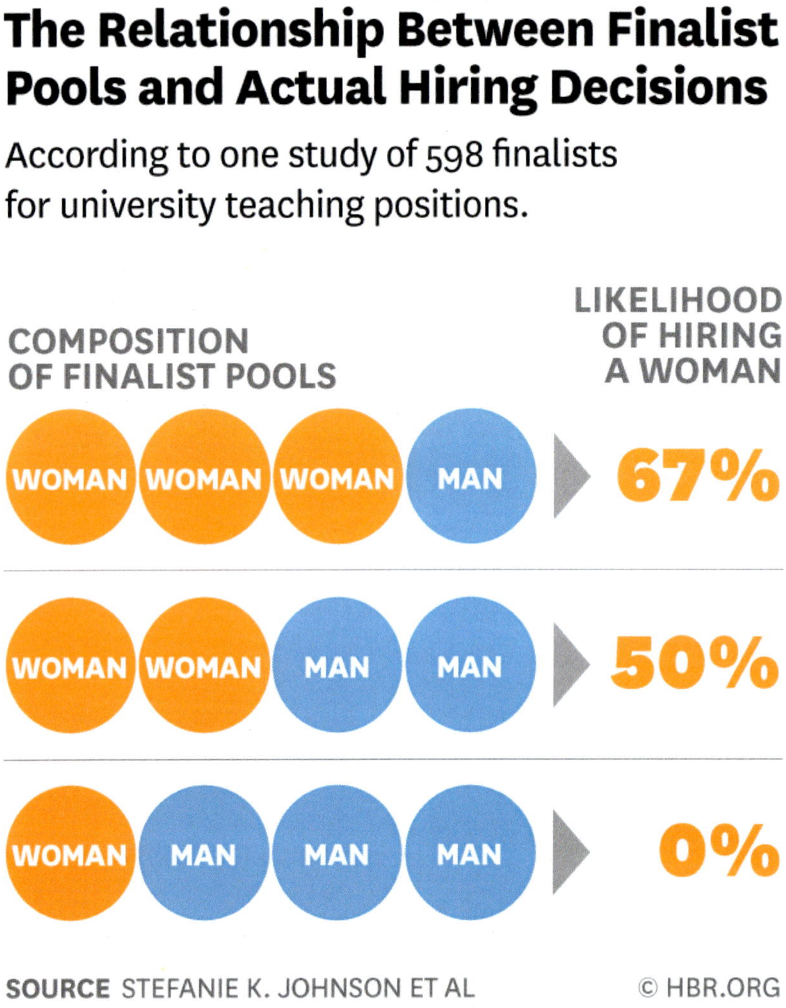

The Relationship Between Finalist Pools and Actual Hiring Decisions

According to one study of 598 finalists for university teaching positions.

Composition of Finalist Pools	Likelihood of Hiring a Woman
WOMAN, WOMAN, WOMAN, MAN	67%
WOMAN, WOMAN, MAN, MAN	50%
WOMAN, MAN, MAN, MAN	0%

SOURCE: STEFANIE K. JOHNSON ET AL © HBR.ORG

In 2016, researchers Stefanie Johnson, David Hekman, and Elsa Chan found that when a majority of the candidate finalists were white (demonstrating the status quo), decision makers tended to recommend hiring a white candidate. But when there were two minorities or women in the pool of finalists, the status quo changed, resulting in a woman or minority becoming the favored candidate.

This means that when the candidate pool has one diverse candidate, the myths about the candidate's skills and abilities will be filtered through unconscious bias. If that person is hired, the unconscious bias persists because the assumption is that the individual HAD to be hired to fulfil the quota (or the diversity goal that was ill-defined).

As Figure 1 suggests, placing more diverse candidates in the hiring pool, greatly improves your chances of hiring diverse talent because of merit.

Training the search committee or hiring team is essential to an equitable outcome for all candidates. Recruiting, interviewing and selecting new employees is typically not part of this group's day to day work or activities. Annual training and regular learning interventions ensures that your organization is fully ready and educated with the necessary tools for a successful hire. Further, reminding the hiring teams that all candidates must be treated the same throughout the process, helps to reduce bias.

The hiring process is confidential and should be treated as such. It is incredibly important to maintain the confidentiality of the applicant's personal information, the work of the search team, and other details that could potentially bias the decision-making process. For this reason, many larger organizations have turned to Anonymous Applications as a best practice. Nevertheless, social media makes it relatively easy to find information about applicants outside of the application that was submitted to the organization. Be careful that this "intel" does not bias the committee with superfluous information (e.g., nationality, age, gender identity, disability, veteran status, neighborhood, religion, family status, etc.) that has no bearing on the knowledge, skills and abilities of the applicant.

Further, as a best practice, the organization should eliminate loopholes that do not intentionally discriminate against individuals but have the effect of screening out potentially great diverse candidates. For example, certain executives are able to hire individuals who are allowed to bypass the formal interviewing process. To close the loophole, the organization must institute a formal interviewing policy where at least three (3) candidates are considered for each position. Another loophole is allowing key hiring decisions to rest in the hands of one person. Think about why universities employ a search committee to select an institutional President; corporations utilize a Board committee to select an enterprise-wide CEO; and nonprofits engage the Board of Directors to select an Executive Director. In the same manner, key positions and promotions (e.g., C-Suite, Vice President, Director, etc.) may achieve more diversity if the decision was made by an unbiased hiring team.

Describing the roles and responsibilities of an engaged hiring team will eliminate any confusion about what is expected. The team members should:

- Understand all job-related criteria for the open position
- Maintain the confidentiality of all information throughout the search process
- Review applicant materials prior to the interview
- Participate in all interviews and meetings
- Share responsibility for ensuring the fair and equitable treatment of all applicants
- Take clear, job-related, fact-based notes; assume the notes may be called into question
- Assist with welcoming the new employee(s)

In areas of higher education there is a myth that underrepresented faculty has a multitude of options available to them and this makes them hard to attract and retain. There is no data to support this myth. It is a scapegoating tactic, where blame is placed on the powerless. Data actually shows that it takes underrepresented faculty members twice as long as their white counterparts to secure a tenure track position. Typically, a conversation about "fit" follows the evaluation of underrepresented applicants. Fit is another word for "they do not look like the rest of us". D&I leaders should be prepared for these types of evaluations and proactively educate the search committee about the legal liability for discriminatory and exclusionary evaluations. Additionally, as the market becomes more competitive for students, the lack of diverse faculty representation will certainly derail future enrollment efforts. Reviewing the demographic projections and providing education about biases will be critical diversity training topics for search committees.

Consideration of candidates without partiality for or against a candidate is best achieved by using unbiased selection criteria and terminology. Being aware of cultural norms and staying professional throughout the interviewing process is essential to ensuring that your organization appears to be thoughtful in hiring.

Cultural bias often manifests itself during interviews. **Cultural bias** can be defined as "interpreting and judging phenomenon according to standards inherent to one's own culture". A blind spot occurs because some individuals never consider that many households do things differently, or other individuals have dissimilar worldviews and customs. Cultural nuances may include:

Physical Closeness
Members of some cultures stand shoulder to shoulder for professional conversation; others separate by two or three feet. There are also variations within cultures by gender. You won't be able to memorize all of the cultures of the world. But what you can do is to very consciously and kindly, allow the other person to determine how close he or she wishes to remain in proximity to you.

Saying Hello
Keep your hands to yourself, no hugging. Among most North Americans, as with the French, a quick, firm handshake is just plain friendly. But with Ecuadorans, it is used as a signal of unusual respect. In many countries, a polite handshake is far limper than the U.S. version. In Muslim countries, your offer of a simple handshake, between genders, can force your conversational partner to either do something they consider morally wrong or embarrass you publicly by refusing your hand.

Facial Expressions
Watch your face-- and theirs. The three most important things to watch on faces are: transparency, smiles, and eye contact.

- *Smiles:* To most cultures in the world, smiles simply express happiness, pleasure, and ease. Among Puerto Ricans, a quick smile can mean "Please," or "What can I do for you?" or "Thank you." The difference depends on eye expression and forehead movements. Japanese men sometimes hide anger, sorrow, embarrassment, or distrust with laughter and smiles. Koreans interpret easy smiles as indicative of a person's shallowness or thoughtlessness.

- *Eye Contact:* Where do you gaze, and for how long? From one country to the next, there is marked disagreement on the answer. Americans are fond of the thought that they cannot trust anyone who does not look them in the eye. In fact, the average duration of eye contact among North Americans is only about three seconds. So, relax your standards for eye contact because you may find that eye contact means different things to different people. Even some African Americans believe that avoiding prolonged eye contact demonstrates respect. Although this behavior has its roots in slavery, it is still taught by some parents today. Generally, Americans do not look steadily into the eyes of someone with whom they are speaking, unless they are feeling romantic. Make eye contact when you begin to speak, then look away, and then, periodically, return to the eyes of the person to whom you are talking. This may increase the comfort level of candidates.

ASSESSING CANDIDATE QUALIFICATIONS

The interview is the time to get to know the candidate, their personality, their willingness to do the work and ability to meet the needs of the organization. A clear and concise method for evaluating and assessing each candidate assists the search team in making the appropriate decision in who is the most qualified candidate.

All interviewers should base their decisions on the job description, or the tasks, traits, styles and skills that are required to do the job. This will require asking behaviorally based questions about the Candidate's work experience and background. According to Inc. Magazine, asking a candidate a question such as: "How important do you feel honesty and integrity are in the workplace?" is an opinion-based question that could be rehearsed and insincere. In the "9 Most Common Behavioral Interview Questions and Answers", author Jeff Haden says, "you can't rely on what candidates say they will do; you can learn a lot from things they have already done". Haden suggests asking questions such as:

- "Tell me about a major mistake you made, and what you did to correct it"
- "How did you respond the last time a customer or co-worker got upset with you"
- "Describe how you operate in a fast moving, high pressure environment"

For best results, interviewers should ask all of the candidates the same questions. Of course, if necessary, the interviewers can ask simple follow-up questions such as: what happened next? Or how did everything work out? These techniques, and more, could be tactics that you provide in a training session for interviewers.

Assessing Whether the Candidate Values Diversity
During the interview process, a diversity statement with corresponding questions should be shared with all candidates regardless of the position. Any employer who is serious about Diversity and Inclusion will have a statement or vision about Diversity and Inclusion, and the statement will make it clear that all people who work for, and interact with, the company should be valued and respected. Candidates who are uncomfortable with questions specific to diversity will not become comfortable after hiring.

Sample Diversity Statement
[Organization or Institution] values diversity among [leadership, management, frontline employees, faculty, staff and students] and we have made a commitment to promoting and enhancing equity and inclusion in our [organization or institution]. We believe that a shared commitment to [teaching and service] within a diverse environment fosters collegiality and advances our central mission. We would like to discuss your experience with and views regarding diversity:

- In your opinion, what's the best way to ensure that diversity is viewed as a strength?
- What do you see as the most challenging aspects of an increasingly diverse community?
- What have you done, formally or informally, to meet such challenges?
- How would you incorporate equity and inclusion into your work?
- How have you worked with others to foster the creation of climates receptive to inclusion?
- Have you ever mentored, supported or encouraged someone from outside your area of expertise? What about individuals of color, women, or international students or colleagues?
- In what ways have you integrated multicultural issues as part of your professional development?

Next, assess what you heard:

- Is the candidate at ease discussing diversity-related issues and their significance to the organization? Or is the candidate reluctant to discuss diversity issues?
- Does the candidate use gender-neutral language? Or was the conversation replete with common stereotypes?
- Does the candidate address all the members of the interview committee?
- How does the candidate show experience, concern, commitment or willingness to advance the organization's diversity efforts?

A candidate should be assessed and evaluated against selection criteria that is specific to the position. Selection criteria is based on the qualifications stated in the job description and is weighted relative to the importance of the criterion. Criteria grids are created prior to interviewing or candidate selection. Each member of the hiring team completes a grid for each candidate and only uses the information on the form to rate or rank candidates. Use of the form maintains focus on the candidate's ability to perform the essential functions of the job.

FIGURE 2. SAMPLE SELECTION CRITERIA GRID

Position: Operations Manager

Applicant Name: Jayne Green

	Criteria	Notes	Point Range	Points Awarded
1	Knowledge: degrees, certifications, licenses, etc.			
2	Ability: years of experience, transferrable experience, etc.			
3	Skills: software, hardware, sales, teaching, marketing, etc.			
4	Job specific requirements			
	TOTAL POINTS		0-100	

Additional notes:

Invite for Interview: ☐ YES ☐ NO

ONBOARDING, ENGAGING & RETAINING DIVERSE EMPLOYEES

Many companies already know that wages and benefits are important to employees, but compensation alone is not enough to retain the talent that your organization needs to excel. As stated earlier, interviewing a diverse pool and hiring the best candidate is just the beginning. Now it's time to supplement the diversity recruiting process with value-added and comprehensive interventions: onboarding, engagement, and retention.

Onboarding

Monster.com reports 30 percent of external new hires turn over within the first two years of employment. Retention statistics from other organizations, including the Society for Human Resources Management (SHRM), show that turnover can be as much as 50 percent in the first 18 months of employment.

Two decades ago, according to the Bureau of Labor Statistics, the average number of jobs held in one person's career was six. Today, the average number of jobs held is 11. And according to the Bureau of Labor Statistics, the cost for replacing an employee is over 25 percent of their annual salary. According to PeopleAdmin, "Onboarding is more than just new hire orientation. Onboarding is a process. Orientation is an event – the first step in the onboarding process."

In an organization with an effective onboarding process, for example, there will be a trained individual who is responsible for taking the time to explain the unwritten rules of the organization. The individual must be trained because employers should not have an individual who spews all of the negative stuff about the company in the first week. Training will advise the individual that some things will be appropriate to say to a new hire, while other issues are professionally inappropriate.

The trained "onboarder" will also learn how to do proper introductions. Instead of "This is Mary who will be working in Marketing", the onboarder will say, "Mary is an award-winning Executive with a Master's Degree in Marketing Communications and 15 years of experience in the field. She will be heading up our Marketing Department." The second introduction distinguishes Mary as an elite professional and ensures that Mary is not perceived to be a token or Affirmative Action hire. This type of introduction will also ensure that Mary receives respect and inclusion at the outset. Utilizing employee or business resource groups for onboarding is a great strategy for guaranteeing that diverse new hires experience onboarding through the lens of people who have a vested interest in seeing diverse workers succeed.

PeopleAdmin suggests that "a sound onboarding process spans 1-2 years and includes constant communication, feedback, and performance measurement — all keys to employee longevity and loyalty. Onboarding follows the employee lifecycle for mentoring and development and includes automation for consistent and timely tracking of onboarding events. Seamlessly transitioning the candidate through the new hire and onboarding experience, then into the performance management process matriculates the new employee and ensures success."

Other ideas for the onboarding process include: defining what success looks like; sharing information about the culture and management; allowing the new hire to "visit" resource group events/meetings; introducing the new employee to other recently hired workers; explaining team dynamics; or letting the new hire ask questions about the way that things work in the organization.

From Onboarding to Employee Engagement
After onboarding, organizations should transition to engagement; but what is employee engagement exactly? *Employee Engagement* can be defined as the level of commitment and involvement a worker has towards his/her employer and its values.

It is important to note that the employee engagement process is a two-way relationship between employer and employee. Managers are integral to this process. "For companies that rely on people as their primary source of competitive advantage, having innovative and customer focused employees is the most crucial factor in winning and keeping business," says Mike Ryan, senior vice president of Madison Performance Group, a global reward and recognition consulting firm. "Many firms overlook the importance of the manager's role in driving employee engagement, but there is a lot of evidence that shows employees perform better when they feel their manager understands their job and rewards them accordingly."

Engaged employees will stay with the company, in spite of being offered higher pay elsewhere; they will be an advocate for the company, its products and services; and they will contribute to bottom line business success. Engaged employees also normally perform better and are more motivated. Research indicates that there is a significant link between employee engagement and profitability. Thus, employee engagement is critical to any organization that seeks not only to retain valued employees, but also increase its level of performance.

Factors of Engagement
Many organizational factors influence employee engagement and retention such as:

- *A culture of respect, where outstanding work is valued*
- *Availability of constructive feedback, regular dialogue with one's supervisor, and mentoring*
- *Opportunity for advancement and professional development*
- *Fair and appropriate reward, recognition and incentive systems*
- *The level of supervisory engagement, and the leadership team's degree of transparency*
- *Clear job expectations and employee perceptions of job importance*
- *Adequate tools to complete work responsibilities*
- *Motivation from quality working relationships with peers, superiors, and subordinates*

Many other factors exist that might apply to your particular business and the importance of these factors will also vary within your organization.

Engagement Essentials
How will you know to what degree your employees are engaged? The best tool to obtain baseline organizational engagement data is with a comprehensive employee satisfaction survey. A well administered satisfaction survey will indicate on what level of engagement your employees are operating. Customizable surveys will provide you with a starting point towards your efforts to optimize employee engagement.

The key to successful employee satisfaction surveys is to pay close attention to the feedback from your staff. This is the only way to identify their specific concerns. When leaders listen, employees respond by becoming more engaged. This results in increased productivity and employee retention. It can't be said enough: *engaged employees are much more likely to be satisfied in their positions, remain with the organization, be promoted, and strive for higher levels of performance.*

Listening to employee ideas, acting on employee contributions and actively involving employees in decision making are essential to employee engagement.

Taking Action to Improve Employee Engagement

Nothing is more discouraging to employees than to be asked for their feedback and see no movement towards resolution of their issues. Even the smallest actions taken to address concerns will let your staff know that their input is valued. Feeling valued boosts morale and encourages future input.

Taking action starts with listening to employee feedback. Then the feedback data needs to be analyzed. Next, a definitive action plan will need to be put in place to change the culture and organizational practices. And finally, the plan must be implemented. It is important that employee engagement is not viewed as a one-time action. Employee engagement should be a continuous process of measuring, analyzing, defining and implementing.

What is the Alternative to Employee Engagement?

Conditions that prevent employee engagement seldom alleviate themselves. They should be assessed and addressed as soon as possible. Left to multiply, employee dissatisfaction issues can result in:

- *Higher employee turnover* - Employees leave, taking their reservoir of knowledge and experience to another workplace, possibly a competitor
- *Diminished performance* - Competency of the workforce is reduced, at least short term, until new employees are trained
- *Lost training dollars* - Time and money invested in training and development programs for departing workers is wasted
- *Lower morale* - Remaining employees can be overburdened with new duties, compounding the unresolved issues that already prevent their full engagement

The End Goal: Retain Talented Diverse Employees

In summary, listen to your employees, and remember that inclusion and engagement are continuous processes. Insist upon increased engagement at the managerial level, and create a customized employee satisfaction survey to assess your current level of employee engagement. The information that your employees supply will provide direction. Identify recurring issues, make a plan, and take action towards improvement.

Making a concerted effort to retain talented diverse employees will benefit everyone. In the long-run, it will save money in recruiting and training, as well as produce a return on investment in future recruiting efforts—especially as the demographics continue to change. Employee retention efforts will also go a long way towards customer/student/patient/client satisfaction and retention.

References:

Haden, Jeff. "9 Most Common Behavioral Interview Questions and Answers". Inc. Magazine, August 25, 2017. Retrieved from: https://www.inc.com/jeff-haden/9-most-common-behavioral-interview-questions-and-a.html

Johnson S., Hekman D., and Chan E. "If There's Only One Woman in Your Candidate Pool, There's Statistically No Chance She'll Be Hired" Harvard Business Review, April 26, 2016. Retrieved from: https://hbr.org/2016/04/if-theres-only-one-woman-in-your-candidate-pool-theres-statistically-no-chance-shell-be-hired

PeopleAdmin, Inc. "What is Onboarding Exactly" November 10, 2017. Retrieved from: https://www.peopleadmin.com/2013/01/what-is-onboarding-exactly/

Kelly, Lila. "Challenges in Recruiting and Hiring Diverse Employees". Retrieved from: http://lilakelly.com/challenges-in-recruiting-and-hiring-diverse-employees/

Bates, Steve. "Use Social Media Smartly When Hiring". Society for Human Resource Management (SHRM), March 13, 2013. Retrieved from: https://www.shrm.org/resourcesandtools/hr-topics/technology/pages/be-smart-when-using-social-media-for-hiring.aspx

Krogstad, Jens Manuel. "Social media preferences vary by race and ethnicity". Pew Research Center, February 3, 2015. Retrieved from: http://www.pewresearch.org/fact-tank/2015/02/03/social-media-preferences-vary-by-race-and-ethnicity/

CDP EXAM STUDY GUIDE © 2018-2020

Sample Test Questions
DIVERSITY RECRUITING & RETENTION

1. Diversity recruiting fails for all of the following reasons EXCEPT:
   A. Focusing on inclusion and retention
   B. Hiring candidates because of their diversity
   C. Underutilizing employee referrals

2. This can be defined as "interpreting and judging phenomenon according to standards inherent to one's own culture":
   A. In-group bias
   B. Blind spot
   C. Cultural bias

3. As a best practice, organizations should eliminate _____, which doesn't intentionally discriminate against individuals, but passively screens out diverse candidates.
   A. Recruiters
   B. Loopholes
   C. Programs

4. Diversity recruiting is different from recruiting traditional candidates.
   A. True
   B. False

5. Employee retention can be defined as the level of commitment and involvement an employee has towards his/her employer and its values.
   A. True
   B. False

6. The New Hire Orientation provides a sufficient onboarding experience for new hires.
   A. True
   B. False

7. Candidates should be assessed and evaluated against selection criteria that is specific to:
   A. A manager's preferences
   B. The need for representation
   C. The applicable job description

Sample Test Questions:
DIVERSITY RECRUITING & RETENTION (cont'd)

8. Attaining employee engagement entails listening to employees and remembering that this is a:
   A. Matter of productivity
   B. One-time occurrence
   C. Continuous process

9. Research shows that when diversity is increased in the candidate finalist pool, the likelihood that a diverse candidate is hired:
   A. Increases
   B. Decreases
   C. Remains the same

10. Which of the following is <u>most likely</u> to be true?
    A. Diversity recruiting broadens the pool to allow the best qualified candidate to get the job.
    B. Diversity recruiting is simply a matter of getting the right diverse candidate in the door.
    C. Search committees are only useful for hiring diverse candidates in certain industries.

11. Tools such as the Candidate Selection Grid allow an organization to:
    A. Consistently screen out employees who lack 'fit'
    B. Assign additional value to diverse candidates
    C. Compare and rank candidates equally

12. Maintaining the candidate's confidentiality or anonymity during the search process:
    A. Will ensure discrimination
    B. Can reduce or eliminate bias
    C. Adds unnecessary complexity

13. Strategic interventions must augment diversity recruiting efforts to preclude:
    A. Supervisors from rewarding diverse new hires for the wrong attitudes and behaviors.
    B. Talented diverse workers from being treated as tokens or Affirmative Action hires.
    C. Traditional candidates from being excluded from employment opportunities.

REINVENTING DIVERSITY TRAINING

> *Diversity, in and of itself, can be a highly charged and emotional topic when discussing key issues, such as race. While employees may not gather negative predispositions in the workplace, employees can bring them to the workplace from other sources; which makes them a workplace problem. Negative attitudes towards diverse groups affects teamwork, productivity, client service, student learning, morale, and inclusion.*
>
> *In this day and age, if an organization is going to be successful, it must be able to deal with diversity effectively, or risk competitive positioning and sustainability. Therefore, it is up to the Diversity and Inclusion practitioner to use diversity training as a vehicle to change the organizational culture and prepare for the future of work.*

OVERALL OBJECTIVES AND COMPETENCIES

The overarching purpose of this competency is to design, present and evaluate training sessions that result in: the acquisition of new skills, the practice of intentional behaviors, and/or a positive change in the organizational culture.

BACKGROUND AND CONTEXT

From Forbes, to Harvard Business Review, to Fast Company, more and more attention is being paid to the failures of diversity training over the last few years. At one point, companies rushed to conduct diversity training; today, in spite of all of the harassment and discrimination complaints that are being levied in the workplace, no one is calling for more training.

The courts have ruled that training is the first defense in a workplace harassment or discrimination lawsuit, but the way that Diversity and Inclusion (D&I) leaders are approaching training today is driving its bad reputation. First, some diversity trainers use **Food, Fun**, and **Friends** as an incentive to entice workers to attend learning sessions. No other workplace training program uses "the 3 F's" as a strategy. Yet, there are D&I practitioners who feel that it is necessary to cheapen the learning experience with food and games so that employees will want to participate. From the C-Suite's perspective (e.g., CEO, President, Provost, Executive Director, Governor, Secretary, etc.), this type of training is not valuable if "a problem" is not immediately looming over the organization.

Second, in this field, good public speakers can say, "I live diversity everyday so that makes me an expert diversity trainer." The individual may have a little knowledge or skill, but not enough to prevent employees or the organization from having a bad training experience. This has a cascading, cooling effect on subsequent D&I work. Nevertheless, a company who hires a diversity trainer without the proper skill is akin to hiring a person who does household finance and says, "I'm so good at managing the household budget, I believe I can be a great accountant. Let me manage your multi-million-dollar budget and file your corporate taxes." It just doesn't happen, and it doesn't happen for a reason. Therefore, employers are partly to blame for the lack of effectiveness in diversity training. They should exercise the same caution in hiring a D&I trainer, as they do in hiring an accountant. After all, organizations can't hire an inexperienced trainer and then say that training doesn't work.

Third, unclear goals and hazy expectations result in change being slow or non-existent. In *Why So Many Diversity Programs Fail*, author Lydia Dishman cites a 2016 U.S. Equal Employment Opportunity Commission report to illustrate that diversity training is having the unintended effect of reducing or marginally increasing the number of diverse people in key positions at companies with more than 100 workers. A national aggregate of all industries between 1985 and 2014 indicates an increase from 3.0% to 3.3% of black men in management roles, and an increase from 22% to 29% of white women in management through the year 2000, and no movement since then. Even for executive roles, after Ursula Burns left Xerox in 2016, there are no black female CEO's at Fortune 500 companies. According to Fortune Magazine, there are 3 black males, 9 Hispanic and 32 female CEO's at the end of 2017.

It's important to ask questions to determine how to improve these results. Specifically:

1) With all of the diversity training that has occurred over the last two decades, why are the numbers so dismal?
2) How can diversity training be improved so that it delivers more organizational value?
3) How will we know that diversity training is succeeding?

This competency is designed to delve into such difficult questions. Let's start with the assumption that everyone cannot facilitate diversity training. The practitioner must be knowledgeable, skilled and experienced. Next, diversity training cannot be a simplistic initiative. It should utilize best practices to ensure that it aligns with organizational goals, the strategic Diversity and Inclusion plan, and customer expectations. Finally, the training must be designed to engage employees in the design, delivery and furtherance of learning. It cannot be a program that *solely* depends on one diversity practitioner to assess learner needs, communicate expectations, develop the curriculum, facilitate the training, and evaluate the results.

In the past, diversity training was primarily conducted to: (1) blame or remind whites about the ills of slavery, racism, sexism, and discriminatory practices that have plagued communities of color or women for centuries; (2) educate white employees about "The _____ Experience" in America; (3) enable workers to be more sensitive to, and accepting of, differences; and (4) redress lawsuits or fulfill the minimum requirements of the law. The historical perspective provides context for a discussion about impact, value, and effectiveness. Nevertheless, the historical perspective is no longer relevant in delivering meaningful Diversity and Inclusion education and training in an environment that is powered by globalization, changing demographics, and capricious competitive. Today, organizations need diversity practitioners to adjust their strategy in order to cultivate innovation, sustainability, and inclusive excellence. Figure 1 explains the history of the field.

FIGURE 1:
DIVERSITY PIONEERS IN THE HISTORY OF DIVERSITY EDUCATION

By Billy E. Vaughn, Ph.D.

Introduction

Diversity education is becoming a solution for many businesses. In the European Union, it is offered to small and medium-sized businesses to develop their capacity to include people across states and cultures in the union. Australia's government utilizes diversity education to end a history of discrimination against Aboriginal and Islander people. Asia finds it useful for increasing productivity in multinational companies, and for addressing the historical challenges of achieving harmony between Muslim and Hindu citizens. South Africa has implemented diversity education to adjust to the removal of the Apartheid system. The United States has offered diversity education for decades, although the rationale for its use has changed over time.

Diversity Training and Education in the United States

Many organizations, communities, military sectors, and higher education institutions have been conducting some form of diversity education since the 1960s in the United States. Businesses used diversity training in the late 1980s and throughout the 90s to protect against and settle civil rights suits. Many organizations now assume that diversity education can boost productivity and innovation in an increasingly diverse work environment. The assumptions about the value of diversity training, as a result of its changing functions and uses, have evolved over the decades.

Basically, diversity education started as a reaction to the civil rights movement and violent demonstrations by activists determined to send a clear message to Americans of European descent that black people would no longer remain voiceless regarding their treatment as citizens. Social change, until a more stable society prevailed, was the rationale for the education, which primarily focused on training to increase sensitivity towards and awareness of racial differences.

Encounter groups became a popular training method for bringing white and black Americans together for honest and emotional discussions about race relations. The military employed encounter groups in what is perhaps the largest scale diversity education experiment ever conducted. Many of the facilitators viewed the "encounter" among racial groups participating in diversity training as successful when at least one white American admitted that he or she was racist and was tearful about racial discrimination and white supremacy.

Employing a black-white pair of facilitators was considered essential for exposing participants to the two race relations perspective and to model cross-racial collaboration. The facilitators were typically men, and the white facilitator was most valued if he could openly show emotions about his own journey in discovering his deep-seated racism.

Facilitators saw their work as a way to achieve equality in a world that had historically oppressed those with less social, political, and economic power. Confronting white Americans who made excuses for, or denied their racism, was common in this diversity training approach. The goal was to increase white American sensitivity to the effects of racial inequity.

White American participants tended to respond to confrontation in sensitivity training in three important ways. One group of whites became more insightful about the barriers to race relations as a result of being put on the hot seat during the encounters. Another group became more resistant to racial harmony as they fought against accepting the facilitators' label of them as racists. A third group became what the military referred to as "fanatics."

These individuals began advocating against any forms of racial injustice after the training. H. R. Day's research on diversity training in the military indicates that the Defense Department Race Relations Institute reduced the amount of training hours and curtailed the use of the "hot seat" techniques in response to negative evaluations by many participants who completed the training. Diversity training in corporations also began to change as Affirmative Action laws were being curtailed by the federal government.

While gender diversity education began to emerge during the 1970s and 1980s, diversity education in the United States expanded in the 1990s to focus on barriers to Inclusion for other identity groups. Differences in ability, ethnicity, religion, sexual orientation, and other worldviews began to appear in education and training.

Some diversity pioneers argue that the broader view of diversity has "watered down" the focus on race to the extent that it is no longer seriously dealt with in training. Their assumption is that focusing on prejudice towards other groups does not activate the visceral reaction needed for individuals, organizations, and the society as whole to deal with core discrimination issues.

Previous research showed that people in the United States had negative reactions towards people who were gay or lesbian. It seems that many Americans shared an anti-gay and lesbian attitude, primarily based on religious beliefs. However, even the attitude towards gays and lesbians has become more positive, as indicated by the success of the movie Brokeback Mountain about two cowboy lovers, and the introduction of state and local legislation that protects their rights.

Multiculturalism refers to the Inclusion of the full range of identity groups in education. The goal is to take into consideration each of the diverse ways people identify as cultural beings. This perspective has become the most widely used approach today in diversity education. The Inclusion of other identity groups poses the challenges of maintaining focus on unresolved racial discrimination and effectively covering the many different identity groups.

The current focus on white privilege training is one sector of diversity work that maintains a place for racism in diversity education. White privilege education involves challenging white people to consider the benefits they reap individually as a member of the racial group with the most social, political, and economic power.

While white privilege, multiculturalism, and racism work are each very important, diversity professionals must keep in mind that organizations vary in diversity education needs. Determining how to meet these needs requires the trainer to possess critical thinking skills and an ability to facilitate issues outside of her or his cultural experience. The capable diversity professional has the ability to determine when race education is the suitable intervention, when gender orientation is called for, and/or when addressing homophobia is necessary, etc.

Discussions about gender differences, sexual orientation, Native American identity, Latino empowerment, white privilege, etc., provide a rich context for understanding the complexity of American diversity. Today's savvy diversity trainer has the expertise to take a multicultural perspective in facilitating and training, and he or she commands knowledge of the range of identity groups. Giving each identity group the attention it deserves is no small matter as a result.

The reality of global mobilization has required an even broader view of diversity due to working with an increasingly cross-national audience. The use of the label African American, for example, is complicated by white and black Africans immigrating to the United States. An organization may have employees from the former Yugoslavia, refugees from Somalia, guest workers from India, and people with limited English-speaking skills--just to name a few modern diversity challenges. Religious diversity accompanies globalism, which is also included in modern diversity education.

It is likely that this identity group complexity prompted diversity professionals like Judith Katz to focus on promoting inclusive organizations. The objective is to remove the barriers to productivity for every member of the organization with particular concern for historically excluded group members.

Another recent change is the emphasis on diversity education, rather than diversity training. While the use of one term versus another is regularly debated, it is a valuable exchange of ideas. From the author's perspective, the term diversity education both broadens the view of what diversity programs within organizations are about and manages the often-negative connotation that diversity training activates. Perhaps more important is that the term allows us to distinguish between diversity training and other programmatic activities among diversity practices.

In addition, diversity expertise has changed over time, which partly reflects changing demands and the growth in the field's body of knowledge. A description of the profession before the rise of the chief diversity officer tells us a lot about what diversity professionals faced as consultants.

Diversity Pioneers

Diversity professionals are hired on staff in organizations that understand that diversity is capital and harnessing it in the service of productivity requires a long-term commitment. An in-house diversity professional is responsible for leading a diversity initiative within an organization. Some have the title Chief Diversity Officer or Vice President of Diversity, while others are considered Diversity Coordinators or Steering Committee Chairs.

Regardless of what they are called, these positions are becoming increasingly prevalent in organizations. Not long ago, a human resource officer would hire a consultant or trainer to handle a diversity matter with sensitivity-awareness training as the expected solution.

Diversity pioneers laid the foundation for the emergence of today's diversity leaders. A diversity pioneer is someone who has been in the profession for more than 20 years, which includes those who have served either as an in-house or consulting professional. The in-house professionals are activists for diversity, inclusion and fairness.

Here is a list of diversity pioneers in the United States:

- Elsie Cross
- Price Cobb
- Sybil Evans
- John Fernandez
- Lee Gardenswartz
- Lewis Griggs
- Ed Hubbard
- Judith Katz
- Frances Kendall
- Fred Miller
- Patricia Pope
- Ann Rowe
- Donna Springer
- Roosevelt Thomas

Few diversity pioneers had specialized training when starting out in the business. Lewis Griggs, for example, is a Stanford MBA. Judith Katz had a more closely related background with a doctorate from University of Massachusetts that focused on race relations. She also taught in the University of Oklahoma Human Relations Program for 10 years prior to entering the business sector as a fulltime consultant.

Each diversity pioneer had to learn about how to navigate the landmines in diversity work while on the front lines as consultants, trainers, and educators.

What the pioneers may have lacked in credentials specific to the diversity profession, they more than made up for with the bumps and bruises they endured in the trenches of just doing the work.

Raising the Bar

Judith Katz was a student activist for social justice in the late 1960s. Judith began her diversity profession by focusing on racism from a white American perspective. By the mid-1980s, she was working for The Kaleel Jamison Consulting Group. Affirmative action was at its height, and many companies utilized independent diversity professionals to provide programs to help increase the numbers of African Americans and women employees. Some organizations utilized diversity training to safeguard against civil rights suits during this time. Much of the training "focused primarily on black-white racial issues and sexism", according to Judith, "with little if any attention given to Latinos, Asians, sexual orientation, age or people with disabilities."

Judith also noticed that the business case in those days emphasized diversity as doing the right thing, rather than as a business imperative. People were expected to fit into the existing organizational culture. It was difficult at the time to effect real organizational change.

"The major change is that diversity is now accepted as a key business driver, rather than diversity for diversity's sake." This was accompanied by a shift away from the confrontational approach common in the early stages of diversity education history.

According to Judith, "for some folks, diversity was about compliance (the concern about law suits); for others, it was about increasing individual diversity awareness. The confrontational approach to raising individual awareness did not create systems change in the long run. Some individuals became more aware; but the very systems, structures and processes often remained unchanged. Judith notes that many organizations still approach diversity from a compliance perspective. However, more and more organizational leaders are going well beyond compliance. They understand that "if you are not leveraging diversity, you are not in the game of business today."

Judith is concerned about the challenges that continue to face diversity professionals as well as Chief Diversity Officers. The following is a list of some of her concerns for in-house professionals who lead diversity initiatives:

• *Diversity leaders must contend with organizational executives who give lip service to the diversity initiative without putting their hearts and souls into it or offer it the necessary resources for success.*

• *As a result, diversity leaders too often shoulder the full weight of the diversity initiative.*

• *They can get too buried in the work to be effective.*

• *They are expected to partner with many different parts of the organization, which contributes to additional stress.*

• *They work alone and are expected to single-handedly get a very difficult job done.*

• *They are expected to manage a highly political role while getting their job done and legally protecting the organization.*

The result is that leading the diversity initiative can be a very difficult, demanding, and lonely job from Judith's perspective. Judith believes that leaders of organizations need to "raise its bar" for expectations in delivering results from the diversity initiative. This is the best way to support the Diversity Officer. A good example is to make people in the organization accountable for contributing to promoting Inclusion-- especially managers and supervisors. Linking bonuses and merit pay to clear Diversity and Inclusion metrics is seldom given serious consideration in even the top fifty companies for diversity. Nevertheless, this obviously raises the bar of expectations and performance. Thanks to Judith, diversity consultants and trainers have a role model. She is one of the few who can successfully engage business leaders in serious discussions about organizational Inclusion.

Valuing Diversity
Valuing diversity is a term that is used in making a case for Diversity and Inclusion—thanks to Lewis Griggs. When he coined the words during the early 1980s, his clients thought it was "too touchy-feely". It wasn't affirmative action or equal employment opportunity language. One African American male colleague told him that the terminology was downright dangerous because white America was not ready to value people for their differences. But, fortunately for us, he had a vision.

Lewis is a European American who came to diversity work through his own individual growth experiences. Griggs says, "While doing international training during the early 1980s, I realized that people from other countries had more knowledge about me as an American than I had about them. This meant that the 'other' person had more power over me in our interactions. I discovered how ethnocentric I was". Griggs figured that if he was ethnocentric about people from other countries, then "Could I be ethnocentric here in the United States?"

Griggs continued to do ground breaking work. He developed a series of valuing diversity videos. He developed one of the first online diversity training programs. Lewis created the annual diversity conference offered by the Society for Human Resource Management (SHRM). Thanks to Lewis, increasing numbers of organizations have embraced the idea that we need to value differences.

Avoiding a Backlash
The higher education sector started offering diversity courses in the general education curricula during the 1980s. Stanford University and the California State University at Fullerton, dared to offer mandatory cultural diversity courses to fulfill general education requirements. There was considerable debate among academicians about whether or not the canon needed protection against including diversity courses.

Dr. Billy Vaughn found himself in the middle of the cultural wars as a new assistant professor with a joint appointment in Ethnic Studies and Psychology. His training made it easy to interweave cultural differences into developmental, social, and cognitive psychology courses. He also taught mandatory general education diversity courses. The primarily European American, politically conservative students, were very resistant to the required courses.

Students resisted less as the courses integrated into the curricula over the years, but many continued to struggle with the material due to difficulty accepting values and beliefs different from their own.

Recruitment of historically excluded group members, especially students of color, was the primary focus at most universities. No one would seriously listen to ideas about creating an inclusive organization before increasing the numbers of students of color. The attitude was "let's just get as many students of color as possible and worry about how to retain them later". Retaining and graduating these historically excluded students became major problems as the numbers of recruits increased.

Dr. Vaughn also witnessed incredible gains in attracting students of historically excluded groups and creating an inclusive environment—only to see those gains undermined by changes in the leadership and economic climate. The lesson learned is that sustainable Diversity and Inclusion initiatives require an on-going commitment to remove all the barriers that can lead to reverting to old ways of doing business. Diversity and Inclusion must, for example, be incorporated into each new initiative that comes along in order to protect the organization from moving back to earlier Inclusion stages.

As economic, political, and global changes required new ways of solving old problems, the pioneers experienced many bumps in the road. This brief history suggests that their sheer determination and commitment built an invaluable foundation from which we all can draw meaningful lessons.

Billy Vaughn, PhD is Editor-in-Chief for Strategic Diversity & Inclusion Management magazine and faculty director for the DTUI.com Diversity Professional Certification program.

WHY EMPLOYEES HATE DIVERSITY TRAINING

EMPLOYEE FEEDBACK

My company, a household name, mandates diversity training annually for all employees. My attitude toward Affirmative Action actually changed and became extremely negative after years of this crap. They've discovered that employees treat diversity training as a ludicrous and insulting joke so they've switched to feel-good boomer tripe like age discrimination and "non-controversial" diversity issues. I don't know anyone who takes this garbage seriously and it has actually hardened discriminatory attitudes, especially now that we have a lot of employees (especially contractors) overseas whose work ethic and language issues are huge barriers to getting anything accomplished.

So many work remotely (from home, mobile, or at customer sites) that diversity training is all online now rather than in a town hall setting. The online stuff just dumbs everything down further. It's easier to race through and ignore, though. We're actually measured on nonsense like this for our reviews. Amazing!

Over the years, diversity training has become an awkward and controversial issue, causing many employers to resist using diversity training as an educational tool. The following is an employee comment pertaining to diversity training.

It is common for an organization to receive negative comments on evaluation forms or in-person after diversity training. Below is a list of words used describe how some employees feel after diversity training:

- *Forced*
- *Chastised*
- *Humiliated*
- *Harassed*
- *Demonized*
- *Fed up*
- *Tired*
- *Uncomfortable*
- *Baffled*
- *Threatened*
- *Annoyed*
- *Weary*
- *Guarded*
- *Prejudiced*

Critics assert that negative feelings regarding diversity training actually leads to increased lawsuits from Caucasian and underrepresented employees. Nevertheless, the conclusion should not be, "we're not getting good reviews, so let's stop this show". Instead, as agents of change, Diversity and Inclusion practitioners must say, "how can we fix diversity training so that it accomplishes what is intended?"

DIVERSITY TRAINING & THE LAW

There have been many workplace issues related to diversity training. The following is a synopsis of punitive cases.

Texaco (1996)
By the early 1990's, Texaco was the only company selling gasoline under the same brand name in all 50 U.S. states, making it a nationally recognized brand amongst its competitors. Texaco consistently made the Fortune 100 list for 50 years and even regularly appeared on the Fortune 20 list until a class-action lawsuit changed everything.

Bari-Ellen Roberts was a senior financial analyst in Texaco's Harrison, N.Y.-based finance department. She, and at least 1,500 current and former African American employees, filed the largest discrimination lawsuit in U.S. history for actions that took place between 1991 and 1994. Mrs. Roberts filed her lawsuit after she was consistently denied chances for advancement, seminars, and foreign travel, while less-qualified white employees—people she had trained—advanced in their careers.

At meetings, Texaco executives were recorded making disparaging remarks about minorities and discussing the disposal of documents related to the class-action discrimination suit. In a diversity training session, one executive was recorded joking about "black jellybeans sticking to the bottom" of the bag during a learning exercise. A former white male executive released the tapes to the media—compounding the company's woes.

The response was swift. Civil rights groups called for boycotts. Texaco's stock price dropped several percentage points. Federal prosecutors launched a criminal investigation into obstruction-of-justice charges. The firestorm of negative publicity was so intense that the company settled the racial-discrimination case 2 weeks later, agreeing to pay more than $175 million over the next five years. The diversity debacle made for fascinating reading for weeks, but more important, it illustrated the power of diversity on the bottom line. Within 3 years, one of the most recognizable brands in America was forced to seek cover through a merger-acquisition.

Hartman v. Pena (1995)
The Federal Aviation Administration was sued for sexual harassment following a 3-day offsite diversity training program in which a white employee was ridiculed for refusing to participate in a role-reversal exercise where males walked between two lines of females and were subjected to sexual comments and touching. He ultimately took part in the "Soul Train Line" and was groped. The acts that took place during the training exercise, the court held, may have been severe enough that a reasonable person could perceive the environment to be hostile or abusive. This case is a perfect example of the stark contrast between intent and impact. The training was designed to expand horizons and sensitize men to women's experiences. However, good intentions are irrelevant if the effect is offensive to a reasonable recipient. After a federal judge refused to dismiss the case, the agency had to pay a settlement to the employee.

Target (2013)
Three former employees sued Target for discrimination claiming that their supervisors, who were nearly all Caucasians, frequently used racial slurs when talking to Hispanic employees. When the problem was reported to human resources, Target bosses retaliated, and eventually fired the three workers. The employees cited a document entitled, *"Organization Effectiveness, Employee, and Labor Relations Multi-Cultural Tips"* as proof that discrimination exists. The company circulated the document to distribution warehouse managers, which featured suggestions on how to manage Hispanic employees. According to the lawsuit, the document stated:

    a. **Food** - not everyone eats tacos and burritos
    b. **Music** - not everyone dances to salsa
    c. **Dress** - not everyone wears a sombrero
    d. **Mexicans** - lower education level, some may be undocumented
    e. **Cubans** - Political refugees, legal status, higher education level and
    f. **Instructions** – to save face, they may say "OK, OK" and pretend that they got the message, when they really do not understand

The document was offensive, but not discriminatory in and of itself. It merely supported the allegation that discrimination exists.

In each of the cases listed above, the employer was liable for diversity education that went wrong. Some of the diversity training exercises, in particular, were professionally inappropriate. From jelly beans to a Soul Train Line, the desire for participants to have fun overrode good judgement about the training exercises. There are many ways for training participants to enjoy a program; however, the goal of "enjoyment" must go beyond trivial activities. Perhaps, diversity training exercises should transition towards practicing skills that are useful, relevant and indicative of professional excellence.

Beyond Compliance with the Law
It is not easy to move people across continents. Companies that want to relocate their employees have to manage issues such as arranging employees' visas, securing work permits and coordinating housing. This task often discourages CEOs from expanding to certain regions. Additionally, a U.S.-based worker relocating to Germany, for example, may have to attend language classes or need training to adjust to the new culture. The law does not mandate it, but cultural training could make or break business dealings or even one's career.

For example, Hong Kong, Taiwan, and Tibet are major regions in China. Under the One-China policy, there is only one sovereign state. In fact, China has a history of reprimanding companies that offend the Chinese government's official policies. Marriott, Delta Airlines, Zara, Medtronic, Qantas, and others have recently faced China's wrath because an employee at each company mistakenly referenced one of China's major regions as a "country". Adequate training can reduce many of the difficulties that come with doing business in other nations such as China. Going beyond black and white, towards helping an organization avoid social media and branding gaffes will prove to be valuable training for any employer that does business globally.

The Office of Diversity can also offer training for employees who work in different cultures. For example, a sales manager, human resource executive, and finance professional must understand the cultures and nuances of doing business and working with people in other nations. While some organizations clearly have a dedicated person who handles education for different regions, many employers do not. Or in some cases, departments such as social media and marketing may be left to figure out the cultural dynamics on their own. It is a good practice for the D&I leader to ensure that the organization is aware that diversity extends beyond language and identity, to customs, expectations, nonverbal communications, preferences, and practices. There are many resources (e.g., educational institutions, nonprofits, and the State Department) that D&I can tap to ensure that the learning is relevant and useful. And, because the learning is relevant to the work that employees are expected to perform, food and fun is not a mainstay.

In the U.S., multinational employers face many challenges as well. Understanding the laws (federal, state, and local) and the multi-layered regulatory environment pertaining to harassment and discrimination can be daunting. Additionally, what is acceptable in America may not be customary in other countries. For example, in the U.S., criticism of Affirmative Action is legal and protected against retaliation by Title VII of the Civil Rights Act. Court rulings that have upheld private-sector Affirmative Action programs, such as *Sisco v. J.S. Alberici Const. Co.* (8th Cir. 1981), have allowed employees to sue employers who retaliate against them for criticizing Affirmative Action. Thus, a Diversity Trainer who believes that employees should not voice their grievances about Diversity and Inclusion during an educational session risks exposing the employer to lawsuits.

Anger and frustration may express itself in different ways. In America's public sector, the employer may face a First Amendment lawsuit. The California Department of Corrections attempted to fire John Wallace after he angrily denounced its affirmative action plan to the Hispanic female employee he perceived as benefiting from it. However, in the *California Department of Corrections v. State Personnel Board*, 59 Cal.App.4th 131 (1997), the California Court of Appeals, found that his criticisms of the plan were protected by the First Amendment, and barred Wallace's firing. As more multi-national companies look to do business in the United States through mergers and acquisitions or importing/exporting, there is a prime opportunity to provide education about the multi-layered cultural and political environment in America.

For example, in addition to U.S. EEO laws, several North American states—California, Connecticut, and Maine—mandate harassment training for supervisors and/or employees (see Figure 2).

FIGURE 2: STATES WITH MANDATORY HARASSMENT TRAINING

	CALIFORNIA Sexual Harassment Training Requirements	**CONNECTICUT** Sexual Harassment Training Requirements	**MAINE** Sexual Harassment Training Requirements
Which employers must comply with the state training law?	All employers with **50 or more** employees (FT, PT and Temporary) and/or contractors (as defined by statute) for each working day in any consecutive 20 week period during the current or prior training year. All employees must be counted even if they do not reside in or work in California.	All employers (including the state and political subdivisions) with **50 or more** employees and partners for a minimum of 13 weeks during the training year. No express requirement that all 50 must work or reside in the state of Connecticut.	The law requires sexual harassment training for all workplaces with 15 or more employees. For purposes of the discrimination statute, even employees outside of the state employed by someone in the state and employers outside the state with in-state employees should be counted. Arguably, a similar analysis applies under the training law.
What kind of training is mandated?	Sexual harassment training	Sexual harassment training	Sexual harassment training
Is there a minimum 'hours' requirement for sexual harassment training?	Yes. A covered employer must provide at least 2 hours of sexual harassment training. For e-learning, the course must take at least 2 hours to complete on-line. California sexual harassment training can be broken into smaller segments as authorized by the statute. Bookmarking features (like those available with ELT products) are permitted by regulation.	Yes. Covered employers must provide a minimum of 2 hours of sexual harassment training and education.	There is no minimum 'hours' requirement under state law.
Are employers required to provide learners with a refresher course on sexual harassment?	Yes, sexual harassment training is required once every 2 years. Organizations should use either an "individual" or a "training year" tracking method to determine when retraining is required.	The Commission "encourages" but does not mandate sexual harassment training once every three years. A refresher course should be an upgrade of legal interpretations and related developments concerning sexual harassment.	There is no sexual harassment retraining obligation under state law.

Why Diversity Training is Still Needed

Even in the absence of a state or federal law mandating employee training, employers should expose all workers to periodic diversity and non-discrimination training. EEOC and US Supreme Court guidelines recommend periodic Equal Employment Opportunity (EEO) training for all employees. Likewise, training is essential if employers wish to establish a defense to claims of harassment and discrimination.

From the employee perspective, some workers appreciate the effort that diversity training makes to facilitate a more inclusive environment. Consider the following employee comment.

> **EMPLOYEE FEEDBACK**
>
> *You may not like to be treated like a child due to repetitive diversity training, but you need it. Here at (Fortune 500 name omitted), where there apparently is no training in minority-related issues, I can tell you that every time I hear co-workers make rude comments about homosexuals working at chocolate factories or auditioning to be the next Tinkerbell, (including some hateful remarks from management themselves), I get stung a bit. Since I'm very well-liked in the store but am also very masculine and "in the closet", I often get the urge to walk up behind them while they're laughing and say "Guess what? I happen to be one of those people." I'd just love to see the color drain from their faces as they struggle to atone for their hurtful comments. Nevertheless, the thought has also often occurred to me that doing so might open myself up to even worse treatment from some of my co-workers, including the possibility of being given the more "menial" tasks in the store on a more regular basis.*
>
> *As a retail associate, you naturally have to grow a thick skin to deflect the angry outbursts of customers in a level-headed manner. Nevertheless, I would have expected more intellect and integrity from my own superiors, but, then again, it will be quite satisfying to walk into (Fortune 500 name omitted) ten years into the future when I have my Ph.D. and see the same people working at the same dead-end jobs trying to make themselves feel better about themselves by degrading what they consider to be the "weaker" segments of society.*
>
> *If you don't want to constantly be subjected to diversity seminars, then start acting like freakin' adults! Just think of the damage I could do to the company right now through litigation if I happened to secretly record some of these tirades and submit them to my family attorney. Nobody should have to enter their workplace and feel discriminated against or uncomfortable around their co-workers. Just remember "Red and Yellow, Black and White, they are precious in his sight!"*

This individual wanted to prove a point to his co-workers. Some employees prove their point with lawsuits; others use workplace violence like the San Bernardino shooters. Students likewise react to teasing, bullying, and intolerant behaviors on campuses with school shootings—which have increased in numbers over the last few years.

TOP REASONS WHY DIVERSITY TRAINING FAILS

Diversity trainers can learn from critics, as well as employees and industry veterans. Once again, the overarching purpose of this guide is to make diversity training better by learning from mistakes and providing better experiences for employees. The following excerpt lists the top 10 reasons why diversity training programs sometimes fail.

Successful vs. Failed Diversity Programs
by Mauricio Velásquez · President, The Diversity Training Group

10. Diversity training is coming out of the Equal Employment Opportunity (EEO)/Affirmative Action (AA) Office. This is the kiss of death. Diversity training must come from the whole organization through a Diversity Steering Committee made up of employees from a representative cross-section of the organization. Do not give the EEO/AA backlash camp ammunition for their resistance.

9. Diversity training is being done because it is the "right" thing or "moral" thing to do. The organization does not understand the connection between diversity and the bottom line. I want to emphasize that these are good and valid reasons but in corporate America, make the business case for diversity training first. (This welfare approach to diversity training plays into the hands of those making the EEO/AA argument – backlash).

8. Training is all the organization is doing. The organization is not reviewing or scrutinizing their hiring, promotion, leadership development, and business practices. Do you have a formal, inclusive mentoring program in place? Are you a homogenous company (senior and upper management) marketing and selling to a heterogeneous or diverse marketplace? Or, will a heterogeneous company (your competitor) understand and anticipate the needs of your heterogeneous or diverse marketplace more effectively than you and your homogeneous company?

7. The diversity training has management's support (they will provide the resources), but not their commitment (management or senior management in particular, does not attend training or does not "walk the talk", e.g., Texaco). Management's lack of participation is all the evidence that the rest of the organization needs to resist the training and consider it the next fad—they will wait, and it will pass.

6. The training being conducted is "off-the-shelf" and not custom designed to meet the unique needs of the particular organization. Participants in the generic workshop are overheard asking themselves, "What does this have to do with me?" Thus, the training fails because participants were not engaged, not interested, and did not find the training practical, pertinent, and compelling.

5. Training is being developed and lead solely by external diversity consultants and trainers. The training is thus the consultant's program and not a program developed by the employees of the organization, for the organization. No ownership or buy-in is solicited and the program eventually perishes. The external diversity trainer becomes the "fall guy."

> 4. Diversity training was designed and developed without a formal needs analysis or diagnosis of the organization. Therefore, interventions are not applicable nor reasonable—leaving employees to question, "Who in the ivory tower developed this program? What do they know?"
>
> 3. Your diversity training program is awareness-based but provides no skills and no practical "hands-on" tools. People are heard saying, "This was great but now what? What am I supposed to do now? I go back to my workplace tomorrow."
>
> 2. Internal resources are not formed, developed, and encouraged (i.e., internal diversity change agents, facilitators, and an internal resource center and/or office of diversity). You haven't formed an internal diversity steering committee and haven't trained and developed internal change agents to "keep the fires burning." You have not continued the work once the external diversity trainer has moved on.
>
> 1. Your diversity training had no formal follow-up. Many of the action items had no owners and no one revisited the training. Training alone is not the cure-all panacea. You need to have internally driven initiatives supported by senior management commitment as well as ongoing attention and training from internal as well as external subject matter experts.

Diversity training may also fail because we place a considerable amount of attention on sensitivity training. While "sensitivity" training may occasionally lead to awareness, in most cases, it results in political correctness. Simma Lieberman, Workplace Culture Strategist, asserts in a blog entitled *Why Sensitivity Training is Insensitive and Patronizing*, "When I observe people from one group wanting to be 'sensitive' to someone from another group I see them not really treating the other person as a 'peer' but rather being "charitable". The Meta message is that in this relationship 'I am superior to you; you are like a child to me. I have to understand that you are not as smart or cannot speak for yourself. Further, if you make a mistake, or do not understand, it is because being from your group you are not expected to do well so I must be "sensitive" to you and say it is ok. I think of you as being part of a "special" group and not as a colleague.' "

Professor Rochelle Ford, Ph.D., APR, suggests that diversity trainers define terms, connect the training to the business imperative and establish expectations. She notes research where Loriann Roberson et al., addresses these issues in the Journal of Organizational Behavior. "The researchers explain that broad definitions of diversity can make training more palatable to participants, reducing potential backlash toward training. At the same time, they caution that broad definitions may reduce the immediate application of skills by many participants after the training. They suggest using a narrow definition of diversity when implementing skills-oriented diversity training."

FACILITATING BETTER TRAINING PROGRAMS

The Houston Chronicle published an article called, "*The Purpose of Internal Training for Employees*" by Shelagh Dillon. In it, the author asserts that, "the purpose of internal training is to create a motivated, skilled, and effective workforce through which organizational goals are achieved".

The problem with most diversity training is that the facilitator is trying to change the minds of participants about Diversity and Inclusion, and he/she is not trying to change their skills. As with any other training session, if you change someone's skills, you will change their mind. However, the emphasis has to move away from an individual focus toward addressing organizational goals.

In "*Individual and Environmental Factors Influencing the Use of Transfer Strategies After Diversity Training*", Loriann Roberson et al., reminds D&I leaders that "Among the learning outcomes, skill learning is the only significant predictor of transfer strategy use." In other words, training must have a clearly defined outcome, seek the transfer of particular skills, and ensure that the learning is consistently put to use. This paradigm shift is a clear departure from how most diversity training is conducted today.

Hence, as a best practice, D&I leaders must formulate a comprehensive system from which to develop diversity training programs. Do not confuse comprehensive with complex. Complex infers that confusion can arise due to the intricate nature of multiple systems; comprehensiveness entails taking the time to build a better platform for effectiveness. Although developing a new framework for training is more time consuming, it will yield an incredible return on investment and be easier for learners to apply on the job over the long-term.

The Assessment
No diversity training program should begin with a D&I leader "assuming" they know what the organization needs. Diversity practitioners require data to justify the training, as well as to understand what is ultimately going to help or hinder one's efforts. An assessment will provide the framework that D&I leaders need to properly diagnose the issues and recommend the appropriate course of action. In one instance, a school district employed two different diversity trainers who both led with race-based training. Nevertheless, the school's diversity issue had little to do with race. In fact, insight from U.S. Census demographic projections showed that changing demographics translated into different expectations for a high quality educational experience, and socioeconomic changes required an adjustment to the school's instructional strategy. An assessment would have saved the school a lot of time and money. Hence, without a proper assessment, diversity training can be likened to a doctor placing a Band-Aid on a gunshot wound.

The assessment is also one of the first steps to improving learning experiences. Imagine the school employees who had to sit through the same diversity training program twice. Therefore, it is the D&I leader's goal to find out what employees know, think, and want. The diversity practitioner may have to: talk to managers one-on-one; hold focus groups (including a diverse range of employees of all races, positions, tenures, etc.); conduct research (i.e., demographics, industry trends, competitors, etc.); analyze performance evaluations; examine equal opportunity complaints and pending lawsuits; and review previous surveys or conduct new surveys for customers/students and employees.

In the assessment phase, the diversity practitioner must distinguish between organizational, operational and personal needs. According to Professor Rochelle Ford, Ph.D., APR, "Organizational needs include the broad goals of the organization. Operational needs pertain to the knowledge, skills and abilities needed for the organization to function. At the personal level, you examine what employees need to perform their tasks well."

Who Should Participate in the Training Design & Instruction?

Engaging a diversity training task force, members of the Diversity Council, or Resource Group affiliates would be a great way to extend training design and delivery beyond the Office of Diversity and into the functional areas of the organization. These individuals can assist with curriculum development, integration into work practices, and evaluation. They can also facilitate learning exercises during the training session. Additionally, D&I leaders can consult with Human Resources and supervisors to determine how to introduce core concepts into other training curriculum so that learning can be sustained and reinforced.

Executives can play a key role as well. Perhaps senior level leaders can serve as an Executive Sponsor for different trainings that take place throughout the year. As Executive Sponsor, the individual would be responsible for communicating the importance of the training, introducing the topic during the training session, or providing a foreword in the curriculum. Never forget that employees want to see their peers and senior executives involved in these types of programs.

The question that arises at employers of all sizes is: "should all employees be mandated to participate in diversity training?" The answer depends on where the organization falls on the Diversity and Inclusion continuum. Are you holding the training session for one or two employees who have a problem? This type of issue may be resolved better with coaching and/or your discipline policy. If there is a particular group that is having problems and needs diversity training, make sure that you use the session to communicate expectations and describe how employees will be held accountable for their behaviors.

If employees have never been exposed to diversity training, it would make sense to hold mandatory sessions. Nevertheless, make sure that the sessions have content that is linked to organizational strategies and objectives. After the training is completed, there needs to be follow-up to encourage the sustainability of the training by supporting Diversity and Inclusion in the workplace. This may include revising policies and releasing the revisions after the training session, as well as ensuring that management demonstrates inclusiveness and the ability to work together in spite of their differences.

Are employees relatively "diversity savvy"? Meaning, have they had diversity training in the past or elsewhere? If so, the diversity leader may want to consider offering a voluntary session. Unfortunately, those who attend voluntary sessions may not necessarily be the ones who really need diversity education. A better way would be to ask managers to designate a few departmental representatives to participate and speak to their entire units about what occurred during the training sessions. In this manner, the individuals could serve as ambassadors with a purpose of educating co-workers. Ask managers to select a mix of employees (not just the people of color or the women) to ensure that a broad perspective is provided about what was taught.

D&I practitioners can also choose great topics for diversity savvy organizations. Diversity training does not need to be called "diversity training" in order for it to be diversity training. Finally, make sure that the training is connected to professional outcomes like promotions or key assignments—this will surely fill up the room if employees understood the "What's In It For Me (W.I.I.F.M.)".

Requiring new or recently promoted managers to participate in mandatory diversity training is a good way to develop their leadership skills, as well as build accountability by establishing performance standards. Additionally, with changes in management expectations, technology, and flexible employee scheduling, it is advantageous to keep current supervisors knowledgeable about recent legislation, court cases, and the impact of demographic trends on the business. In global organizations, update senior leadership about changes in the international diversity landscape (i.e., the location of satellite offices, customers, supply chain, and employees).

Diversity Training in the Education Sector

More colleges and universities are providing mandatory diversity education for students. Beyond an introductory diversity class, institutions must think about how pedagogy, the campus climate, and student-run organizations support Diversity and Inclusion throughout a student's matriculation. Instead of asking how to expose students to Diversity and Inclusion, campus leaders must determine, "How can we do a better job in preparing students for the future workforce?"

Culturally Responsive Teaching is a pedagogy that recognizes the importance of including students' cultural references in all aspects of learning (Ladson-Billings, 1994). Research has shown that no one teaching strategy will consistently engage all learners. The key is helping students relate lesson content to their own backgrounds. There is growing evidence that strong, continual engagement among diverse students requires a holistic approach—an approach where the how, what, and why of teaching are unified and meaningful (Ogbu, 1995).

Some of the characteristics of culturally responsive teaching are:

- Positive perspectives on parents and families
- Communication of high expectations
- Learning within the context of culture
- Student-centered instruction
- Culturally mediated instruction
- Reshaping the curriculum
- Teacher as facilitator

Teaching in a way that is culturally responsive is complex task that requires time and effort. The following case study provides an example.

CASE STUDY: CULTURALLY RESPONSIVE TEACHING

Source: Wlodkowski, Raymond J. & Ginsberg, Margery B. (1995) *A Framework for Culturally Responsive Teaching*. ASCD Educational Leadership, Sept. 1995 | Volume 53 | Number 1. Strengthening Student Engagement p. 17-21

The norm that Mr. Clark, a U.S. history teacher, is aiming for is "sharing the ownership of knowing." The topic is the notion of cultural pluralism, and, later, the roles that our socioeconomic backgrounds play in our lives. Clark uses the procedures of collaborative learning and critical questioning to facilitate student comprehension of the concepts of "melting pot," "social class," and other terms.

> Clark asks the class to first brainstorm words that are associated with culture. Students volunteer "language," "ethnicity," "gender," "religion," "food preference," and so forth. In pairs, students then talk to their partner about ways in which they believe they are culturally similar and distinct from each other.
>
> After 15 minutes, the teacher asks students to note three observations about the concept of culture. The most prevalent response is that "we were surprised at how much we have in common." Clark indicates that he sees this as well. He asks the class, "If we have such commonality, why do some groups of people in the United States have such difficulty becoming economically secure?" Note what happens as students struggle over whose perceptions are the most accurate.
>
> **First student**: Some have more difficulty because of discrimination, because people have prejudices against people whose skin is a different color from theirs.
>
> **Second student**: I don't think it's that simple. Look how many people of color are doing well. We've got generals, mayors, and corporation executives. There's a black middle class and they are economically secure.
>
> **Third student**: Yeah, that might be so, but it isn't as many people as you think. The newspapers just make a big deal about minorities succeeding.
>
> Clark's ground rules (structure) for this conversation endorse honesty in offering opinions and forbid putdowns, so the tone of this exchange is respectful. Interest in the topic intensifies as a result of the exchange. Clark acknowledges the different points of view and asks the class: "What questions might provide insights or clarify the differences between these viewpoints?" The class breaks into small groups after which Clark records the suggested questions. Some that emerge:
>
> - *Which ethnic groups are most economically successful? Least successful?*
> - *What proportion of each ethnic group is lower income, middle income, upper income?*
> - *Are more people of color economically successful today than 20 years ago? 100 years ago?*
> - *What is the relationship of educational opportunity to income status?*
> - *Do middle- and upper-class African Americans and Latinos encounter more discrimination than do European Americans?*
> - *Is there a difference in the quality of family and community support among middle- and upper-income African Americans, European Americans, and Latinos?*
>
> As a result of the discussion, students begin to see how the viewpoints about race and socioeconomic backgrounds are part of a broad and complex picture. The difference of opinion has become a stimulus for deeper learning. Students then divide into three groups: one to conduct library research of relevant documents and studies; one to read and analyze relevant biographies and autobiographies; and one to interview community members who represent different cultures.

In *Beyond Diversity Awareness: Culturally Responsive Teaching for Social Change*, Susan Santone, Executive Director at Creative Change Educational Solutions says, a culturally responsive educator can:

- Identify their own biases and recognize their impacts on different student groups
- Regularly research and learn about other cultures

- Challenge the deficit thinking that assumes students of color are less capable and motivated
- Identify how biases and deficit narratives manifest in disciplinary practices, such as the disproportionate suspensions of black children
- Challenge other forms of institutional discrimination within the school
- Create an inclusive environment that leverages the strengths of students' cultures, languages, experiences, families, and communities
- Integrate citizenship, critical thinking, and social justice into the core subject areas
- Deliver effective learning experiences about race, class, gender, culture, etc.

There are a variety of educational formats that may be used including: presentations, lectures, panel discussions, community forums, film and music analyses, workshops, plays, festivals, art, etc.

Diversity Training in the Public Sector
In the public sector, Diversity and Inclusion training provides three important qualities. First, it allows government and quasi-governmental agencies to make full use of unique employee skill sets. Second, it enables state and local agencies to stay in tune with the changing needs of different demographic groups. Third, it facilitates innovation and problem solving.

The U.S. Intelligence Community has had many obstacles that have traditionally led to intelligence failures; this was clearly illustrated in the ill-advised decision to go to war with Iraq over "weapons of mass destruction". Intragency and interagency breakdowns were indicative of hardened attitudes against change, insular organizations, resistance to external recommendations and insistence on preserving the status quo (Priest, 2005). However, Diversity and Inclusion training led to improvements in the performance culture (Pincus and Baker, 2005) including:

- Agencies encouraging dissent, not smothering it
- Intelligence teams moving away from the tradition of searching for consensus in favor of inspiring open debate and diverse views

NASA defines its organizational culture as the values, norms, beliefs, and practices that characterize the institution's functioning. Today, NASA has one of the strongest Diversity and Inclusion management programs in the Federal government. Like the U.S. Intelligence Community, NASA's advancement was driven by failure aboard the Columbia Space Shuttle. Causes that contributed to the Columbia accident included (NASA, 2003):

- An organizational culture that squelched dissent
- A performance culture that stifled differences of opinion
- Resistance to external criticism and doubt
- Imposition of the "party line vision… (which) led to flawed decision-making, self-deception, introversion, and diminished curiosity"
- Organizational barriers that prevented open, effective communication

The key for government agencies, whether federal, state, or local, is to become proactive about Diversity and Inclusion education. Reactive agencies only consider Diversity and Inclusion after a failure, lawsuit, or riot; but imagine how much time and effort these organizations could save if they took steps to pre-empt these types of problems.

What is Appropriate in Diversity Training?

Sometimes diversity trainers like to use techniques that are emotionally jarring—even shocking, to some extent. Although well intended, many of these tactics may be inappropriate for the workplace.

To determine the appropriateness of a training practice, consider the organizational culture. In conservative cultures, crude and offensive antics will produce complaints. Simultaneously, in environments where the culture is more laid back and relaxed, some employees may resent the "in-your-face" type of diversity training.

The best approach to diversity training involves conducting an assessment prior to arranging any learning sessions. Understanding the employee's developmental needs allows for customized content that addresses specific business concerns. For example:

- In the Information Technology (IT) department, do employees have more systems issues with older workers? If so, that unit may be better served with generational diversity training.

- In the Development Office, how many diverse donors have been approached by your organization over the last year? This particular unit may need to learn about the giving potential of diverse individuals, as well as women- and minority-owned enterprises.

- In the Customer Service department, how many complaints are fielded from diverse customers? This particular unit may need to learn about the need to value <u>all</u> customers and how to deliver 5-star service to everyone.

In these scenarios, the training content and curriculum will be focused on skills and tools that employees can take back to their jobs and apply immediately. By using lecture, employee experiences, and work-related simulations, a trainer can ensure that Diversity and Inclusion education has impact.

Additionally, you want to go beyond simply setting a date, selecting a trainer, and scheduling attendees. This is called "planning an event". Diversity and Inclusion leaders must strive to construct an educational experience, in which employees are engaged and encouraged to lead cultural competence, as well as drive culture change.

The Business Case for Diversity and Inclusion Training

Clearly, diversity training is different from other types of professional development programs. Therefore, from time to time, you may need to justify its existence. There are several methods that you can use to make your case for diversity training:

- Track the ratio of employee opportunities. A scorecard can be created that tracks hiring, promotions, and turnover by category. The scorecard will provide visible evidence of the organization's success in providing evenhandedness in employee opportunities.

- Develop an organizational health survey with questions that specifically target the organization's inclusive practices. This confidential survey will be administered to all employees in the organization. It is important to evaluate the organization in its entirety and among its individual work groups. The results of this information will identify if the diversity training yielded a positive influence on the work group or if tools for Inclusion were used correctly. Questions should focus on corporate policy, local management, the execution of policies, and the effectiveness of training. Perhaps, include a question that asks if the tools and techniques taught in the session are supported by managers. Also, consider tracking employee advancement, key assignments, and other rewards, before and after the training.

- <u>Evaluate the competitive landscape.</u> Providing information about shifts in demographic trends, customer expectations, employee preferences, and other industry changes, **as well as** how well the competition is or is not meeting market needs can offer insight to supervisors and senior executives. For example, if a diversity practitioner conducted a trend analysis to compare Baby Boomers, Generation Xers and Millennials with Generation Z purchasing habits, it could have had a ground-breaking impact on strategic decisions at Toys "R" Us. Although the company dominated its sector for decades, Toys "R" Us was ultimately caught by surprise when they realized that Generation Z kids were primarily buying toys at Target, Walmart and Amazon. Nevertheless, this topic will be a valuable case study for a diversity training session.

Each of these techniques will also produce baseline data that you can use to evaluate the impact of the training.

Diversity and Inclusion training presents an opportunity for employees to learn, as well as for the D&I leader to refresh and/or refine key skills. Go beyond the role of a trainer in diversity development by being a:

- **Leader**—set the example and become a role model
- **Technical Expert**—on organizational culture, Equity, Diversity, and Inclusion
- **Team Builder**—pull people into a unified team
- **Peace Keeper**—act as a mediator
- **Pot Stirrer**—bring controversy out into the open
- **Devil's Advocate**—raise issues for better understanding by assuming opposing positions on controversial topics
- **Cheerleader**—praise people for demonstrating Inclusion, cultural competence, or change management techniques
- **Counselor**—provide intimate feedback

When instructing a training session, some Diversity Facilitation Techniques should include:

- Drawing People Out:
  - "What do others think?" or "What do you think?"
  - "I've heard from (name) so far...are there any other thoughts?"
  - "And what else?"
  - Silence (20-30 seconds)—gives the learners a chance to reflect. Longer periods of silence can be used to force people to talk due to the uncomfortable nature of silence in a group.
  - "You look like you have something to say..."

- Interpreting comments:
  - Compare the comments with the tone (e.g., most questions are <u>not really questions</u>)
  - Assess, but don't assume, the person's intent-vs-wording
  - Consider past experiences and personality

- Use your intuition
- Shift paradigms and filters

- Clarifying thoughts/comments
    - Use models and experience
    - Seek multiple points of view
    - Look for similarities/differences among people
    - Ensure that you do not exhibit facilitator bias; demonstrate impartiality

- Sensing group energy
    - Spark energy within the group
    - Take breaks; watch your timing

- Balancing the group

- Handling objections
    - Try not to personalize (the learners will become defensive)
    - Reflect/deflect
    - Encourage conversation
    - Remember to breath

- Treating learners with respect; leading by example:
    - Accept and support others in the group
    - Encourage individual responsibility
    - Delineate between being right-vs-being successful in the training session
    - Understand the difference between influence and dominance (e.g., don't try to pull rank)
    - Establish confidentiality/trust
    - Don't preach or "Talk at" participants
    - Demonstrate active listening
    - Diffuse conflicts with examples/stories that reflect each perspective of those in disagreement. *Remember, diversity of thought does not require agreement. There should be healthy and natural differences in analysis, approach, and expectations, to name a few.*

Using Consultants

If you are a consultant, using all of these tools will help clients construct a meaningful training program, which may ultimately lead to more business for you. If your organization is going to use consultants, make sure the consultant is supported before, during, and after the training program.

The consultant's primary role is to assist organizations with certain areas of inclusiveness work. While the consultant may act as an educator, a catalyst for deeper change, a resource, or a facilitator, the leadership of the process remains within your organization. The Inclusiveness Committee, D&I staff, Board Members, and President/CEO have the power, and the greater responsibility, to lead the process of becoming more inclusive.

There are generally four categories of work for which to hire the services of a consultant or a consulting team:

1. Overall Guidance: The consultant works with the Inclusiveness Committee throughout the diversity initiative to plan and execute the effort and act as a meeting, or process, facilitator.

2. Information Gatherer: The consultant designs and collects data during the information-gathering phase. Consultants can be particularly useful in collecting qualitative data through interviews and focus groups, since their neutral position with the organization can lead to responses that are more honest from internal and external stakeholders.

In this phase, the consultant can also help you develop curriculum that is tailored for your organization or customized by department/division.

3. Cultural Competency Builder/Diversity Trainer: The consultant facilitates diversity/inclusiveness training sessions to create an inclusive and culturally competent culture. The consultant may also help stakeholders become more aware of the organizational climate for diverse communities, as well as more intentional about doing business better. In this instance, you may want to use one consultant/consulting team for all of the trainings. Alternatively, you may wish to bring in content specialists for different educational sessions and use an "integrating facilitator" to provide continuity between trainings.

4. Evaluator: The consultant creates an evaluation plan to assess the efficacy of training and/or to measure the progress of your diversity efforts.

The consultant's role can be a combination of the tasks above, or just one. The work will depend on the organization's needs, the consultant's expertise, and your budget. Nevertheless, evaluating the training should be a forethought and not an after-thought. If your initial conversations do not include any discussions about measurement or evaluation, then this may not be the best consultant for your organization.

Throughout this process, the performance expectations as well as reporting requirements must be clear. Therefore, issue a Request for Proposals (RFP), check references, and negotiate with the consultant that you select.

MEASURING DIVERSITY TRAINING

There is no one prescription for success in diversity training. However, three components will drive better results—experience, Inclusion, and outcomes.

1. **Experience** relates to the end-user. From an Information Technology perspective, new software is always tested. For example, a beta test is the second phase of software testing in which a sampling of the intended audience tries the product out. Beta testing can be considered "pre-release testing", "user acceptance testing", or end user testing. In this phase of software development, applications are subjected to real world testing by the intended audience for the software. The experiences of the early users are forwarded back to the developers who make final changes before releasing the software commercially. Can you do a "Beta test" with your Diversity and Inclusion training? You bet! It's called a pilot and you can test your training program, curriculum, or components of the learning session with a small group before rolling it out enterprise-wide.

After the pilot, the diversity practitioner can gather meaningful participant feedback to make improvements to the program, or to share the program's successes. The D&I leader can also institute and test support mechanisms in order to reinforce learning after the session concludes.

Piloting a program can eliminate costly mistakes that will make or break a diversity training initiative. It can also help D&I leaders to ascertain the answer to questions such as: beyond planning for an event, how can we create an *experience* that participants will find relevant, useful, and impactful?

2. **Inclusion** pertains to your ability to configure a program that incorporates diverse perspectives in every aspect of learning. From planning the experience, to developing curriculum, to communicating expectations for results, your job is to include as many people as possible.

   Inclusion facilitates ownership. The reason why D&I practitioners experience so much resistance to diversity training is because they create a training program **for** participants, not **with** them.

3. **Outcomes** apply to quantitative and qualitative results. Quantitative results from Diversity and Inclusion training may include increased sales or student enrollment, a surge in diverse representation in management or in business functions, more constituents served, better client retention numbers, and other key organizational indicators. Qualitative results may include improved teamwork, communication, decision-making, and Cross-Cultural Competency building.

   Prior to facilitating any training, you must determine what types of outcomes you want to produce. Next, determine how you will acquire baseline data, and track improvements over time. Measurement is useful because it allows you to make improvements. Additionally, you may have to attach supplemental components to sustain the initial learning and improve your training outcomes. These components may include webinars, computer-based training, 6- or 12-month post-training assessments, coaching, mentoring, supplemental readings, collaborative assignments, and other interventions. For superior outcomes, D&I leaders will take a multi-faceted approach to employee education. Take the time to think through the *best* way to achieve desired outcomes.

Both the Society for Diversity and The Society for Human Resource Management (SHRM) acknowledge that many companies struggle with effectively measuring the results of diversity initiatives. In part, the challenge lies in determining what measures will yield useful information. For others, this task is complicated because access to the right type of baseline data is limited. While measuring the effect of diversity training can be difficult, there are several quantitative measures that can be used.

By effectively measuring diversity results with tangible and quantifiable organizational data, diversity practitioners and senior leaders can better justify the business rationale for Diversity and Inclusion, as well as ascertain the impact of diversity on key business drivers and culture.

Traditionally, the following tools have been used to measure diversity training:

- Training session evaluations
- Equal employment opportunity and affirmative action metrics
- Employee attitude surveys
- Cultural audits
- Focus groups
- Customer surveys
- Management and employee evaluations
- Accountability and incentive assessments

However, research shows that measures outside of EEO and HR data are likely to be more comprehensive and better demonstrate the business impact of diversity management. By establishing broader organizational metrics in the following five categories, diversity leaders can better measure the return on investment in diversity training:

1) Changes in organizational culture (e.g., communication, teamwork, risk-taking, etc.)
2) Improvements in Accountability (e.g., management, compliance, etc.)
3) Shifts in productivity
4) Programmatic measures facilitating better recruitment and retention of students, staff, patients, clients or constituents
5) Innovation resulting in costs savings or increased profits

Other examples of meaningful data include:

- Level of participation in the organization's diversity training strategy formulation
- Number of diverse employees who get promoted after participating in training
- Percentage of diversity objectives aligned with key strategic business objectives that are tied to bonus and compensation systems
- Overall organizational climate and culture ratings and their effects on all represented groups after training

There are many tangible factors to measure. However, it is up to the diversity practitioner to think of what can be measured, how to do it effectively, and what is most valuable to the senior leadership. Training must be relevant to employees' jobs, and clearly connected to business goals. This presents an opportunity for diversity practitioners to target specific organizational components for change.

At the end of the day, an evaluation should help D&I leaders to continually make improvements so that employees can build upon their knowledge, skills and abilities. Diversity training is necessary, but it is one of many tools that can help you advance equity and inclusion from point A to point B, point B to point C, point C to point D, and so on. Diversity training, however, is not a panacea for all of the organization's ills and should not be the focal point of your Diversity and Inclusion strategy. It must be understood that diversity training has limitations. Nevertheless, diversity training is an important aspect of organizational competency in this area called Diversity and Inclusion. Therefore, if your diversity training is not working, do not do away with it, fix it.

References:

Dishman, Lydia. *Why So Many Diversity Programs Fail*. Fast Company, June 23, 2016. Retrieved from: https://www.fastcompany.com/3061198/why-so-many-diversity-programs-fail

Vaughn Ph.D., Billy E. *Diversity Pioneers in the History of Diversity Education.* Ezine Articles, February 15, 2018. Retrieved from: http://ezinearticles.com/?Diversity-Pioneers-In-The-History-Of-Diversity-Education&id=988500

Ladson-Billings, G. (1994). *The Dreamkeepers*. San Francisco: Jossey-Bass Publishing Co.

Velasquez, Mauricio. *The Top Ten Reasons Diversity Programs Succeed/Fail.* Retrieved from: http://home.diversitydtg.com/article/best-practices-inclusive-strategies/the-top-ten-reasons-diversity-programs-succeed-fail

Lieberman, Simma. *Why Sensitivity Training is Insensitive and Patronizing.* February 2, 2016. Retrieved from: http://simmalieberman.com/why-sensitivity-training-is-insensitive-and-patronizing-2/

Ford Ph.D., APR, Rochelle L. Diversity Dimensions: Needs assessment helps ensure effective diversity training. The Public Relations Society of America, July 2004. Retrieved from: http://apps.prsa.org/Intelligence/Tactics/Articles/view/6C-070440/101/Diversity_Dimensions_Needs_assessment_helps_ensure#.WsOG9i7wbIU

Roberson, Loriann; Kulik, Carol T. and Pepper, Molly B. *Designing Effective Diversity Training: Influence of Group Composition and Trainee Experience.* Wiley & Sons, 2001. Journal of Organizational Behavior, Volume 22, Issue 8, pp. 871-885

Roberson, Loriann; Kulik, Carol T. and Pepper, Molly B. *Individual and Environmental Factors Influencing the Use and Transfer of Strategies After Diversity Training.* Sage Journals, February 1, 2009. Available at: http://journals.sagepub.com/doi/abs/10.1177/1059601108329732?journalCode=gomb

National Aeronautics and Space Administration (2003). *Report of Columbia Accident Investigation Board*, Volume I

Santone, Susan. Beyond Diversity Awareness: Culturally Responsive Teaching for Social Change. LinkedIn, January 14, 2016. Available at: https://www.linkedin.com/pulse/beyond-diversity-awareness-culturally-responsive-teaching-santone/

Ogbu, J. U. (1995). *Understanding Cultural Diversity and Learning*. In Handbook of Research on Multicultural Education, edited by J. A. Banks and C. A. M. Banks. New York: Macmillan. Retrieved January 12, 2018

Pincus, Walter and Baker, Peter. *Dissent on Intelligence is Critical*, Washington Post, March 30, 2005.

Priest, Dana. *Panel Warns on Headstrong Agencies.* Washington Post, April 1, 2005, on findings of Commission on the Intelligence Capabilities Regarding Weapons of Mass Destruction, February 2004.

Sample Test Questions:
REINVENTING DIVERSITY TRAINING

1. Examples of meaningful data used to measure the effectiveness of a training program should NOT include:
   A. The breadth of innovation resulting in cost savings or increased profits
   B. The number of diverse employees who get promoted after participating in training
   C. The total number of employees that participated in the training session

2. What must diversity trainers ensure before conducting any diversity training?
   A. That it is approved by a diverse group of managers
   B. That content contains discussions about expectations
   C. That it is closely aligned with the company's strategy

3. How can accountability for diversity be built into an organization?
   A. With quarterly employee behavior reviews
   B. Through ongoing monitoring and employee testing
   C. By establishing performance standards

4. Who employed the first and largest scale diversity education experiment ever conducted?
   A. The U.S. military
   B. Xerox Corporation
   C. The American Red Cross

5. Which state has mandatory Sexual Harassment Training requirements?
   A. Indiana
   B. Connecticut
   C. Texas

6. All of the following are great facilitation techniques in diversity training EXCEPT:
   A. Eliminating group discussions
   B. Addressing past experiences
   C. Handling objections

7. An encounter group was successful when at least:
   A. Half of the employees rated the training with high remarks on the evaluation forms
   B. One white American admitted to being a racist and was tearful about discrimination
   C. One supervisor reported positive employee changes within their business unit

Sample Test Questions:
REINVENTING DIVERSITY TRAINING (cont'd)

8. Diversity leaders can measure training's return on investment better by reporting:
    A. Equal Employment Opportunity and Affirmative Action metrics
    B. Levels of participation in training strategy formulation
    C. Class evaluation results from employees and managers

9. The following individual is noted as a Diversity Pioneer in the "History of Diversity Education":
    A. Lewis Griggs
    B. Dr. Shirley Davis
    C. Dr. Martin Luther King Jr.

10. Over the years, diversity training has become less awkward and controversial.
    A. True
    B. False

11. These three components drive better results in diversity training: experience, cultural competency, and outcomes.
    A. True
    B. False

inclusion

12. Training content and curriculum should NOT focus on skills or tools that employees can use on the job.
    A. True
    B. False

13. The purpose of a training pilot is to:
    A. Delay solving "the problem" until management commits more time and resources
    B. Understand how diversity can advance learning and professional development
    C. "Beta-test" the training program to determine where improvements must be made

HANDLING DIFFICULT CONVERSATIONS

> *The art of getting your message across effectively is a vital part of being a successful Diversity practitioner. Few Diversity practitioners, however, are able to transfer critical information or deliver succinct, compelling messages with clarity. Not only will effective multicultural communication skills improve business relationships, but it will also serve as an example to other workplace leaders.*

OVERALL OBJECTIVES AND COMPETENCIES

This competency seeks to guide Diversity and Inclusion practitioners in their efforts to confidently initiate and mediate complex discussions about diversity; as well as develop an effective message of Inclusion for employees, students, patients, customers, Board members, suppliers, partners, or other stakeholders.

BACKGROUND AND CONTEXT

Effective communication can be defined as the process of meaningful interaction when what is received and understood is what was directed. Communication includes written, spoken, and non-verbal behaviors that have the goal to affect the knowledge or behavior of another person.

Contrary to popular opinion, effective communication skills are not talents that individuals are born with; it is an acquired skill that allows for cooperation and collaboration.

As it relates to multicultural audiences, verbal language is just one small piece of the communication effort. The explicit fact that diverse groups speak a variety of languages is considered tangible evidence of cultural difference. As far back as the classical period, the connection between human culture and language has been noted as a point of contention relative to effective communication. The ancient Greeks used language to distinguish between people who were civilized and those considered to be barbarous (individuals who spoke unintelligible languages). Similarly, we as humans in almost every realm, use language as a means of identifying with the cultural nuance of groups. Even among speakers of one language, several different ways of using the language exists; with each language utilized to signal affiliation with particular subgroups within a larger culture.

According to the United Nations, the top three languages with the largest number of native speakers are Mandarin Chinese, Spanish, and English [UNESCO October 2015: World Education Forum]. Languages not only differ in pronunciation, vocabulary, and/or grammar, it also differs through "cultures of speaking". Some cultures for example have elaborate systems of signaling social distance through linguistic means. This can be demonstrated by distinguishing between addressing some people by first name and others by surname, as well as in titles such as "Mrs.", "boy", "Doctor" or "Your Honor". In other languages, such systems may be highly complex and codified in the entire grammar and vocabulary of the language.

For any language spoken, effective communication requires certain elements—Sender, Message, Channel, and Receiver.

FIGURE 1: MODEL OF COMMUNICATION

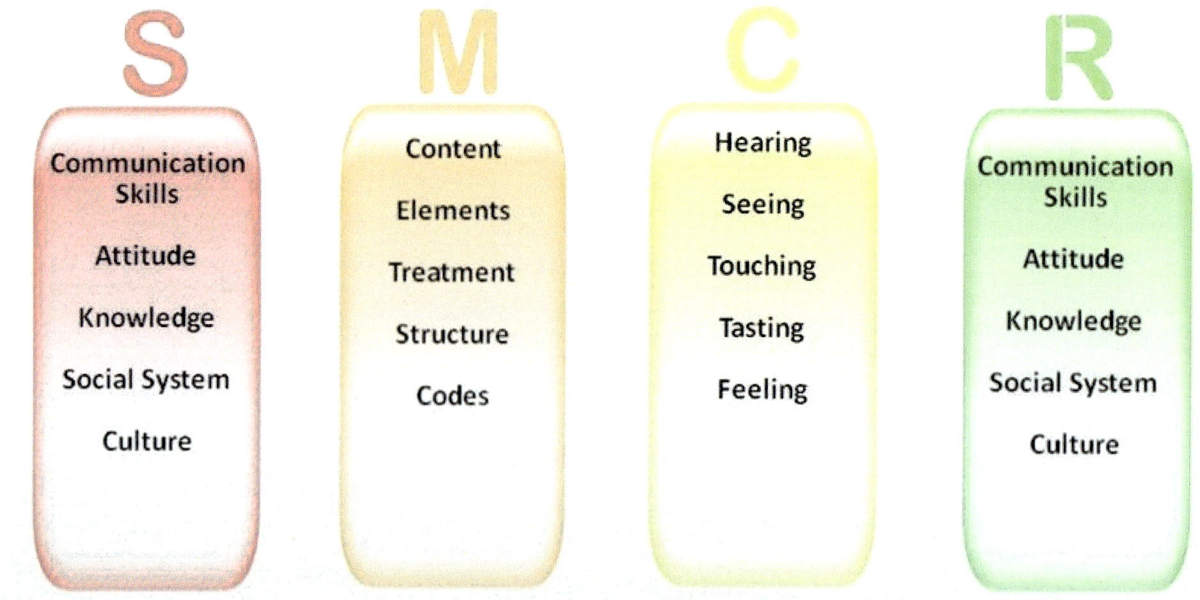

S	M	C	R
Communication Skills	Content	Hearing	Communication Skills
Attitude	Elements	Seeing	Attitude
Knowledge	Treatment	Touching	Knowledge
Social System	Structure	Tasting	Social System
Culture	Codes	Feeling	Culture

BLOCKS TO EFFECTIVE COMMUNICATION AT WORK

Even if the message is appropriately delivered through one or more channels, the receiver may not interpret or respond to the message as intended. Thus, breaking down barriers is one of the first steps towards good communication.

Some believe Diversity and Inclusion is a highly charged topic because a few folks love racism so much. In actuality, there may be factions of the population that unconsciously benefit, or anticipate benefiting, from unequal or unfair systems. This global phenomenon does not require a universal favorite target for inequity nor does it mandate *active* participation in inequality or discrimination; it merely entails allowing the status quo to remain. Hence, initiating a workplace discussion about Diversity and Inclusion requires delving into a conversation about benefits or What's In It for Me (WIIFM). It also requires recognizing blocks to talking about sharing power and resources.

In the workplace, common barriers to effective communication with similar or different groups include:

- Me-too-ism
- Moralizing, Preaching & Being Judgmental
- Group-Think
- Giving Unsolicited Advice
- Focusing on Differences (e.g., Shifts, Job Duties)
- Defensiveness, Arguing or Disagreeing
- Analyzing or Interpreting

In addition to verbal barriers, there are several parameters that may be perceived differently by people of diverse cultures. These may include:

- *Perception of Time:* In some countries, like China and Japan, punctuality is considered important and being late would be considered as an insult. However, in countries such as those in South America and the Middle East, being on time does not carry the same sense of urgency.

- *Perception of Space:* The concept of "personal space" also varies from country to country. In certain countries, like America, it is considered respectful to maintain a distance while interacting. However, in other countries like Italy, keeping your distance or moving away from close interactions may be considered cold and unfriendly.

- *Nonverbal Communication:* This describes the process of conveying meaning in the form of unspoken messages. Research shows that the majority of our communication is nonverbal.

  Nonverbal communication includes gestures, body language or posture; facial expressions and eye contact; object communication such as clothing, hairstyles, architecture, symbols, and tone of voice, as well as through an aggregate of the above. Non-verbal communication is also called a silent language because it plays a key role in multicultural employment relations by indicating indirectness, politeness, or ambiguity. For example, because written communications (e.g., email correspondence) are void of nonverbal cues, they must be worded particularly to communicate clearly using just the language in the message. Oftentimes, written communications lack the context of non-verbal signals, and result in misunderstandings.

The Use of Global English
The ability to speak a second or third language is clearly an advantage for any global leader. Nevertheless, English is frequently the language used in global business even though English is not the language spoken by the majority of people in the world. In *English: The Language of Global Business*, author Dorie Clark adds, "English will maintain and grow its dominance, moving from "a marker of the elite" in years past to "a basic skill needed for the entire workforce, in the same way that literacy has been transformed in the last two centuries from an elite privilege into a basic requirement for informed citizenship."

Yet, in the absence of being bilingual or multilingual, it is very important for native English speakers to be sensitive to the fact that English is a foreign language for many of their associates around the world, and the extent to which English is understood and spoken varies widely. This becomes a valid point to stress because it speaks specifically to the issue of effective communication.

In countries such as Japan, English is generally studied in junior high and high school, but the method of instruction emphasizes reading and grammar. Therefore, many Japanese may have more familiarity with written English than spoken English. The Japanese are also very shy and hesitant to speak for fear of making a mistake. In this instance, being sensitive to non-verbal communication is essential to the communication process. Without considering the non-verbal aspect of the communication process, the Japanese speaker could be inadvertently insulted through embarrassment. Another factor to consider is that non-native English speakers around the world may be more familiar with British English than American English, or vice versa. The degree to which your colleagues speak English may also vary by region, occupation, educational background, level of international experience, etc.

Native and bilingual English speakers should learn to adjust the way that they speak when interacting with those who are less fluent in order to facilitate successful communication and minimize or prevent communication breakdowns.

Cultural Considerations
Communication is more than just speaking, listening, writing, and reading. When communication is most effective, it involves information gathering and teamwork. In a global economy, this supports cross-cultural communications. In fact, cultural considerations make up the third component of a global communication process:

1) Subject Matter
2) Medium of Delivery
3) Cultural Considerations

Of the three components, cultural considerations are generally ignored because the term carries some ambiguity. For our purposes, culture is defined as the way in which each of us is programmed to behave in a certain environment. The present definition acknowledges the breath of culture and respects the fact that culture is dynamic (ever changing) and not static.

Nevertheless, cultures are like icebergs; some features are apparent to anyone who is not in a fog, while others are deeply hidden due to the fog. Above-the-surface features include overt behaviors such as how people:

- Dress
- Eat
- Walk
- Talk
- Relate to one another
- Conduct themselves during public ceremonies such as weddings or funerals
- Use social distance

Other aspects are so far below the surface that they are hard to understand if you are not accustomed to that culture. We may see evidence of these aspects, but we usually cannot pinpoint them precisely, and may not have a clue as to their origin. This might include such things as:

- How we encode and retrieve information
- Our definition of justice
- What music appeals to us
- How to properly parent

- How we define beauty or ugliness
- The meaning attached to "teaching" stories
- What "well-educated" means
- What constitutes status

Technology, transportation, and changes in living styles have begun to blur many of the surface distinctions between different cultures. Some cultures are adopting Western dress and music, however deeper differences remain relative to effective communication. For instance, compare the respect due to elders in some Asian, Latin, and African societies versus the lack of deference shown in some parts of North America. Alternatively, contrast the practice of arranging marriages in some Middle-Eastern and African countries with the Western practice of selecting your own mate. While there is some surface convergence, there is divergence as well. In fact, the world seems to become more tribal as opportunities for communication expand. Many large metropolitan cities, such as Chicago, New York, Philadelphia, and Los Angeles have culturally ethnic divisions within the city.

High/Low Context Culture
One of the deep or hidden aspects that differentiate cultures is the amount of context (clarity) a culture's members expect in social interactions. People who study such things divide cultures into those societies that are high-context, and those that are low-context (Beyond Culture; Edward T. Hall, Anthropologist).

In general, high context cultures place great importance on:

- Ambience
- Decorum
- The relative status of the participants in a communication
- The manner of a message's delivery

High context cultural attitudes might be expressed with the phrase, "*It's not what you said, it's how you said it*". For Asians and Latin Americans, members of high-context societies, the following three items are as important as the work:

- Issues
- Circumstances
- Relationships

Low context cultures tend to want to ignore such things and emphasize the content of a communication. Well defined, direct or explicit may be a better way of describing the low context culture. Attitudes that might be expressed by low context cultures can be coined in the phrases "*cut to the chase*" or "*get to the point*".

Geographic & Social Distance
When working in a global environment, effective communication can be very difficult. Since the per diem cost of gathering people from all over the world could easily reach tens of thousands of dollars, the best that can be hoped for in this kind of a multicultural team situation is an environment that fosters the building of a shared culture. A mutually agreed upon context, wherein this "virtual" culture can develop, thrive, and benefit from the individual richness of its members, is critical to organizational productivity, teamwork, engagement, and inclusion.

A case to illustrate the point is people, programmed differently, with superficial knowledge of each other, now have to communicate in a way that makes meaning clear and does not provoke misunderstanding. The message might be anything from a simple local proposal saying "fund this program" to an attempt by a global organization to communicate a vision to employees in fifty countries. In effect, distance alone can make communicating with a virtual team quite difficult.

Herein lies the problem: the sender wants a particular reaction to a message. The challenge is to get the same desired reaction from many different groups. The best way to get the information you need is to talk to a person from the group with whom you are communicating.

For example, while they may not be in other countries, executives are typically distinguished by an exclusive location (e.g., the 52nd floor) or by a separate building (e.g., City Hall for a Mayor or the Administrative Offices for a college President). The physical distance dictates a unique culture that is distinct from the standard employee population, and the resulting social distance often makes communication with senior executives more difficult. A common challenge among many Diversity and Inclusion professionals is that they lack support from executive leadership. The best person to target for information about how to get more senior level support is the CEO, President, or Division Head. Asking an executive for input could provide you with valuable information to reach senior management with the business case for Diversity and Inclusion. A diversity practitioner can ask questions such as:

- What is the best way to communicate my message?
- How do you think other senior executives will respond?
- How do I get the leadership to respond in this manner?

It is impossible to learn about each of the cultures with whom you must communicate, or to even anticipate with whom you might encounter during the course of your work. The best that can be expected is to try to find a common denominator and work from there. Hence, it is important to gain support from upper level management because they can open the door of acceptance for diversity within the organization.

Creating communication hierarchies in which there are D&I Champions who are responsible for collecting data, sharing information, or recruiting volunteers, is a great strategy for expanding responsibility for D&I beyond the Office of Diversity. This is particularly helpful in the case of virtual teams, where employees are often isolated from others. Also, using face-to-face technology platforms (i.e., Skype, web conferencing, etc.) to facilitate communication will help to dismantle any distrust issues that may arise due to geographic dispersion.

HOW GENDER INFLUENCES COMMUNICATION

Although at times, distinctions in women and men communication styles seem to be minor, part of understanding multicultural communications involves the fact that men and women are similar, as well as different. For example, both women and men can be nurturing, aggressive, task-oriented, or sentimental.

Nevertheless, studies indicate that women, more so than men, are sensitive to the interpersonal meanings that lie "between the lines" in the messages they exchange with males. That is, societal expectations often make women responsible for regulating intimacy in interpersonal relationships. For that reason, it is argued that women pay more attention than men to the underlying meanings about intimacy that verbal messages imply. Men on the other hand, more so than women, are more sensitive to "between the lines meanings" about status. For men, societal expectations are that they must negotiate hierarchy, or who is the captain and who is the crew.

The difference between interpersonal vs. status implications of messages typically leads women to expect relationships to be based on interdependence (mutual dependence) and cooperation. Women more frequently emphasize the similarities between themselves and others and try to make decisions that make everyone happy. In contrast, it is more typical for men to expect relationships to be based on independence and competition. Men more frequently emphasize the differences between themselves and others, and often make decisions based on their personal needs or desires.

These characteristics in the workplace are observed primarily in the ways that women and men communicate and/or lead. Women tend to be the relationship specialists and men tend to be task specialists. Women are typically experts in "rapport talk", which refers to the types of communication that build, maintain, and strengthen relationships. Rapport talk reflects skills in sharing, nurturing, supporting, expressing emotions, and empathizing. Men are typically experts in task accomplishment, as well as addressing questions about facts. They are experts in "report talk", which refers to the types of communication that analyzes issues and solves problems. Report talk reflects skills of being competitive, analyzing, and focusing aggressively on task accomplishment.

These differences can create specific and commonly experienced misunderstandings. Here are two examples:

Misunderstanding #1

He:	I'm really tired. I have so much work to do—I don't know how I'm going to get it done!
She:	Me, too. There just aren't enough hours in the day!
He:	There you go again! You never think my contributions to this project are good enough!

In this conversation, she is trying to communicate something like "We're partners and share similar experiences". Her intended 'between the lines' message is: "I understand what you're going through; you're not alone". The 'between the lines' message he hears emphasizes competition for status: "What are you complaining about? You aren't any better than I am!" or "Your contributions to this project aren't any more significant than mine!"

Misunderstanding #2

She:	I'm really tired. I have so much work to do—I don't know how I'm going to get it done!
He:	Why don't you take a day off and rest, if you're so tired?
She:	(sarcastically) Thanks a lot! You think my contribution to this project is so trivial that I can do nothing and the difference won't even be noticed?

Here, he is trying to communicate something like "Oh, you need advice and analysis? I'll focus on the details and facts and offer a solution". His intended 'between the lines' message is: "I will help you solve your problem because I think I know something that might help". The 'between the lines' message she hears him saying: "I don't want to understand your feelings; I'm different from you and I know what you should do".

The problems here result from some subtle differences in the ways that women and men approach problems. Women *sometimes* deal with problems (especially emotional concerns) by talking about them, sharing their feelings, and matching experiences with others. This can be frustrating to men, who *more typically* deal with problems by focusing on the facts and seeking an immediate solution. Occasionally, men perceive women to be ungrateful for the advice and solutions they offer and ponder in frustration why women do not want to resolve their problems! Similarly, when men offer a solution, rather than talking about a problem, women may feel hurt, dissatisfied, and put-down by the lack of empathy that men show.

What does all this mean? One extremely important observation is that perception, especially based on interpersonal feelings, may become reality if communication is not effective. Understanding differences is the key to working them out. When we misunderstand one another, we often think that the other's motives are not reasonable, are mean spirited, or worse! Clarity, however, may not occur until after the gender conflict has been resolved.

It is important to experience feelings of surprise, disappointment and, yes, anger as a response to an ineffective communication attempt. The counter measure, however, to these responses is to seek a better understanding prior to reacting to an ambiguous message. So, the next time you feel surprised, disappointed, or angry at someone's response to something you have said, ask yourself if he or she may have "misunderstood" the message. Is the other responding to your problems with a solution, when you wanted to receive sympathy? Is the other responding to your message of empathy with a message of status? If so, you will be able to help the other to understand the source of your miscommunication and avoid the hurt feelings and conflicts that sometimes follow.

In addition to distinct communication styles, men and women often use different processes for decision-making and leadership. In order to facilitate equality and inclusion, it is important to understand the strengths and styles that different genders bring to the workplace.

1. *Attitude towards tasks vs. relationships.* Women tend to be more relationship oriented and accomplish tasks by building relationships first. They know with whom to partner and are comfortable asking others to get things done. Men tend to be more task-oriented and go straight to the task. They build their relationships when they are in the midst of the task or project.

2. *Way of Processing Information.* When women have to make a decision, they will often process and look at options aloud, while men tend to process internally until they come up with a solution. Women often think that the man is being unresponsive to suggestions because of this and men often think that women are looking for approval or do not know what they are doing when they process aloud. Some men think that a woman's way of processing is a sign of weakness.

3. *Leadership Style.* Women are more relationship-oriented and they tend to lead by consensus. Men tend to be more hierarchical and include only the people closest to them at their level in the decision-making process, when they think it is necessary.

4. *Communication Styles*. In non-verbal behavior, women will nod their head to show that they are listening. Men leave the conversation thinking that a head nod means agreement and will be surprised to find out that the woman did not agree at all. When a woman is speaking to a man and he does not say anything, but he stays in neutral body language, a woman will interpret that as the man is bored or is not listening to what she is saying. This can lead the woman to become very uncomfortable and repeat what she is saying or ask the man each time if he understands what she is saying. The man then interprets that as insecurity, or talking too much, which leads him to think she is not assertive or confident enough to be a leader.

Women will actually use more direct eye contact in conversation to create relationship and connection, while many men take that as a challenge to their power or position. Women will also approach a man from the front while men often approach from the side at an angle, which is how each of them tends to stand or sit when talking to others. Men interpret the face-to-face as too personal or aggressive, and women will interpret the talking side to side as though he is not being upfront or even hiding something from her.

5. *Talk time*. Men take up more time and space at meetings, while women try to make sure there is more equality in the room. Despite stereotypes, studies have shown that men talk more than women talk. Men interrupt women and talk over them much more than women interrupt men. All of this can lead to the type of miscommunication based on assumptions of why members of the other gender are using certain verbal and non-verbal behaviors. These miscommunications can result in team breakdown—people not listening to each other, as well as a loss of good ideas.

While most women are in the workforce full-time, there is still bias amongst certain men in leadership roles that stop women from advancing up the ladder, such as:

- The only style or way to lead is the hierarchical one
- Most women can't be leaders because they are not "strategic"
- Women are not in the workforce on a permanent basis and don't really want to move up
- A woman is a b---- or too aggressive if she communicates "like a man"

Because some of these men are married to women who work in the home, they have a harder time conceptualizing how a woman could run an organization, and therefore are not as objective when making hiring and promotion decisions.

Effective communications with the opposite sex, as well as gender equity, are both very important workplace concepts. Accordingly, there is a need to make a difference by using the following gender communication strategies.

1. *Take this synopsis with a grain of salt*. It is important not to use this information to stereotype all men or all women. Of course, not everyone fits within these generalizations. These are research-based cultural norms where majorities of men and women have displayed some of these characteristics. Many of these behaviors are based on acculturation and learning, while some of them are based on how our brains work.

2. *Seek understanding*. Both men and women need to be conscious of each other's styles of communication-- both verbal and non-verbal-- in order to avoid miscommunication and work together better.

3. *Realize* unconscious stereotypes and biases and be open to breaking through them in order to leverage each other's strengths.

4. *Recognize* that many different styles of leadership can be effective.

5. *Men, be conscious* of how much time and space you use in meetings or group interactions. Make room for the contributions of women. When asked for a decision by a woman or for your opinion— if you are an internal processor—let her know you are in process of thinking about it so she knows she is heard.

6. *Women, get comfortable* asserting more space for yourselves. When dealing with men in decision-making, try to stop yourself from processing aloud. If you do process aloud, let the man know that this is a process you use for decision-making and you are not asking him what to do.

7. *Finally, get information*. Learn more about male and female styles of communication and be willing to use both. You need both to deal with the complexity and diversity of situations in today's world both personally and professionally. Do not be afraid to recognize differences. Once you detect variances, it will be easier to have open discussions in order to find similarities and use those differences to achieve greater goals together.

LISTENING & PROVIDING FEEDBACK

When a Diversity and Inclusion practitioner is in search of information, consensus, or building a working relationship, attentive listening is a must. When speaking in a way that will garner a response is required, it is not necessary to dominate the conversation. Also, use silence confidently as a tool to encourage hesitant speakers. Repeat key words silently as you hear them to help you remember what is said.

Active listening is a communication technique that requires the listener to understand, interpret, and evaluate what (s)he hears. The ability to listen actively can improve personal relationships by reducing conflicts, strengthening cooperation, and fostering understanding. This is a vital skill for individuals in the field of Diversity and Inclusion.

Active listening is best demonstrated by asking open-ended questions. This can further engage and stimulate audiences if you keep your responses brief. Figure 2 shows the degree to which an individual listens to the responses-- by repeating, paraphrasing, and reflecting.

FIGURE 2

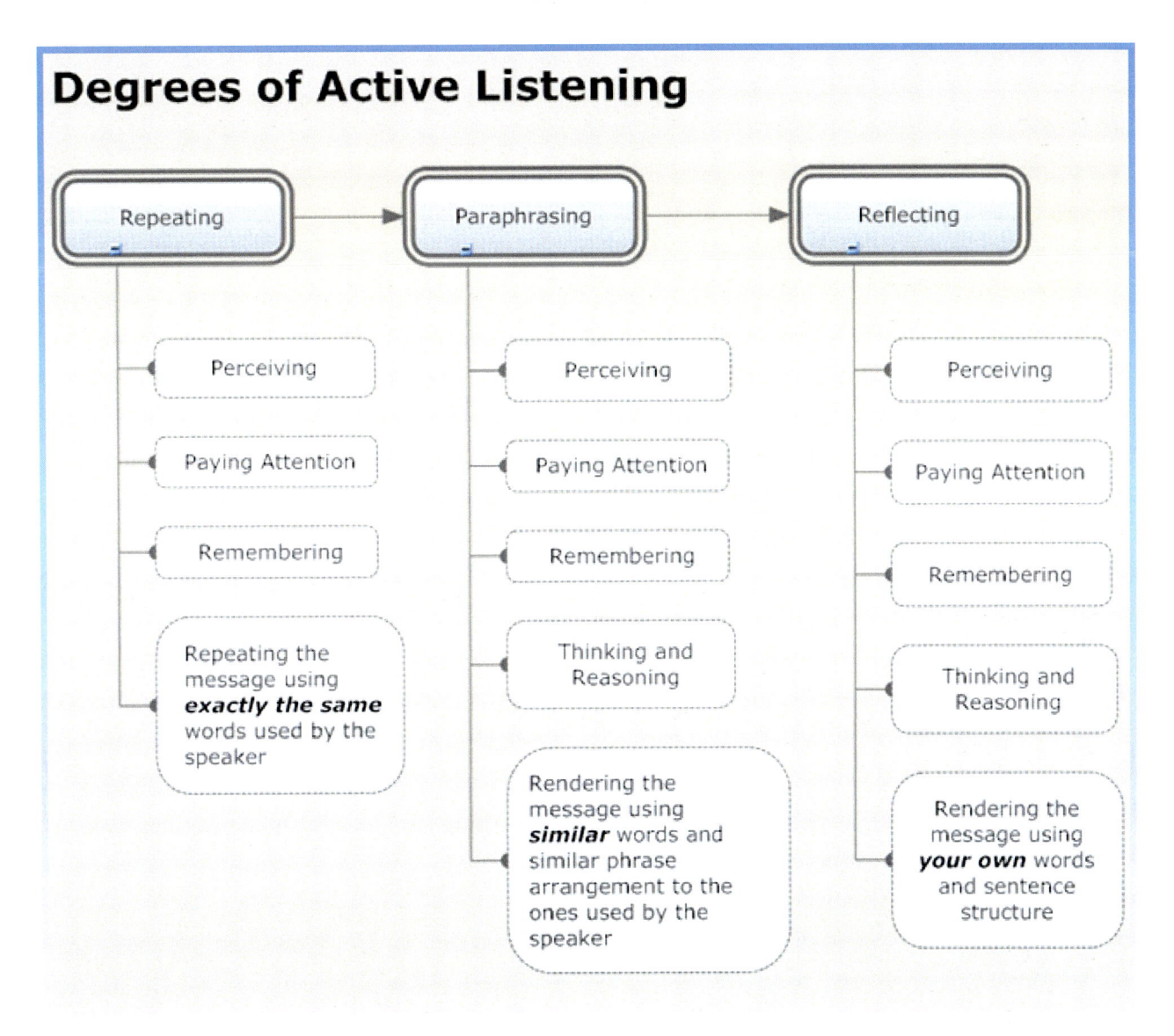

Degrees of Active Listening

Repeating → **Paraphrasing** → **Reflecting**

Repeating:
- Perceiving
- Paying Attention
- Remembering
- Repeating the message using **exactly the same** words used by the speaker

Paraphrasing:
- Perceiving
- Paying Attention
- Remembering
- Thinking and Reasoning
- Rendering the message using **similar** words and similar phrase arrangement to the ones used by the speaker

Reflecting:
- Perceiving
- Paying Attention
- Remembering
- Thinking and Reasoning
- Rendering the message using **your own** words and sentence structure

When interacting, people often are not listening attentively. They may be distracted, thinking about other things, or contemplating what they are going to say next (the latter case is particularly true in conflict situations or disagreements). Active listening is a structured way of paying attention, and responding, to others by focusing attention on the speaker.

All elements of communication, including listening, may be affected by barriers that can impede the flow of conversation. Such barriers include distractions, trigger words, vocabulary, and limited attention span.

Listening barriers may be psychological or physical (e.g. noise and visual distractions). Cultural differences, including speakers' accents, vocabulary, and misunderstandings due to cultural assumptions, often obstruct the listening process as well. Figure 3 illustrates that any of these can interfere with listening to a message.

FIGURE 3: MODEL OF COMMUNICATION

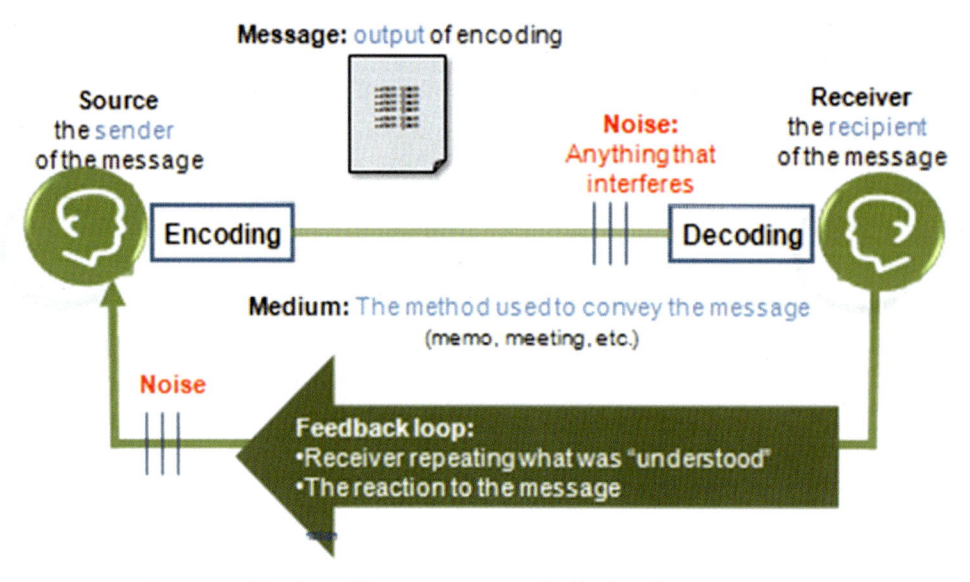

Message: output of encoding

Source the sender of the message

Noise: Anything that interferes

Receiver the recipient of the message

Encoding → Decoding

Medium: The method used to convey the message (memo, meeting, etc.)

Noise

Feedback loop:
- Receiver repeating what was "understood"
- The reaction to the message

Source: Project Management Global Solutions, 2010

Frequently, the listener's personal interpretations, attitudes, biases, and prejudices lead to ineffective communication. For this reason, managing a difficult conversation about Diversity and Inclusion can be a matter as simple as listening—without walls of resistance.

Being able to demonstrate respect in communications, as well as displaying a willingness to listen, is more important than anything you can verbalize. Remember, people watch what you do before they listen to what you say.

CONFRONTING DIFFICULT ISSUES

It has been said that we need to facilitate conversations about Diversity and Inclusion in order to engender better understanding, foster teamwork, and resolve conflict. The question is, how do you initiate a conversation about an issue that has the potential to spiral out of control? For instance, if someone asserts that your work is racist, what do you do? If an employee claims that your senior leadership team is not doing enough about discrimination, how do you respond? Alternatively, how do you tell an executive that his or her behavior is inappropriate?

First, you cannot "ignore it", because *it will not go away* on its own. Not only can the problem escalate into a lawsuit, but it usually affects other employees. Second, allowing diversity problems to linger is counterintuitive to your efforts to change the organizational culture.

There are several ways to handle a potentially contentious conversation. First, we must understand that some Caucasian individuals may claim that they are a victim of racism or reverse discrimination. There may also be Latinos, Asians or Native Americans who feels that they have been victims of racism or discrimination and no one has taken them seriously. Likewise, there may African Americans who associate nearly every unpleasant action with racism.

In any situation that a person alleges an 'ism' (e.g., racism, sexism, ageism, etc.) it is up to the accused to ask, "*What makes you say that?*" Or "*What did I do that was racist/sexists/ageist?*" Getting to the root of the accusation and demonstrating empathy may actually solve the problem. This technique can be practiced during training as a tool to stimulate a professional conversation instead of devolving into a quarrel or "Me-too" exchange.

If merely venting one's frustration does not help, the accused should continue to ask the employee questions such as "*What could have been done differently?*" or "*How do we prevent this in the future?*" If an employee discloses an –ism to a D&I professional, this is a great time to suggest taking their concerns to management anonymously. Also, before doling out advice, ask if they would like to hear your views about the situation. This approach is illustrated in Figure 4 where you should aspire to be an active and constructive listener.

FIGURE 4: ACTIVE LISTENING FOR D&I LEADERS

FOLLOWERS	Don't Listen	Say They're Listening	Actively Listening
Passive & Silent	Unquestioning faithful	Uncomplaining Optimists	Silent Majority
Active & Negative	Combative Contestants	Disillusioned Cynics	Potential Converts
Active & Constructive	Potential Deserters	Potential Cynics	Creatively Engaged

LEADERS

Source: Amplify Disturbance, 2010

For a group conversation about a workplace conflict, you want to avoid "stacking the deck" where everyone is complaining about some unfair and unfortunate situation. Instead, begin the meeting with a non-threatening topic. You could inquire about how individuals grew up, and how today's families are different. Alternatively, you could ask long-time employees to describe how the organization was different when they first started, or probe how the industry has changed over the years. Discussing change in a neutral context will set the stage for a hard-core discussion. Once you begin the conversation, do not simply ask what is wrong, make sure you seek solutions. Asking "How do we fix it?" is a great way to get employees thinking and engaged in the healing process.

According to Charles M. Blow, writer for the New York Times, whenever you initiate a conversation about race, gender, LGBTQ+, age, different abilities, or other unique characteristics, it cannot be an insular, circular, or one-dimensional dialogue. The conversation should be a multi-directional discussion that includes historical information, presents data, and shares personal experiences. Additionally, the group should explore the stereotypes and privileges of the majority group. Much more than a training session, this type of dialogue presents an opportunity for employees to learn from each other, build relationships across difference, and explore new paradigms. Do not forget to follow-up on the conversation. Change occurs not with one conversation, but over a series of conversations. Be sure to plan an agenda for each meeting.

Giving Feedback
In the event that you need to address inappropriate comments or behavior in the workplace, provide feedback to the offender. Keep in mind, it is the Supervisor's responsibility to address errant behavior; but occasionally, the D&I leader may need to provide feedback or equip someone else to provide feedback. The following criteria for giving constructive feedback provides a straightforward way to let individuals know how their behavior negatively affects others.

- *Describe specific behavior*
  Effective feedback describes observable actions, rather than assigning meaning to activities. Be descriptive, not judgmental.

- *Express feelings*
  Good feedback tells someone how you feel about what he or she did. It is okay to say you are mad, frustrated, confused, or upset—so long as you direct your feelings toward the *behavior*, not the person.

- *Request alternatives*
  Good feedback is proactive in asking for an alternative behavior, rather than just "dumping" the negative. State what you would like to see the person do instead.

- *Consider everyone's needs*
  Give effective feedback with the needs and feelings of both the sender and receiver in mind.

- *Time it well*
  Choose the time and situation for the feedback strategically. Try to do it as soon as possible after the incident. However, do not do it in the heat of the moment unless you can maintain your composure. Also, avoid a public discussion unless it is an issue for the entire team to discuss.

> **FIGURE 5: EXAMPLE OF EFFECTIVE FEEDBACK**
>
> After the meeting you can say:
>
> "Pat, remember that joke you made in the meeting today?" *(timing)*
>
> "Well, I feel uncomfortable laughing at someone else's expense." *(express feelings)*
>
> "Could you / Would you tell jokes that are neutral, and don't cut anyone down?" *(request alternative)*
>
> "I really like your sense of humor, and I'd like your jokes a lot more if they were upbeat." *(consider everyone's needs)*

Giving feedback is important, and again, you can give feedback regardless of your position. Instead of talking about a person who does things wrong or complaining about their performance, a true leader will give feedback and work to help that person improve. Even if the person initially rejects your feedback, the most important thing is that you did your part, and your motives are right.

References:

Clark, Dorie. *English - The Language of Global Business?* Forbes, October 26, 2012. Retrieved from:
https://www.forbes.com/sites/dorieclark/2012/10/26/english-the-language-of-global-business/#1906bb6ab57e

Hall, Edward T. *Beyond Culture.* Anchor Books, 1977

Ferrell, Jared Z. and Herb, Kelsey C. *Improving Communication in Virtual Teams.* Society for Industrial and Organizational Psychological, SIOP White Paper Series, October 2012. Available at:
https://www.siop.org/WhitePapers/Visibility/VirtualTeams.pdf

Blow, Charles. *Constructing a Conversation on Race.* New York Times, August 2014. Retrieved from:
http://www.nytimes.com/2014/08/21/opinion/charles-blow-constructing-a-conversation-on-race.html?_r=0

Sample Test Questions:
HANDLING DIFFICULT CONVERSATIONS

1. Studies indicate that some men tend to communicate with an emphasis on:
   A. Interdependence and cooperation
   B. Independence and competition
   C. Aggression and intimacy

2. Giving constructive feedback includes all of the following criteria EXCEPT:
   A. Timing it well
   B. Requesting alternatives
   C. Documenting the feedback

3. The three main components to any communications are:
   A. Subject matter, medium of delivery, and cultural considerations
   B. Sender, receiver, and message
   C. Language, context, and listening

4. According to the United Nations, all are top three languages in the world EXCEPT:
   A. Mandarin
   B. Spanish
   C. German

5. In communication, "perception of space" refers to:
   A. The distance one maintains while interacting
   B. The sense of urgency when one sets a meeting
   C. The nonverbal cues given during a meeting

6. Silent language such as gestures, eye contact, and tone of voice convey information and is known as:
   A. Intercultural communication
   B. Nonverbal communication
   C. Cultural communication

HANDLING DIFFICULT CONVERSATIONS (cont'd)

7. Thinking and reasoning is a degree of active listening that is involved in reflecting but is **NOT** involved in this degree of active listening:
   A. Remembering
   B. Paraphrasing
   C. Repeating

8. This physical listening barrier includes anything that interferes with communication:
   A. Feedback
   B. Bias
   C. Noise

9. Characteristics of effective feedback include:
   A. Only allowing managers to give feedback during appraisals
   B. Being true to your generation and speaking your mind
   C. Describing specific behavior and requesting alternatives

10. When giving effective feedback, direct your feelings toward the person, not the behavior.
    A. True
    B. False

11. Active listening is a structured way of listening and responding to others, focusing attention on the speaker.
    A. True
    B. False

12. If a D&I issue hasn't spiraled out of control, you should ignore the problem until it goes away.
    A. True
    B. False

13. Women may communicate in a way that fosters interdependence and cooperation.
    A. True
    B. False

RESOURCE GROUPS & DIVERSITY COUNCILS

> *Employee Resource Groups (ERGs) and Diversity Councils have become driving forces in organizational Diversity and Inclusion initiatives. Not only are they central to business strategies, but they can solve problems and serve as a public relations vehicle for the organization. As the next generation of Diversity and Inclusion thought leaders, these groups will become increasingly important.*

OVERALL OBJECTIVES AND COMPETENCIES

The purpose of this competency is to empower Diversity and Inclusion (D&I) leaders to collaborate with, and delegate to, internal allies in order to analyze the organizational climate, integrate D&I within business units, and achieve mission-centered objectives.

BACKGROUND AND CONTEXT

The first politically oriented affinity group surfaced during the anarchist and workers movement in the late 19th century. These anarchists fought fascism in Spain during the Spanish Civil War. Small circles of good friends, called "tertulias" would meet at cafes to discuss ideas and plan actions. In 1888, during a period of intense class conflict in Europe and of local insurrection in Spain, the Anarchist Organization of the Spanish Region made "tertulias" the preferred form of organization.

Decades later, the Iberian Anarchist Federation (FAI), which contained 50,000 activists, organized into affinity groups and confederated into local, regional, and national councils. Wherever several FAI affinity groups existed, they formed a local federation. Committees coordinated local federations, which consisted of one mandated delegate from each affinity group. Mandated delegates were sent from local federations to regional committees and finally to the Peninsular Committee. Affinity groups remained autonomous as they carried out education, organized protests, and supported local struggles. The intimacy of the groups made police infiltration difficult.

In July 1936, Francisco Franco, along with a group of fascist generals, launched a military revolt to take power from Spain's government. Spanish workers and peasants armed themselves and defeated the military throughout much of the country, particularly in Anarchist strongholds. Millions of Spaniards took action to restructure society along revolutionary lines—being careful not to revive the treacherous Spanish government.

Factories, transportation, communications, and even wholesale and retail stores were taken over and run collectively; an estimated 1200-1800 self-managed workers' collectives were formed. Worker 'self-management' effectively replaced the remnants of government and private institutions, providing for life's everyday necessities—food, clothing, shelter, and public services. The experience of working in non-hierarchical affinity groups created the conditions for 6 million people in Spain to reorganize society along revolutionary principles—taking charge of workplaces, agriculture, and communities without bosses and government.

The idea of large-scale, affinity group-based organization arrived in the United States on April 30, 1977, when 2,500 people, who were organized into affinity groups, occupied a Seabrook, New Hampshire nuclear power plant. The growing anti-nuclear power and disarmament movements adopted the affinity model and used it in many successful actions throughout the late 1970s and 1980s. Since then, the Central American solidarity movement, Gay Rights movement, Earth First and Earth Liberation movements, as well as many others have used the affinity group structure.

Today, as organized unions are on the decline, workers are finding a new voice in affinity groups (e.g., Diversity Councils and Resource Groups). Workers around the world are organizing with a purpose of changing corporate cultures and fostering inclusive business strategies.

Catalyst, a global research organization, found that there are different types of employee groups that employers can leverage to facilitate cultural change and manage Diversity and Inclusion successfully. In the Catalyst Information Center March 2013 report entitled, "*First Step: Diversity Councils*", these groups are listed as:

- **Advisory Board:** Unlike the members of a board of directors, an advisory board's members have no fiduciary responsibility to the organization or its stakeholders. These individuals serve in more of a mentorship capacity, and it is likely that there is a combination of external (e.g., community leaders) and internal (e.g., employees) members.

- **Diversity Council:** A diversity council serves as an advisory board to an organization and is made up of employees and/or external experts who "lead, advocate for, coordinate, inform, and/or monitor the Strategic Diversity Management process".

- **Executive Diversity Council:** Membership for this type of diversity council consists of leaders representing all business functions of the enterprise and is usually led by the chairman/CEO and the Chief Diversity Officer. This team is responsible for developing a company's overall integrated Diversity strategy.

- **Employee Resource Groups:** ERGs are voluntary, employee-led groups that can have a few members or a few thousand. Diversity councils and employee resource groups often collaborate when the group's leadership works as a council to oversee ground-level network activities.

According to the Society for Diversity, some organizations have advanced the concept of ERGs:

- **Business Resource Groups:** BRGs strategically impact the organization through intersectional, employee-led groups whose sole purpose is to solve real-life business problems, generate enterprise-wide opportunities through cross-functional collaboration, and offer long-term efficacy in pursuit of D&I goals.

For purposes of this competency, we will focus on the Diversity Council and Employee Resource Groups. Both employee-led groups provide an opportunity to leverage the knowledge, skills, and resources of workers, without assuming additional staff costs. Further, the Office of Diversity and Inclusion can extend its organization-wide impact with participation from high-profile employees.

DIVERSITY COUNCILS

Diversity is a complex issue that takes a lot of time and effort to fully integrate into business practices. For many organizations, diversity councils present a viable solution to increasing the capacity and effectiveness of the Office of Diversity.

A diversity council is a group of people who are charged with monitoring and making recommendations about hiring, retention, discrimination, and harassment, as well as other areas of diversity management. These volunteer employees serve as an advisory board to help senior management understand and enact diversity initiatives. Members of the council advocate for more inclusive practices within an organization, as well as monitor the implementation of the strategic diversity plan. They often gather data, help improve communications within the organization, recommend policies, and educate other employees about diversity.

The diversity council may work with a diversity practitioner or an Inclusion consultant. Alternatively, the Chairperson or Co-Chairperson of the diversity council may work in lieu of a full-time diversity practitioner. This is the approach used by many law firms. Nevertheless, the diversity council should be a fundamental part of the organizational structure. Effective diversity councils take leadership on diversity and offer innovative strategies to make inclusion a reality within the organization.

The majority of diversity councils meet quarterly, while others meet on a monthly basis. Members of the group represent every facet of the organization. These groups can be small or large, depending on the needs of the business. Positions held on the diversity council should not be permanent. Membership should rotate at regular intervals to ensure fairness and Inclusion. For example, a member may serve for 2 or 3 years, with several rotating seats available throughout the year. Senior managers should continually make recommendations for high-potential and influential employees to serve on the diversity council.

Two of the most common types of diversity councils are **internal diversity councils** and **external diversity councils**. An internal diversity council is comprised of employees within the company; an external diversity council functions similarly to a board of advisors. It may be comprised of educational and community leaders, business executives, or practitioners from the diversity industry. In large multinational organizations, as well as those that have been defendants in discrimination lawsuits, external diversity councils can be useful tools.

According to DiversityInc., external councils are rare—less than 10 percent of companies use them. That is why occasionally, organizations will have both types of councils or a hybrid of the two. Both types help an organization's reputation and can minimize or resolve diversity-related issues before they become liabilities.

Giving one group too much power, or power without accountability, is a sure path to trouble, and it is a common problem among diversity councils. According to Prism International, a diversity consulting organization, diversity should not "belong" to the council. Rather, responsibility for diversity initiatives should permeate all facets of an organization. Additionally, diversity councils could be perceived as just another grievance committee. Thus, CEOs should set the tone and scope of work for the council, as well as define a purpose linked to business objectives.

The Society for Diversity suggests that large organizations utilize more than one diversity council. To bolster the probability of success for diversity councils, a good idea might be to create a separate council for each location or division with 500 or more employees to ensure diversity objectives are accomplished. Moreover, your organization may need councils to address regional diversity concerns. Consider these questions to assess the need for regional or multiple diversity councils:

- Are there field offices, or divisions, in your organization with high levels of under-representation, or over-representation, of certain groups?
- Is the disability, religious, and caregiver accommodations sufficient?
- Are there high-levels of turnover among diverse groups in a field office or division?
- Are D&I directives from headquarters ignored or fulfilled haphazardly?

Having multiple diversity councils can ensure these issues are addressed quickly and completely. Furthermore, when operating globally, different diversity councils can address local inclusion issues. For example, depending on the country, issues with women, religion, LGBTQ+, or harassment may be exacerbated based on local customs. If an organization employs more than one diversity council, it would be advantageous to have a central coordinating body to track goals, nuances, and results of the council.

The council must have executive participation, a clear and focused mandate, expert facilitation, and a time-bound agenda. If the council has members drawn from a cross section of the organization, it may provide more meaningful input concerning relevant workplace issues. Accordingly, it is most important for a diversity council to set and achieve goals— which means having an agenda linked to organizational objectives.

How to Form a Diversity Council
Before starting a diversity council, *determine its intended purpose first*. Then, form the council with members that can achieve the objectives. Forming a council sounds simple, and it is. However, most councils are formed in reverse order. Typically, a group of interested people is convened and left largely on their own to figure out what to do. In this way, it may take them several years to "figure out" how to create a diversity plan or how to move Diversity and Inclusion forward. By providing direction in the construction of the council, this process is more effective and meaningful.

Creating a council charter will provide direction for the group. A council charter outlines the diversity council's vision, mission, objectives, leadership assignments, membership criteria, responsibilities, and operational procedures. The charter also serves as a reminder to volunteers that employees who serve on the council are expected to achieve organizational goals.
So, what does a successful diversity council look like? Once the purpose is established, consider these questions as a guide to ensure effectiveness in composition and mission of the council:

- What levels, functions, backgrounds, skills, and perspectives are needed to achieve the objective?

- Is there sufficient representation of diversity's dimensions on the team (i.e., Caucasian men, older/younger employees, different departments, various geographic locations, etc.)?
- Are the team members culturally competent and stellar role models?
- Has the necessary work been done to ensure that the council's recommendations will be heard and implemented?

During implementation, a well-focused diversity council can make many vital contributions. Potential roles include providing feedback, training, and serving as engaged mentors. The Association of Diversity Councils identified **10 recommendations for every diversity council:**

- A clear and approved charter
- Well defined mission and vision
- Executive support and participation
- Members that represent a cross-section of the organization
- A structure that reflects the culture of the organization
- A system and process to track and measure progress
- A strategic communications plan that reports progress and broadcasts diversity messages via multiple media sources
- A strong understanding of the organization's business objectives
- Links to other major company functions (HR, Communications, Operations, etc.)
- On-going member education and team building

According to the Harvard Business Review, diversity is good for business. Having a diversity council as a symbol of the organization's commitment to Diversity and Inclusion sends a clear message. It tells your customers, students, employees, and community that you are serious about creating opportunity for all individuals. It also demonstrates your organization's dedication to serving everyone well.

Nevertheless, Inclusion is hard work. A diversity council presents a strategic solution to spreading the work around to multiple individuals and to empowering an independent body to provide oversight of diversity initiatives. Councils heighten awareness of diversity issues and make employees more sensitive to inclusive practices. Moreover, with diverse representation, diversity councils are more acceptable for inspiring Diversity and Inclusion Champions.

EMPLOYEE RESOURCE GROUPS (ERGs)

Employee Resource Groups (also commonly referred to as Affinity Groups, Associate Resource Groups, Employee Network Groups, and Business Resource Partners) are independent, voluntary groups of employees who share common interests, backgrounds, and/or goals. Employee Resource Groups (ERGs) are forums for employees that create and foster an inclusive environment in which employees feel challenged, empowered, and supported in developing and maximizing their personal potential and value to the organization.
ERG's offer employees the opportunity to:

- Network and engage in dialogue with other employees who have common interests and goals
- Develop new skills-- enabling employees to learn, grow and achieve
- Play a role in initiatives that positively affect employees throughout the company

- Become more involved in surrounding communities
- Foster a creative, innovative work atmosphere
- Improve communication and inclusion across the organization
- Develop metrics on diversity progress
- Track recruitment and retention
- Coach new hires
- Identifying new markets, donors, customers, agents, vendors & students
- Serve as external ambassadors
- Participate in fundraising, or sales and marketing efforts
- Recommend systemic interventions to diversity barriers
- Conduct Executive Briefings

Many organizations have both an Employee Resource Group and a Diversity Council. The difference between the two is that the ERG is a group of employees who share similar interests and goals, while the Diversity Council may be a part of the internal organizational structure by functioning as an advisory board to the President/CEO, Diversity Officer, or senior executive team. Both groups have a specific plan of action, and both are expected to obtain measurable results.

CASE STUDY

Aerospace Corporation has made significant progress from 0.01 percent women in their technical workforce in 1962 to 12.5 percent women in 1993. Its recruitment of women is aided by the involvement of many women who serve as mentors, by policies and practices that are attractive to women, and by many dedicated people who are working toward creating a positive climate that contributes to the successful recruitment of women.

Women's committees or networks within a company can be vitally important influences on the recruitment and retention of women. The Women's Network at Aerospace has been not only a leader for change, but also a strong support system that has helped women gain confidence. Issues addressed through the Women's Network include:

- *Developing a maternity leave policy*
- *Equalizing employee benefits for secretarial and technical staff*
- *Establishing awards for women*
- *Researching and making recommendations to the president and executive staff on female candidates for the board of directors*

Employee Resource Groups are invaluable assets to universities, corporations, nonprofits, and government agencies. The effective resource group:

- Reduces social isolation
- Can help increase Diversity and Inclusion in the management ranks
- Aids in recruiting and retaining superior diverse talent
- Has a plan
- Tackles real life problems
- Works together with the other employee resource groups

Some educational institutions and corporations provide each resource group with a small budget to manage. The ERG may use the funds for professional development, philanthropy, marketing, and other business expenses.

Forming Special Groups
Employee Resource Groups exist for all types of employees: Women, Blacks, Latinos, Asians, Veterans, LGBTQ+, individuals with disabilities, caregivers, single parents, new dads, Millennials, Gen Xers, Baby Boomers, and more. Not only are these groups a viable source of support, but they can also be strategic to the organization's achievement of Diversity and Inclusion goals. However, like the Diversity Council, ERG's must be built around organizational goals—not individual issues.

Today, more organizations are shifting away from uni-dimensional identifiers for groups. For instance, there may be a transgender that does not want to participate in the LGBTQ+ network, or a multi-racial employee that does not feel comfortable participating in the African American network. Additionally, some companies do not want employee resource groups developed around "Affirmative Action" labels. Therefore, organizations are creating names for the groups that are consistent with business functions, such as the Talent Development Resource Group, Market Outreach Network, or the Strategic Alliances Group.

The creation of Business Resource Groups (BRGs) is a relatively recent development in the D&I space. BRGs are designed to strategically impact the organization and are particularly effective in identifying real business pain-points and driving real-life solutions. BRG's particularly bring value because they offer long-term functionality as organizations transition away from uni-dimensional groups. ERGs have evolved into BRGs because the latter makes room for overlapping or intersecting dimensions of diversity. Some organizations have already fully transitioned to BRGs while others employ a hybrid concept, where the most active ERGs remain and everyone else is rolled into a BRG. If there is a specific need that must be addressed, it is possible for the BRG to form temporary or permanent committees/task forces to address the requirement.

Additionally, some employers have wondered whether to allow Caucasian men to form a Resource Group, and the answer is yes! Using the BRG framework, the group may be called "Global Managers Network", or the "Innovation Network" in order to be representative of the titles or work that they perform, since many white males are in leadership positions. Current and aspiring global supervisors would be welcome. Keep in mind, some employees may still have negative reactions to forming an ERG for white men. Therefore, diversity practitioners must prepare justification for such a group, and in some cases, expect backlash from the underrepresented groups who believe that D&I efforts should only focus on them. Of the utmost importance is understanding the imperative that all groups are allowed the opportunity to be represented and feel welcomed.

Keep in mind, diversity is *not* Affirmative Action. Including Caucasian males is an important part of one's strategic Inclusion efforts. First, white men are the minority in many occupations, such as nursing, K-12 education, and on many college campuses. It would behoove an educational institution to develop a strategy to increase representation among Caucasian men, as well as all other diverse students, faculty and staff. Second, white men will soon be the minority around the world, and it is equally important to ensure engagement and professional development. Caucasian men may not request an ERG for themselves, in fear of being labeled a racist or Klansman, or some other unflattering name. However, depending on your business strategy, it may make sense to voluntarily offer one.

Jennifer Brown, President and CEO of Jennifer Brown Consulting, created the ERG Progression Model in Figure 1 to illustrate the transition from Affinity Groups to ERGs to BRGs.

FIGURE 1.

ERG Evolution: Affinity Groups to BRGs

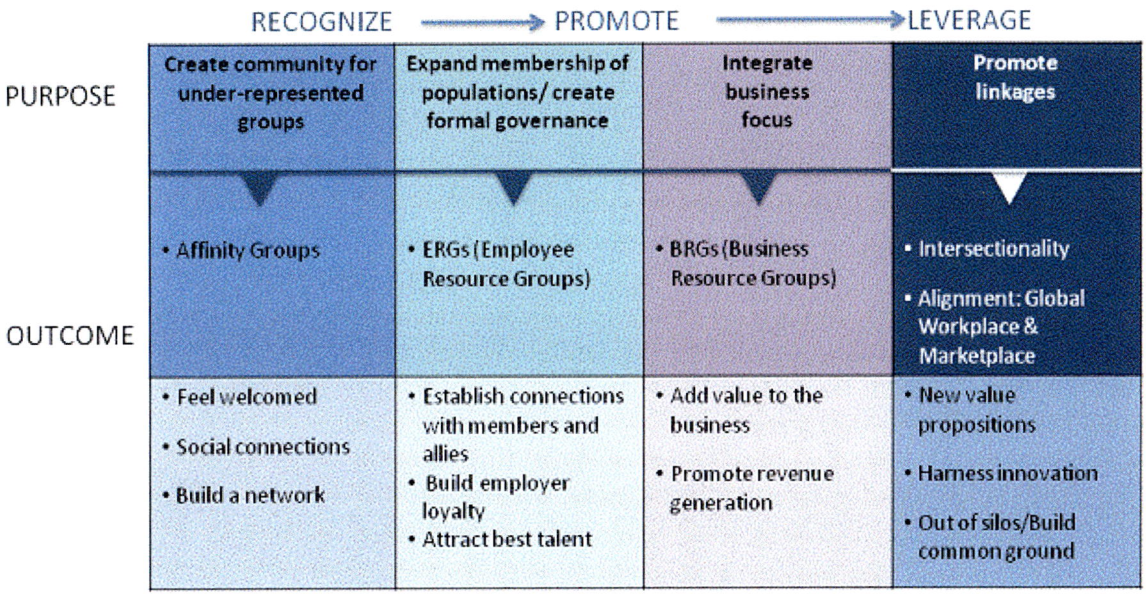

	RECOGNIZE →	PROMOTE →	→ LEVERAGE	
PURPOSE	Create community for under-represented groups	Expand membership of populations/ create formal governance	Integrate business focus	Promote linkages
OUTCOME	• Affinity Groups	• ERGs (Employee Resource Groups)	• BRGs (Business Resource Groups)	• Intersectionality • Alignment: Global Workplace & Marketplace
	• Feel welcomed • Social connections • Build a network	• Establish connections with members and allies • Build employer loyalty • Attract best talent	• Add value to the business • Promote revenue generation	• New value propositions • Harness innovation • Out of silos/Build common ground

Source: Association for Talent Development, 2016

According to Nadine Vogel, disability expert, President and Founder of Springboard Consulting LLC, employees with disabilities are also unlikely to come forward and ask their employer to create a networking group. As a result, companies may believe that there is no interest in such a group. Vogel adds, "It has nothing to do with interest; it has to do with the fear of repercussions if there isn't company support for the group".

Vogel says organizations may find that it is best to create two different disability-related groups: one for employees with a disability and one for employees with a child or dependent with special needs. She asserts, "The parents group sometimes has a hard time sitting in the same room with the adults with disabilities; the issues are different. Companies have later separated the groups and said that it worked much better."

Vogel says disability-related groups, if formed, should be structured the same as other employee resource groups. She states, "There needs to be a sense that there is a business imperative. They should talk about the mission and intent behind such a group. What are you hoping these groups are going to do?"

Likewise, when forming an ERG for the LGBTQ+ community, it is important to consider the support you will need to ensure participation, address negative reactions, and achieve the goals of the group. Some employees may be reluctant to participate in fear of "coming out of the closet". Furthermore, in foreign countries, the group may not have high levels of participation due to cultural ideals of masculinity, femininity, or religious beliefs. These issues may have to be resolved before expecting widespread participation in an LGBTQ+ resource group. Some employers have added "A" for "And Allies" to the end of LGBTQ+, so as not to distinguish between the LGBTQ+ community and its allies, who may be heterosexual.

Examples of initial goals include reviewing the employer's LGBTQ+ related policies and making recommendations for policy improvements, as well as evaluating the LGBTQ+ inclusiveness of the organization's diversity training programs. Other initiatives may include identifying opportunities for the organization to engage LGBTQ+ consumers, such as obtaining a booth at an LGBTQ+ pride event, launching an LGBTQ+ inclusive advertising campaign, and strategic philanthropy to LGBTQ+ community-based organizations.

About Selecting an Executive Sponsor

The executive sponsor fills an important and multi-faceted role. He or she alternates between coach and tiebreaker, advocate and adversary. Additionally, he or she can clearly proselytize the value of Diversity and Inclusion to the business. A 2005 research study reported that project success rates were proportional to the organization's sponsorship capabilities. Concurrently, the combination of fuzzy role definitions and the misinterpretation of priorities mean that more often than not, executive sponsors do not measure up.

You have doubtlessly seen an ivory tower manager somewhere in your company. He or she is the one that never leaves the office. Sometimes he or she shuts his door to avoid interruptions. In this case, the acronym MBWA does not mean, "management by walking around," but "management by *waiting* around". If no one walks through the doorway or schedules a meeting, the perception is that everything is good.

This type of Figurehead may agree to be an executive sponsor. However, he/she will do little to support Diversity and Inclusion efforts by sponsoring exactly what is requested—no more, no less. If the ERG initiative is successful, this individual will be proud to represent it at the next executive management meeting off site. If the initiative fails, he or she will point an index finger in the direction of the D&I leader. Then he/she will close the door and hide behind the undeserved title that invited the sponsorship request in the first place—until the next sponsorship opportunity rolls around.

Generally, there is no rulebook for the role of executive sponsors. Therefore, each sponsor must personify the role. The executive sponsor is most likely adding the role to an already full plate. Consequently, the person must be comfortable with the additional time demands of the role. Additionally, Diversity and Inclusion practitioners should understand how the potential sponsor operates in crisis mode in the event that a problem arises.

Of course, the best way to choose an executive sponsor is not to choose one at all, but for the sponsor to self-select. With most Diversity and Inclusion initiatives, an executive in an influential position must envision the desired outcome and support its success. He or she must have the energy to propel the initiative forward, the organizational authority to get people to listen, the passion to evangelize the benefits, and the time management skills to participate at the level needed. In this role, he or she performs a service to the project and to the company by setting an example of good project sponsorship and solid leadership.

The second-best sponsors are those who vet the role that is requested of them. They ask what needs to be done, decide whether they could contribute, and inherently know that they will be effective before saying yes.

Ideally, each ERG would have an Executive Sponsor. This helps ensure senior management accountability for Diversity and Inclusion objectives, and it is a good way for executives to maintain visible support of Diversity and Inclusion efforts. The role of Executive Sponsor can be for a term (e.g., one year) and/or the position can rotate—giving senior executives an opportunity to learn about multiple facets of diversity as well as about employee concerns and objectives. From the employee perspective, it provides an opportunity to build relationships with senior level executives and stay focused on organizational objectives.

Today, securing Executive and Leadership support for ERG's is no longer the challenge. The biggest challenge is overcoming the passive resistance exhibited by business-unit leaders and middle managers during program execution.

Leaders often tend to withhold support of initiatives perceived to be a distraction, or perhaps less important than other drivers of productivity and goal achievement. However, by establishing a clear and measurable approach, it often becomes illogical for leaders to withhold their support as they come to realize the real potential to enhance key business drivers that Resource Groups can provide. Again, this is where Executive Sponsors can play a key role in garnering support from, and making a connection to, mid-level managers and business unit leaders.

HOW TO FORM AN EMPLOYEE RESOURCE GROUP

As illustrated in Figure 2, the smartest organization will form an ERG with the purpose of being able to measure the group's impact. The group should be structured carefully so that:

- There is a business reason for the existence of each group
- A minimum number of documented members participate
- An annual plan of activities and events can be developed and maintained
- A succession plan is built into the leadership model to ensure continuity
- A sponsor from the executive level can lead the ERG accountability and evaluation process

FIGURE 2: ATTRIBUTES OF EFFECTIVE RESOURCE GROUPS

Purpose → Planning → Protocol → Partnerships

Source: The Society for Diversity, 2011

By structuring the group properly, your organization can avoid common pitfalls such as:

- *Peer Pressure to Conduct Activities Outside the Scope of the Charter*
- *Gossip or Gripe Sessions; Glorified Book Clubs*
- *Unfocused or Inactive Groups; "Events Based" Diversity Initiatives*
- *Inability to Work with Other Groups to Achieve Goals or Pool Resources*

Additionally, make sure the ERG is within the confines of the law. ERG's cannot:

- *Discuss Union Issues (such as work hours, assignments, pay or promotions)*
- *Show Favoritism in Group Formation*
- *Exclude Individuals from Participation*

Within each group, there will be structural roles and meeting specific roles. For example, a structural role would be a Chairperson, Vice Chairperson, Treasurer, or Secretary. An example of a meeting specific role would be facilitator, note taker, peacekeeper, or refreshments coordinator.

Pertaining to group development, each ERG should have a charter detailing the: *mission, target audience, short & long-term goals, plan of action, timeline, budget, key partners, and measurable benefits to the organization.*

This means that each Employee Resource Group will have a diversity plan and annual evaluation criteria. These plans should support the overall Diversity and Inclusion strategy, which will support the overall organizational strategy.

Within every organization, there are high performing groups and underperforming groups. In the event that a group performs well, you may want to provide more opportunities for corporate visibility and recognition. If a group underperforms, you may have to take proactive action to assist in the group's success. This may require replacing an ERG leader or providing coaching from a sponsor or higher performing group. At any rate, you cannot allow an underperforming group to remain dormant.

ERGs need to understand the functional and organizational business goals and ask, "How can we help?" The diversity practitioner must then make sure that the visible work of the ERG is tied to business drivers, and that the ERGs are not just doing one-off events. Here, purpose and vision are the key components of effectiveness.

By employing these methods, human resource and diversity leaders will know how to help ERGs move forward. By advancing a clear plan that includes goals, metrics, measurement tools, and strategies, ERGs can be instrumental in advancing organizational Diversity and Inclusion efforts.

Partnering with Other Groups
ERG's may need to partner with other affinity groups or community organizations to advance corporate Diversity and Inclusion goals. Before partnering, the ERG should address the following questions in respect to working with **internal** groups:

- What guidelines will be in place for joint projects?
- What communication vehicles will work best to keep everyone in the loop?
- How can duplication of effort be avoided?

- What process will be used to refer individuals to other groups?
- How will best practices be shared with current and new groups?

When working with **external** groups, such as other ERG's within a university system, nonprofit organizations, or other outside affinity groups, the ERG must address these questions:

- Which community-based organizations support the mission?
- What is the best way to coordinate activities & initiatives (i.e., events, seminars, fundraising, or support for legislation)?
- Where should joint activities & accomplishments be publicized?

By working together on certain projects, ERG's can supplement their accomplishments and gain additional support, internally and externally. This will positively affect sustainability and add to the credibility of the overall Diversity and Inclusion strategy.

References:

Building a Diverse Work Force: Scientists and Engineers in the Office of Naval Research (1997). National Academies Press: Washington, DC. Appendix D: Examples of Successful Diversity Initiatives in Other Organizations

Derven, Marjorie. *What's Next for Employee Resource Groups?* Association for Talent Development, January 22, 2016. Retrieved from: https://www.td.org/insights/whats-next-for-employee-resource-groups

Sample Test Questions:
RESOURCE GROUPS & DIVERSITY COUNCILS

1. The four P's of an effective Employee Resource Group are: Purpose, Plan, Protocol, and
   A. Prevention
   B. Partnerships
   C. Participation

2. The two types of roles that Employee Resource Groups need to establish for participants pertain to:
   A. Chairperson and Facilitator
   B. Chairperson and Vice-Chairperson
   C. Organizational structure and meeting specific

3. A(n) _____ is the organizational document that describes an Employee Resource Group's mission, goals and plan of action.
   A. Charter
   B. Agenda
   C. Strategic Plan

4. Affinity groups started with these individuals, who were a small group of friends that met to discuss ideas and plan actions.
   A. Allies
   B. Tertulias
   C. Strategists

5. A Diversity Council is a group of employees who serve as a(n):
   A. Advisory Board
   B. Rubber Stamp
   C. Workers Union

6. Are there white male resource group best practices?
   A. White males are only allies in other groups and cannot have their own group.
   B. No, because white males do not need an employee resource group in the work place.
   C. Yes, a white male resource group is an important part of a diversity program.

7. Legally, Employee Resource Groups are not permitted to discuss union issues such as:
   A. Work hours
   B. Strategic plan goals
   C. Equal pay

RESOURCE GROUPS & DIVERSITY COUNCILS (cont'd)

8. When starting a Diversity Council, most organizations:
   A. Determine the intended purpose first, and then choose members
   B. Choose members based on their passion for Diversity and Inclusion
   C. Recruit members first, and then develop the purpose

9. All of the following meaningful contributions can be made by a well-focused Diversity Council EXCEPT:
   A. Teaching and training
   B. Providing feedback
   C. Gossiping and complaining

10. For employee resource groups, the role of an executive sponsor is to:
    A. Serve as a figurehead
    B. Advocate and coach
    C. Manage the project

11. Securing Executive and Leadership support for ERG's is no longer the challenge.
    A. True
    B. False

12. The Employee Resource Group and Diversity Council are the same so companies can advance their diversity efforts by choosing one or the other.
    A. True
    B. False

13. As organized unions are on the decline, workers are finding a voice in Affinity groups.
    A. True
    B. False

EMPOWERING WOMEN IN THE WORKPLACE

> *Oftentimes, when we refer to Women in the workplace, we speak as if we are talking about one monolithic group, with similar backgrounds, interests, needs, ideas and expectations. The reality is that women are as diverse as the general population, and we should acknowledge that a one-size fits all approach is not sufficient for addressing the needs of such a sizable component of the educational landscape, workforce, and marketplace. Additionally, women can have multiple overlapping or intersecting identities– making representation with just one female a skewed approach to diversity.*

OVERALL OBJECTIVES AND COMPETENCIES

The purpose of this competency is to develop interventions that will eliminate the gender gap in compensation, promote work-life integration, build a diverse pipeline, and increase the overall inclusion of women in the workplace.

BACKGROUND AND CONTEXT

In 1941, nearly 7 million American women entered the workforce, thanks to a shortage of workers during World War II. With this significant influx of women in the workforce, and the following legislation and accomplishments, the workplace was forever changed:

- 1963 – **The Equal Pay Act** made it illegal to pay women less than men for the same job--although today on average, women are still being paid 20-40% less than men, depending on the occupation and the woman's race/ethnicity.
- 1964 – **Title VII of the Civil Rights Act** banned discrimination in employment on the basis of race and sex.
- 1970's – Women began to flood colleges and graduate schools, entering professions such as medicine, law, and business.
- 1976 – **The Pregnancy Discrimination Act** banned employment discrimination against pregnant women.
- 1986 – **Meritor Savings Bank v. Vinson** was a landmark decision in which The Supreme Court declared sexual harassment as a form of illegal discrimination.
- 2009 – President Obama signed the Lilly Ledbetter Fair Pay Act, which allows women to seek redress for grievances six months after receiving any discriminatory paycheck.
- 2009-2010 – According to the U.S. Department of Education, women earned the majority of degrees at all levels (Associates, Bachelors, Masters, and Doctorate) within each racial/ethnic group.
- 2016 – One hundred and five (105) Women served in the U.S. Congress.

Despite these significant events and ground-breaking legislation, many statistics show that women continue to lag far behind their male counterparts in terms of compensation, promotions, and development. Catalyst cites 10 issues of importance to women when it comes to advancing within organizations:

1) Flexible work arrangements - allowing employees to manage career and personal priorities.
2) Equal pay – ensuring that women do not continue to lag behind men in pay.
3) Race and gender bias – removing biases against women of color based on race/ethnicity, culture, language, and other distinctions.
4) Access to hot jobs – offering women more high-visibility and mission-critical roles.
5) Role models – providing access to senior or successful female role models.
6) Sponsorship – encouraging more leaders to sponsor or advocate for highly qualified women
7) Sexual harassment – preventing harassment from affecting women at all levels.
8) Non-inclusive workplaces
9) Double-bind – eliminating the fact that women leaders are viewed as being *either* competent *or* liked.
10) LGBTQ+ protection – including LGBTQ+ women in all of the power structures.

Globally, actions to remedy the disparities in compensation and benefits are underway. The International Monetary Fund (IMF) has raised issues around women in the workforce in its regular reviews of the economies of Japan, Italy, Germany and other nations. IMF asserts that putting more women in jobs is good for the world economy-- citing research that predicts a permanent rise in Gross Domestic Product (GDP), from 4 percent in France and Germany to 34 percent in Egypt, once the employment gap between men and women closes in those countries. Gender parity is also predicted to increase GDP by 12 percent among all Organization for Economic Cooperation and Development (OECD) countries.

IMF has been recommending ways to give women more incentives to join the labor force across the world. In crisis-hit Portugal, for example, tax policy discriminates against second-earners, as it does in France and the United States. Because second-income earners in these countries tend to be women, the tax policy can act as a disincentive for women entering the labor force.

In Germany, there is no tax on what is considered "mini jobs." These are jobs that pay less than 450 euros per month. Currently, one in five German workers has such employment. These positions make it easier to balance work and motherhood. Yet "mini-jobs" have also been blamed for trapping people in low-paid employment, without benefits or the chance for advancement. Hence, the IMF is suggesting that Germany takes measures to promote full-benefit jobs by lowering the tax bills for low-wage earners.

In its last annual assessment of the Italian economy, the IMF recommended measures to address Italy's very low female employment rate -- one of the lowest among the developed economies of the OECD. The IMF recommended that Italy make provisions for more child-care and maternity support. Additionally, it was suggested that "reducing the marginal tax rates for married second earners would help raise female labor participation" in Italy.

The IMF made similar recommendations in its most recent evaluation of the Japanese economy, calling for the full integration of Japanese women into the economy to compensate for the nation's demographic decline and spur growth. The government of Prime Minister Shinzo Abe has pledged to provide child-care facilities in Japan for all starting in 2017.

According to Business Insider, since 2012, Prime Minister Abe has sought to put more women into the labor force in the hopes of increasing Japan's growth potential. The effort has been nicknamed *womenomics*. "The basic thinking behind this strategy is that more women working means an increase in both potential output and improvement in women's income, which, theoretically, means that they will be able to spend more as consumers."

Around the world, embracing women in the workplace is a labor shortage solution and the key to economic development. At issue are those actions and policies that would ensure work-life integration, inclusion in leadership roles, and gender equality.

There is no simple solution to addressing gender employment issues. At best, it requires a commitment from employers, legislators, families and individuals in the broader community, in order to develop solutions and effect genuine change.

DEFINING & PROMOTING GENDER EQUALITY IN THE WORKPLACE

What is gender equality? This question is often asked; however, for many organizations there is no clear definition of gender equality. Usually when we have no clear definition for something, we become susceptible to disaster, heated debates, and arguments that are meaningless in resolving matters.

Removing these debates in the workplace is important so that all individuals can effectively contribute to the company's strategic goals. The truest definition of **gender equality** is when men and women share equal rights and responsibilities. However, while understanding the definition is valuable, companies should turn their attention to addressing issues of gender inequality in their individual workplaces—because doing so allows employees to build stronger alliances, as well as enables the entire team to contribute to organizational success.

Women entering the workforce have had an inadvertent effect on society. For instance, birthrates have decreased significantly, contributing to an impending labor shortage in developed nations. In the United States, where fertility rates remain high, 20% of women are childless, which is twice as many as 30 years ago, according to the Centers for Disease Control and Prevention (CDC).

To curb the decline in the birthrate in recent decades, some European governments have re-evaluated their family policies. Germany's example is especially instructive. In Germany, a parent who stays home with a child receives 67% of his or her current net income for up to 12 months. Although the state's family policies are now among the most generous in Europe, they have failed to boost the birthrate or reverse the figures for childless women.

Germany's policies provide considerable financial help; however, they essentially encourage mothers to quit the work force (recent figures show that only 15% of fathers take advantage of the leave). Only an astonishing 14% of German mothers with one child resumes full-time work. Thus, the family policies end up promoting the role of *father-provider*, while mothers in effect feel the need to choose between family and work from the moment the first child is born-- an especially risky proposition when one in three German marriages ends in divorce.

In this situation, where a high number of mothers are able to stay at home, but the birthrate remains exceptionally low, the message is clear: Women do not want policies that serve only to support mothers in their family life. For women to want children, they require policies that support the full range of their needs, roles and ambitions: maternal, financial, and professional.

The varying European experiences show that the highest birthrates exist in the countries with the highest rates of working women. Therefore, it is in society's interest to support working motherhood, which requires considerable public investment. Generous leave is not, in and of itself, an incentive. To raise more than one child, a mother must have access to high-quality, full-day child care, as well as income equality, flexible work hours and partners sharing family-related tasks. These are the essential components that will allow women to be mothers without forgoing their other aspirations.

Ruth Mayhaw, eHow contributing writer asserts, "It is important to acknowledge that where gender inequality exists, it is generally women who are excluded or disadvantaged in relation to decision-making and access to economic and social resources." While there is urgency to include all women, organizations must be intentional in their efforts to develop, promote, and retain multicultural women so that economic and social gaps do not persist.

Carol Evans, President of Working Mother Media, says:

> I've heard white women say, privately, that they do not see color; that they are always "nice" to women of color; that they feel united with women of color in the struggle to gain equal rights from men. These are great sentiments, but I've also heard white women acknowledge that as we pushed our way up the ladder of success into the all-male hierarchy, we did not reach out and bring many women of color up with us. We were so busy feeling left out and pushed back by the male power structure that we didn't see that women of color felt the same way about us as we felt about the men. This is the kind of unbridled honest dialogue that will push us forward.
>
> The most difficult topic we must address is trust. We've discovered that African-American women trust white women only half as much as they trust every other group. Companies need to face the barriers that still exist in promoting multicultural women through the ranks and create programs to give a voice to these issues within their own walls.

By analyzing these areas, and implementing and enforcing policies, processes, and procedures to close any gaps, gender equality is truly established because men and women share not only the same opportunities, but also the same constraints.

CLOSING THE GENDER COMPENSATION GAP

Compared to other countries, France has always been rather late in adopting gender equality as a goal and designing policies to achieve it. Nevertheless, after the success of its gender quota law for Boards of Directors, France realized that it can do more to foster pay equity with legislation. By the end of 2017, men were still paid on average 9% more than women in France despite equal pay laws going back 45 years. Across the 28 EU member states, the average "unexplained" gender pay gap is a little higher than France's at 11.5%, according to 2017 Eurostat figures.

France is determined to improve its gap. According to BBC News, in 2018, the French government proposed a plan to crackdown on unions and employers with a fine for those organizations that persist in paying men and women unequally. The law would monitor unexplained pay gaps with technology and increase compliance oversight with four times the current number of spot checks. The fine could reach 0.01% of the total payroll for firms who do not comply by 2020.

In 1963, American women who worked full-time, year-round earned 58.9% of what men did in similar jobs with similar hours. Today, women generally make 80% of a man's salary, according to the most recent figures from the U.S. Census Bureau. Keep in mind, that eighty cents on the dollar is roughly the pay gap for white women. The gap is even higher for black and Latino women, as evidenced in Figure 1.

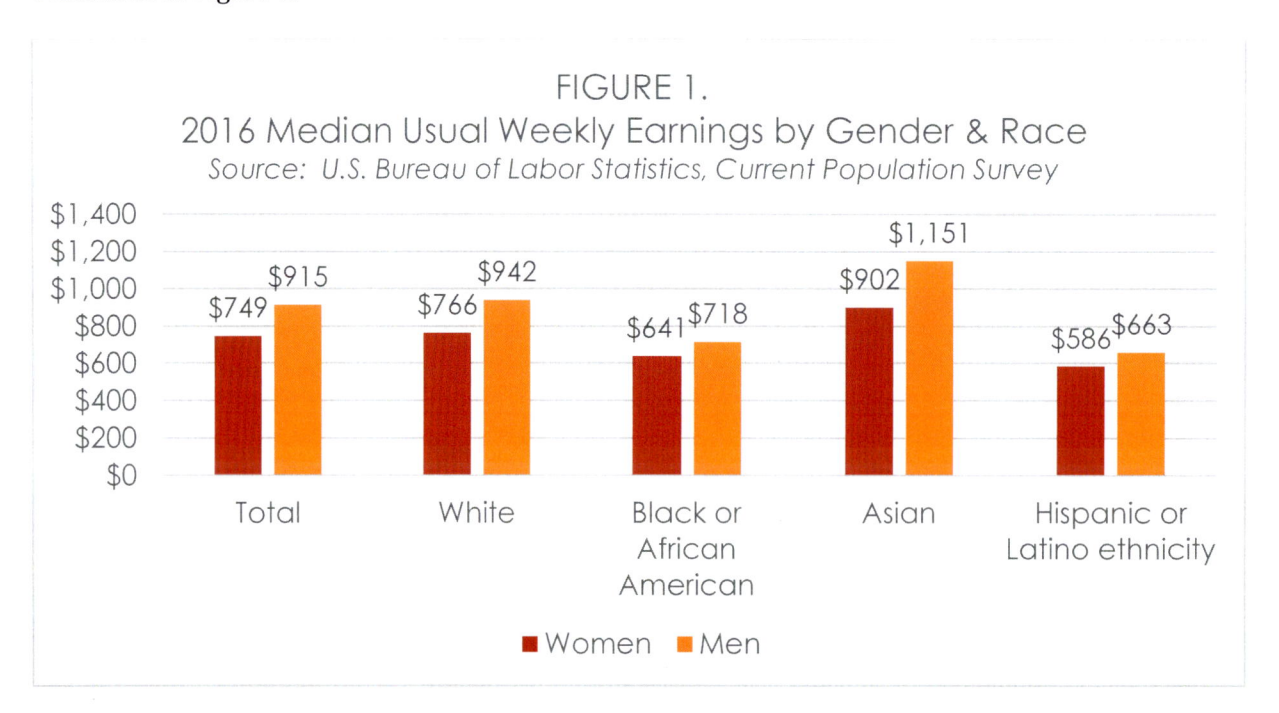

FIGURE 1.
2016 Median Usual Weekly Earnings by Gender & Race
Source: U.S. Bureau of Labor Statistics, Current Population Survey

Category	Women	Men
Total	$749	$915
White	$766	$942
Black or African American	$641	$718
Asian	$902	$1,151
Hispanic or Latino ethnicity	$586	$663

According to an October 2017 report by McKinsey & Company entitled *Women in the Workplace*, "One of the most powerful reasons for the lack of progress is a simple one: we have blind spots when it comes to diversity, and we can't solve problems that we don't see or understand clearly. Many employees think women are well represented in leadership when they see only a few. And because they've become comfortable with the status quo, they don't feel any urgency for change. Further, many men don't fully grasp the barriers that hold women back at work. As a result, they are less committed to gender diversity, and we can't get there without them. Many companies also overlook the realities of women of color, who face the greatest obstacles and receive the least support. When companies take a one-size-fits-all approach to advancing females, women of color end up underserved and left behind."

As we look towards the workforce of the future, organizations must get better at empowering Women of Color, as well as females with other underrepresented and/or intersecting dimensions of diversity. In order to improve, diversity leaders must be intentional about their inclusion efforts.

Education also plays a factor in American compensation, as the pay gap increases with education. Figure 2 illustrates the earnings gap by educational attainment and sex.

FIGURE 2.
U.S. Weekly Earnings in 2016 by Educational Attainment and Sex

Source: Bureau of Labor Statistics

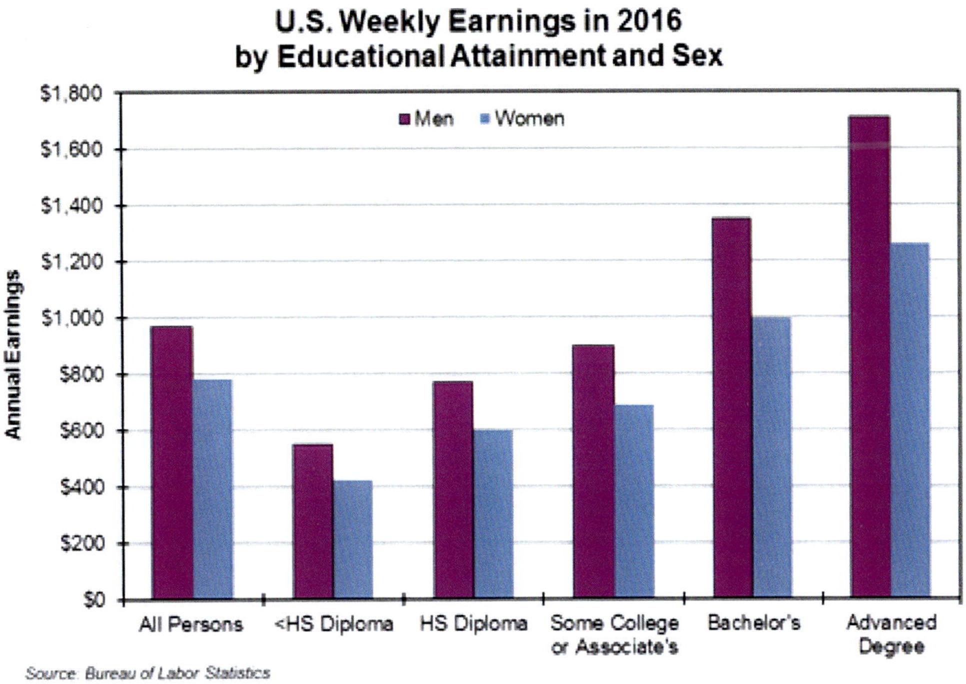

According to some experts, women earn less than men for a several reasons, including their college majors, occupations, and the number of hours they work. Today, women still tend to enter lower-paid fields such as education and social sciences, while men typically major in engineering and computer science.

Closing the gender compensation gap requires effort from several sources. Employers must act fairly without discrimination, the government must enforce current laws better, and women can do more research on salary data as well as become good negotiators. Some research has found that women are less likely to negotiate for higher salaries, and other studies have shown that women who do negotiate are perceived differently than men and may be penalized for negotiating.

As discussed in *EEO Laws in the U.S. and Abroad*, some states have begun to pass laws barring pay history questions during the interviewing process. According to the National Women's Law Center (NWLC), "Employers' requests for an applicant's salary history in the hiring process, and reliance on that information to determine compensation, forces women and, especially women of color, to carry lower earnings and pay discrimination with them from job to job." The NWLC found that:

- Some employers use salary history to determine a new hire's starting pay, providing a standard percentage increase over the new hire's previous salary or otherwise directly correlating the new hire's pay to her salary history.

- Some employers use salary history to screen out job applicants whose salaries, the employer determines, are too high or too low to allow them to be considered for the job. The employer assumes that someone whose salary is "too high" would not be interested in a lower-paying job and that someone whose salary is "too low" does not have sufficient skill, knowledge, or experiencc for the position.

- Some employers ask for salary history as part of the salary negotiation. Even if the employer is willing to pay an applicant significantly more than she previously made, the negotiation is likely to be affected by "anchoring," a cognitive tendency to heavily weight the first piece of information encountered during a decision-making process. Because of this cognitive bias, a low prior salary may have an outsized effect on the salary negotiation and the employer's perception of a reasonable salary for the employee, depressing the resulting salary offer.

- Some employers use salary history to evaluate and compare applicants' job responsibilities and achievements. As with screening, this practice assumes that prior salaries are an accurate measure of an applicant's experience and achievements, and not the product of discrimination, bias, or other factors that are simply irrelevant to the employer's business.

CASE STUDY

Xerox Corporate Research and Technology (CRT) is working towards making Xerox Corp. "the employer of choice for women and minorities." To meet its goal, a "Women's Council" was formed in 1991 to provide advice to senior management on issues related to recruiting and retaining women. Council members identified five problem areas:

- *The number of women in corporate research*
- *Career development*
- *Salary equity*
- *Working environment*
- *Benefits*

As a result, the following recommendations have been made:

- *Improve hiring and promotions*
- *Establish linkages with universities*
- *Create lateral hiring opportunities into other units of Xerox*
- *Allow cross-laboratory promotions*

Through the formation of the "Women Managers Roundtable," the company is introducing a change in culture from the top.

A best practice in gender compensation is to pay talent in accord with the job description. Therefore, any discrepancies in salary can be attributed to skill, required/preferred education, experience, etc. These divergences may be legally defensible so long as other factors are not considered such as race, sex, disability, age, sexual orientation, religion, etc.

Other Strategies That Help Close the Compensation Gap
In 2009, The Shriver Report was released, and its findings astonished many in education, government, and the workplace.

The Shriver Report describes how a woman's nation changes everything. For the first time in American history, women are half of all U.S. workers and mothers are the primary breadwinners or co-breadwinners in nearly two-thirds of American families. This is a dramatic shift from just a generation ago (in 1967, women made up only one-third of all workers).

When we look over the 21st Century, much has changed in families:

- Moms aren't home all day watching babies or waiting for the kids to come home from school. Yet, affordable, high-quality child care and flexible work hours are in short supply.
- Workplaces are no longer the domain of men. In fact, every worker under 40 has had either a mother in the workforce or has worked with women in some capacity during their entire careers.
- Most dual-income households share parental responsibilities, yet it is assumed that only women prefer to sacrifice their careers for their children and families.
- Women are no longer playing the role of the dependent, self-sacrificing spouse. They are pursuing advanced degrees, obtaining corporate leadership positions, and even filing for divorce at unprecedented rates.
- In some cases, women are the primary breadwinner in the household. If she is paid less, and her spouse is unemployed, it affects the family's viability.
- More than 66% of women serve as the lead financial decision maker at home, according to data from the Citibank-Owned Women & Co. Research Study, "Women & Affluence 2010: The Era of Financial Responsibility".

The Shriver Report asserts, "Government policies and laws continue to rely on an outdated model of the American family. And, despite the existence of innovative practices in corporate America, most employers fail to acknowledge or accommodate the daily juggling act their workers perform; they are oblivious to the fact that their employees are now more likely to be women; and they ignore the fact that men now share in domestic duties."

Families need more flexible work schedules, comprehensive child care policies, redesigned family and medical leave, and equal pay. As stated earlier in the October 2017 McKinsey report pertaining to blind spots, acknowledging that the workplace and the marketplace have changed is one of the keys to closing the gaps. Additionally, organizations must identify opportunities for women to advance—professionally and personally. Keep in mind, that advancing women does not necessarily mean that men must take a back seat; it simply means that everyone is doing their share to transform the American workplace into one of fairness and equality. Figure 3 identifies other opportunities to help women succeed.

FIGURE 3: HELPING WOMEN MOVE UP	
What organizations can do	**What women can do**
1) Formalize succession planning. 2) Recognize performance equally. 3) Monitor gender differences in salary. 4) Democratize development experiences. 5) Provide women with mentors. 6) Internationalize women's experiences. 7) Provide support for leadership transitions. 8) Make HR policies more family friendly.	1) Make intentions clear. 2) Consider multinational assignments. 3) Counteract behavioral stereotypes. 4) Seek opportunities. 5) Stay positive and take informed risks. 6) Choose wisely (women are already earning more than men in 80 fields). 7) Work full-time (i.e., time is money).
(Source: SHRM, 2009)	

The Role of HR & Diversity Professionals

HR and diversity professionals are the primary points for ensuring the rest of the workplace is practicing fairness. These roles must partner to increase knowledge of employment laws, and think strategically to anticipate future challenges—thus improving the organization's competitive advantage.

Some corporations have launched Employee Resource Groups for women, or they have entire business units that focus on women's issues. On college campuses alike, forward thinking institutions have appointed an individual to serve as the liaison for women. It is up to HR and the Office of Diversity to work together to determine the best approach to facilitate gender equality and identify support mechanisms to advance organizational objectives.

The San Francisco Department on the Status of Women and Calvert Group, Ltd. identified seven major areas where organizations may take steps to affect change in gender inequality. The areas are: employment and compensation; work-life balance and career development; health, safety and freedom from violence; management and governance; business, supply chain and marketing practices; civic and community engagement; and leadership, transparency and accountability.

HR and diversity professionals can evaluate the organization's programs and make recommendations to top level leaders for changing those programs that are not friendly to women's advancement and success.

PREPARING WOMEN FOR LEADERSHIP POSITIONS

At the 2011 TED Conference, Facebook's Chief Operating Officer (COO), Sheryl Sandberg asserted:

> For all the ceilings that have been shattered, we still have a real problem. Women became 50 percent of the college graduates in the United States in 1981. Since then, we have slowly and steadily made progress, earning increasingly more of the college degrees, taking more of the entry-level jobs, going into previously male-dominated fields, moving up each step of

the ladder. But there is one big exception to this improvement -- the top jobs. Thirty years later, we have not come close to holding our proportionate share of positions of power in any industry.

Sandberg added:

> Moreover, in the 2008 election, women lost seats in Congress for the first time in three decades. Across the corporate sector, women have held 15 to 16 percent of the C-level jobs and Board seats since 2002. Globally, only nine of 190 countries are led by women. So even as people worry about boys falling behind girls in education and write articles with headlines like "The End of Men," we have to acknowledge that men still run the world.

In fact, Senator Hillary Clinton made a second presidential run in 2016. She received the most votes and delegates in the 2016 Democratic primaries and formally accepted her party's nomination for President of the United States on July 28, 2016 with vice presidential running mate Senator Tim Kaine. She became the first female candidate to be nominated for president by a major U.S. political party. Nevertheless, as the most experienced candidate in the history of Presidential politics, Clinton lost the general election to Republican opponent Donald J. Trump, despite winning a plurality of the popular vote. For all of the conversations about less qualified diverse people, her experience became a snare that signified corruption. In fact, the nickname "Crooked Hillary" drove voters to choose a male candidate without any experience for the Office of the President of the United States. What's even more interesting is the number of women who did not believe that Clinton was a viable candidate.

One of the biggest issues in the workplace is the perceived lack of support for women by other women. If D&I leaders are honest, men are not the only individuals engaging in unfair pay and inequitable workplace practices—some women are too. The Harvard Business Review published an article entitled, *Women Rising: The Unseen Barriers,* in which it is acknowledged that "many women have worked hard to take gender out of the equation—to simply be recognized for their skills and talents." By attributing their success to merit alone, some women attempt to navigate, or negate, the existence of gender bias. The authors of Women Rising assert that "more than 25 years ago the social psychologist Faye Crosby stumbled on a surprising phenomenon: Most women are unaware of having personally been victims of gender discrimination and deny it even when it is objectively true and they see that women in general experience it."

Recognizing that women are diverse is one issue but creating a safe space in which females can strongly identify as a woman is another co-existing challenge. Marianne Cooper explains in *Why Women (Sometimes) Don't Help Other Women*, "For women with low levels of gender identification—who think their gender should be irrelevant at work and for whom connecting with other women is not important—being on the receiving end of gender bias forces the realization that others see them first and foremost as women. And because of negative stereotypes about women, like that they are less competent than men, individual women can be concerned that their career path may be stunted if they are primarily seen as just a woman and therefore not a good fit for leadership.

To get around these kinds of gendered barriers, these women try to set themselves apart from other women. They do this by pursuing an individual strategy of advancement that centers on distancing themselves from other women. One way they do this is through displaying Queen Bee behaviors such as describing themselves in more typically masculine terms and denigrating other women ("I'm not like other women. I've always prioritized my career")."

Cooper adds, "This kind of response is not even unique to women. It's actually an approach used by many marginalized groups to overcome damaging views held about their group. For example, research has found that some gay men try to distance themselves from stereotypes about gays being effeminate by emphasizing hyper-masculine traits and holding negative beliefs about effeminate gays. Social distancing then is a strategy many individuals use who are trying to avoid, escape, or navigate the social disadvantage of the group to which they belong."

Preparing women for leadership positions requires a thorough assessment of the existing policies, procedures, and culture that govern how opportunities are provided. This means, at a minimum, making sure that you understand the needs of the organization by conducting an in-depth analysis of the available support systems for gender equity, as well as examining the following:

- **Training & Development** – to increase its long-term effectiveness, training must be equally accessible and designed so that learning outcomes consider the needs of women.

- **Mentoring & Coaching** – while one of the best approaches to prepare women for leadership roles, mentors must be trained for sensitivity to women's needs.

- **Succession Planning** – talent review processes should be calibrated to effectively identify and rate the potential of female employees for senior leadership positions.

- **Global Concerns** – leaders must be aware of the laws, religions, and traditions that govern the countries they operate in, and adjust their programs for women to be successful.

It is important to note that without the supporting organizational structures, any strategies to help women become more promotable, will likely be 'eaten for lunch' by the existing culture. This means that in order for new strategies to succeed, the execution must include strong communication plans, accountability, and measurable outcomes to ensure that they are implemented well and sustained throughout all locations, divisions, and departments.

CASE STUDY

Jim Turley, former Chairman and CEO of Ernst & Young, described an incident in which he was called out for disregarding women's contributions: "I like to facilitate our board discussions by getting right into the more contentious points, and we were having a discussion around a particular topic. Three women on the board made individual comments that were similar in direction, which I didn't respond to. Not long after they spoke, a fourth person, who happened to be a man, made a comment in line with what the women had been saying, and I picked up on his comment. I said, 'I think Jeff's got it right,' not even aware of what I had just done. To their great credit, the women didn't embarrass me publicly. They pulled me to the side, and they said, 'Jim, we know you didn't mean for this to be the way it was received, but this is what happened.' They played it back to me, and they said that that's what happens to women throughout their careers. It was a learning moment for me."

Like the Ernst & Young Board Meeting scenario, D&I leaders may be placed in a comprising position when they do have to provide feedback for actions that were unfair or exclusive. This requires courage, as well as the ability to present alternative behaviors to remedy future problems.

ASSESSING WORKPLACE FAIRNESS & FAMILY FRIENDLINESS

As indicated in Figure 3, "Helping Women Move Up", HR and diversity professionals must play a pivotal role in ensuring that workplace policies are family friendly and fair. Policies support and encourage women to thrive in the workplace; therefore, if they do not already exist organizations should strive to develop policies that ensure inclusive cultures are established and supported. Two best practices regarding fairness and equity in the workplace include establishing a process for proper documentation and regular evaluation of the organization's total reward system—which consists of compensation, benefits, performance appraisals, training and development, and career opportunities. Benchmark tools, such as employee compensation and benefits surveys, can also be useful.

SHRM's recent report, **2013 Employee Benefits: An Overview of Employee Benefits Offerings in the U.S.,** lists a broad range of benefits that companies offer to help create fair environments: 53% have flextime; 35% offer a compressed workweek; 34% have on-site lactation/mother's rooms; 20% offer mentoring programs; 19% have shift flexibility; 58% offer telecommuting; 10% allow job sharing; 16% offer paid maternity leave and 15% offer paid paternity leave; 12% offer a child care referral service; 4% offer subsidized child care; and 3% offer prepared take-home meals. One percent (1%) of employers offer unique programs such as on-ramping programs for family members dealing with elder care issues and for parents re-entering the workforce. By providing such benefits, organizations demonstrate that fairness matters in their workplace.

Through a systematic assessment, HR and diversity professionals can obtain a true picture of the situation and determine what needs to be done. Figure 4 presents examples of actions that HR and diversity professionals can take to evaluate fairness in their workplace.

FIGURE 4: ACTIONS TO EVALUATE FAIRNESS IN THE WORKPLACE

Action	Examples
Examine the Organizational Culture	- *Review HR policies and practices to determine if they are fair and inclusive (e.g., pay differences, hiring practices, history of promotions to senior positions, affirmative action plans, etc.).* - *Examine the organization's informal culture: look at subtle behaviors, traditions, norms, and unwritten rules.* - *Through surveys and focus groups, determine employee perceptions about the organization's culture, their career expectations and what drives their intentions to stay or leave.* - *Identify the organization's best practices that support advancement for women.* - *Map the strengths and weaknesses of policies and programs.*

Drive Change Through Management Commitment	• Utilize sponsorships to strengthen executive commitment to talent management, including women in senior positions. • Ensure that diversity is a key business measurement for success and that it is communicated to all employees by top management. • Require line management accountability for advancing women by incorporating it in performance goals. • Train line managers to raise awareness of, and understand barriers to, advancement for women. • Engage managers as mentors or sponsors of Employee Resource Groups for women.
Foster Inclusion	• Establish and lead a change-management diversity program for managers and employees. • Confirm diversity's inclusion in all employment brand communications. • Develop a list of women to include in annual succession planning activities. • Develop and implement retention programs for women. • Ensure all programs for women do not unintentionally exclude multicultural females.
Educate and Support Women in Career Development	• Emphasize the importance of women acquiring line management experience. • Encourage mentoring via informal and formal programs. • Utilize successful senior-level women as role models. • Support the development and utilization of women and diverse networks inside and outside the organization. • Create and implement leadership development programs for women, including international assignments if applicable. • Train women in critical skills such as negotiating, developing confidence, managing emotions, delegating, and risk taking.
Measure for Change	• Monitor the impact of recruiting strategies designed to attract women to senior levels of the organization. • Track the advancement of women within the organization (e.g., hiring, job rotations, transfers, international assignments, promotions). • Determine who gets access to leadership and management training and development opportunities. • Evaluate differences between salaries at parallel levels within the organization. • Measure and compare turnover for women and other groups within the organization. • Explore reasons why women and other diverse groups leave the organization.

Adapted from: Lockwood, N. (2004). *The glass ceiling: Domestic and international perspectives.* Alexandria, VA: Society for Human Resource Management.

Gender equity and equality in the workplace must be approached strategically—as a long-term process, not as a single event—with a focus on positively impacting the bottom line and fostering a workplace of choice for the brightest and most talented employees. Organizations must transition from coordinating a one-time event or initiative, towards implementing comprehensive interventions. From a tactical perspective, men must be included in the conversation about empowering and advancing women. As companions in the household, same sex partners, and/or team members at work, men have a lot to contribute to the conversation about fairness and equality for women. Men can also learn about different leadership and communication styles that are effective, as well as share skills and strategies that work. When men feel as if they are a part of the solution, they may play are greater role in working towards equity.

While quotas are not legal, organizations can set targets or goals for recruiting, engaging, and retaining women at every level of the organization. Finally, when organizations remember that all dimensions of women are valuable, its goals for including women will go a long way towards innovation, better management, and sustainability.

References:

Center for American Women and Politics, "*Women in the US Congress 2016/CAWP*", 2017. Available at https://www.cawp.rutgers.edu/women-us-congress-2016. Accessed: 5-Dec-2017

Catalyst: Workplaces that Work for Women, "*10 Big Issues Women Face at Work and What Leaders Can Do to Help*". Available at: https://www.catalyst.org. Accessed: 7-Dec-2017

Holodny, Elena. *This might be the 'silver lining' for Japan.* Business Insider, April 9, 2016. Retrieved from: http://www.businessinsider.com/japanese-women-entering-workforce-2016-4

BBC News. *France labour: Firms to be fined over gender pay gap.* March 7, 2018. Retrieved from: http://www.bbc.com/news/world-europe-43320041

McKinsey & Company. *Women in the Workplace 2017.* October 2017 Report. Retrieved from: https://www.mckinsey.com/global-themes/gender-equality/women-in-the-workplace-2017

National Women's Law Center. *Asking for Salary History Perpetuates Pay Discrimination from Job to Job.* June 9, 2017. Retrieved from: https://nwlc.org/resources/asking-for-salary-history-perpetuates-pay-discrimination-from-job-to-job/

Shriver, Maria et al. *The Shriver Report: A Women's Nation Changes Everything.* Center for American Progress, October 2009. Retrieved from: https://www.americanprogress.org/issues/women/reports/2009/10/16/6789/the-shriver-report/

Ibarra, Herminia et al. *Women Rising: The Unseen Barriers.* Harvard Business Review, September 2013. Retrieved from: https://hbr.org/2013/09/women-rising-the-unseen-barriers

Cooper, Marianne. *Why Women (Sometimes) Don't Help Other Women.* The Atlantic, June 23, 2016. Retrieved from: https://www.theatlantic.com/business/archive/2016/06/queen-bee/488144/

2010 The San Francisco Department on the Status of Women and Calvert Group, Ltd. "*Gender Equality Principles, Building a 21st Century Workplace*", 2010. Available: genderprinciples.org/principles.php. Accessed: 5-Dec-2017

Groysberg, Boris and Connolly, Katherine. *Great Leaders Who Make the Mix Work*, (2013). Harvard Business Review. Retrieved from: https://hbr.org/2013/09/great-leaders-who-make-the-mix-work

Building a Diverse Work Force: Scientists and Engineers in the Office of Naval Research (1997). National Academies Press: Washington, DC. Appendix D: Examples of Successful Diversity Initiatives in Other Organizations

U.S. Equal Employment Opportunity Commission (EEOC), *Laws Enforced by EEOC*, (2017). Retrieved from https://www.eeoc.gov/laws/statutes/

Sample Test Questions:
EMPOWERING WOMEN IN THE WORKPLACE

1. Pertaining to work-life programs that promote equity for women, more companies offer this type of benefit compared to all other benefits.
   A. Flex time
   B. Mentoring
   C. Job sharing

2. Globally, organizations must be aware of the laws, religions, and traditions that govern the countries they operate in, and:
   A. Provide standard programs for women in each country of operation
   B. Adjust programs for women according to country customs
   C. Avoid hiring women in countries where discrimination is still high

3. Talent Review processes identify qualified candidates for promotions by:
   A. Calibrating the performance potential ratings of male and female employees
   B. Considering all relevant factors for promotional opportunities for men and women
   C. Creating management tracks for the best qualified male and female employees

4. Which training program is likely to help reduce the gender gap in promotions?
   A. Talent management
   B. Recruiting practices
   C. Diversity & Inclusion

5. Which of the following strategies will BEST help to close the gender compensation gap?
   A. Training senior leaders to encourage compensation plan changes
   B. Creating an analysis that highlights promotional challenges for women
   C. Evaluating pay equity among male and female employees and managers

6. Women in the workplace still lag behind their male counterparts in compensation because:
   A. The economy has not fully recovered from the recession
   B. Women tend to work part-time jobs or enter lower-paid fields
   C. Fewer development opportunities exist in executive level jobs

7. Men should be involved in the gender equity discussion because they are:
   A. Responsible for harassment, discrimination and inequity
   B. Companions, same sex partners and team members at work
   C. The only individuals who can lead inclusion in the workplace

Sample Test Questions:
EMPOWERING WOMEN IN THE WORKPLACE (cont'd)

8. The truest definition of gender equality in the workplace is when:
   A. Men and women share equal rights and responsibilities
   B. Women are compensated equally with their male counterparts
   C. Women hold significant leadership positions within the organization

9. While mentoring and coaching are among the best approaches to prepare women for leadership roles, male mentors and coaches must be:
   A. Trained for sensitivity to women's needs
   B. Experienced and senior level leaders
   C. Dedicated to mentoring/coaching for one year

10. Two key best practices regarding fairness and equity in the workplace are (1) establishing a process for proper documentation and (2):
    A. Introducing new family friendly events and policies annually
    B. Preventing harassment and sexist remarks in the workplace
    C. Regularly evaluating the organization's total reward strategy

11. According to the Bureau of Labor Statistics, the pay gap between American males and females decreases with education.
    A. True
    B. False

12. Companies should analyze the gender composition of the board of directors, executive leadership team, and staff, and make adjustments as necessary.
    A. True
    B. False

13. Providing women with mentoring, international work experience, and communication skills training can lead to entity-wide cultural change.
    A. True
    B. False

DISABILITY & SPECIAL NEEDS ACCOMMODATIONS

> *The disabilities that exist in the workplace stem from a variety of factors, and they may or may not be disclosed by an employee. To minimize legal issues in the work place, and enhance positive employee relations with the disabled workforce, managers and supervisors must be knowledgeable about the needs of individuals with disabilities, aware of related legislation, and sensitive to the responsibilities of caregivers.*

OVERALL OBJECTIVES AND COMPETENCIES

The purpose of this competency is to encourage employees to eliminate the stereotypes associated with workers who have visible and non-visible disabilities; help supervisors to provide appropriate accommodations upon request; and ensure disabled individuals are fully engaged in the workplace.

BACKGROUND AND CONTEXT

We often hear the term "disability" being used loosely. But different organizations classify disability differently. For example, workers compensation uses the term 'disability' when an employee is injured or becomes sick on the job. If an employee has a temporary work-related injury that lasts more than 7 days and results in lost time from work, then the employee may be eligible for compensation at a percentage of his/her normal salary. All medical care is covered by the workers comp insurance carrier, self-insured employer, or state operated plan, and it is separate from group health coverage. An employee must be released to return to work after sustaining a job-related injury. Otherwise, an injured worker may return to work on light or modified duty.

Under workers comp, there may be different disability classifications such as:

- **Temporary Total Disability**: When a worker is *completely* disabled for a limited period. The employee is expected to eventually recover and return to work
- **Temporary Partial Disability**: The employee is still able to work, but in a reduced capacity until he/she recovers and returns to his/her original post
- **Permanent Partial Disability**: The employee suffers from a permanent injury, but is still able to perform work in a reduced capacity (e.g., a machinist lost a finger)
- **Permanent and Total Disability**: The employee no longer possesses the capacity to work

Workers comp varies from state-to-state.

If a person is disabled for any reason, Short Term Disability (STD) insurance provides coverage for a limited amount of time. One can receive benefits after a short waiting period of up to 14 days. The individual generally receives a regular payment over the course of one year, depending on the program. Long-Term Disability (LTD) pays you a portion of your income after you run out of both sick leave and STD. The average LTD benefit lasts 36 months. Both STD and LTD can be employer sponsored or voluntary insurance programs.

The definition of disability under the U.S. Social Security Administration is also different from other programs. All employees contribute to Social Security with every pay check. However, Social Security only pays for total disability. No benefits are payable for partial disability or for short-term disability. Hence, disability under Social Security is based on your inability to work. The Social Security Administration considers you disabled under Social Security rules if:

- You cannot do work that you did before;
- They decide that you cannot adjust to other work because of your medical condition(s); **and**
- Your disability has lasted or is expected to last for at least one year or to result in death.

Social Security applies one of the strictest definitions of disability. Social Security program rules assume that working families have access to other resources to provide support during periods of short-term disabilities, including workers' compensation, insurance, savings, and investments. Social Security disability benefits may be paid to individuals who: were born with a disability; incurred a disability as a result of a disease, accident or injury; sustained a disability while on the job; or experienced a disability while in the military.

FIGURE 1. COMPARISON OF DISABILITY PROGRAMS
Source: The Society for Diversity, 2018

Workers Compensation Disability	Short-Term or Long Term Disability	Social Security Disability	U.S. EEOC enforced Americans with Disabilities Act (ADA) and Amendments
• *Insurance* pays when an individual is injured, or becomes sick, on the job • Varies by State • Provided by an employer	• *Insurance* pays for any type of disability that is expected to last short term (14 days to 1 year) or long-term (at least 6-months or longer) • Purchased by an individual and/or provided by an employer	• *Insurance* pays only for total disability • Administered by the federal government, U.S. Social Security Administration • All employees contribute every time they receive a paycheck	• Employees work for an equal opportunity employer • No compensation for individuals unless they work • Employers provide harassment and discrimination-free workplaces, as well as reasonable accommodations

Disability law also varies from country to country. For example, the European Commission Directive requires employers and training providers to make 'reasonable accommodations' to meet the needs of disabled people. National laws determine the exact form of implementation and member states can impose more demanding requirements if they wish, but this Directive sets a common standard. Therefore, the obligation on employers and training providers is not absolute.

For example, they are not required to pay costs beyond those that the business could stand, or accept severe disruption to overall training programs. The Directive makes the correct assumption that most adjustments require only small-scale changes and that the requirement to make 'reasonable accommodations' will considerably improve the labor-market position of disabled people.

The Fundamental Law for Disabled Persons, which took force in 1993 in Japan, serves as the base of welfare policies in the nation; it was revised in 2004. The revised law sets forth, 'full participation and equality,' as its guiding philosophy, and intends to maintain the individual livelihood and dignity of people with disabilities. The Fundamental Law states that opportunities for people with disabilities to take part in Japanese society must be secured, discrimination based upon a person's disability must be abolished, and the equal rights of people with disabilities in Japan must be protected. The Fundamental Law for Disabled Persons also mandates that municipal government both draw up and implement programs which support the independence and social participation of Japanese citizens with disabilities. The Law also has provisions related to nursing and medical care, pensions, living support, vocational training and employment, education, barrier-free institutions, information, housing, prevention of the causes of disabilities, and additional areas to ensure that the needs of people with disabilities in Japan are met.

Federal law in Russia guarantees that physical infrastructure be accessible to people with disabilities, though it lacks concrete enforcement mechanisms. In 2012, Russia ratified the UN Convention on the Rights of Persons with Disabilities, which binds it to developing accessible physical infrastructure, among other provisions. Nevertheless, millions of people with disabilities in Russia continue to face significant barriers to participation in society. Discrimination and lack of accessibility impacts everything from the delivery of healthcare to education to employment. According to a 2013 report entitled, *"Barriers Everywhere: Lack of Accessibility for People with Disabilities in Russia"* by Human Rights Watch, at least 13 million people with disabilities live in Russia, or approximately 9 percent of the population.

For the purposes of this study guide, we will focus on the U.S. Equal Employment Opportunity Commission's definition of disability through the Americans with Disabilities Act (ADA), and its relevance to Inclusion in the workplace and at educational institutions. Under this standard of disability, the expectation is that individuals with disabilities will obtain and retain gainful employment, and if necessary, employers will make reasonable accommodations to ensure full participation in the workforce by persons with disabilities. As of May 2015 about 29 million Americans ages 16 or older were regarded as having a disability and are not institutionalized, according to the U.S Department of Labor's Bureau of Labor Statistics (BLS); the total is 817,000 over the previous year. This number didn't include the thousands of men and women returning home from wars in Iraq and Afghanistan with physical and mental disabilities, who are seeking to reenter the workforce.

The ADA prohibits employment discrimination against qualified individuals with disabilities. It prohibits employers with 15 or more workers from discriminating against qualified individuals with disabilities, with regard to applications, hiring, discharge, compensation, advancement, training, or other conditions, or privileges of employment. It also says employers must make reasonable accommodations for physical or mental limitations unless doing so imposes an undue hardship on the business.

In general, EEOC defines a **reasonable accommodation** as "any change in the work environment or in the way things are customarily done that enables an individual with a disability to enjoy equal employment opportunities." There are three categories of reasonable accommodations:

(i) Modifications or adjustments to a job application process that enable a qualified applicant with a disability to be considered for the position such qualified applicant desires; or

(ii) Modifications or adjustments to the work environment, or to the manner or circumstances under which the position held or desired is customarily performed, that enable a qualified individual with a disability to perform the essential functions of that position; or

(iii) Modifications or adjustments that enable a covered entity's employee with a disability to enjoy equal benefits and privileges of employment as are enjoyed by its other similarly situated employees without disabilities.

An **undue hardship** is defined as a "significant difficulty or expense incurred by a covered entity" with respect to the provision of an accommodation. In the event of an undue hardship, an employer would have an affirmative defense against a discrimination claim. Nevertheless, in order to determine whether a proposed accommodation imposes an undue hardship on an employer, the following factors must be considered:

1. The nature and net cost of the accommodation, taking into consideration the availability of tax credits and deductions, or outside funding;

2. The overall financial resources of the facility or facilities involved in the provision of the reasonable accommodation, the number of persons employed at such facility, and the effect on expenses and resources;

3. The overall financial resources of the covered entity, the overall size of the business of the covered entity with respect to the number of its employees, and the number, type, and location of its facilities;

4. The type of operation or operations of the covered entity, including the composition, structure, and functions of the workforce, and the geographic separateness and administrative or fiscal relationship of the facility or facilities in question to the covered entity; and

5. The impact of the accommodation upon the operation of the facility, including the impact on the ability of other employees to perform their duties and the impact on the facility's ability to conduct business. 29 C.F.R. § 1630.2(p).

It's always a best practice to consider each accommodation on a case by case basis; as there isn't a one-size fits all process that will work for every employee or employer.

The ADA does not list specific disabilities. Instead, the Equal Employment Opportunity Commission (EEOC) guidelines say that someone is disabled when he or she has a physical or mental impairment that "substantially limits" one or more major life activities.

Like so many other areas of diversity, the term "disability" can be difficult to define. The World Health Organization provides clarification, which can be applied universally.

> **Disability is an umbrella term, covering impairments, activity limitations, and participation restrictions. An *impairment* is a problem in body function or structure; an *activity limitation* is a difficulty encountered by an individual in executing a task or action; while a *participation restriction* is a problem experienced by an individual who may not be able to fully involve themselves in life's daily pursuits.**
>
> Thus, **disability is a complex phenomenon, reflecting an interaction between features of a person's body and features of the society in which he or she lives.**
>
> —*World Health Organization*

Under the ADA, impairments include any physiological disorder or condition, cosmetic disfigurement, or anatomical loss affecting one or more body systems, or any mental or psychological disorder. The ADA also prohibits discrimination against people with HIV/AIDS. Additionally, numerous state laws provide protection for people with an HIV/AIDS infection. Avert.org estimates that "36.7 million people (including 1.8 million children) were living with HIV in 2016. Since the start of the epidemic, an estimated 78 million people have become infected with HIV and 35 million people have died of AIDS-related illnesses. One-million people died globally of AIDS-related illnesses in 2016."

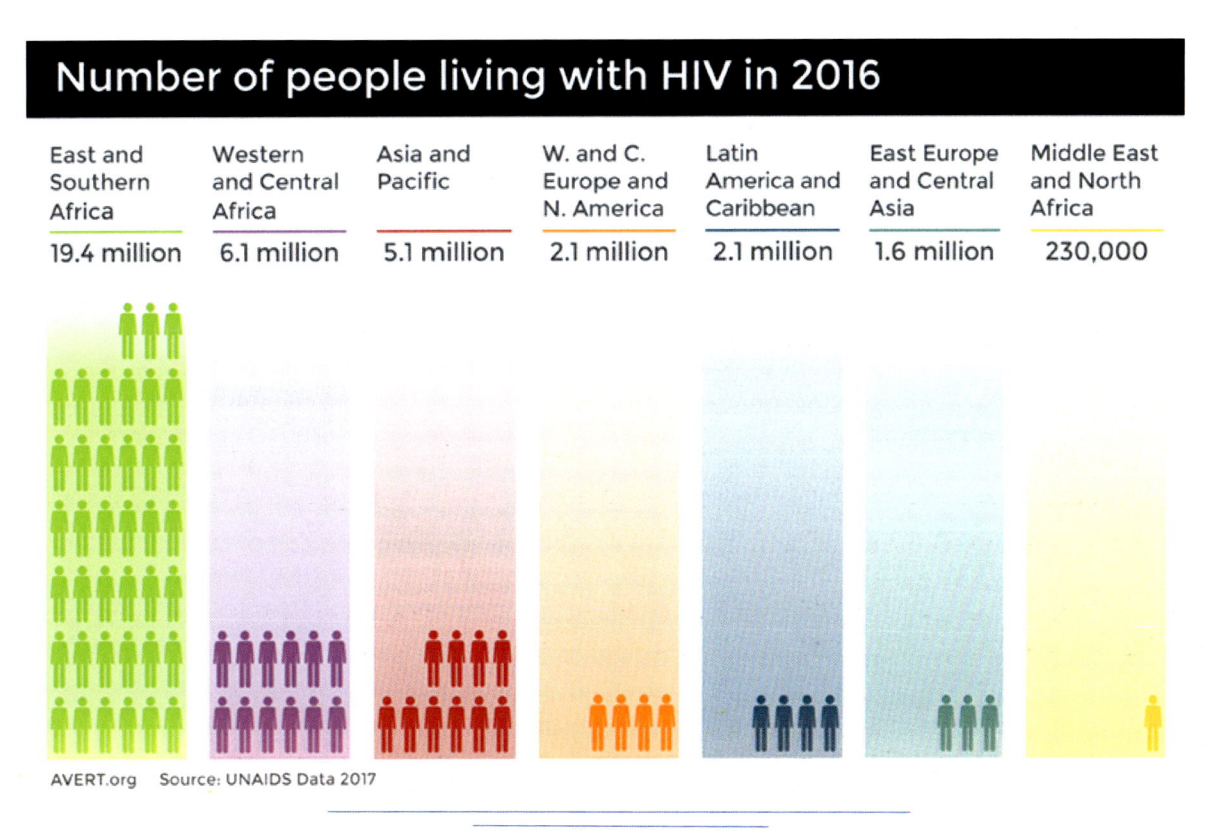

Number of people living with HIV in 2016

East and Southern Africa	Western and Central Africa	Asia and Pacific	W. and C. Europe and N. America	Latin America and Caribbean	East Europe and Central Asia	Middle East and North Africa
19.4 million	6.1 million	5.1 million	2.1 million	2.1 million	1.6 million	230,000

AVERT.org   Source: UNAIDS Data 2017

U.S. EEO law specifies several conditions that are not considered disabilities, such as homosexuality, bisexuality, voyeurism, compulsive gambling, pyromania, and certain disorders resulting from the illegal use of drugs.

Since the initial passing of the ADA, the landscape of the work force has dramatically changed. Many lawsuits have surfaced, alleging violations of the ADA. However, in the majority of the lawsuits, employers prevailed. A key reason was that, under the ADA, employees failed to show that they were disabled and qualified to do the job. Another key reason was that employees were not proving that their disability was "substantially limiting" one or more of their major life activities. As a result, in 2008 the ADA Amendment Act became effective.

The EEOC had been interpreting the ADA's 'substantially limiting' definition very narrowly. The "New" ADA, as this Act is called, makes it much easier for employees to show that their disabilities are limiting, and that one or more of their 'major life activities' have been impacted.

Outside of defining the term 'disability' there are other words within this particular competency that have changed. Some people in the field use the term "differently abled" instead of disabled. They believe that there is a negative connotation associated with 'disability' and 'differently abled' is less offensive in the workplace or on campuses. While differently abled is inclusive, the EEOC and many countries have laws on the books specifically referring to the word "disability" and therefore, our terminology should be inclusive, but it should also be legal where appropriate.

It is a misperception to label a disabled worker as "sick" or "ill", as individuals may have obtained the disability in a variety of different ways. Additionally, the word "handicapped" should not be used to label people or their capabilities. This term originally described someone who could not work and went begging with their cap in hand. This, however, is not the true origin of the word. It originated in the 17th century in a lottery game known as 'hand-in-cap', which involved players placing money in a cap. It moved later into horse racing where it meant bringing the strongest competitors back to the field by giving them extra weight to carry. In golf, it became the number of strokes a player could subtract from his score to give him a chance against better players, so a bigger handicap is actually an advantage in golf. Only in 1915 did 'handicap' become a term to describe disabled people, when it was used to label crippled children. Today, both terms 'handicapped' and 'crippled', have since become outdated language in the field of Diversity and Inclusion. Nevertheless, handicapped placards or parking spaces are still used in relation to vehicle permits.

The American Psychological Association style guide states that, when identifying a person with an impairment, the person's name or pronoun should come first, and descriptions of the impairment/disability should be used so that the impairment is identified, but it does not modify the person (person first language). Negative examples are "the blind", or, "the autistic man". Terminology that is more affirmative includes "a person who is visually impaired" or "he has autism". The style guide also states that a person's adaptive equipment should be described functionally as something that assists a person, not as something that limits a person, e.g., "a woman who uses a wheelchair" rather than "a woman confined to a wheelchair." When speaking of a person with a disability, a negative phrase would be to say that the individual "is courageous", implying the person has courage because he/she has a disability. An affirmative phrase would be "a person is productive".

By understanding social and legal behavior pertaining to disabilities, as well as being knowledgeable about the visible and non-visible disabilities that exist within the workplace, diversity practitioners will be in a better position to reduce lawsuits and facilitate positive employee relationships.

Workers with disabilities make up another dimension of diversity in the workplace, and like the other dimensions, can add valuable viewpoints and perspectives that contribute to the effectiveness of any organization.

OTHER DISABILITY RELATED LEGISLATION

Globally, there are approximately 1.3 billion people with disabilities and their buying power is estimated to be greater than $1.2 trillion USD, according to SenseAbility.

In the workplace, employees with disabilities extend the definition diversity beyond Black and White, male and female, or Political Correctness. In the "*Top 5 Benefits of Hiring People with Disabilities*", the Chicago Lighthouse describes the advantages of a disabled workforce. Among the key benefits are tax credits, fewer workplace injuries, and higher job retention. Many studies have shown that people with disabilities take less time-off, and that they are more likely to stay on the job longer than non-disabled workers.

Recently, the Chicago Lighthouse studied the retention rate of employees in its Illinois Tollway call center, which employs people who are blind, visually impaired, disabled, and Veterans (as well as people without disabilities). On average, the employees with vision loss or other disabilities, and Veterans, had a retention rate of 1.7 years. In contrast, the retention rate for employees without disabilities, or that were not Veterans, was only 0.9 years. Beyond talent retention and productivity benefits, there are also advantages to complying with global legislation pertaining to employing individuals with disabilities.

In countries such as Japan, Italy, and Spain, quotas exist whereby employers must hire a certain percentage of the disabled population or pay a fine. The Chinese government also sets a minimum quota of disabled workers for companies to hire or employ. The national average is 1.5 percent of a firm's workforce, but the rate can differ by province. The quota does not apply to companies under three years old and with a workforce of less than 20. Companies that don't meet this quota have to pay into a fund called the *Baozhang Jin*. The fee varies according to location, but the majority of companies choose to pay into the fund rather than employ the requisite number of disabled workers. Reluctance to train disabled staff and difficulty integrating them into the company structure are commonly cited reasons for the high unemployment rate amongst China's disabled population.

These commonly cited excuses are not restricted to China; employers around the world struggle with discerning myth from reality in this dimension of diversity. Outside of the ADA, the U.S. has sought to combat disability stereotypes and economic exclusion with additional disability-related legislation.

THE VOCATIONAL REHABILITATION ACT OF 1973
The Vocational Rehabilitation Act of 1973 requires employers with federal contracts of more than $2,500 to take affirmative action in employing persons with disabilities. It does not require hiring unqualified people, but it does require an employer to take steps to accommodate a worker that is disabled unless doing so imposes an undue hardship on the employer. This Act is related to the ADA in that both laws stipulate that employers do not have to accommodate a worker with a disability if that accommodation imposes an undue hardship.

THE PREGNANCY DISCRIMINATION ACT OF 1978
The Pregnancy Act of 1978 prohibits using pregnancy, childbirth, or related medical conditions to discriminate in hiring, promotions, suspension, discharge, or in any other term or condition of employment. Furthermore, under the act, if an employer offers its employees disability coverage, then it must treat pregnancy and childbirth like any other disability, and include it in the plan as a covered condition. Employers are exempt from providing medical coverage for elective abortions (except in the case that the mother's life is threatened) but are required to provide disability and sick leave for women who are recovering from an abortion.

THE VIETNAM ERA VETERANS' READJUSTMENT ASSISTANCE ACT
About 150,000 Vietnam veterans came home wounded, and at least 21,000 were permanently disabled. The Vietnam Era Veterans' Readjustment Assistance Act (VEVRAA) of 1974 required covered federal government contractors and subcontractors to take affirmative action to employ veterans and prevent discrimination against such individuals. In addition, VEVRAA required contractors and subcontractors to list their employment openings with the appropriate employment service delivery system, and give veterans priority when receiving system referrals.

UNIFORMED SERVICES EMPLOYMENT AND REEMPLOYMENT RIGHTS ACT (USERRA)
The Uniformed Services Employment and Reemployment Rights Act ("USERRA") is a federal law that provides reemployment rights to returning veterans and other members of uniformed services. Under USERRA, an individual who leaves his or her civilian job for military service is entitled to return to the job with accrued seniority if he or she satisfies the eligibility requirements set forth under USERRA. USERRA applies to all employees regardless of the size of the employer.

With the largest group of veterans returning to the workplace since World War II, companies must establish best practices and disability management procedures to ensure they are appropriately addressing the needs of the 'workplace warriors' as they reintegrate into civilian roles. This effect will be felt for decades, as veterans from Iraq and Afghanistan return to the workplace—some with disabilities that they didn't have before being deployed.

A guide called *"Workplace Warrior: The Corporate Response to Deployment and Reintegration"* identified the challenges that returning employees face and the resources that employers can use to support them. It was co-authored by the Workplace Warrior Think Tank, convened by the non-profit Disability Management Employer Coalition (DMEC) and three disability insurers: The Hartford, MetLife, and Unum.

While it is important to understand disability-related legislation and terminology, it is by educating all levels of the work force that organizations will collectively become more knowledgeable about, and sensitive to, individuals with disabilities.

VISIBLE AND NON-VISIBLE DISABILITIES

Just about every workplace has employees with non-visible disabilities. In many workplaces, the population with non-visible disabilities is sizable; however, the organizational culture determines whether a worker will disclose the disability and/or request an accommodation.

Employers must create an environment that supports workers with visible or non-visible disabilities. The reason some employees choose not to disclose their non-visible disabilities is because they have learned the hard way that every organization is not supportive of workers with differing abilities, as evidenced by the following story.

CASE STUDY

"In a previous Fortune 500 job, someone called HR because they thought I was being abused," Kimberly McCabe told SHRM Online. Her non-visible condition, Von Willebrand's Disease, results in heavy menstrual bleeding, anemia and bruising. When she explained her situation to HR and her colleagues, they apologized profusely. However, that wasn't the only awkward experience McCabe had. "I was once called into my boss's office and scolded for going to the toilet too frequently," she said of another employer. "I was too embarrassed to make an issue."

But the reactions at other workplaces have been better. In June 2007, McCabe joined a technology firm and decided to explain the situation to her small workgroup. "They were so incredibly supportive. They never made me feel bad or embarrassed in any way," she said. "I once had a mild hemorrhage and was really weak for a few days. They were a dream come true; they checked to make sure I was OK, asked if I needed to take time off, and inquired what they could do to make me feel better."

Educating the Workplace
According to the 2010 U.S. Census, the African American community has the highest rate of disability at 20.3 percent, slightly higher than the overall disability rate of 18.7%. Although people have come to better understand and accept different types of disabilities, a stigma remains attached to the disabled community. Blacks with a disability are not only subject to this stigma but also to the additional forces of race discrimination. African American women who have a disability face tremendous discrimination due to their condition, race, and gender. Dr. Eddie Glenn of Howard University describes this situation as the "triple jeopardy" syndrome.

In "*Getting Support, Supporting Others: A Handbook for Working with Non-Visible Disabilities*", produced by Ernst & Young (E&Y) for the benefit of employees and people managers, non-visible disabilities are grouped into three broad categories:

- Chronic health conditions and illnesses (such as diabetes and cancer).
- Sensory impairments (such as hearing loss, low vision, and mobility limitations).
- Mental health and learning disabilities (such as depression, anxiety disorders, and attention-deficit hyperactivity disorder).

E&Y uses "non-visible" rather than "hidden" or "invisible" to refer to disabilities that are not obviously apparent, to avoid any implication of concealment or shame.

How Common are Specific Disabilities?

- Difficulty walking/climbing stairs — **30.6 million**
- Require assistance of others with everyday tasks — **12.0 million**
- Vision difficulty (partial or total) — **8.1 million**
- Hearing difficulty — **7.6 million**
- Using a wheelchair — **3.6 million**
- Alzheimer's, senility or dementia — **2.4 million**

Source: Americans with Disabilities: 2010, from Survey of Income and Program Participation

United States Census Bureau
U.S. Department of Commerce
Economics and Statistics Administration
U.S. CENSUS BUREAU

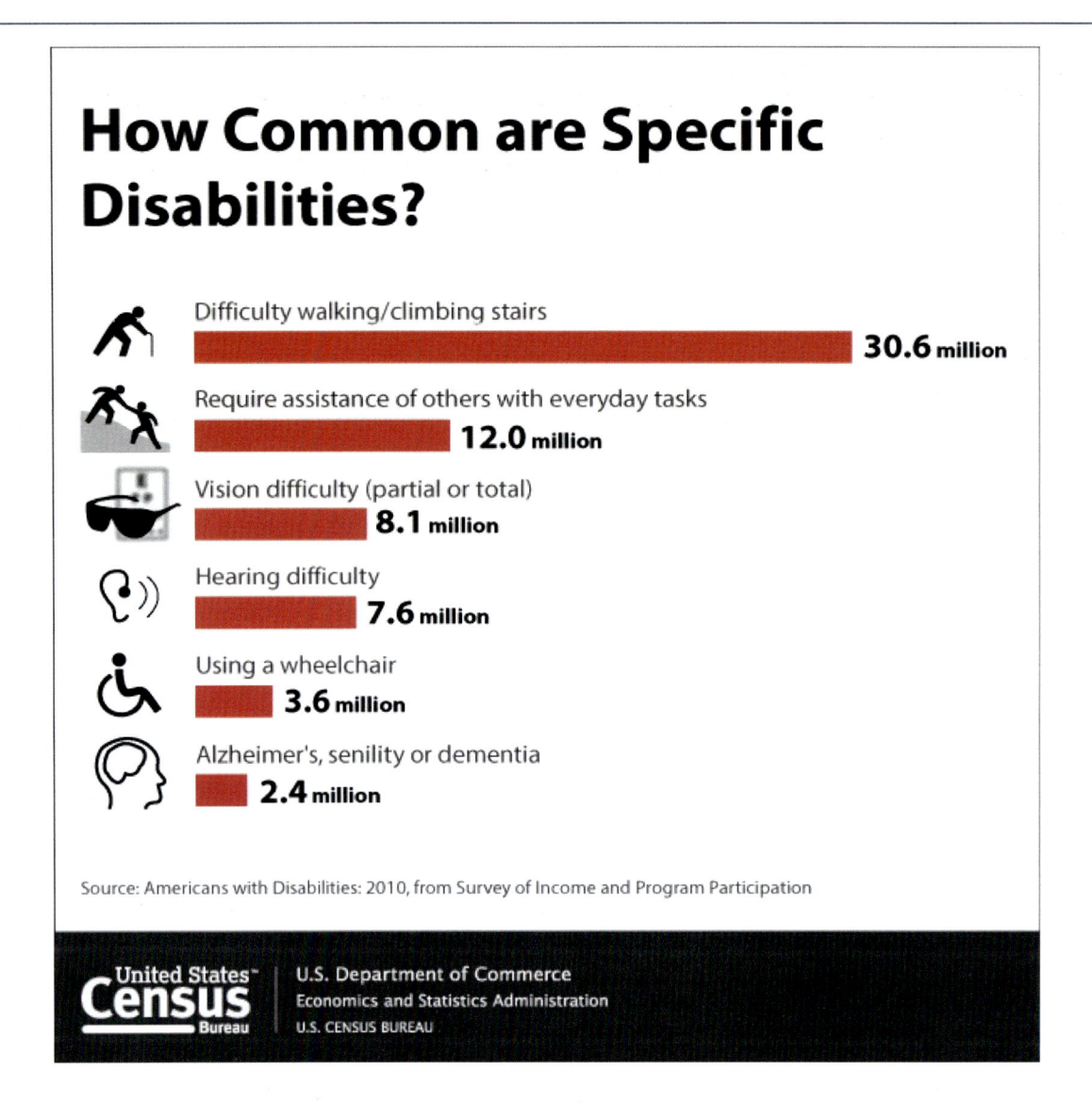

Employers who are committed to inclusive cultures make objective employment decisions without regard to visible or non-visible disabilities. They ensure that they hire workers who are qualified to do the job, minimizing the employee's concerns about the disability.

Because non-visible disabilities are unseen, they cannot be cited as a reason a candidate is not hired. However, once a candidate with a non-visible disability is hired, and discloses his/her disability, education of the workforce is vital to Inclusion, as well as ensuring that other workers are sensitive to not treating them differently.

If An Employee Reveals A Disability, A Manager Should:
- Ask for signs of what to look for if the employee is under medical distress, and what the manager should do in addition to calling 911
- Ask where the employee keeps emergency medicine
- Research the condition on the web
- Avoid making comments like "Oh, I'm so sorry", or "Oh, you poor thing!"

What Is the Office of Diversity's Role?
- Provide education to avoid assumptions and discrimination, as well as raise awareness
- Develop an inclusive definition of diversity
- Celebrate and communicate the organization's commitment to different abilities
- Utilize employee resource groups and community-based organizations to support workers with disabilities

On college campuses, in particular, there may be a dedicated office that handles disability issues. This does not preclude the Office of Diversity from partnering with the disability services unit; it just presents another opportunity for the Office of Diversity to demonstrate knowledge, best practices, and Inclusion of disability into organizational diversity efforts. In this instance, diversity practitioners must 'bridge the gap', versus allowing both units to operate in a stand-a-lone capacity.

REASONABLE ACCOMODATIONS

> "Reasonable accommodation" means necessary and appropriate modifications and adjustments not imposing a disproportionate or undue burden, where needed in a particular case, to ensure that persons with disabilities enjoy or exercise equal human rights and fundamental freedoms as others."
>
> - The United Nations

When an employee discloses a disability, he/she may request a workplace accommodation for that disability. If so, it is wise for the supervisor to initiate a discussion with the employee to better determine appropriate accommodations. This discussion, also known as the interactive process, requires careful planning and guidance from legal, HR, Diversity and Inclusion, or the in-house disability expert.

While the employer and the employee share responsibility for initiating the interactive process, it is important that the employer understands that they typically have a higher level of responsibility to ensure that this process goes smoothly. Court rulings that assess the adequacy of interactive processes also rely heavily on the phrase *'act in good faith'* and use it as a centerpiece to judge compliance efforts.

Purposes Served by the Interactive Process
The importance of the interactive process is to develop a procedure to compile information about one or more of the following:

- Learning the specific essential job functions that the employee is unable to perform due to a disability.
- Understanding the employee's ideas pertaining to specific accommodation(s) that the employee feels he or she needs.
- Requesting additional information, including general data about the condition, that justifies an employee's specific accommodation request. This applies when the employer and/or the employer's medical evaluator disagree with the justification given by the employee for a specific accommodation.

- Facilitating a negotiation that results in a mutual agreement about the specific accommodation(s) that will enable the employee to perform his or her essential functions.
- Explaining the accommodation that the employer is willing to provide and, if appropriate, providing the employer's rationale for imposing an accommodation different from the accommodation requested by the employee.
- Informing the employee about the employer's inability to provide a reasonable accommodation due to an undue hardship on the employer's part.

FIGURE 2. (SOURCE: SHRM)
The ADA Decision-Making Cycle

Phase 1: Evaluate information to determine if employee or applicant is "qualified but disabled."

Phase 2: If "yes," analyze essential job functions, determine if accommodation is requested or needed. If "no," clearly document all findings and discussions. Accommodation process ends.

Phase 3: Perform Interactive Process

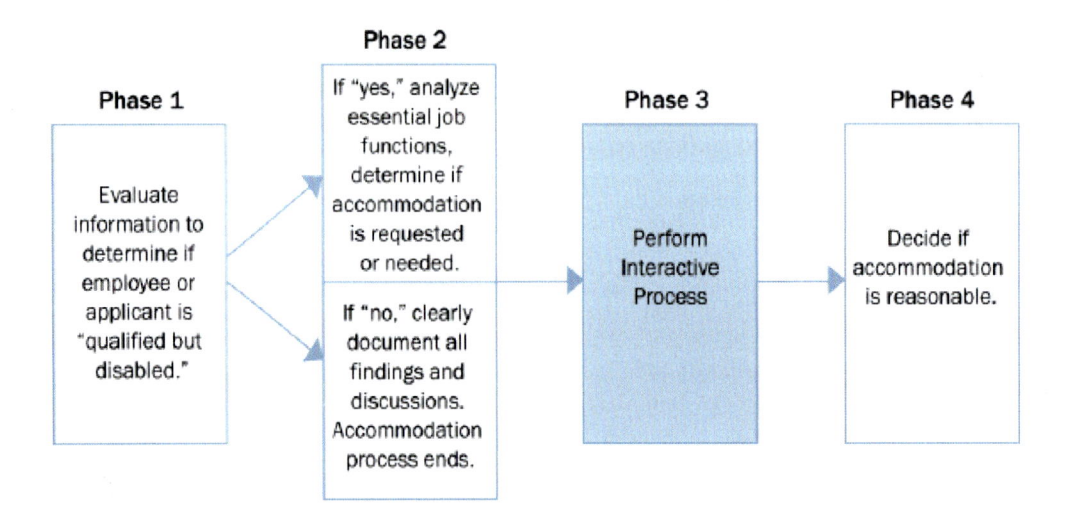

Phase 4: Decide if accommodation is reasonable.

Figure 2 depicts a typical four-phase ADA reasonable accommodation decision tree and illustrates where the interactive process fits.

Requesting Medical Information
Many requests for accommodation will be so simple that additional medical information and/or negotiation is unnecessary. In these situations, Diversity or HR should document the content of the meeting(s), memorialize the agreement, and conclude the process.

There are times however, when this process is not as simple. First and foremost, a diversity professional's normal sensitivity to the privacy considerations of the employee's personal information, including medical data, is an important starting point for the interactive process. No one from the Office of Diversity, Human Resources, nor any manager or supervisor, should initiate an inquiry into aspects of an employee's medical diagnosis, his or her symptoms, medications that he or she may be taking, types of doctors providing treatment, or the history of a disability.

Initiating such a medical inquiry is forbidden. Employees may bring these items into discussions, and if they do, diversity professionals should exercise appropriate caution in discussing them. The purpose of the Interactive Process is to determine whether a reasonable accommodation can be made to enable the employee to perform the requirements of a job.

Therefore, Diversity or HR's inquiry should seek to answer: *what exactly does the employee need to allow him or her to perform the essential functions of his or her position?* Throughout the interactive process, it is especially important for diversity, HR and supervisors to avoid making unwarranted assumptions about the impact of an employee's disability. Assumptions, especially those that derive from stereotypes, reinforce the fears of people with disabilities that they will not be given a fair chance to demonstrate their capabilities.

Assigning and Reassigning Employees with Disabilities
Some employers offer disabled workers light duty or alternative jobs to satisfy requests for reasonable accommodations; this is approved by the ADA. But in the event that an organization cannot agree with the employee on a reasonable workplace (or job) modification, it may be necessary to accommodate the worker with a reassignment.

Companies sometimes seek to limit reassigning jobs because of its disruption on workforce management. Employers are only required to reassign a disabled employee when that worker is unable to perform his/her present job. They are not required to reassign or promote them simply based on the fact that they have a disability. Employers are also not required to promote the disabled employee as a reasonable accommodation reassignment.
It is important to remember that:

- Job reassignment to vacant positions can be considered as a mandated option under the ADA
- A disabled worker is qualified for protection under the ADA, if he can perform other open positions at the company, not just the job he had been doing

Determining a reasonable accommodation under ADA should be a cooperative and interactive process, with the employee and employer working in good faith to find the best possible solution. Once again, providing accommodations may not be expensive or difficult. Most importantly, the process is designed to ensure that you are in legal compliance and that you promote employee satisfaction and inclusion.

Diversity and HR professionals can apply all of these techniques to design and implement an interactive process that will achieve both spirit and letter compliance with the law. By using a Diversity or HR professional's interpersonal skills (and their knowledge of the requirements of the ADA), employees and their employers can learn each other's perspectives and negotiate many different solutions, as well as preserve good employee relations.

INTEGRATING WORKERS WITH DISABILITIES INTO THE WORKPLACE

Employees who are: 1) already disabled, 2) disabled in a workplace injury, 3) disabled due to an illness, injury, or accident outside of work, 4) disabled due to age-related health issues, or 5) disabled veterans returning to the workforce, will all require careful consideration in order to integrate them into the workplace effectively and avoid issues of discrimination.

The key to remember is that there are many candidates and employees who are already highly skilled. They just happen to have a disability. Not only should we evaluate the physical working environment, we must also assess the organizational culture. Supervisors will really lead the way in ensuring that myths about disabled workers are dispelled, and that these individuals are not singled out because of their different abilities.

Returning Veterans

Because veterans can have visible or non-visible disabilities, handling their return to the workplace requires the same interactive process as any other worker with a disability. The employer, however, must also be knowledgeable about the laws specifically related to veterans, such as USERRA.

The perception exists that it is expensive to return veterans to the work force, and that they require more training than other employees. This is not true. Veterans are disciplined; they are team players; and they are dedicated to fulfilling goals. Even with disabilities, veterans are strong leaders who are used to working with advanced technologies. Employers committed to diversity can engage with agencies that help returning veterans and establish partnerships to obtain valuable resources about interviewing, hiring and developing veterans so that their skills can be put to good use. By being proactive, employers can collectively help returning veterans, as well as other members of the work force.

Assistive Technology

Assistive Technology is a generic term for devices and modifications that help overcome or remove a disability (i.e., wheelchair, prosthetics, etc.). The first recorded example of the use of a prosthesis dates back to 1800 BCE. The wheelchair dates back to the 17th century. The curb cut is a related structural innovation. Other examples are standing frames, text telephones, accessible keyboards, large print, Braille, and speech recognition computer software. People with disabilities often develop personal or community adaptations, such as strategies to suppress tics (e.g., due to Tourette's syndrome) in public, or sign language in deaf communities.

As the personal computer has become more ubiquitous, various organizations have developed software and hardware to make computers more accessible for people with disabilities. For example, the LOMAK keyboard was designed in New Zealand specifically for persons with disabilities. Some software and hardware, such as Voice Finger, SmartboxAT's The Grid, Freedom Scientific's JAWS, the Free and Open Source alternative Orca, etc., have been specifically designed for people with disabilities while other software and hardware, such as Nuance's Dragon NaturallySpeaking, were not developed specifically for people with disabilities, but can be used to increase accessibility.

The Internet is also used by disability activists and nonprofits to network and further their goals. Organizations, such as AbilityNet and U Can Do IT in the U.S., provide assessment services that determine which assistive technologies will best help an employee. These organizations also train individuals with disabilities on how to use computer-based assistive technology. Federal programs like Ability One, provide employment opportunities to more than 45,000 individuals who are blind or have significant disabilities; including approximately 3,000 Veterans. Hence, if one of your strategic diversity plan goals is to include more veterans or disabled employees in your workplace, it may be a good idea to research different technical products and service providers that can assist with the integration.

Inclusion signifies going beyond the law to develop a culture that values the contributions of all workers—in whatever state that different abilities manifest. Becoming more knowledgeable about the workplace constraints, challenges and stereotypes facing individuals with disabilities will go a long way in facilitating cultural competence and Inclusion. Additionally, Inclusion can help our organizations to leverage the positive and innovative mindsets that exist in workers with disabilities.

In order to accomplish this feat, first we must include disability in our diversity framework (i.e., definition of diversity, diversity planning, resource groups, etc.). Second, D&I leaders should gather baseline data and track how the culture is becoming more inclusive for disabled workers, students, patients, customers, etc. Third, the organization must continuously build competency around the interactive process, accommodations, assistive technology and caregivers.

BEST PRACTICES FOR EMPLOYEES WITH CAREGIVING RESPONSIBILITIES

On Sharecare.com, Deborah Raines, RN, of the Honor Society for Nursing, says "a caregiver is a broad term for any person who provides assistance for another person who cannot live independently due to developmental, physical, emotional or psychological needs."

Dr. Eric Pfeifer, author of *The Art of Caregiving in Alzheimer's Disease*, states "what a caregiver does depends on what that other person needs to have done for them. And that may depend on the stage or the severity of the illness or disability. In some cases, and at some stages of a disease, it may involve giving only a little bit of help: steadying the person's gait, combing their hair, helping them to get dressed or helping them to get to the bathroom on time. In other cases it can go much further, to the point, in fact, where the caregiver does virtually everything for the other person."

Raines adds, "Examples of caregivers are prevalent in society: Parents are caregivers to children, children are caregivers to elderly parents, physicians and nurses are caregivers to patients. Caregivers may have specialized training and the caregiver role may be paid (for hire) or volunteer."

The Benefits of Including Caregivers
Currently, many workers juggle both work and caregiving responsibilities. Those responsibilities extend not only to spouses and children, but also to parents, other older family members, and/or relatives with disabilities.

Employers adopting flexible workplace policies that help employees achieve a satisfactory work-life integration may not only experience decreased complaints of unlawful discrimination, but may also benefit their workers, their customer base, and their bottom line. Numerous studies have found that flexible workplace policies enhance employee productivity, reduce absenteeism, lower costs, and appear to positively affect profits. They also aid recruitment and retention efforts-- allowing employers to retain a talented, knowledgeable workforce, as well as save the money and time that would otherwise have been spent recruiting, interviewing, selecting and training new employees.

The benefits of these programs remain constant regardless of the economic climate, and some employers have implemented workplace flexibility programs as an alternative to workforce reductions. Such programs not only enable employers to "go lean without being mean," but they also can position organizations to rebound quickly once business improves.

Family & Medical Leave
The Family and Medical Leave Act (FMLA) is designed to help employees balance their work and family responsibilities by allowing them to take reasonable unpaid leave for family and medical reasons. It also seeks to accommodate the legitimate interests of employers and promote equal employment opportunity for men and women.

FMLA applies to all public agencies, public and private elementary and secondary schools, and companies with 50 or more employees. These employers must provide an eligible employee with up to 12 weeks of unpaid leave each year for any of the following reasons:

- For the birth and care of an employee's newborn child;
- For adoption or foster care placement;
- To care for an immediate family member (spouse, child, or parent) with a serious health condition;
- When the employee can't work due to a serious health condition;
- For any qualifying exigency arising out of the fact that a spouse, son, daughter, or parent is a military member on covered active duty or on call for covered active duty status.

Employees are eligible for leave if they have worked for their employer at least 1,250 hours over the past 12 months, and work at a location where the company employs 50 or more employees within 75 miles. Whether an employee has worked the minimum 1,250 hours of service is in accordance with Fair Labor Standards Act (FLSA) principles for determining compensable hours of work.

An eligible employee may also take up to 26 work weeks of leave during a "single 12-month period" to care for a covered service member with a serious injury or illness, when the employee is the spouse, son, daughter, parent, or next of kin of the service member. The "single 12-month period" for military caregiver leave is different from the 12-month period used for other FMLA leave reasons.

Time taken off work due to pregnancy complications can be counted against the 12 weeks of family and medical leave. Nevertheless, if an employee and his/her spouse both work for the same employer, they cannot each take 12 weeks off for the birth of a child, when adopting a child, or to care for a parent with a serious health condition.

Keep in mind, the households of today are much different than they were 50 years ago. While women, particularly women of color, remain disproportionately likely to exercise primary caregiving responsibilities, men have increasingly assumed household chores and caregiving duties for children, parents and relatives with disabilities. Thus, in order to avoid stereotypes, discrimination, and non-compliance, men and women should have equal opportunities to take family leave.

The eligible employee must provide 30 days advance notice for foreseeable events. The employer is allowed to ask the employee to obtain certification from a medical provider testifying to the need for the employee to take the leave for themselves or for the family member. The employer can delay the start of FMLA for 30 days if the employee does not provide advance notice, and/or until the employee can provide certification from a medical provider. Upon completion of the leave, the employer is allowed to require the employee to obtain a certification of fitness to return to work when the leave was due to the employee's own health concerns.

Best Practices
The following are examples of employer best practices that go beyond federal nondiscrimination requirements. These practices are also designed to remove barriers to equal employment opportunity.

- *Be aware of, and train managers about, the legal obligations that may impact decisions pertaining to the treatment of workers with caregiving responsibilities. The education should include training on how to discern when an accommodation is being requested. The organization should also implement processes to ensure that new leaders are trained when they are promoted. All supervisors should receive regular updates with case law changes.* This includes federal employment statutes and regulations, such as the Americans with Disabilities Act of 1990, as amended; the Equal Pay Act of 1963, as amended; the Pregnancy Discrimination Act; Title VII of the Civil Rights Act of 1964, as amended; the Family and Medical Leave Act (FMLA); the Employee Retirement Income Security Act (ERISA), and Executive Order 13152.

    - An employee tells the supervisor that he/she can't use the manual blood pressure machine because he/she has arthritis and it hurts. (This is a request for a reasonable accommodation). It will be necessary to provide this employee with an automatic blood pressure machine.
    - An employee tells the supervisor he/she is having trouble getting to work on time because of the medical treatment that he/she is undergoing. (This is a request for a reasonable accommodation). Supervisors must be familiar with the ADA accommodation process to connect the dots.

- *Develop, disseminate, and enforce a strong EEO policy* that clearly addresses the types of conduct that might constitute unlawful discrimination against caregivers based on characteristics protected by federal anti-discrimination laws. An effective policy that addresses caregiver protections under the law should:

    - Define relevant terms, including "caregiver" and "caregiving responsibilities."
        - Provide an inclusive definition of "family" that extends beyond children and spouses and covers any individual for whom the applicant or employee has primary caregiving responsibilities.

    - Describe common stereotypes or biases about caregivers that may result in unlawful conduct, including assuming that:
        - Female workers' caregiving responsibilities will interfere with their ability to succeed in a fast-paced environment;
        - Female staff who work part-time or take advantage of flexible work arrangements are less committed to their jobs than full-time employees;
        - Male workers do not, or should not, have significant caregiving responsibilities;
        - Female workers prefer, or should prefer, to spend time with their families rather than work;
        - Female workers who are caregivers are less capable than other workers; and
        - Pregnant workers are less reliable than other workers.

    - Provide examples of prohibited conduct related to caregiving, such as:
        - Asking female applicants and employees, but not male applicants and employees, about their child care responsibilities;
        - Making stereotypical comments about pregnant workers or female caregivers;
        - Treating female workers without caregiving responsibilities more favorably than female caregivers;

- Steering women with caregiving responsibilities to less prestigious or lower-paid positions;
- Treating women of color who have caregiving responsibilities differently than other workers with caregiving responsibilities due to gender, race and/or national origin-based stereotypes;
- Treating male workers with caregiving responsibilities more, or less, favorably than female workers with caregiving responsibilities;
- Denying male workers', but not female workers', requests for leave related to caregiving responsibilities; and
- Providing reasonable accommodations for temporary medical conditions but not for pregnancy.

- Prohibit retaliation against individuals who report discrimination or harassment based on caregiving responsibilities or who provide related information.

- Identify an office or person that staff may contact if they have questions or need to file a complaint related to caregiver discrimination. This will typically be HR or the Office of Diversity.

- *Ensure that managers at all levels are aware of, and comply with, the organization's work-life policies.* In particular, front-line supervisors, middle management and other managers who regularly interact with employees or who are responsible for assignments, leave approval, schedules, promotions and other employment terms, conditions and benefits, should be familiar with the organization's work-life policies and supportive of employees who take advantage of available programs.

  - Provide incentives for managers to ensure that their employees are aware of work-life integration programs and empower supervisors to support employees who choose to take advantage of such opportunities.

  - Assess supervisors' willingness to assist employees who have caregiving responsibilities on supervisors' performance evaluations.

- *Respond to complaints of caregiver discrimination efficiently and effectively.* Investigate complaints promptly and thoroughly. Take corrective action and implement corrective and preventive measures as necessary to resolve the situation and prevent problems from arising in the future.

- *Protect against retaliation.* Provide clear and credible assurances that if employees make complaints or provide information related to complaints about unfair treatment of caregivers, the employer will protect them from retaliation. Ensure that these anti-retaliation measures are enforced.

Recruitment, Hiring, and Promotion

- *Focus on the applicant's qualifications* for the job in question. Do not ask questions about the applicant's or employee's children, plans to start a family, pregnancy, or other caregiving-related issues during interviews or performance reviews. Don't write anything regarding the applicants' appearance related to their disability status on the interview notes.

- *Review employment policies and practices*—particularly those related to hiring, promotion, pay, benefits, attendance, and leave—to determine whether they disadvantage workers with caregiving responsibilities.

- *Develop specific, job-related qualification standards* for each position that reflects the duties, functions, and competencies of the position and minimizes the potential for gender stereotyping or other unlawful discrimination against caregivers. Make sure these standards are consistently applied when choosing among candidates.

    - Example: Employer A posts a job opening for a marketing director. The position requires frequent interaction with company executives, marketing staff, and external vendors. Alexis and David apply for the position. Both have extensive marketing experience; however, Alexis is the primary caregiver for her elderly father, who has Alzheimer's disease, and requests to work from home part-time, while David is available to work on-site full-time.

        Employer A selects Alexis for the position based on her familiarity with many of the top vendors in the industry, noting that she can communicate with relevant parties via phone and e-mail on the days that she is not in the office. In this situation, Employer A evaluated both candidates and made the selection decision based on specific, job-related criteria.

    - Example: Same facts as above, except Employer A selects David for the position, commenting that, while it sympathizes with Alexis's family situation, it is concerned that her desire to prioritize family responsibilities over work responsibilities would have a detrimental effect on the company's marketing strategy, potentially discouraging future clients and decreasing revenue. Employer A should not have based its selection decision on Alexis's caregiving responsibilities.

- *Ensure that job openings, acting positions, and promotions are communicated* to all eligible employees regardless of caregiving responsibilities.

    - Do not assume that certain employees (for example, mothers of young children or single parents) will not be interested in positions that require significant travel, working long or unusual hours, or relocation.

- *Implement recruitment practices that target individuals with caregiving responsibilities* who are looking to enter or return to the workplace.

    - Advertise positions in parenting magazines and other publications and web sites that are directed at caregivers.

- *Identify and remove barriers to re-entry* for individuals who have taken leaves of absence from the workforce due to caregiving responsibilities or other personal reasons.

    - When reviewing and comparing applicants' or employees' work histories for hiring or promotional purposes, focus on work experience and accomplishments and give the same weight to cumulative relevant experience that would be given to workers with uninterrupted service.

        - Example: Employer B posts a Customer Service Manager position. Joanne and Tim apply. Both have approximately three years of customer service experience; however,

Joanne's experience is spread over a five-year period due to two maternity leaves, while Tim's experience is uninterrupted by medical leave. Employer B selects Tim, reasoning that his continuous service demonstrates his commitment to his career. Employer B discriminated against Joanne if it refused to consider her for the job based on her use of maternity leave.

- Example: Same facts as above, except that Tim worked for Employer B in a customer service capacity, while Joann worked for a different company. If Employer B selected Tim based on his knowledge of and demonstrated commitment to the company, Employer B's decision was not discriminatory.

- Example: Employer C invites employees who are on personal leaves of absence to attend company-sponsored training and networking events to familiarize them with the latest industry developments. Employer C also recruits these employees, on a voluntary basis, to work on temporary assignments.

o As a best practice, employers should provide the skills and training necessary to enhance the competitiveness and competency of employees while they are on leaves of absence.

- *Ensure that employment decisions are well-documented and transparent* (to the extent possible).
  o To prevent misunderstandings, clearly explain the reasoning behind employment decisions to relevant parties.
  o Retain records relevant to decisions about hiring, promotion, performance, pay, leave, benefits, awards, and other employment determinations for at least the length of time required by statute.

Terms, Conditions, and Privileges of Employment

- *Monitor compensation practices and performance appraisal systems* for patterns of potential discrimination against caregivers. Ensure that performance appraisals are based on employees' actual job performance and not on stereotypes about caregivers.

- *Review workplace policies that limit employee flexibility*, such as fixed hours of work and mandatory overtime, to ensure that they are necessary to business operations.

- *Encourage employees to request flexible work arrangements* that allow them to balance work and personal responsibilities. Work with employees to create customized flexible work arrangements that meet the specific needs of the employee and employer. Ensure that managers do not discourage employees from requesting flexible work arrangements or penalize employees who make such requests. Flexible work arrangements may include:

  o Flextime Programs. Flextime policies generally permit employees to vary their work day start and stop times within a certain range, such as allowing an employee to arrive at work at any time between 8:00 and 9:30 a.m. and then work for 8 hours.

  o Flexible Week Opportunities. Flexible week opportunities may include compressed work weeks, such as a workweek consisting of four ten-hour work days.

  o Telecommuting, Work-at-Home, or Flexplace Programs. These options enable employees to work from home or alternate office locations.

- Part-time work opportunities. Part-time workers should receive proportionate wages and benefits compared with full-time workers. Similarly, part-time workers should receive proportionate credit for relevant experience needed to qualify for promotions, training programs, or other employment opportunities.

    - Example: José works 3 days a week and spends the other 2 days caring for his young children. José should receive 3/5 of the wages and benefits he would receive if he worked full-time.

    - Example: Employer D posts a job that requires three years of relevant work experience. Nadia and Jermaine apply for the job. Both have the required qualifications and three years of work experience; however, Nadia has worked full-time for the past three years, while Jermaine has worked three days a week for the past five years while caring for his father, who has Parkinson's disease. Employer D should base its decision on the applicants' qualifications and experience, rather than on their schedules.

- Job sharing. Job sharing programs permit two employees to share one full-time position. In general, employees participating in job sharing programs receive a proportionate share of the salary and benefits.

- *If overtime is required, make it as family-friendly as possible.* Determine whether a voluntary, rather than mandatory, overtime system would meet the needs of the organization. If not, permit employees to schedule overtime in advance so they can arrange for child care, elder care, or other caregiving responsibilities.

    - Example: Employer E requires employees to work overtime during peak periods to meet customer demand. Employer E first asks for volunteers and then, if necessary, requires employees to sign up for any remaining shifts. Employer E circulates the overtime schedule in advance to enable employees to adjust their personal obligations accordingly.

- *Reassign job duties that employees are unable to perform* because of pregnancy or other caregiving responsibilities.

    - Example: Suriya's doctor recommends a 15-pound lifting restriction during her pregnancy. Employer F adjusts Suriya's workload by reassigning her heavy lifting duties to one of her co-workers and assigning Suriya some of the co-worker's duties.

    - Example: Jack and Lily work on the same team. Jack requests permission to readjust his schedule so that he can leave work early to pick up his daughter from pre-school. Lily requests a delayed start time so that she can take her mother to her weekly physical therapy sessions. Amar, their supervisor, grants both requests on the condition that Jack represent the team at early morning meetings and Lily represent the team at late afternoon meetings.

- *Provide reasonable personal or sick leave to allow employees to engage in caregiving* even if not required to do so by the Family and Medical Leave Act of 1993 (FMLA).

- o To the extent feasible, permit employees to take leave with little notice in case of an emergency and to use leave in short increments, rather than full days or weeks. Caregiving issues may arise suddenly and unexpectedly, and may be resolved in a relatively short amount of time.

    - For example, a child or elderly parent may get sick during the day and need to see a doctor. Or, a parent may need to make a quick phone call to ensure that his or her child got home from school safely.

    - With appropriate communication procedures and leave policies in place, these situations may be addressed with minimal inconvenience or cost to the employer.

  o Establish leave donation banks that enable employees to voluntarily contribute their leave to co-workers. Some organizations have "use it or lose it" leave policies which prohibit employees from accruing and retaining large amounts of leave. Leave donation banks ensure that leave time does not go to waste, and it fosters an atmosphere of collegiality and cooperation.

- *Promote an inclusive workplace culture.* Cultivate a professional work environment that recognizes and appreciates the contributions of all staff members and demonstrates respect for employees' personal lives and obligations.

    - Example: Employer G ensures that all employees, including individuals who work part-time or have flexible work schedules, are eligible to receive awards and recognition for their achievements.
    - Example: Employer H schedules all-staff meetings and events on "core days" when employees who work flexible schedules are in the office and able to attend.

- *Develop the potential of employees, supervisors, and executives* without regard to caregiving or other personal responsibilities.

  o Provide training to all workers, including caregivers, to provide them with the information necessary to perform their jobs well.

    - Example: When Nejib has to miss Employer I's annual training session to take his wife to the doctor, Nejib's supervisor e-mails him copies of the training presentations and handouts and provides him with contact information for the presenters in the event he has questions or comments. In this situation, Employer I ensured that Nejib has both access to the information presented and the ability to follow up with the appropriate individuals, as necessary, for additional information.

- *Ensure that employees are given equal opportunity to participate on complex or high-profile work assignments* that will enhance their skills and experience, as well as help them ascend to upper-level positions.

- Example: Employer J solicits assistance from employees on a large-scale project for an important client. Nicole has a flexible work schedule that enables her to work from home several days a week so she can care for her young son. Nicole volunteers to assist with the project and is selected for the team. The majority of work for the project can be performed off-site and circulated electronically to team members. Nicole also volunteers to come to the office for meetings with the client.

  - Example: Same facts as above, except Nicole is not selected for the project. Necessary files and equipment are stored on-site and cannot be removed. Furthermore, impromptu team meetings occur frequently so project members can discuss new developments and share information. As a result, it would be very difficult for an employee who works remotely to participate in this assignment. Employer J is justified in refusing Nicole's request to participate on this basis.

- *Provide employees with equal access to workplace networks* to facilitate the development of professional relationships and the exchange of ideas and information.

  - Example: Employer K has a mentoring program that matches experienced employees with more recent hires. All employees, including employees who work part-time or have a flexible work schedule, are eligible to participate in the program.

- *Provide support, resources, and/or referral services* that offer caregiver-related information to employees. Such services may include referral services for local child care centers or assisted living facilities, home health care, parenting education classes, college financing classes, or a toll-free caregiver hotline that provides guidance and advice to employees who have work-life integration questions or concerns.

Studies have demonstrated that flexible work policies have a positive impact on employee engagement and organizational productivity and profitability. The practices outlined above have the potential to benefit all workers, regardless of caregiver-status. Furthermore, these practices have the potential to benefit employers, enabling them to recruit and retain talented, productive, committed employees. Finally, these practices will help ensure that all workers enjoy equal opportunity to compete, advance, and succeed in the workplace.

References:

Human Rights Watch. "*Barriers Everywhere: Lack of Accessibility for People with Disabilities in Russia*", September 11, 2013. Available at: https://www.hrw.org/report/2013/09/11/barriers-everywhere/lack-accessibility-people-disabilities-russia

U.S. Equal Employment Opportunity Commission. "*Enforcement Guidance: Reasonable Accommodation and Undue Hardship Under the Americans with Disabilities Act*", October 17, 2002. Available at: https://www.eeoc.gov/policy/docs/accommodation.html

Avert. "*2016 Global HIV Statistics*", September 1, 2017. Available at: https://www.avert.org/global-hiv-and-aids-statistics

The Chicago Lighthouse. "*Top Benefits of Hiring People with Disabilities*", October 5, 2016. Available at: https://chicagolighthouse.org/sandys-view/top-5-benefits-hiring-people-disabilities/

Disability Management Employer Corporation. "*Workplace Warrior: The Corporate Response to Deployment and Reintegration*", March 22, 2007. Available at: https://dmec.org/2007/03/22/2007-think-tank-white-paper-workplace-warriors-the-corporate-response-to-deployment-and-reintegration/

Ernst & Young. "*Getting Support, Supporting Others: A Handbook for Working with Non-Visible Disabilities*", 2010. Available at: http://www.ey.com/Publication/vwLUAssets/Getting-support-handbook-non-visible-disabilities/$FILE/Getting-support-handbook-non-visible-disabilities.pdf

Sharecare.com. "*What's a caregiver?*" Available at: https://www.sharecare.com/health/caregiving/whats-a-caregiver

CDP EXAM STUDY GUIDE © 2018-2020

Sample Test Questions:
DISABILITY & SPECIAL NEEDS ACCOMMODATIONS

1. Providing a necessary and appropriate modification to a job position or the workplace is called:
   A. An undue burden
   B. The interactive process
   C. A reasonable accommodation

2. Assistive Technology is a generic term for devices and modifications that:
   A. Enable disabled workers to move
   B. Guide individuals with visual impairments
   C. Help overcome or remove a disability

3. An employer should **NOT** initiate a medical inquiry into an employee's:
   A. Prescriptions and treatment history
   B. Ability to perform the job
   C. Need for workplace modifications

4. Which term below is considered outdated when referring to a person?
   A. Handicapped
   B. Differently abled
   C. Disabled

5. Which is NOT an example of an employer's commitment to develop an inclusive environment?
   A. Handling disability accommodation requests with confidentiality and respect
   B. Hiring people with disabilities who may not be the best qualified for the job
   C. Encouraging employees to be receptive of fellow employees with disabilities

6. Extra job-related training and support is always required for employees with disabilities.
   A. True
   B. False

7. Under the ADA, an employer may refuse to hire an individual or fire a current employee who uses drugs illegally.
   A. True
   B. False

Sample Test Questions:
DISABILITY & SPECIAL NEEDS ACCOMMODATIONS (cont'd)

8. The ADA does NOT apply to people with AIDS.
   A. True
   B. False

9. Which of the following is considered a "nonvisible disability"?
   A. Behavior problems
   B. Diabetes
   C. A phantom limb

10. An example of a reasonable workplace accommodation may consist of:
    A. Modified or light duty
    B. Purchasing expensive equipment
    C. Promoting the worker

11. Which is TRUE concerning FMLA?
    A. FMLA provides up to 12 weeks of paid leave for all employees and their spouses
    B. FMLA allows an employee to care for a family member with a serious health condition
    C. FMLA only applies to female employees with 1,250 hours over the past 12 months

12. Which is NOT a common misconception about employees with caregiving responsibilities?
    A. Both male and female workers may have significant caregiving responsibilities
    B. Female employees prefer to spend time with their families instead of working
    C. Pregnant workers are less committed and reliable than other employees

13. A relationship exists between the Americans with Disabilities Act (ADA) and which Act below?
    A. The Vocational Rehabilitation Act of 1973
    B. The Genetic Information Nondiscrimination Act
    C. Employee Retirement Income Security Act (ERISA)

GENERATIONAL INTELLIGENCE

> ***CAUTION!***
>
> *A fundamental danger of working to dispel stereotypes is the inherent risk that you may reinforce biases instead of eliminating them.*
>
> *In respect to evaluating multiple generations in the workplace, the key is to acquire and apply knowledge that will provide insights into the different generation's interests, needs, and behaviors. Thereby, D&I leaders will ensure that organizations remain focused on strategy and not stereotypes.*

OVERALL OBJECTIVES AND COMPETENCIES

The purpose of this competency is prepare the workplace for changes in the organizational scope and structure by acknowledging generational differences in the approach to work, as well as in expectations for management.

BACKGROUND AND CONTEXT

Karl Mannheim, (March 27, 1893– January 9, 1947) a Hungarian-born sociologist, was influential in the first half of the 20th century as one of the founders of the sociology of knowledge. He defined a "generation" as a group of people born around the same period resulting in a shared experience of significant events and social changes. Such experiences influence their worldview and affect their attitudes, beliefs, and perceptions. People born in the same general timeframe were raised similarly, and share traditions and culture that often shape a "collective" peer personality. This collective worldview not only helps them to define themselves, but also their attitudes about members of different generations. Factors that help to give a generation this collective identity are (Wyatt, 1993):

1. Sharing in a traumatic or formative event such as 9-11 for Millennials, the assassination of a political leader (President John F. Kennedy for Boomers), or a nation's involvement in war (World War II for Veterans);

2. A dramatic shift in the nation's demography, such as the disproportionate increase of one age cohort relative to another (the Baby Boomer generation that affects the current and future distribution of resources, such as jobs and social security);

3. Privileged intervals or historical "luck" that occurs when a generation comes of age in a time of optimism and opportunity, such as the Veterans entering the workforce after World War II when the economy was growing rapidly;

4. Creation of a sacred space when a particular event or place defines the values and spirit of a generation such as the Woodstock concert for the Baby Boomers; and

5. Mentors or generational heroes who provide models for a generation about values such as courage, morality, justice, and holiness to incorporate into their own lives. For example, such models for the Boomers might include Dr. Martin Luther King, Jr. and for the Veterans or Traditionalists, President Franklin D. Roosevelt.

Generational groups are not sharply delineated nor mutually exclusive because of:

1. The number of people born on the cusp or cut-off line of a generation's defining birth years and;

2. The "crossover effect." For example, the assassination of John F. Kennedy, the *Challenger* disaster, and the terrorist attacks of September 11, 2001, had a profound effect on members of all generations—although these were formative moments for the generations coming of age during the time.

FIVE GENERATIONS IN THE MAKING

Each country defines its generational periods differently. Accordingly, D&I practitioners must be careful to cite the source when referencing generational data, as various Internet authors apply different time periods to each generational group. The U.S. Census, Pew Research Center, SHRM, and Nielsen, are a few of the reliable resources for generational data.

Until recently, the conversation about different generations involved just four groups, which are categorized in Figure 1.

FIGURE 1:

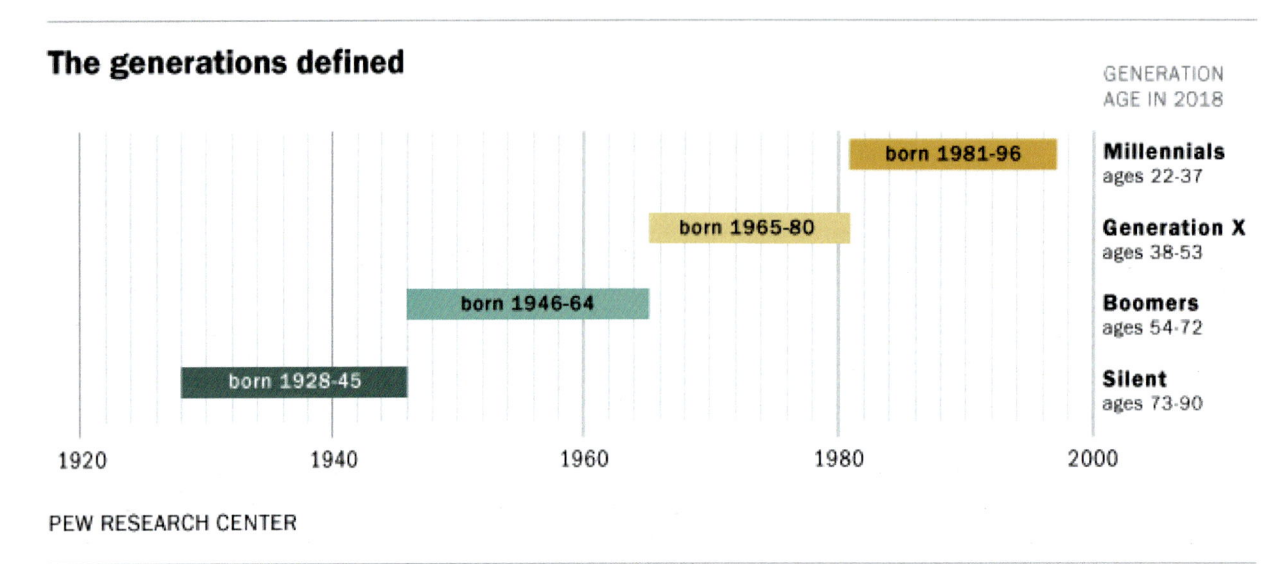

The generations defined

Generation	Birth Years	Age in 2018
Millennials	born 1981-96	ages 22-37
Generation X	born 1965-80	ages 38-53
Boomers	born 1946-64	ages 54-72
Silent	born 1928-45	ages 73-90

PEW RESEARCH CENTER

Generation Z or iGen is the latest cohort to be added to the education and workplace prospectus. While most are still getting to know this group, D&I leaders can employ generational intelligence to provide a competitive advantage to their respective organizations or clients.

FIGURE 2:

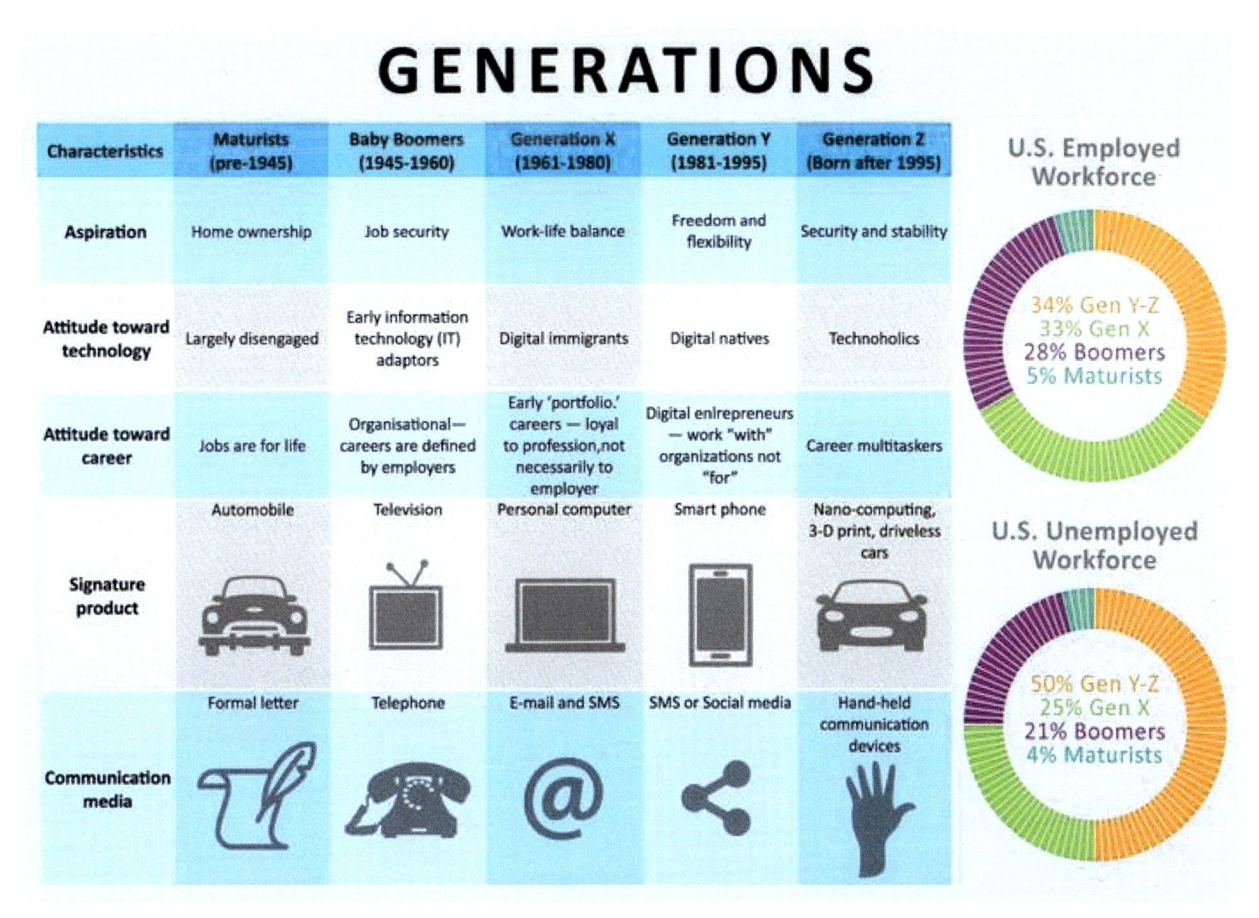

GENERATIONS

Characteristics	Maturists (pre-1945)	Baby Boomers (1945-1960)	Generation X (1961-1980)	Generation Y (1981-1995)	Generation Z (Born after 1995)
Aspiration	Home ownership	Job security	Work-life balance	Freedom and flexibility	Security and stability
Attitude toward technology	Largely disengaged	Early information technology (IT) adaptors	Digital immigrants	Digital natives	Technoholics
Attitude toward career	Jobs are for life	Organisational— careers are defined by employers	Early 'portfolio.' careers — loyal to profession, not necessarily to employer	Digital entrepreneurs — work "with" organizations not "for"	Career multitaskers
Signature product	Automobile	Television	Personal computer	Smart phone	Nano-computing, 3-D print, driverless cars
Communication media	Formal letter	Telephone	E-mail and SMS	SMS or Social media	Hand-held communication devices

U.S. Employed Workforce
- 34% Gen Y-Z
- 33% Gen X
- 28% Boomers
- 5% Maturists

U.S. Unemployed Workforce
- 50% Gen Y-Z
- 25% Gen X
- 21% Boomers
- 4% Maturists

Source: Vecteezy.com

With Generation Z, several different generations are working side-by-side in organizations around the world. This mixing of generations adds valuable diversity to the workforce, but also lends itself to potential conflicts and complications. In addition to age differences, each of these generations is at a different stage in their career cycles. This observation may seem straightforward, but it is also important to note that the generations will expect human resource variations in promotions, training and development, work assignments, paid time off, and employee benefits, to name a few.

According to the new Pew Research Center analysis of U.S. Census Bureau data, Millennials are the largest generation in the U.S. workforce. They surpassed Baby Boomer employees in 2014, and in 2015, Millennial workers topped Generation X to become the largest share of the American labor force. Nevertheless, Generation Z is projected to be even larger. See Figure 3.

FIGURE 3:

GENERATIONAL COMPOSITION

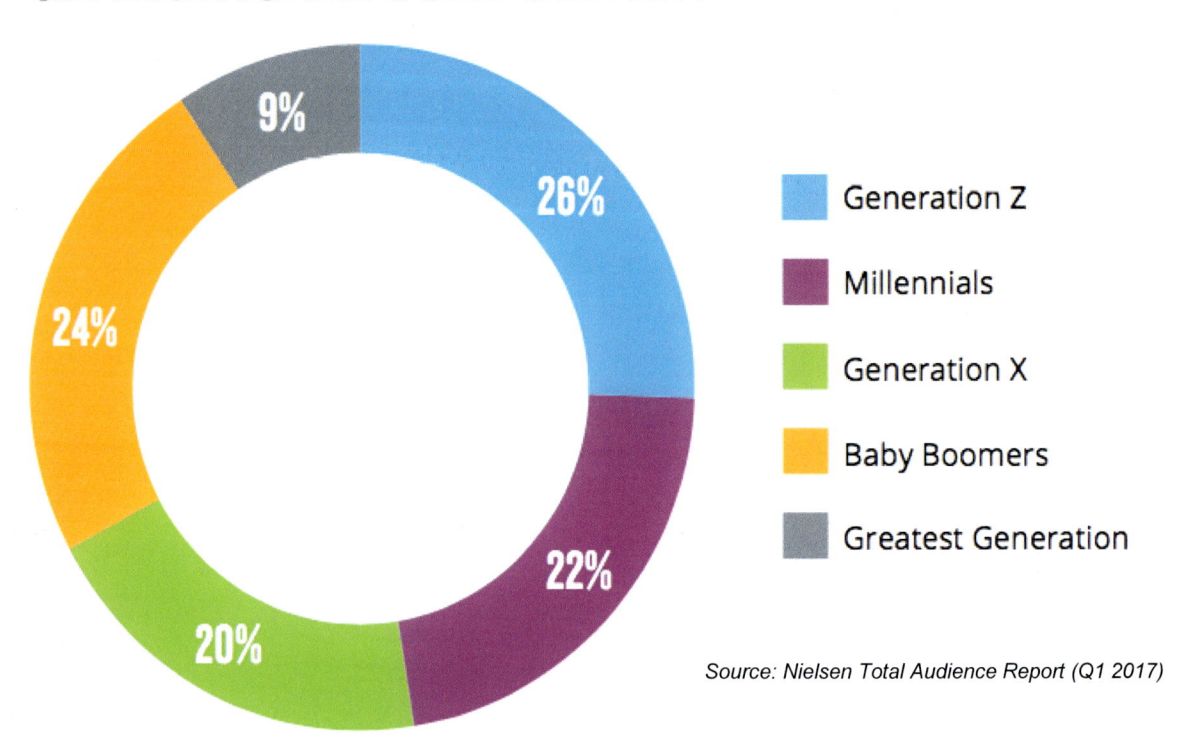

- Generation Z — 26%
- Millennials — 22%
- Generation X — 20%
- Baby Boomers — 24%
- Greatest Generation — 9%

Source: Nielsen Total Audience Report (Q1 2017)

Millennial generation witnessed the advent of "helicopter parents". A helicopter parent is a mom or dad who pays extremely close attention to a child's or children's experiences and problems, particularly at educational institutions and in the workplace. Helicopter parents are so named because, like helicopters, they hover overhead. The term gained wide currency when American college administrators began using it in the early 2000's as the Millennial Generation began reaching college age. Their Baby-Boomer parents earned notoriety for practices such as calling their children each morning to wake them up for class and complaining to their professors about grades the children had received. Employers also reported similar behavior with parents attending job fairs and showing up with candidates for job interviews. The rise of the cell phone is often blamed for the explosion of helicopter parenting.

In Today's Parent, Emma Waverman asserts that Helicopter Parents are old news. In *Snowplow parenting: The latest controversial technique*, Waverman defines a snowplow parent as "a person who constantly forces obstacles out of their kids' paths. They have their eye on the future success of their child, and anyone or anything that stands in their way has to be removed." She adds that while helicopter parents are motivated by fear, snowplow parents are driven by something else. Waverman says, "Snowplow parents may also micro-manage when it comes to diet and education, but they do so with an eye on the future. They want to remove any pain or difficulties from their children's paths so that their kids can succeed. They are the parents sitting in the principal's office asking about extra courses or for special allowances for their child. According to educators, there is a sense of entitlement to snowplowers: They blame the school when things go wrong and never accept anything less than first place for their child."

Another challenge is the proliferation of misinformation and stereotypes about each generational group. There are a myriad of ways to dispel the myths and foster cooperation, teamwork, and leadership.

> **Case Study #1: Leverage your young workforce's expertise**
> Ron Garrow, Chief Human Resources Officer at MasterCard, is not a technophobe, but he readily admits that social media didn't come easily to him — at least at first. "I recognized that I had a lot to learn about operating in this new world," says Ron, who is 51.
>
> So he volunteered to take part in a reciprocal mentoring program run by one of MasterCard's internal business resource groups. The program partners young employees with older colleagues to work on tech skills. Ron was assigned a coach, Rebecca Kaufman — 24 years old and an avid social media user — who taught him how to use Twitter and how to get more out of professional networking sites, such as LinkedIn. "Rebecca has shaped my thinking in terms of how I operate in the social space," says Ron. "I now carve out time in my day to get on LinkedIn and I have a [better appreciation for] the importance of social media."
>
> Working with Rebecca also helped Ron relate to Millennials as both the consumers and workforce of the future — a critical insight considering the changes taking place in MasterCard's industry. "This new generation is shaping the future in terms of purchasing habits: They don't use cash to buy things; they use electronic means. [As a result,] MasterCard's job descriptions have changed." Rebecca also benefits from the relationship: Ron provides professional counsel and is also helping improve her communication skills.
>
> Today hundreds of MasterCard employees take part in the program, which is currently offered in five offices. "There's a contagion going on — people are raising their hands and saying: 'I want a mentor.' It's really about making yourself vulnerable," he says.
>
> Source: Knight, Rebecca. Harvard Business Review, 2014. *Managing People from 5 Generations*. Retrieved from: https://hbr.org/2014/09/managing-people-from-5-generations

Successfully engaging and retaining multiple generations in the workplace is an asset because each group brings unique strengths, ideas, and experiences to the organizations with which they work. Stereotypes, however, reinforce generational conflicts and biases against these individuals. Stereotypes exist pertaining to skills (e.g., technology, communication, problem solving, coping, etc.), level of engagement, drive, and more. Nevertheless, there exists an opportunity for organizations to foster collaboration and leadership while preparing to employ and serve individuals across multiple dimensions of diversity.

> **Case Study #2: Motivate your employees with incentives that matter to them**
>
> Kris Snyder — the founder and CEO of Vox Mobile, the mobile technology management company based in Cleveland, Ohio — offers his 130 employees a veritable cafeteria of benefits, compensation, and work assignments. "I think of my employees as a cast of characters," says Kris, who is 42. "Everyone's needs are different, so we can't be a one-size-fits-all [employer]."
>
> The majority of Vox Mobile's sales force — about 85% — are just out of school and on their first or second job. Its leadership team, however, is comprised of people in their 30s and 40s. To appeal to these different age groups, he has developed different sets of employee perks based mainly on where these two age groups are in their personal and professional lives. "I noticed that these groups have different motivations and, therefore, they need different incentives," he says.
>
> "There are no hard and fast rules, but generally speaking, my Gen Y workers want us to fund their LinkedIn accounts; they like things like branded gear and company-sponsored happy hours — they're more social and they're not going home right after work. Gen Xers don't care about logoed backpacks; instead they are looking at our 401(k) matching plan and our healthcare provisions."
>
> The different incentive packages and perks will likely shift along with the company's demographics, says Kris. "As we build and grow and as the company goes through different stages, the makeup of our workforce will change, too," says Kris. "We will navigate those changes and experiment with new ways to incentivize employees."
>
> Source: Knight, Rebecca. Harvard Business Review, 2014. *Managing People from 5 Generations*. Retrieved from: https://hbr.org/2014/09/managing-people-from-5-generations

DIVERSITY AND INCLUSION PROFESSIONAL COMPETENCIES

Key to the role of a Diversity and Inclusion practitioner is understanding and working with the varied experiences, values, perspectives, work styles, and attitudes of the existing and emerging workforce. In addition to the overall definition of Generational Intelligence in this regard, the more specific components of this competence should guide your understanding of what practitioners need to know and what skills they must have in order to address issues arising from generational differences in the workplace.

D&I practitioners must develop intergenerational skills in:

3. **Team-Building and Effectiveness**
   A team's composition brings together the perspectives, attitudes, values, and other dimensions of its members that affect work behavior and team interaction.

Generational differences play a key role in building an effective team. Knowing the ways in which different generations approach the workplace, how to motivate each successfully, what rewards and incentives lead to high performance, and the leadership styles each prefer will all affect the success of any team.

4. **Recruitment and Retention**
   Not everyone is attracted to and retained in the workplace by the same organizational values, incentives, and rewards. Therefore, from the first steps of recruiting to the on-going efforts of retention, an organization must use its understanding of what values, incentives, and rewards appeal to each generation in the recruitment process, as well as in its longer-term retention and professional development planning.

5. **Performance Appraisal and Evaluation**
   Carrying out successful performance appraisals and evaluations are some of the most difficult processes and requirements for managers and supervisors. It is the rare person who finds these tasks easy to do and/or does them in such a way that all the parties involved feel satisfied in the process. Furthermore, these activities can become more difficult than usual when people from different generations are evaluating each other. This may be particularly true when a younger supervisor, for example, a Millennial, evaluates a Baby Boomer. What are the key values of both generations that must be taken into account during this process? What are the preferred modes of evaluation for each generation? How does one provide feedback to each generation in the most effective way?

6. **Professional Development**
   Employees at different life stages have different professional development expectations. For example, Baby Boomers may be most interested in "end of career" planning, while Millennials want to know how to develop their experience, knowledge, and skills to move up the management ladder. Others, such as Generation Xers, may need mid-career advice, including support and training for a career change within the organization, transfer to another division, or an overseas assignment. Each needs a career plan with goals, specific steps, timelines, and commitments from people within the organization.

7. **Multi-Generational Knowledge Transmission**
   While there is often more focus on the problems that arise from multiple generations in the workplace, many advantages also emerge. Different generations bring distinct knowledge, skill sets, and perspectives to work problems and issues that can foster effectiveness and innovation. Each generation's unique contributions, however, must flow up and down the organization. Therefore, management needs to create an atmosphere of openness to different ideas, whether they emanate from a Veteran, Baby Boomer, Gen Xer, or Millennial. They must also engage questions—even if the answers are contrary to the way that things are currently done.

   Before they leave the workforce, Veterans and Baby Boomers must find ways to transmit their knowledge and skill to the generations that remain. Because Baby Boomers, in particular, occupy such a large percentage of the global marketplace and are transforming entire communities, organizations must glean valuable insights from these individuals pertaining to the marketplace. From a historical context, institutional information and industry data are also indispensable resources in a knowledge-economy.

8. Global Business

Some organizations reluctantly assess how their industries and the needs of the workforce change; hence they are slow to adapt to the new workplace realities. For example, many organizations are still operating under the premise that most of the women who are having children are teenagers or in their early twenties. When in fact, the New York Times cites a 2018 Pew Report where "highly educated women, those over 40, and women who have never been married" are more likely to be mothers. Nevertheless, the erroneous assumption about when women have children is likely to negatively impact caregiver policies, key assignments, travel and relocation offers, paid time off, benefits, promotional opportunities, and other employment decisions for females in the mid-career stage. Therefore, management teams must be cognizant of the changes that have occurred in the workplace within the last few decades.

Since the arrival of the industrial age, organizations have hired human capital under the auspices that talent is disposable. When times were good, they increased the employee population. When times were bad, they would release talent to control costs. As a result, employees were considered to be an expense item on the balance sheet.

As the world migrates to the current service and information age, the nature of the employee contract will change dramatically. Human capital can no longer be valued for what they produce, but rather they must be valued for what is in their heads. With this change, the employee transitions from being a cost to being a non-owned corporate asset.

Using this framework—that talent is the most valuable asset in the organization—entails tailoring business functions such as recruiting, communications, IT, and benefits coordination to the generation, as well as delivering the format in various languages to account for the ethnic makeup of the workplace.

From a global sustainability perspective, organizations must have a strategy to recruit, engage, and retain the talent that will lead it into the future. According to an Organization for Economic Cooperation and Development (OECD) report, in 2005, 60% of the 25-34-year-olds with a tertiary education were in OECD countries. By 2013, the division between OECD and non-OECD G20 countries was about even, and by 2030 the picture will have reversed, with 70% of all graduates coming from non-OECD G20 countries. The non-OECD G20 group consists of the BRIC countries of Brazil, Russia, India and China, plus Argentine, Indonesia, South Africa and Saudi Arabia.

In dealing with global generational issues however, it is very important to recognize that each country faces very different problems and that the generalizations that may work in addressing this issue in the United States will not be successful in other parts of the world. It is also true that even in the U.S., different regions and states will have exclusive generational issues arising from the diverse employee populations that comprise the hiring pools.

Additionally, many global organizations actually lease the services of workers (e.g., contractors, temporary workers, etc.) rather than having a formal employment relationship. Changing the classification of some employees solidifies the existence of generational differences within our organizations. Hence, there is a need to approach the generational groups with fairness, but in the same token, with dissimilar ways. See Figure 4.

Figure 4: Relating to Generational Differences in the Workforce
(Source: Expressworks International, Nov. 21, 2017)

Characteristics	Maturists (pre-1945)	Baby Boomers (1945-1960)	Generation X (1961-1980)	Generation Y (1981-1995)	Generation Z (Born after 1995)
Formative experiences	Second World War, Rationing, Fixed-gender roles, Rock n' Roll, Nuclear families, Defined gender roles (particularly for women)	Cold War, Post-War Boom, "Swinging Sixties", Apollo Moon landings, Youth culture, Woodstock, Family-oriented, Rise of the teenager	End of Cold War, Fall of Berlin Wall, Reagan / Gorbachev, Thatcherism, Live Aid, Introduction of first PC, Early mobile technology, Latch-key kids; rising levels of divorce	9/11 terrorist attacks, PlayStation, Social media, Invasion of Iraq, Reality TV, Google Earth, Glastonbury	Economic downturn, Global warming, Global focus, Mobile devices, Energy crisis, Arab Spring, Produce own media, Cloud computing, Wiki-leaks
Percent of Global Population	5%	15%	20%	27%	32%
Aspiration	Home ownership	Job security	Work-life balance	Freedom and flexibility	Security and stability
Attitude toward technology	Largely disengaged	Early information technology (IT) adaptors	Digital Immigrants	Digital Natives	"Technoholics" - entirely dependent on IT; limited grasp of alternatives
Attitude toward career	Jobs are for life	Organizational: careers are defined by employers	Early "portfolio" careers - loyal to profession, not necessarily to employer	Digital entrepreneurs - work "with" organizations not "for"	Career multitaskers - will move seamlessly between organizations and "pop-up" businesses
Communication media	Formal letter	Telephone	E-mail and text message	Text or social media	Hand-held (or integrated into clothing) communication devices
Communication preference	Face-to-face	Face-to-face ideally, but telephone or email if required	Text messaging or email	Online and mobile (text messaging)	Facetime
Technology Milestone	Car	TV	PC	Smartphone	AR/VR

Naturally, there will be differences in thinking styles (e.g., holistic, analytical, etc.), thought processes (e.g., perceptual, attentional, etc.), and cognitive functions (e.g., verbal, visual-spatial, etc.) in all of the groups. Each generation is also characterized by a distinct perspective. These nuances are further complicated by culture, gender, socio-economic status, and educational attainment, to name a few. Therefore, managers and team members must learn to relate to each individual's situation.

Broadly speaking, all of the groups have strengths or weaknesses, however it is important not to generalize or assume. Focusing on each individual will be much more constructive, and lead to fewer frustrations.

Figure 5 illustrates how each generational group rates their own strengths and weaknesses.

FIGURE 5.

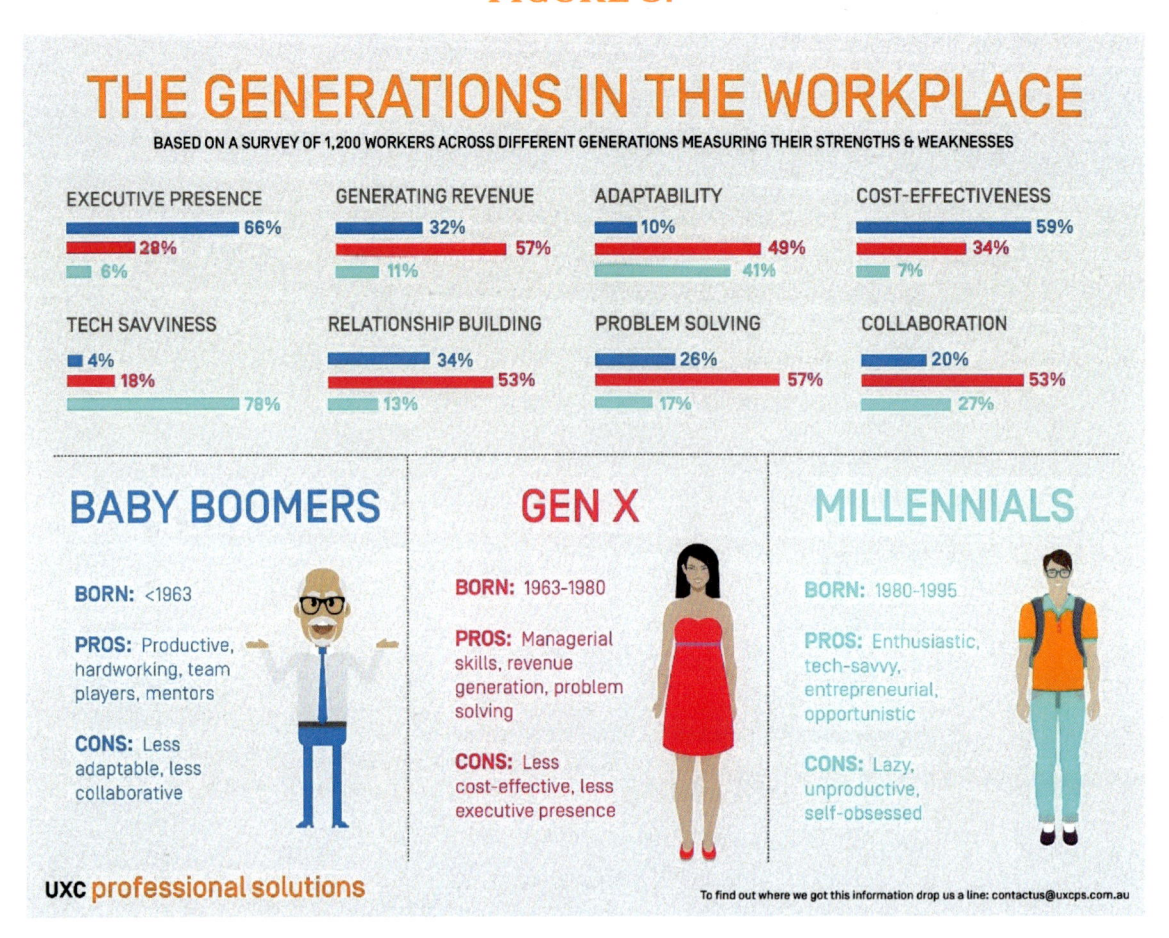

THE GENERATIONS IN THE WORKPLACE
BASED ON A SURVEY OF 1,200 WORKERS ACROSS DIFFERENT GENERATIONS MEASURING THEIR STRENGTHS & WEAKNESSES

Category	Baby Boomers	Gen X	Millennials
EXECUTIVE PRESENCE	66%	28%	6%
GENERATING REVENUE	32%	57%	11%
ADAPTABILITY	10%	49%	41%
COST-EFFECTIVENESS	59%	34%	7%
TECH SAVVINESS	4%	18%	78%
RELATIONSHIP BUILDING	34%	53%	13%
PROBLEM SOLVING	26%	57%	17%
COLLABORATION	20%	53%	27%

BABY BOOMERS
BORN: <1963
PROS: Productive, hardworking, team players, mentors
CONS: Less adaptable, less collaborative

GEN X
BORN: 1963-1980
PROS: Managerial skills, revenue generation, problem solving
CONS: Less cost-effective, less executive presence

MILLENNIALS
BORN: 1980-1995
PROS: Enthusiastic, tech-savvy, entrepreneurial, opportunistic
CONS: Lazy, unproductive, self-obsessed

UXC professional solutions
To find out where we got this information drop us a line: contactus@uxcps.com.au

To foster skills in working with multiple generations in an ever-changing organizational environment, open dialogue is essential in order to learn and understand the differences between the groups. Strategies to initiate discussion may consist of asking questions to solicit individuals' perspectives about how they grew up, as well as about family dynamics (e.g., parenting, meals, discipline, etc.) at that time. To expand upon this theme, participants may be encouraged to describe their own generation, and individuals may share whether they agree or disagree with generational stereotypes about their group and why. Questions may also be tailored to facilitate conversations about how the workplace has since changed, such as organizational policies (e.g., time-off), practices (e.g., mentoring), and expectations (e.g., promotions). These conversation starters provide a positive forum for open dialogue and self-reflection of employees' understanding of generational diversity.

In order to establish a broader approach to generational Inclusion, synergism is necessary. As the sum is greater than the parts, so the outcomes will span the generational gaps. Beyond employees, discussions about generational diversity must be facilitated regarding everyone that interacts with the organization, from customers to the Board of Directors. Focus on tapping into the resources of a diverse organization by asking questions that are thought provoking. For example, in respect to customers/students, determine if products/services will appeal to individuals in all age groups. Pertaining to the Board of Directors, ask if there is a Generation Xer or a Millennial. In regards to retirement projections, has a process been established for building "bench strength"?

In terms of activities to increase awareness, diversity practitioners can increase experiential learning and cultivate generational synergism by:

- *Sharing videos that illustrate generational differences;*
- *Reviewing the benefits package to determine whether the benefit offerings accommodate all career stages and generational needs;*
- *Developing an Employee Value Proposition--for each generation--which would list what is attractive about working for the organization; and*
- *Creating profiles of four ideal managers (with one from each generation). Place the profiles and pictures in easy to access locations (i.e., the website, break room, etc.).*

Non-monetary motivators designed for different generations may provide valuable options to increase productivity and retention as well. For example, the opportunity to utilize analytical and strategic thinking skills for temporary or part time assignments is a great use for Veteran and Baby Boomer talent. On the other hand, for Generation Xers and Millennials, the provision of opportunities to work with the latest technology or to travel to satellite locations would be desirable.

While the Millennials appreciate a management style that consists of close supervision and feedback, Generation Xers would be de-motivated. The creation of experiences or programs that capitalize on the generations' strengths, while simultaneously aligning the outcomes with your organization's mission and vision, supports a win-win scenario (Schwarz, 2008). Reframing the leaders' ability to build on the strengths and weaknesses of the generations serves as a catalyst to achieve the desired organizational culture (Dittman, 2005).

By understanding and embracing generational differences, D&I leaders will be better equipped to expand the definition of diversity and to foster the alignment of an institution's organizational culture with its mission and vision. This proactive approach—designed to search, value, respect, and effectively incorporate generational diversity—enhances communication, spans the gaps between generations, and promotes collaboration among organizations and their employees.

A NEW APPROACH TO AGING

Today, people grow older differently than their grandparents did. Sixty-five no longer marks the normal retirement age, and more people than ever are living 20-30 years into retirement. The aging of the population will have wide-ranging implications for every country around the world. As the United States ages over the next several decades, its older population will become more racially and ethnically diverse. Projecting the size and structure of the older population, in terms of age, sex, race, and Hispanic origin, is important to public and private interests, both socially and economically. The projected growth of the older population in the United States will present challenges to policy makers and programs such as Social Security and Medicare.

For example, Social Security has proven itself vital in protecting older Americans from poverty in old age. However, Social Security was never designed to help promote second careers, or new forms of productivity among older people. Similarly, Medicare has proven to be an important means of guaranteeing access to healthcare for older people but it was never designed to address the problems of long-term care for older people who need the day-to-day help in order to remain in their own homes.

Indeed, healthcare has changed dramatically for seniors. Not only do more American seniors have health care coverage, but the quality of that care is exceptional. This has led to longer life expectancy, cures for previously untreatable ailments, and prescription drugs to treat all other medical problems. This means that seniors are more likely to have a better quality of life in old age. As a result, instead of retiring in nursing homes, seniors are more likely to live at home and receive home health care or outpatient care. Additionally, these individuals are more likely to be cared for by a family member, which has created a new phenomenon all over the world.

The **Sandwich Generation** is a term that reflects the byproduct of people aging at home. Essentially, the Sandwich Generation is "a generation of people who care for their aging parents while supporting their own children". According to a 2013 Pew Research Center survey, nearly half (47%) of adults in their 40s and 50s have a parent age 65 or older, and are either raising a young child or financially supporting a grown child (age 18 or older). About one-in-seven middle-aged adults (15%) are providing financial support to both an aging parent and a child.

FIGURE 6.

Middle-Aged Adults "Sandwiched" Between Aging Parents and Kids

% of adults ages 40 to 59 who ...

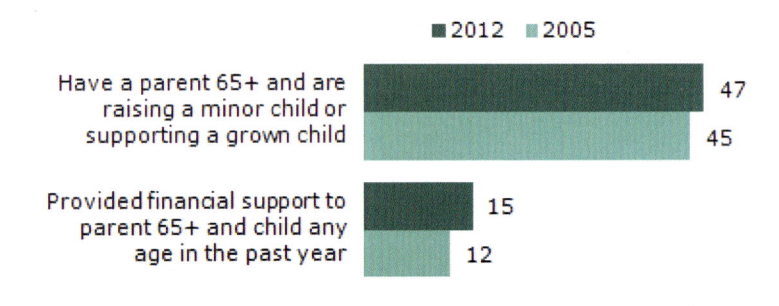

	2012	2005
Have a parent 65+ and are raising a minor child or supporting a grown child	47	45
Provided financial support to parent 65+ and child any age in the past year	15	12

Note: Based on all adults ages 40 to 59; for 2012, n=844; for 2005, n=1,185.

PEW RESEARCH CENTER   Q21,27, P1,3,4

Who is in the Sandwich Generation? According to the Pew Report, Sandwich Generation "members are mostly middle-aged: 71% of this group falls between age 40 and 59. An additional 19% are younger than 40 and 10% are age 60 or older. Men and women are equally likely to be members of the sandwich generation. Hispanics are more likely than whites or blacks to be in this situation. More affluent adults, those with annual household incomes of $100,000 or more, are more likely than less affluent adults to be in the sandwich generation. Additionally, married adults are more likely than unmarried adults to be sandwiched between their parents and their children: 36% of those who are married fall into the sandwich generation, compared with 13% of those who are unmarried."

The Sandwich phenomenon is due in part to what the U.S. Census Bureau calls the "Delayer Boom", or the number of American women who decided to have children later in life. In this scenario, highly educated women initially delay childbearing but are more likely to have children in their 30s. The Census Bureau report entitled, "Fertility of American Women: 2010" found that:

- *In 2000, women aged 25 to 34 with at least a bachelor's degree had fewer total children and were less likely to have ever given birth compared with women who had less than a high school education. By 2010 (10 years later), these same women with at least a bachelor's degree had 1.7 births, while women who had less than a high school education had 2.5 births.*

- *Foreign-born women were more likely to have had a baby than were native-born women by the age of 40 to 44, at 87 percent compared with 80 percent.*

- *More than half (55 percent) of women who had a child in 2009 were in the labor force. Of those women, about one third (34 percent) were working full time, 14 percent were working part time, and 7 percent were unemployed.*

- *Almost one-quarter (23 percent) of women with a birth in 2009 reported living in households with family incomes of at least $75,000. At the other end of the income scale, about one in five (21 percent) were living in families with incomes under $20,000.*

- *By age 40 to 44, white non-Hispanic women (20.6 percent) were more likely to be childless than Hispanic women (12.4 percent), black women (17.2 percent) and Asian women (15.9 percent). Black women were also more likely to be childless than Hispanic women. Asian women did not differ from black or Hispanic women.*

There has been a small but significant increase in the number of childless women in their early 30s since the 2010 report, according to recently released data from the U.S. Census Bureau's Current Population Survey's fertility supplement. In 2006, 26.2 percent of women ages 30 to 34 were childless, meaning they had never given birth to a child. By 2016, that number had risen about 4 percentage points to 30.8 percent. The Census Bureau's latest report on young adults captures the ongoing trend of delaying marriage and childbearing among those aged 18 to 34. This delayer boom will also have an impact on the workplace, as well as on future generations.

The U.S. Census Bureau reports that by 2030, all of the Baby Boomers will have moved into the ranks of the older population. This will result in a shift of the age structure, from 13 percent of the population aged 65 and older in 2010 to 19 percent in 2030. In 2010, 60 percent of the U.S. population was aged 20–64. By 2030, as the Baby Boomers age, the proportion in these working ages will drop to 55 percent.

Immigration is expected to play an important role in how the age structure of the United States changes over the next four decades. As Baby Boomers age and retire from the workforce, younger immigrants will replace the Baby Boomer labor force. In other words, the country's aging has slowed somewhat by the immigration of younger people. These immigrants will also contribute to Social Security coffers, and fill technical and professional positions in unprecedented percentages.

While the older population is not as racially and ethnically diverse as the younger population, the population is projected to substantially increase its racial and ethnic diversity over the next four decades. Additionally, while all of the racial and ethnic groups will become older, the degree of aging that is projected to occur within each group varies greatly. In terms of race, the share of the population that is White alone is projected to decrease by about 10 percentage points among those 65 years and over, and by about 9 percentage points among those 85 years and over, through 2050. Meanwhile, all other racial groups are projected to see an increase in their shares of the population.

The 85 years and over population is less racially diverse than the 65 years and older population, but it is projected to see a similar increase in diversity through 2050. Although the older population is not expected to become majority-minority in the next four decades, it is projected to be 42 percent minority in 2050, up from 20 percent in 2010.

Seniors in the Workplace
The recession was not kind to older Americans. Low stock prices depleted their savings and many retirees were forced back into the workplace to survive. In a 2011 survey by the Associated Press and LifeGoesStrong.com, one in four baby boomers still working said they will never retire. Moreover, nearly 60 percent said their workplace retirement plans, personal investments, or real estate lost value during the economic crisis in the last decade. Because of that, 42 percent in that group are delaying retirement plans.

At a time when they are supposed to be enjoying their golden years, many senior citizens are competing for jobs against younger applicants at places like movie theaters, grocery stores, and restaurants. Nevertheless, ageism is real. There are dozens of myths that must be dispelled such as older workers are slower on technology or are resistant to change. Additionally, our language may perpetuate employment stereotypes. In *Hiring in the Age of Ageism*, Kate Rockwood asserts that we are noticing "a shift in hiring managers' vocabulary away from 'experienced' and 'seasoned' and toward 'high-potential' and 'energetic.' That's where [employers] need to be careful, since such terms can be viewed as a code for 'young'." SHRM notes that "in a youth-obsessed employment market, age discrimination could cost your company strong candidates and diverse teams".

There are many benefits to hiring older workers. According to one AARP report on *The Business Case for Hiring 50+ Workers*, older employees are more likely to demonstrate loyalty, motivation, as well as the soft skills that today's employers need. Those traits offer a good model for younger workers. Furthermore, a number of companies with older customers are hiring more seniors because they can identify with clients' needs.

UP NEXT: I-GEN

The word *iGeneration* is derived from Apple's suite of popular products, encompassing the iPod, iPhone, iPad, and iWatch, to name a few. This generation prefers to FaceTime, use touch screens, watch short video clips online (e.g., YouTube), wear headphones, and work in small groups of high performers. To the iGeneration, the Internet is not limited to home or work computers; it is something you can access in your pocket.

Also known as Generation Z or iGen, this group was born in the late 1990's and is more technologically advanced than all other generations before it. A recent study by Einstein Medical Center in Philadelphia found that "Children younger than a year old are using smartphones and tablets before they know how to walk - some are even making phone calls. Three quarters of children are using the devices by the time they're two years old, and almost all of them are plugged into mobile media by the time they're four." In other words, by the time the iGen cohort becomes teenagers, they are technology experts with 10 or more years of experience. In some suburban school districts, students are learning keyboarding and coding as young as kindergarten. Even in urban areas, students are provided with laptops or tablets as early as middle or high school. Globally, youth are participating in international robot-building competitions.

From social media, to video games, to the proliferation of mobile technology, iGen has the potential to be among the smartest and most competitive employees yet. Concurrently, iGen represents a change in methods, attitudes, and values. Organizations may have to re-think:

- The layout of buildings (e.g., away from individual offices/classrooms into open concept spaces).
- How work groups operate (e.g., with more focus on team accomplishments versus individual achievements).
- How learning is facilitated (e.g., with short, how-to videos versus all day sessions).
- How often technology is upgraded or updated.
- Organizational transparency (e.g., in regard to decision-making, pay, promotions, and discipline).

Additionally, a larger proportion of iGen members are multi-racial. In fact, Census 2010 reported that the multi-racial population has increased almost 50% since 2000, making it the fastest growing youth group in the country. This means that different racial and ethnic groups **must** be included in succession planning and pipeline development. Further, one of the prominent features of iGen is the non-traditional household. According to the 2010 U.S. Census, both men and women are getting married at a later age, and there are more same-sex couples raising children.

In terms of marketing, "iGen is a generation born with consumer-driven capitalism at its core and altruism at its heart. We recognized that iGen'ers only care about information if it is relevant to them and, since the power of brand-engagement is in the hands of the consumer, they will serve as their own gatekeepers. This trend is already evident in early studies: 60% of iGen expects relevant advertisements and 46% prefer funny advertisements", according to Stefan Pollack, author of *Disrupted, From Gen Y to iGen: Communicating with the Next Generation.* Hence, iGen is a cohort that is indiscriminately focused on me, myself, and I.

A marked difference between Millennials and iGen is that older members of the former remember life before the takeoff of mass technology, while the latter have been born immersed within it. This generation has also been born completely into an era of postmodernism, multiculturalism, and globalization. Parents of iGen are working part-time in the Gig Economy or becoming stay-at-home parents so that children are raised by them and other family members instead of a day care facility, which forces children to be in groups.

Generation Z has not fully entered the workplace yet. Therefore, it remains to be seen what impact technology will have on their expectations for education and employment.

CONCLUSION

Navigating through the generations with intelligence is crucial to avoiding costly mistakes, and preventing a generational imbalance (i.e., 80% of your workforce is 50 or older, while 20% is younger than age 49). Each age group is necessary for your organization to function effectively, as well as for you to transfer knowledge, skills, and other qualities from generation to generation. This is what will make your organization a great place to work through the ages.

Understanding how education, work and the marketplace should prepare for each generational group is a powerful reminder that diversity efforts must go beyond political correctness and token inclusion, towards planning for the next generation.

References:

Wyatt, David. (1993). *Out of the Sixties: Storytelling and the Vietnam Generation.* New York: Cambridge University Press.

Parker, Kim and Patten, Eileen. Pew Research Center (January 2013). *The Sandwich Generation: Rising Financial Burdens for Middle-Aged Americans.* Retrieved from: http://www.pewsocialtrends.org/2013/01/30/the-sandwich-generation/

Waverman, Emma. Today's Parent (Jan. 14, 2015). *Snowplow parenting: The latest controversial technique.* Available at: https://www.todaysparent.com/blogs/snowplow-parenting-the-latest-controversial-technique/

Miller, Claire Cain. The New York Times (Jan. 18, 2018). *The U.S. Fertility Rate Is Down, Yet More Women Are Mothers.* Available at: https://www.nytimes.com/2018/01/18/upshot/the-us-fertility-rate-is-down-yet-more-women-are-mothers.html

Morrison, Nick. Forbes (Apr. 26, 2015). *The Global Talent Pool Will Have A Different Face by 2030.* Available at: https://www.forbes.com/sites/nickmorrison/2015/04/26/the-global-talent-pool-will-have-a-different-face-by-2030/#1109bb834d14

Schwarz, R. (2008). *Why managing generational differences is important.* Retrieved on 5/10/08 http://www.marsvenusatwork.com/generations/htm

Dittman, M. (2005). *Generational differences at work"* Monitor on Psychology. Retrieved on 11/15/2007 http://www.apa.org/monitor/jun05/generational.html

Monte, Lindsay. (U.S. Census Bureau, Nov. 2017). *Some Delay Childbearing, Others Opt Out.* Available at: https://census.gov/library/stories/2017/11/women-early-thirties.html

Rockwood, Kate. (SHRM, Jan. 22, 2018). *Hiring in the Age of Ageism.* Available at: https://www.shrm.org/hr-today/news/hr-magazine/0218/pages/hiring-in-the-age-of-ageism.aspx

AARP. *The Business Case for Hiring 50+ Workers.* Available at: https://www.aarp.org/aarp-foundation/our-work/income/back-to-work-50-plus/hire-50-plus-workers/

Kabali, Hilda. (Einstein Healthcare Network, Apr. 27, 2015). *Toddler Tweets? Maybe Not So Far Off.* Available at: https://www.einstein.edu/news/toddlertweetsmaybenotsofaroff

Pollack, Stefan. (Pacific Coast Creative Publishing, Jan. 24, 2014). *Disrupted, From Gen Y to iGen: Communicating with the Next Generation.*

Sample Test Questions:
GENERATIONAL INTELLIGENCE

1. **An example of a generational difference in cognitive functioning is:**
   A. Analytical
   B. Visual-Spatial
   C. Attentional

2. **Which of the following words could indicate age discrimination in the hiring process?**
   A. High potential
   B. Experienced
   C. Seasoned

3. **In appealing to Generation Z, organizations may have to re-think all of the following EXCEPT:**
   A. Policies regarding paid time off
   B. The layout of buildings
   C. How learning is facilitated

4. **This phenomenon resulted in a number of American women who decided to have children later in life:**
   A. Snowplow Parenting
   B. Sandwich Generation
   C. Delayer Boom

5. **Social Security has been vital in protecting older Americans from poverty, but it was never designed to:**
   A. Support people in their 100's
   B. Provide in-home healthcare
   C. Promote second careers

6. **Before leaving the workforce, Veterans and Baby Boomers must find ways to transmit their _____ to the generations that remain.**
   A. Stereotypes and biases
   B. Knowledge and skills
   C. Customer Relationships

Sample Test Questions:
GENERATIONAL INTELLIGENCE (cont'd)

7. Marketers should be prepared to engage iGen with information that is:
   A. Face-to-face or formal
   B. Reliant on text messaging
   C. Relevant to them

8. In this current service and information age, human capital cannot be valued for:
   A. What they produce
   B. What they know
   C. How they work

9. A surge of "Helicopter Parents" on college campuses and in the workplace has been aided by:
   A. Cell Phones
   B. Global Marketing
   C. The Delayer Boom

10. Generational groups are not sharply delineated nor mutually exclusive because of:
    A. Longer living cohorts
    B. The labor force shortage
    C. The cross-over effect

11. When managing individuals of different generations, supervisors should not acknowledge differences.
    A. True
    B. False

12. Each country faces the same workplace issues and generalizations about the different generations.
    A. True
    B. False

13. Not everyone is attracted to and retained in the workplace by the same organizational values, incentives, and rewards.
    A. True
    B. False

DESIGNING PROGRAMS FOR VETERANS

> *Veterans returning to the workplace from overseas and combat assignments can face difficult challenges transitioning into the workplace, as well as in civilian life. It is important to understand their experiences without stereotyping or exhibiting biases. We must also create a culture of support that embraces veterans in the workplace and allows them to utilize their leadership skills and talent to get the job done!*

OVERALL OBJECTIVES AND COMPETENCIES

This competency is designed to improve the organization's ability to employ a diverse veteran population by utilizing best practices for optimal workplace performance.

BACKGROUND AND CONTEXT

The United States Armed Forces consist of the Army, Navy, Marine Corps, Air Force, and Coast Guard. The President of the United States is the military's Commander-in-Chief and helps form military policy with the U.S. Department of Defense (DoD), a federal executive department, acting as the principal organ by which military policy is carried out.

The DoD is headed by the Secretary of Defense, who is a civilian and cabinet member. The Defense Secretary is second in the military's chain of command, just below the President, and serves as the principal assistant to the President in all DoD-related matters. To coordinate military action with diplomacy, the President has an advisory National Security Council, headed by a National Security Advisor. Both the President and Secretary of Defense are advised by a seven-member Joint Chiefs of Staff, which includes the head of each of the Defense Department's service branches as well as the chief of the National Guard Bureau. The Chairman of the Joint Chiefs of Staff and the Vice Chairman of the Joint Chiefs of Staff provide leadership.

For over 300 years, American Colonists or United States citizens have been involved in war. Beginning in 1675 with King Philip's War, America has required its citizens to be away from home for long periods of time—fighting for or serving the country. Since the 1900's, the most notable wars include World Wars I & II, the Korean War, the Vietnam War, the Persian Gulf War, and the Invasion of Afghanistan and Iraq. These wars have resulted in millions of veterans who eventually returned home. Many assimilated with little or no problems, while others returned with a service-connected disability resulting from war.

While not all veterans who return home or to the workplace have difficulties readjusting, some do. It is possible for a veteran to deal with feelings of relief, hope, and a desire for things to "return to normal". It is important for Diversity and Inclusion leaders to keep in mind that some of their experiences, emotions, and memories of what they have seen or lived through may be anything BUT normal. Every veteran is different as is every family, but there are some common readjustment factors. Such factors may be affected by:

- The length of time the veteran was away
- The veteran's proximity to active warfare
- The number of times the veteran engaged in warfare
- The age of the veteran
- The veteran's marital status

Not only will veterans experience readjustment factors at home, they must also transition into a civilian work force that has not always welcomed them with open arms. Because of their military experiences, veterans can suffer stereotypes and stigmas on the job. Facing these issues in the workplace can be disheartening for the veterans who voluntarily risked their lives for their country.

According to government statistics, between October 2001 and December 2012, thousands of service members in Iraq, Afghanistan, and surrounding duty stations were wounded in action. Many of them lost a hand or limb, or were severely burned or blinded. Others were diagnosed with hearing loss, post-traumatic stress disorder (PTSD), traumatic brain injury (TBI), and other service-connected disabilities. Despite their injuries, many veterans who leave active duty are still able to work because of medical advances and new technologies.

A NATIONAL FOCUS ON VETERANS

A military veteran is a person who has served or is serving in the armed forces. Outside of the U.S., virtually every nation with a military has veterans, and every country also has challenges serving these veterans after they return from duty. By global standards, the U.S. Department of Veterans Affairs (or VA) provides generous and comprehensive programs and services for veterans. Yet, the VA and Veteran care are generally considered inefficient in the U.S.

Size is one problem. The huge Veteran population and bureaucratic size of the VA possibly contributes to an outdated business model. Smaller countries may have smaller budgets, but they also serve fewer Veterans and have smaller veterans' departments.

In 2014, Veterans Affairs Canada sheds light on the sheer numbers of Veterans in the United States versus other countries. The study determined that Canada, Australia, the United Kingdom and the United States all offer their veterans comparable benefits and services. While there are significant differences in the design, delivery, and type of services available to Veterans in each country, all of these countries provide Veterans re-adjustment support in five common domains: disability compensation, rehabilitation, income support, health services coverage, and career transition support. Some of the differences include the fact that the United States is the only country which provides all Veterans up to 36 months of educational benefits. Additionally, Canada, Australia and the United Kingdom provide a lump-sum award for disabled veterans versus the monthly disability compensation that is provided in the U.S.

Figure 1 illustrates the findings of Veterans Affairs Canada.

FIGURE 1: COUNTRY COMPARISON

Source: Veterans Affairs Canada, 2014 (Note: C$ = Canadian dollars)

Country	Canada	Australia	United Kingdom	United States
Name	Veterans Affairs Canada	Department of Veterans Affairs	Service Personnel and Veterans Agency	United States Department of Veterans Affairs
Total Population	33,500,000	21,200,000	61,100,000	307,200,000
Number of clients served	220,000	415,000	900,000	23,800,000
Number of annual releases	Approximately 4,000 release annually.	Approximately 5,000 release annually.	Approximately 24,000 release annually.	Approximately 200,000 release annually.
Budget (2009-2010)	$3.4 billion C$	$11.13 billion C$	$19.40 billion C$	$100.14 billion C$
Number of staff	3,700	2,100	2,100	278,500
Programs Supporting Transition **	•New Veterans Charter •Disability Awards •Rehabilitation •Financial Benefits •Health Benefits •Job Placement	•Military and Compensation Act •Rehabilitation •Permanent Impairment •Incapacity Payments •Special Rate Disability Pension •Career Transition Assistance Scheme	•Armed Forces Compensation Scheme •Lump-Sum Payment •Guaranteed Income Payment •Career Transition Partnership	•VA Disability Compensation •VA Disability Pension •VA Health Care System •Independent Living Program •Vocational Rehabilitation and Employment Program •Post 9/11 GI Bill

The focus of this competency is the U.S. armed forces, which is the world's third largest military in the world behind China and India respectively, according to the World Atlas. The Atlas reports that although America has the 3rd largest military, its budget is far larger than its closest rival China, which spends $216 billion annually. In fact, on February 9, 2018, Congress passed a spending bill that appropriated $700 billion for the defense base budget.

Over the past decade, approximately 3 million veterans have returned from military service and another one million are expected to return to civilian life over the course of the next 5 years. According to the U.S. Bureau of Labor Statistics (BLS), the veteran unemployment rate was 4.5 percent in 2017. BLS also reported that about 41 percent of Gulf War-era II veterans (those who served after September 2001) had a service-connected disability in August 2017, compared with 24 percent of all veterans.

Since the official end to the Afghanistan and Iraq wars in 2011, the U.S. government has developed a strategic approach to veteran's health, employment, and the prevention of homelessness. The first level of national focus is with the Veterans Administration and partner social service agencies; the second level of national focus is with employers who can provide jobs and government vendors who can provide sub-contracting opportunities through supplier diversity programs.

To be eligible for veteran status in the U.S., an individual must have served in the military for a minimum of 180 days of regular active duty service. The U.S. also requires a last discharge, or release, under honorable conditions. A veteran's record does not have to include wartime service.

Veterans serve for different lengths of time and during different wartime and peacetime periods. They also entered the military at different ages and came from different backgrounds. Some were drafted, while others volunteered. Their differences make each veteran unique and influence the size and overall characteristics of veterans as a group. Generally, veterans can be classified as two main cohorts: "draft era" and "All Volunteer Force" (AVF). Draft-era veterans are mainly those veterans who served in the military during the Vietnam era, Korean War or World War II. In 1973, the draft ended and the AVF began. As depicted in Figure 2, the draft-era military was substantially larger than today's AVF.

FIGURE 2

Number Who Served During Selected Periods
(In millions)

- World War II: 16.1
- Korean War: 5.7
- Vietnam Era: 8.7
- Current active duty strength: 1.3

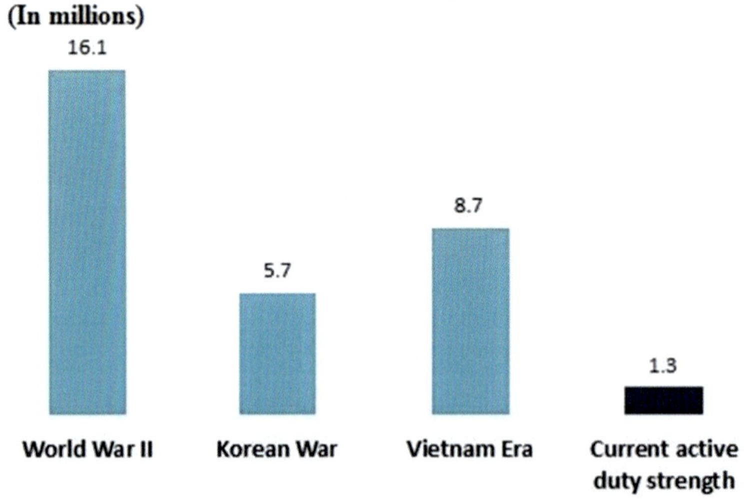

Sources: Department of Defense, Defense Manpower Data Center; Department of Veterans Affairs, Office of Public Affairs.

To put this into perspective, 16 million people served in World War II, 6 million served in the Korean War and 9 million served during the Vietnam era, according to this Department of Defense chart. In contrast, AVF active-duty military strength has remained under 2 million each year since the 1990s. In 2015, there were just under 1 million living World War II veterans, 70 years after the end of the war, while the active duty military size was about 1.3 million service members.

Providing Benefits & Care for Veterans
The United States Department of Veterans Affairs is a government-run military veteran benefit system with Cabinet-level status. It is the United States government's second largest department, after the United States Department of Defense. The VA employs over 300,000 people at hundreds of Veterans Affairs medical facilities, clinics, and benefits offices, and is responsible for administering benefits programs for veterans, their families, and survivors. The benefits provided include disability compensation, pension, education, home loans, life insurance, vocational rehabilitation, survivors' benefits, medical benefits, and burial benefits.

VA categorizes veterans into eight priority groups and several additional subgroups, based on factors such as service-connected disabilities, and one's income and assets (adjusted to the local cost of living). A service-connected disability means that the veteran "is disabled due to an injury or illness that was incurred in or aggravated by military service". Veterans with a 50% or higher service-connected disability as determined by a VA regional office "rating board" (e.g., losing a limb in battle, PTSD, etc.) are provided comprehensive care and medication at no charge. Veterans with lesser qualifying factors who exceed a pre-defined income threshold have to make co-payments for care for non-service-connected ailments and pay a very modest co-payment per 30- to 90-day supply for each prescription medication. VA dental and nursing home care benefits are more restricted.

Reservists and National Guard personnel who served stateside in peacetime settings or have no service-related disabilities generally do not qualify for VA health benefits.

Within the last few years, VA opened hundreds of new convenient outpatient clinics in towns across the United States, as VA's budget was pushed to the limit by the War on Terrorism. In December 2004, it was widely reported that VA's funding crisis had become so severe that it could no longer provide disability ratings to veterans in a timely fashion. This was a problem because until veterans are fully transitioned from the active-duty TRICARE healthcare system to VA, they are on their own with regard to many healthcare costs.

After much scrutiny, as well as administrative and procedural changes, the VA began instituting an improvement process to reduce screening times for returning combat veterans. As part of the improvement process, VA personnel now evaluates combat veterans well before their actual discharge and they receive first priority for patient appointments.

In the *2011 Costs of War* report from Brown University, researchers projected that the cost of caring for veterans of the War on Terror would peak 30-40 years after the end of combat operations. They also predicted that medical and disability costs would ultimately total between $600 billion and $1 trillion for the hundreds of thousands treated by the VA. Simultaneously, the New York Times reported that while the withdrawal of American military forces from Iraq and Afghanistan will save the nation billions of dollars a year, healthcare costs and disability payments are projected to continue rising for decades to come as the population of Iraq and Afghanistan veterans age and become more infirm. BLS reports that more than 4 million troops served in those wars as of 2017.

Estimating the long-term costs of healthcare and other programs for veterans is a complex and contentious art; and no one inside the government makes estimations beyond 10 years. Independent and government experts agree that, for a variety of reasons, the costs are just about certain to continue rising, even as large numbers of World War II and Korean War veterans are dying.

The cost of veterans' care has increased due to improvements in battlefield medicine, equipment, and technology. In fact, more troops today are surviving injuries—90 percent, up from 86 percent in Vietnam—according to the Congressional Budget Office. As a result of these improvements, more troops are coming home with complex and severe wounds. Nevertheless, their resilience and tenacity enables them to be career ready!

TRANSITION ASSISTANCE FOR SEPARATING SERVICE MEMBERS

Service members separating from active duty, including Reservists and Guardsmen demobilizing after serving 180 days on active duty, face numerous challenges as they transition to civilian life.

These challenges include but are not limited to:

- An American economy that is not ready to absorb the numbers of post Afghanistan and Iraq Veterans into the workforce
- How to prudently use the very generous Post 9/11 GI Bill to accomplish college and technical training goals
- A confusing array of services for Veterans in both the public and private sector
- Employers who misunderstand the occurrence and effects of PTSD.

In order to address these challenges, the Department of Defense (DoD) and Veterans Affairs (VA) led an interagency Veterans Employment Initiative Task Force to redesign the Desert Storm-era Transition Assistance Program (TAP). TAP would provide a cohesive, modular, mandatory training to build skills so that separating Service members could meet new career readiness standards (CRS) before they start their civilian careers. The transition training is known as Transition GPS. The training is comprised of interlinked curriculums, services, and processes conducted by six different partners—DoD, the Military Services, VA, Department of Labor (DoL), Small Business Administration (SBA), and the Office of Personnel Management (OPM). The Department of Education (ED) serves in an invaluable consultative role.

While this transformational approach was approved by President Obama in January 2012, the real work of implementing this redesigned, interdependent program had only just begun. The first step was for each of the TAP interagency partners to pilot, modify, and finalize revised curriculums. The next step was to execute the teaching of the curriculums via a seamless process, capitalizing on technology in military installation classrooms. Additionally, a high quality virtual curriculum had to be developed to ensure that geographically dispersed Service Members had access to career readiness training. Routine assessment of curriculum and performance of the overall program also had to be established.

Data collection and sharing processes across the interagency were developed to ensure targeted service delivery across the military to the civilian continuum. An information technology architecture serves as the backbone to both share data and create efficiencies across the TAP interagency "system". Finally, resources had to be committed for the long-term to assure all TAP partners that their interdependent work would take root and endure.

There exists a tremendous opportunity for the private sector to model the redesigned TAP program. Employers, who are eager to tap the talent of transitioning military members, can partner with nonprofit organizations, who are enthusiastic to support America's Veterans in a multitude of ways. A public/private partnership could provide guidance to the TAP interagency effort on how to best prepare Service members for the ever-changing workforce, as well as reintegrate veterans into civilian communities.

Ultimately, an interagency partnership can cultivate mutual respect, collegiality, and shared goals to help Service Members become self-sufficient, thriving veterans.

EMPLOYMENT CHALLENGES FOR VETERANS

Despite numerous education efforts, there are still a lot of myths about veterans. Such myths include beliefs that veterans are less educated; they have alcohol and drug problems; they all have PTSD; or they are ticking time bombs. These stereotypes prevent hiring managers from considering the unique contributions that individuals, with backgrounds as veterans, bring to an organization. Additionally, these negative labels are simply not true for *every* veteran.

FIGURE 3. FEMALE VETERANS

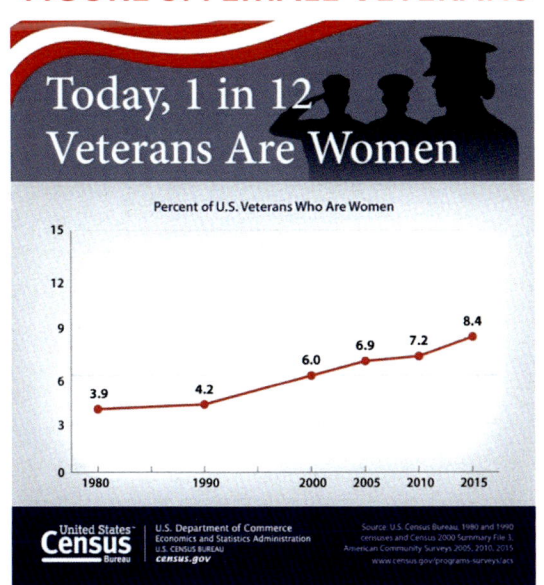

Another fallacy is that all veterans are men. During the last two years of World War I, in 1917-1918, women were allowed to join the U.S. military and have served ever since, according to History.org. In December 2015, Defense Secretary Ash Carter stated that starting in 2016 all combat jobs would be open to women. Today, the U.S. Census reports that 1 in 12 veterans are women.

There was a time when employers did not consider military experience as a marketable background; if the hiring manager disagreed with the purpose of the war, it was even more difficult for a veteran to be hired. Further, if an employer decided to give a veteran a chance, the veteran's use of military terminology (e.g., acronyms) during the interview would be an immediate turn-off because most hiring managers were fearful of asking a veteran to decode the acronym or language.

Unlike soldiers of previous wars, the modern-day soldier has to function in more capacities than they did in the past. Sure, they are expected to fight, but they have to know how to use technology that did not exist before. They have to be leaders amongst their cohort, as well as amongst local populations. Solders also have to be familiar with safety precautions and quickly adjust to changes in military strategy. All of these factors give them valuable skills that they can use in the civilian workforce.

Young veterans, especially Army and Marine riflemen, face stiff competition for the jobs that fit them best. Many employers erroneously believe that veterans are only suitable for fields such as security or police work. This commonly held stereotype is based on the belief that veterans' experiences only involved carrying a weapon and engaging in combat. The military is composed of officers who typically begin their career with at least a bachelor's degree, as well as enlisted men and women who may join shortly after high school. The services encourage continued education while in uniform-- often requiring a college degree for enlisted soldiers, airmen, and sailors in order to advance in rank.

Military service members work in a myriad of 50 career fields and gain experience working with diverse groups of people within the military and in the countries they serve. Figure 4 presents a general illustration of how an employer can translate military experience into civilian employment.

FIGURE 4 - Description of Military Career Fields

Career Field	Enlisted Officer	Career description	Possible Military Titles	Related Civilian Jobs
Business Administration and Operations Careers	E	Business Administration and Operations enlisted personnel record information, fill out reports and maintain files to assist in the operation of military offices. While most Service members in this field work in a typical office environment, some specialize in areas such as health care and work in medical offices. Service members in this field must be very organized and should enjoy working and communicating with others.	*Administrative Specialist; Information Management Specialist; Medical Records Technician; Yeoman*	*Office Clerk; Administrative Assistant; Medical Records Technician; Admitting/ Discharge Clerk*
	O	The success of many military activities and operations depends on the effective management and coordination of administrative functions. Business Administration and Operations officers direct administrative functions and services, such as mail distribution and delivery, records management and financial management. These officers also help analyze and plan administrative systems, which means they must have superior organizational skills and the ability to communicate the systems to the people they manage.	*Supply Officer; Administrative Officer; Chief Staff Officer; Health Services Administrator; Management Analyst and Planner; Purchasing and Contracting Manager; Medical Plans and Operations Officer*	*Contracting Officer; office Manager; Health Services Administrator; human Resources; Information Systems Management; Procurement Services Manager*
Communications Equipment Technologists and Technicians Careers	E	The ability to relay information among air, sea and ground forces is critical in the Military. Communications Equipment Technologists and Technicians are enlisted personnel who operate sophisticated communications systems. They use a variety of technologies and telecommunications equipment such as radios, telephones, antennas, satellites and complex security and network devices. These Service members work in many different situations domestically and abroad, and must have excellent technical and communication skills.	*Electronics Technician; Radar and Sonar Operator; Electronic Instrument and Equipment Repairer; Communications Equipment Operator; Avionics Technician*	*Aircraft Technician/ Electrician; Communication Center Operator; Navigator*
	O	Instant worldwide communication among air, sea, and land forces are vital to military operations. The Services operate some of the largest and most complex communications networks in the world. Communications Equipment Technologists and Technicians officers plan and direct the operation of military communication systems. They also manage personnel in communications centers and relay stations.	*Chief of Operations and Plans; Communications Manager; Satellite Operations Officer; Signal Officer*	*Communications Manager; Software Engineer; Systems Analyst; Information Systems Director*

In *"Out of War, Out of Luck"*, authors Lila Shapiro and Laura Bassett assert that the 2007-2008 financial crisis was unkind to veterans returning from the most recent wars. According to data from the Bureau of Labor Statistics, more than one fifth of 18-24 year old veterans returning from Iraq and Afghanistan were unemployed in 2010. Those who focused on veteran rights and unemployment issues found that number disturbing.

"We're asking our young men and women to go serve in combat and make major sacrifices – not just going into danger for their country, but the sacrifice of time from their lives. It's a moral imperative to actually support them when they get home," said Tim Embree, a legislative associate at Iraq and Afghanistan Veterans of America who served two combat tours in Iraq. "We spend so much money investing in the service members while they're wearing the uniform but then to just waste that? It's a waste of tax dollars," he added.

Embree said one of the biggest challenges for returning veterans could be figuring out how to translate skills they have gained in the service to civilian jobs. This challenge goes both ways -- employers often need help understanding how veteran skills can benefit their businesses.

In Embree's view, long-term unemployment can be one of the most hazardous obstacles for both young veterans coming home from war, and for society."

"Unemployment is one of the most dangerous problems," Embree said. "If a person can't find a job and they're already susceptible to mental or physical injuries, it's going to be a lot more expensive down the road." On the other hand, he said, "if someone has a good job that they can develop in and grow in, they're not going to be homeless. They're not going to be utilizing more and more services because they're not going to need to."

Shapiro and Bassett add, "While the statistics are most dire for young veterans returning home from Afghanistan and Iraq, the problem of unemployment after the military was widespread." If the unemployment issue is not wholly the inability to identify easily transferrable job skills or education, what could it be? Some fear that veterans may experience high-levels of discrimination.

LEGISLATION PROHIBITING EMPLOYMENT DISCRIMINATION

Just as with other groups, such as women, LGBTQ+, and older workers, employment discrimination is alive and well for veterans—regardless of the racial or ethnic group they represent.

In addition to the Americans with Disabilities Act (ADA), several pieces of legislation have been introduced to prevent employment discrimination against returning veterans, and many programs have been designed to help them better assimilate into the workforce.

The Uniformed Services Employment and Reemployment Rights Act
The Uniformed Services Employment and Reemployment Rights Act (USERRA) prohibits discrimination against members of the armed forces. It ensures that employees leaving their jobs to enter the military or return to active reserve duty are guaranteed that they can later resume their civilian jobs without loss of compensation, benefits, or seniority.

USERRA protects civilian job rights and benefits for veterans, members of reserve components, and even individuals activated by the President to provide a Federal Response for National Emergencies. USERRA also makes major improvements in protecting service members' rights and benefits by clarifying the law, improving enforcement mechanisms, and adding Federal Government employees to those employees already eligible to receive U.S. Department of Labor assistance in processing claims of noncompliance.

USERRA applies to all employers in the United States. This includes Federal, state and local governments as well as private and foreign companies operating within the United States and its territories. USERRA also applies to all United States employers operating in foreign countries.

USERRA limits the cumulative length of time that an individual may be absent from work for military duty and retain reemployment rights to five years. The exceptions to the five-year limitation includes initial enlistments lasting more than five years, periodic United States National Guard and reserve training duty, and involuntary active duty extensions and recalls, especially during a time of national emergency. USERRA clearly establishes that reemployment protection does not depend on the timing, frequency, duration, or nature of an individual's service as long as the basic eligibility criteria are met.

USERRA also provides protection for disabled veterans by requiring employers to make reasonable efforts to accommodate the disability. Service members convalescing from injuries received during service or training may have up to two years from the date of completion of service to return to their jobs or apply for reemployment.

Returning service-members are to be reemployed in the job that they would have attained had they not been absent for military service, known as the "escalator principle" (FISHGOLD v. SULLIVAN DRYDOCK & REPAIR CORP., 328 U.S. 275 (1946)), with the same seniority, status and pay, as well as other rights and benefits determined by seniority.

USERRA also mandates that reasonable efforts (such as training or retraining) be made to enable returning service members to refresh or upgrade their skills to help them qualify for reemployment. The law clearly provides for alternative reemployment positions if the service member cannot qualify for the "escalator" position. USERRA also provides that while an individual is performing military service, he or she is deemed to be on a furlough or leave of absence and is entitled to the non-seniority rights and benefits accorded other individuals on comparable types of non-military leaves of absence.

There were many deficiencies within USERRA that affected those in the National Guard and Reserves. In October 2007, Mathew B. Tully, an attorney practicing military law, as well as a Major in the National Guard, was called to give testimony to Congress on these flaws within USERRA. On August 1, 2008, Senators Barack Obama and Edward Kennedy introduced legislation, the Servicemembers Access to Justice Act (SAJA) 2008, to address and repair these flaws.

Specifically, SAJA would make it easier for service members to obtain justice when their employment rights are violated by prohibiting employers from requiring service members to give up their ability to enforce their rights under USERRA in court, in order to get or keep a job. It also adds minimum liquidated damages for willful violations and punitive damages for violations committed with malice. SAJA would also restore the original intent of Congress to protect service members under USERRA by making it clear that USERRA prohibits employers from paying lower wages to service members simply because of their status as a service member, veteran, or applicant to be a service member.

Another amendment to USERRA is the Wounded Veteran Job Security Act, which prohibits discrimination and acts of reprisal against persons who receive treatment for illnesses, injuries, and disabilities incurred in or aggravated by service in the military.

The Vietnam Era Veterans' Readjustment Assistance Act of 1974
The Vietnam Era Veterans' Readjustment Assistance Act (VEVRAA) requires covered federal government contractors and subcontractors to take affirmative action to employ and advance in employment specified categories of veterans protected by the Act. It also prohibits discrimination against veterans.

VEVRAA requires contractors and subcontractors to list their employment openings with the appropriate employment service delivery system, and to give priority to covered veterans who are referred to such openings. Further, VEVRAA requires federal contractors and subcontractors to compile and submit an annual report on the number of current employees who are covered veterans. The Employment Standards Administration's Office of Federal Contract Compliance Programs (OFCCP) within the U.S. Department of Labor (DOL) enforces the affirmative action and mandatory job-listing provisions of VEVRAA.

While some Vietnam War veterans are retired, or are on their way to retiring, a sufficient number are still in the workforce. This speaks volumes about the level of stability, commitment, and skills that veterans can bring into the civilian workforce.

Veterans Employment Preference Points

By law, veterans who are disabled or who served on active duty in the Armed Forces during certain specified time periods or in military campaigns are entitled to preference over non-veterans, both in hiring from competitive lists of eligible workers, and in retention during reductions in force.

The goal of this legislation is not to place a veteran in every vacant Federal job; however, preference does provide a uniform method by which special consideration is given to qualified veterans seeking Federal employment. Preference applies in hiring from civil service examinations, temporary appointments, direct hires, and delegated examining authorities from the U. S. Office of Personnel Management.

Office of Federal Contract Compliance Programs (OFCCP) Regulations

The Office of Federal Contract Compliance Programs (OFCCP) is a division of the U.S. Department of Labor that has been charged with implementing the laws that require equal employment opportunity for anyone working within the government contracting system. As stated in the OFCCP mission statement, this would mean enforcing laws "that ban discrimination and require Federal contractors and subcontractors to take affirmative action to ensure that all individuals have an equal opportunity for employment, without regard to race, color, religion, sex, national origin, disability or status as a Vietnam era or special disabled veteran."

The first thing to keep in mind with OFCCP compliance is that it applies directly to any contractors or subcontractors who have worked on a federal government contract valued at $10,000 USD or more. In other words, OFCCP compliance pertains to virtually every organization.

From a recruiting perspective, OFCCP regulations require contractors to document the following computations or comparisons pertaining to applicants and hires on an annual basis, and maintain them for a period of 3 years:

- The number of applicants who self-identified as, or are otherwise known to be, individuals with disabilities;
- The total number of job openings and total number of jobs filled;
- The total number of applicants for all jobs;
- The number of applicants with disabilities hired; and
- The total number of applicants hired.

In order to comply with this legislation, contractors must have EVERY applicant fill out a disclosure form similar to the EEOC form that most companies use.

Twenty-First Century Communications and Video Accessibility Act of 2010

The Twenty-First Century Communications and Video Accessibility Act of 2010 was intended to ensure that veterans disabled by a hearing or visual impairment could take advantage of evolving technology at work. Figure 5 illustrates what is covered through the Act.

FIGURE 5: COVERED COMPONENTS

Communication Access
- Hearing Aid Compatibility
- Relay Services
- Access to Internet-Based Services & Equipment
- Universal Service
- Emergency Access and Real-Time Text Support

Video Programming
- Video Programming Guides and Menus
- Video Descriptions and Closed Captioning
- User Interfaces
- Access Video Programming Guides and Menus

Homeless Veteran Reintegration Program (HVRP)
The Point-in-Time (PIT) Count is an annual effort led by the U.S. Department of Housing and Urban Development (HUD) to estimate the number of Americans, including Veterans, without safe, stable housing. It is one of the tools used to assess progress each year toward VA's priority goal of ending homelessness among Veterans.

The most recent PIT Count was conducted in January 2017. This national snapshot of Veteran homelessness showed that:

- On a single night in January 2017, just over 40,000 Veterans were experiencing homelessness.
- On the same night, just over 15,000 of the Veterans counted were unsheltered or living on the street.
- Between 2016 and 2017, there was a 1.5 percent increase in the estimated number of homeless Veterans nationwide; however, the majority of the country continued to make progress reducing Veteran homelessness in 2017.
- Still, the estimated number of Veterans experiencing homelessness in the United States has declined by nearly 50 percent since 2010.

The announcement from several government agencies, including the Department of Housing and Urban Development and the Department of Veterans Affairs, attributed the drop to several strategies, including reducing prerequisite "barriers" to get veterans into permanent housing more quickly and focusing housing efforts on chronically homeless and "vulnerable" veterans. In past years, the homeless veteran population was concentrated in California, Texas, Florida, and New York.

In the *2016 Annual Homeless Assessment Report (AHAR) to Congress*, the VA reports that the nation's homeless veterans are predominantly male, with roughly 9 percent being female. The majority of them are single, come from urban areas, and suffer from mental illness, alcohol and/or substance abuse. The report notes that veterans are at a greater risk for homelessness if they are impoverished due to unemployment or underemployment, lack support networks, or reside in overcrowded or substandard housing. About 11% of the total adult homeless population is a veteran. Roughly 45% of all homeless veterans are African American or Hispanic, despite only accounting for 10.4% and 3.4% of the U.S. veteran population, respectively. Homeless veterans are also younger on average than the total veteran population.

The Homeless Veterans Reintegration Program (HVRP) provides services to assist in reintegrating homeless veterans into meaningful employment within the labor force and stimulates the development of effective service delivery systems that will address the complex problems facing homeless veterans. HVRP is the only federal program wholly dedicated to providing employment assistance to homeless veterans.

This comprehensive program provides a variety of employment services to address the complex needs of homeless veterans such as:

- Classroom training
- Job search activities
- Job preparation
- Subsidized trial employment
- On-the-job training
- Job placement
- Placement follow-up services
- Vocational counseling

HVRP programs fill a special need because they serve veterans who may be shunned by other programs and services because of problems such as severe PTSD, long histories of substance abuse, serious psychosocial problems, legal issues, and those who are HIV-positive. These veterans require more time-consuming, specialized, intensive assessment, referrals and counseling than is possible in other programs that work with veterans seeking employment.

According to the Department of Labor, the employment focus of HVRP distinguishes it from most other programs for the homeless, which may concentrate on more immediate needs such as emergency shelter, food, and substance abuse treatment. While these are critical components of any homeless program, the objective of HVRP is to enable homeless veterans to secure and keep jobs that will allow them to re-enter mainstream society as productive citizens.

Veterans may require a wide range of support and services in order to successfully feel included in a high-performing workplace. Nevertheless, it is important not to assume that every veteran requires assistance. Certain veterans have become sensitive to prevailing stereotypes about PTSD, and do not want a "disorder" to be placed in their personnel files. Therefore, some people simply say PTS for Post-Traumatic Stress. Accordingly, HR and diversity professionals must continue to educate the workforce, while emphasizing the strategic value of veterans within our organizations.

OPTIMIZING PROGRAMS FOR VETERANS

The best way to approach designing programs for veterans is to create a multi-faceted strategy to address a variety of different needs that a veteran may have as an employee. There is no one-size-fits-all approach; therefore, Diversity and Inclusion leaders may want to blend mentoring and proactive interventions (nutrition, flexibility, suicide prevention, etc.) with workplace accommodations and support (Employee Assistance Programs, Employee Resource Groups, career pathing, etc.). Figure 6 illustrates an Optimal Approach.

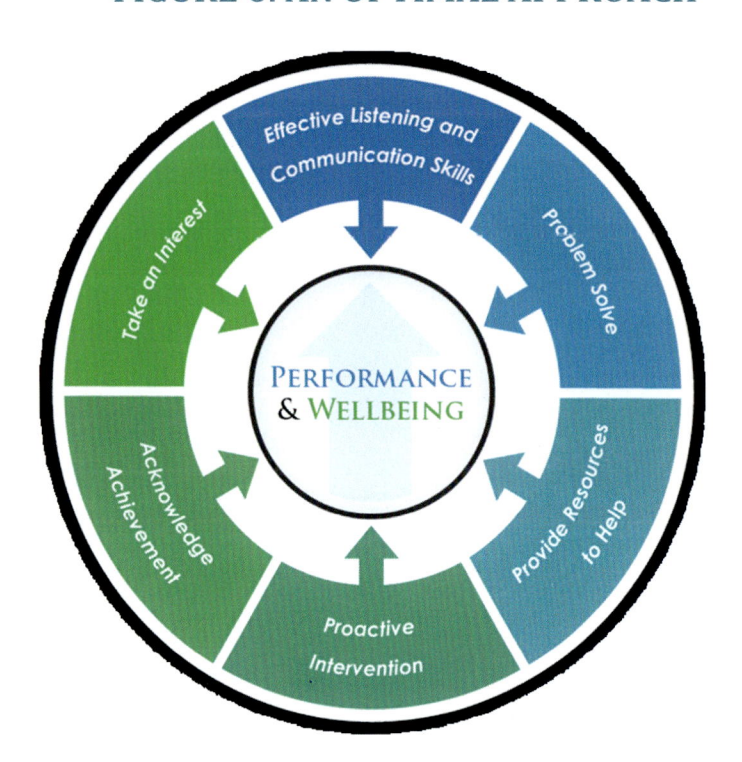

FIGURE 6: AN OPTIMAL APPROACH

Finally, organizational leaders should remember that veterans will represent a myriad of backgrounds and skill levels. Therefore, avoid assuming that a veteran is a 21-year old or even a 65-year old. Veterans with great skills will come in packages of all shapes and sizes!

References:

Veterans Affairs Canada, 2014. *Comparison to Other Countries.* Available at: http://www.veterans.gc.ca/eng/about-us/reports/departmental-audit-evaluation/2009-12-nvc/4-4

U.S. Bureau of Labor Statistics, 2018. *Employment Situation of Veterans Summary.* Available at: https://www.bls.gov/news.release/vet.nr0.htm

Brown University, 2011. *Costs of War Project.* Available at: http://watson.brown.edu/costsofwar/about

Dao, James. New York Times, 2011. *Cost of Treating Veterans Will Rise Long Past Wars.* Available at: https://www.nytimes.com/2011/07/28/us/28veterans.html

Shapiro, Lila and Bassett, Laura. HuffPost, 2011. *Out of War, Out of Luck: For Veterans, Skills Learned In Service Don't Translate To Employment.* Available at: https://www.huffingtonpost.com/2011/04/13/out-of-war-veterans-unemployment_n_848898.html

U.S. Department of Veterans Affairs. *2017 Point-in-Time Count.* Available at: https://www.va.gov/HOMELESS/pit_count.asp

U.S. Department of Housing & Urban Development. *The 2016 Annual Homeless Assessment Report (AHAR) to Congress.* Available at: https://www.hudexchange.info/programs/hdx/guides/ahar/#reports

Sample Test Questions:
DESIGNING PROGRAMS FOR VETERANS

1. To be eligible for veteran status, an individual must serve for 180-days and:
   A. Serve in one or more wars
   B. Get injured while on active duty
   C. Receive an honorable discharge

2. Readjustment issues may be determined by all of the following EXCEPT:
   A. The veteran's proximity to warfare
   B. The veteran's gender and age
   C. Whether the veteran attended college

3. The escalator principle applies to the following legislation:
   A. The ADA
   B. USERRA
   C. ADEA

4. Flaws in USERRA were addressed and repaired in this recent law:
   A. Servicemembers Access to Justice Act
   B. The Family Medical Leave Act
   C. Americans with Disability Act & Amendments

5. This law prohibits employment discrimination and acts of reprisal for treatment of illnesses, injuries, and disabilities incurred in active duty.
   A. Section 508 of the Rehabilitation Act
   B. Americans with Disabilities Act
   C. Wounded Veteran Job Security Act

6. The best way to approach designing programs for veterans is to:
   A. Create a multi-faceted strategy to address a variety of different needs
   B. Design one program that is extremely effective and share the success stories
   C. Fulfil the requirements outlined for employers in USERRA and OFCCP regulations

Sample Test Questions:
DESIGNING PROGRAMS FOR VETERANS (cont'd)

7. The U.S. Armed Forces consist of the:
   A. FBI, CIA, National Security Council, and Department of Defense
   B. Commander-in-Chief and Secretary of Defense
   C. Army, Navy, Marine Corps, Air Force, and Coast Guard

8. _____ can be defined as a disability "due to injury or illness that was incurred in or aggravated by military service".
   A. Post-traumatic stress disorder
   B. Service connected disability
   C. Workers comp disability

9. Modern day soldiers specialize in acquiring all of the following EXCEPT:
   A. Post-traumatic stress disorder
   B. Skills in advanced technology
   C. Knowledge about the military's strategy

10. This may prevent hiring managers from considering the unique contributions that veterans can bring to an organization:
    A. Limited skills and abilities
    B. Stereotypes and biases
    C. Lack of advanced education

11. One of the biggest challenges for veterans returning to the workplace can be figuring out how to:
    A. Use new technology in a civilian environment
    B. Cope with emotional or physical disabilities
    C. Translate military skills into civilian jobs

12. Veterans are most suitable for jobs as security guards or police officers.
    A. True
    B. False

IMMIGRANT GROUPS IN THE WORKPLACE

> *Organizations must be cautious not to pursue an immigrant strategy that will put them at a disadvantage in the workplace and marketplace. As the U.S. population ages rapidly, the labor force will increasingly depend on immigrants and their children to replace current workers and fill new jobs. Therefore, one's commitment to including different immigrant groups will be vital to withstanding competitive pressures, and ensuring organizational sustainability.*

OVERALL OBJECTIVES AND COMPETENCIES

The purpose of this competency is to help organizations modify diversity terminology, policies, and practices to include nationality, as well as create more opportunities for employees to learn about and work in different cultures.

BACKGROUND AND CONTEXT

With new and improved transportation options, people are able to move around the world for better housing, education, healthcare, and employment opportunities. According to the United Nations (UN), 232 million people don't live in the country where they were born. The United States is the world's leader by far as a destination for immigrants. Russia is second and Germany holds the number three spot. Although Germany is home for a little over 1% of the world's population, the nation now views immigration as an advantage due to historically low birth rates.

America has had a long, tenuous relationship with immigrants. Due to the fact that American history books tend to omit important details about the nation's past, and overlook the contributions of different immigrant groups, the country engages in an ongoing struggle with its founding principle. This Founding Principle is actually embedded in the Declaration of Independence: *We hold these truths to be self-evident, that all men are created equal, that they are endowed by their Creator with certain unalienable Rights, that among these are Life, Liberty and the pursuit of Happiness.*

Slavery and the acquisition of sizable territories that were already inhabited by people of color (e.g., Texas, California, Arizona, New Mexico, Nevada, Utah, Wyoming, Colorado, Florida, and Puerto Rico) resulted in large, diverse populations that naturally increased by birth. Today, these individuals are U.S. citizens, and the rich diverse fabric of America shines as a beacon of opportunity for millions of immigrants from other nations. Nevertheless, the colonialist perspective in education causes some to assert, "We have too many immigrants because there so many Latinos in our largest cities." Instead they should ask, "Why are Los Angeles, Las Vegas, and San Antonio Spanish words?"

In other words, it's important to distinguish between American citizens and immigrants, and not to assume that every person of color, or everybody with an accent, is an immigrant. Notwithstanding Native Americans, everyone is technically an immigrant in the U.S. Together, the diverse multitude of people, both citizens and immigrants, have caused the nation to become great over the years.

The Founding Principle alludes to the fact that immigrants come to America for freedom and opportunity. Like every other country around the world however, America has a process for immigration and citizenship. To understand this process, it's important to distinguish between the different terms.

Passport
Countries issue passports to their own citizens. A passport is a government-issued travel document that certifies an individual's identity and nationality for the purpose of international travel. If traveling outside of one's country, a passport is used to regain entry into the country of citizenship. Nations chose which country passports to admit or restrict based on foreign relations, terrorist activity, immigration policies, or other conditions and events.

As of May 2018, holders of a United States passport could travel to 186 countries and territories without a travel visa, or with a visa on arrival, ranking the United States passport 4th in terms of travel freedom (tied with Austrian, British, Dutch, Luxembourgish, Norwegian and Portuguese passports) according to the Henley Passport Index. Japan is rated first, with access to 189 destinations visa-free or visa-on-arrival. Singapore and Germany are second, while third place is shared by six countries: one Asian (South Korea) and the rest European (Finland, France, Italy, Spain, and Sweden) according to the Henley Passport Index, which is a ranking of all the passports of the world according to the number of countries their holders can travel to visa-free. The ranking is based on exclusive data from the International Air Transport Association (IATA).

Visa
Countries provide visas to foreigners. A visa is a conditional authorization granted by a country to a foreigner, allowing them to enter, leave or stay in a country for a specified time period. The most common visa types are tourist, student, work and transit visas.

American employers can temporarily employ foreign workers in specialty occupations in the U.S. through the H-1B Visa Program. The H-1B is a non-immigrant visa under the Immigration and Nationality Act and through the Department of Homeland Security. It allows an employee to stay in America for 3 years, and receive an extension for another 3 years. Nevertheless, recent changes to the law allow the period to be shorter than 3 years, and the process of extension is now more challenging—ensuring greater difficulty for H1-B holders to obtain a Green card.

The regulations define a "specialty occupation" as requiring theoretical and practical application of a body of highly specialized knowledge in a field of human endeavor including but not limited to architecture, engineering, mathematics, physical sciences, social sciences, biotechnology, medicine and health, education, law, accounting, business specialties, theology, and the arts, and requiring the attainment of a bachelor's degree or its equivalent as a minimum (with the exception of fashion models, who must be "of distinguished merit and ability".) Likewise, the foreign worker must possess at least a bachelor's degree or its equivalent and state licensure, if required to practice in that field. H-1B work-authorization is strictly limited to employment by the sponsoring employer.

Recent changes to the law provide that U.S. Immigration officers can seek detailed documentation from employers to establish that they have specific assignments in a specialty occupation for the H-1B beneficiary.

The current law caps the number of workers who may be issued a visa or provided with H-1B status each fiscal year (FY). Excluded from the ceiling are all H-1B non-immigrants who work at (but not necessarily for) universities and non-profit research facilities. This means that contractors working at, but not directly employed by the institutions may be exempt from the cap. Additionally, Free Trade Agreements allow a carve-out from the numerical limit for Chilean and Singapore nationals. Laws also exempt a certain number of foreign nationals from the cap if they hold a master's or higher degree from U.S. universities. Yet, in spite of these exceptions and temporary increases in the annual cap, yearly visa shortfalls began to arise in the mid-2000s.

Globally, an anti-immigrant backlash has been fueled by sentiment that foreign laborers are taking jobs away from American and European citizens. The U.S. Department of Labor (DOL) is responsible for ensuring that foreign workers do not displace or adversely affect wages or working conditions of U.S. employees. While an employer is not required to advertise the position before hiring an H-1B non-immigrant pursuant to the H-1B visa approval, the employer is required to complete and submit a Labor Condition Application (LCA).

By signing the LCA, an employer attests that: (1) the prevailing wage rate for the area of employment will be paid; (2) working conditions of the position will not adversely affect conditions of similarly employed American workers; (3) the place of employment is not experiencing a labor dispute involving a strike or lockout; and (4) that the foreign employee will be given benefits comparable to those offered to other workers with similar jobs. The law requires H-1B workers to be paid the higher of the prevailing wage for the same occupation and geographic location, or the same as the employer pays to similarly situated employees. Other factors, such as age and skill were not permitted to be taken into account for the prevailing wage. Congress changed the program in 2004 to require the Department of Labor to provide four skill-based prevailing wage levels for employers to use.

The taxation of income for H-1B employees depends on whether they are categorized for tax purposes as either non-resident aliens or resident aliens. A non-resident alien for tax purposes is only taxed on income from the United States, while a resident alien for tax purposes is taxed on income from both inside and outside the United States.

The classification is determined based on the "substantial presence test": If the substantial presence test indicates that the H-1B visa holder is a resident, then income taxation is like any other U.S. person and may be filed using Form 1040 and the necessary schedules; otherwise, the visa-holder must file as a non-resident alien using tax form 1040NR or 1040NR-EZ. He or she may claim benefits from tax treaties if they exist between the United States and the visa holder's country of citizenship.

Persons who are in their first year within the United States may choose to be considered a resident for taxation purposes for the entire year, and must pay taxes on their worldwide income for that year. This "First Year Choice" can only be made once in a person's lifetime.

A company can also send employees to work abroad. An expatriate (or in abbreviated form, expat) is a person temporarily or permanently residing in a country and culture other than that of the person's upbringing or legal residence. In common form, the term is often used in the context of professionals sent abroad by their companies, as opposed to locally hired staff or individuals who took it upon themselves to seek work in another country. The differentiation usually comes down to socio-economic factors-- skilled professionals working in another country are described as expatriates, whereas a manual laborer who has moved to another country to earn more money might be labeled an 'immigrant'.

According to the BBC, the word expat is loaded. In *The Difference Between an Expat and an Immigrant*, author Kieran Nash asserts it's a matter of semantics. It carries many connotations, preconceptions and assumptions about class, education and privilege — just as the terms foreign worker, immigrant and migrant call to mind a different set of assumptions.

The term 'expatriate' in some countries also has a legal context used for tax purposes. An expatriate living in a country can receive favorable tax treatment. In this context a person can only be an expatriate if they move to a country, other than their own, to work with the intent of returning to their home country within a period of no more than 5 fiscal years.

Lately, a different type of expatriate has emerged where commuter and short-term assignments are becoming more common and often used by organizations to supplement traditional expatriation. Additionally, personal motivation is becoming more relevant than company assignment. Families might often stay behind when work opportunities amount to months instead of years. The cultural impact of this trend is more significant. Traditional corporate expatriates did not integrate and commonly only associated with the elite of the country they were living in. Modern expatriates form a global middle class with shared work experiences in multi-national corporations-- working and living in the financial and social centers.

In Dubai, the population is predominantly comprised of expatriates, from countries such as India, Pakistan, Bangladesh and the Philippines, with only 20% of the population made up of citizens. In terms of outbound expatriation, the UK has the highest number of expatriates among developed countries with more than three million British living abroad, followed by Germany and Italy. On an annual basis, emigration from the UK has stood at about 400,000 per year for the past 10 years. In terms of expatriate influx, the most popular expatriate destinations are currently Spain, followed by Germany and the UK.

In dealing with expatriates, an international company should recognize their value and have experienced staff to develop written policies and employee benefit programs for expatriates. Salary of internationally assigned personnel customarily consists of standard salary and monetary benefits such as cost of living and/or hardship allowances, supported by non-monetary incentives, such as housing and education. Some companies will completely cover the cost of the education, even at relatively expensive international schools, while others, usually smaller companies, encourage families to find local schooling options.

Family relocation is an important element of successful long-term international assignments. International corporations often have a company-wide policy and coaching system that includes spouses at an earlier stage in the decision-making process, giving spouses an official voice.

Not many companies provide compensation for loss of income of expatriate spouses, although they often do provide other benefits and assistance. The level of support varies, ranging from offering a job-hunting course for spouses at the new location to full service partner support structures, run by volunteering spouses supported by the organization. Spousal employment options, however, vary.

In the U.S. military, for example, the Council of Economic Advisors reports that "spouses of service men and women stationed abroad are particularly disadvantaged, as foreign hosts often do not grant spousal work visas. Additionally, military families typically move every two to three years, requiring frequent labor market adjustments for those who do not have remote work arrangements. In anticipation of frequent moves, employers may be reluctant to hire military spouses or they may offer these workers a lower wage in an attempt to recover turnover costs. Moreover, the U.S. Chamber of Commerce (2017) reports that many military bases are located more than 50 miles from an urban center" which may make daily transportation difficult or even dangerous.

There are several advantages and disadvantages of using expatriate employees to staff international company subsidiaries. Advantages include, permitting closer control and coordination of international subsidiaries and providing a broader global perspective. Disadvantages include high transfer costs, the possibility of encountering local government restrictions, and possibly creating a problem of adaptability to foreign environments.

Research indicates that a significant amount of international business is lost due to ineffective communication such as a lack of foreign language skills. Many English-speaking business people don't bother to learn other languages because they believe that most of the people they do business with in foreign countries can speak English, and if they don't speak English, interpreters can be used. The lack of foreign language knowledge puts the English speakers at a disadvantage. In meetings, for example, the people on the other side can discuss things amongst themselves in their own language without the English speakers understanding, and using interpreters slows everything down. Also, in any socializing after the meetings, the locals will probably feel more comfortable using their own language rather than English.

Working with a visa in a foreign country can be challenging for both the immigrant and his/her family. Diversity and Inclusion leaders, who are aware of these challenges, can play an instrumental role in helping immigrants and/or their family transition successfully.

Permanent Citizenship
A lawful permanent resident can apply for United States citizenship, or naturalization, after five years of residency including a physical presence of 30 months within a five-year period, or three year period if an individual is married to a U.S. citizen. Lawful permanent residency is informally known as having a green card. This is where an immigrant is permanently authorized to live and work in the United States of America. Green cards are valid for 10 years for permanent residents, and 2 years for conditional permanent residents. After this period, the card must be renewed or replaced.

The U.S. Immigration and Nationality Act (INA) stipulates that a person may obtain permanent resident status primarily through the course of the following proceedings:

- Immigration through a family member
- Immigration through employment
- Immigration through investment (from 500,000 to 1 million U.S. dollars)

- Immigration through the diversity lottery
- Immigration through refugee or asylum status
- Immigration through "the registry" provisions of the immigration and nationality act
- Immigration approved by the director of central intelligence

There are annual quotas for each of the categories listed above, except for those seeking asylum and immediate relatives of U.S. citizens (e.g., spouse, minor children, and parents). Also, no more than 7 percent of the visas may be issued to natives of any one country. Currently, individuals from China, India, Mexico and the Philippines are subject to per-country quotas in most of the categories, and the waiting time may take an additional 5–20 years.

Some individuals may resort to unauthorized entry or simply allow their visa to expire in order stay in the United States. Illegal immigration is "the undocumented entry of a person or a group of persons across a country's border, in a way that violates the immigration laws of the destination country, with the intention to remain in the country". At one point, India claimed to have the world's largest number of illegal immigrants, with 20 million immigrants from Bangladesh. That figure has been debunked, but like most countries, it is difficult to determine how many illegal immigrants enter any one country at any given time.

While the foreign-born population is at record levels, immigrants' share of the total population is below the U.S. peak of 15%. This record high level was established during the immigration wave from 1890 to 1920 and was dominated by arrivals from Europe. The modern wave, which began with the passage of border-opening legislation in 1965, has been dominated by arrivals from Latin America (about 50%) and Asia (27%).

The United States welcomes thousands of foreign workers in multiple occupations or employment categories every year. These individuals come from many different nations and have become increasingly important to certain industries, local economic development, and the aging population.

FIGURE 1.

1. Immigrants are a growing part of the labor force

Immigrants make up 13% of the population but 16% of the labor force.

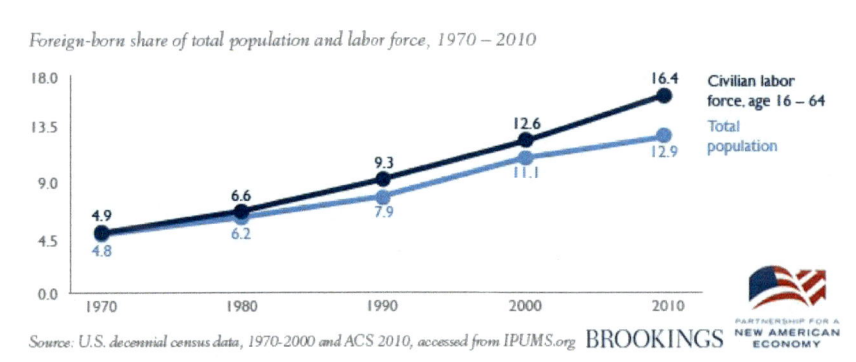

Foreign-born share of total population and labor force, 1970 – 2010

Year	Civilian labor force, age 16–64	Total population
1970	4.9	4.8
1980	6.6	6.2
1990	9.3	7.9
2000	12.6	11.1
2010	16.4	12.9

Source: U.S. decennial census data, 1970-2000 and ACS 2010, accessed from IPUMS.org BROOKINGS NEW AMERICAN ECONOMY

As depicted in Figure 1, in 1970, immigrants made up approximately 5% of the population and 5% of the labor force. Their growth in the labor force began to exceed their population growth by 1990. By 2010, immigrants were 16% of the labor force, but only 13% of the total population.

According to the Brookings Institute, immigrants are over-represented in certain industries. They have a significant presence in industries that demand higher-skilled workers such as information technology and high-tech manufacturing. In both sectors, immigrants make up 23% of all workers. However, they also comprise a large number of workers in industries with a more mixed or primarily low-skilled workforce. These industries include construction, food service, and agriculture where immigrants represent approximately one-fifth of all workers. The highest shares of immigrant workers are found in private households (49% of all workers) and in the accommodations sector (31%) followed by warehousing, management and administration, and agriculture.

From a strategic perspective, Diversity and Inclusion practitioners must use this data to ensure that immigrant groups are properly included in D&I and organizational change efforts. Additionally, efforts must be taken to ensure customers/students/constituents are valued and represented throughout your organization in meaningful ways. Concurrently, suppliers, partners, volunteers, board members, donors, and other stakeholder groups should reflect America's changing demographics.

ASIAN IMMIGRANTS SURPASSING HISPANICS

Among new immigrant arrivals, Asians outnumber Hispanics

% of immigrants arriving in the U.S. in each year who are ...

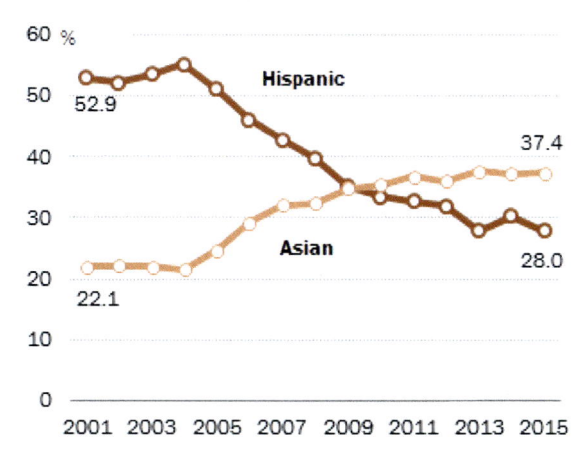

- Hispanic: 52.9 (2001) → 28.0 (2015)
- Asian: 22.1 (2001) → 37.4 (2015)

Note: Figures for 2001 to 2005 are based on the household population and do not include arrivals residing in group quarters. 2015 figure represents only arrivals between Jan. 1 and April 1, 2015. Figures reflect only immigrants who are residing the U.S. as of April 1, 2015. Race and ethnicity based on self-reports. Asians include only single-race non-Hispanics. Hispanics are of any race.
Source: Pew Research Center tabulations of 2001-2015 American Community Surveys (IPUMS).

PEW RESEARCH CENTER

In the last few years, we have heard much about the size, complexity, and growth of the Latino population. However, a new group of immigrants has emerged and is projected to surpass Hispanics. For the first time, the influx of Asians moving into the U.S. has exceeded that of Hispanics, reflecting a slowdown in illegal immigration while American employers increase their demand for highly skilled workers.

An expansive study by the Pew Research Center details what it describes as "the rise of Asian-Americans" a highly diverse and fast-growing group. Mostly foreign-born and naturalized citizens, their numbers have been boosted by increases in visas granted to specialized workers and to wealthy investors as the U.S. economy becomes driven less by manufacturing and more by technology.

By race and ethnicity, more Asian immigrants than Hispanic immigrants have arrived in the U.S. each year since 2010. Asians are projected to become the largest immigrant group in the U.S. by 2055, surpassing Hispanics. In 2065, Pew Research Center estimates indicate that Asians will make up some 38% of all immigrants, Hispanics 31%, whites 20% and blacks 9%. Furthermore, 6 in 10 international students studying at U.S. colleges and universities are most likely to come from Asian countries. Some of these students can live and work in the U.S. after graduation.

In recent years, more than 60% of Asian immigrants ages 25 to 64 graduated from college, double the amount for new arrivals from other continents.

"Like immigrants throughout American history, the new arrivals from Asia are strivers," said Paul Taylor, executive vice president of the Pew Research Center and co-author of a 2012 report on *The Rise of Asian Americans*. "What's distinctive about them is their educational credentials. These are not the tired, poor, huddled masses of Emma Lazarus's famous inscription on the Statue of Liberty. They are the highly skilled workforce of the 21st century."

The findings are part of Pew's broad portrait of Asian-Americans, immigrants or U.S.-born children of immigrants who come mostly from China, the Philippines, India, Vietnam, Korea, and Japan. Now tied with Hispanics as the fastest-growing U.S. group, Asian-Americans are slowly becoming visible as founders of startups in Silicon Valley. They are owners of ethnic eateries, grocery stores, and small businesses in cities across the country, as well as candidates for political office. Asian Americans have also become a key bloc of voters in states such as California, Nevada, and Virginia.

In the 1970's, long before the word globalization achieved common currency, the term "brain drain" was recognized as a problem in many Asian countries. Today, India and China struggle with the concept that the best and brightest men and women are leaving their countries for education and employment opportunities in Western nations. In China, political alienation, low income, poor living conditions, insufficient research facilities, and mismanagement of high-level workers are the major factors pushing intellectuals to seek development opportunities abroad. Nevertheless, once they go abroad, Asians face discrimination in the U.S., as well as in Western Europe.

Like Africa, Asia is a populous continent with many different nations. As defined by the U.S. Census Bureau, "Asian" refers to a person having origins in any of the original peoples of the Far East, Southeast Asia, or the Indian subcontinent, including, Cambodia, China, India, Japan, Korea, Malaysia, Pakistan, the Philippine Islands, Thailand, and Vietnam. Asian population data, as reported to the U.S. Census, includes people who indicated their race(s) as "Asian" or reported entries such as "Asian Indian" "Chinese," "Filipino," "Korean," "Japanese," and "Vietnamese" or other detailed Asian responses.

Asian Americans Lead Others In Education, Income

% with a bachelor's degree or more, among ages 25 and older, 2010

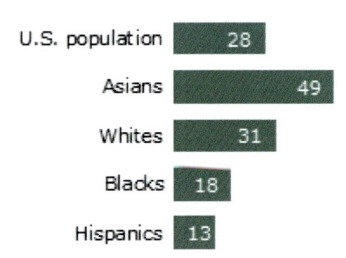

U.S. population	28
Asians	49
Whites	31
Blacks	18
Hispanics	13

Median household income, 2010

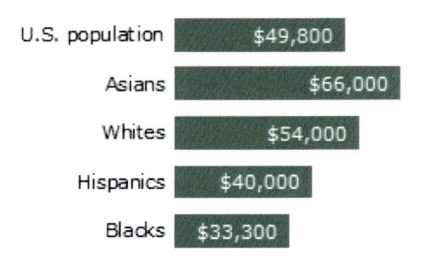

U.S. population	$49,800
Asians	$66,000
Whites	$54,000
Hispanics	$40,000
Blacks	$33,300

Note: Asians include mixed-race Asian population, regardless of Hispanic origin. Whites and blacks include only non-Hispanics. Hispanics are of any race. Household income is based on householders ages 18 and older; race and ethnicity are based on those of household head.

Source: Pew Research Center analysis of 2010 American Community Survey, Integrated Public Use Microdata Sample (IPUMS) files

PEW RESEARCH CENTER

The Largest U.S. Asian Groups

The six largest country of origin groups each number more than a million people

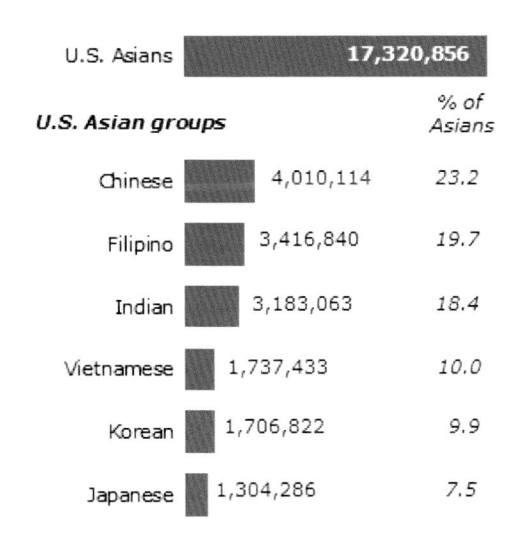

U.S. Asian groups		% of Asians
U.S. Asians	17,320,856	
Chinese	4,010,114	23.2
Filipino	3,416,840	19.7
Indian	3,183,063	18.4
Vietnamese	1,737,433	10.0
Korean	1,706,822	9.9
Japanese	1,304,286	7.5

Note: Based on the total Asian-race population, including adults and children. There is some overlap in the numbers for the six largest Asian groups because people with origins in more than one group—for example, "Chinese and Filipino"—are counted in each group to which they belong.

Source: Pew Research Center analysis based on Elizabeth M. Hoeffel et al., *The Asian Population: 2010*, U.S. Census Bureau, March 2012.

PEW RESEARCH CENTER

According to the 2010 Census, many Asian Americans reside in the West, followed by the South, Northeast, and Midwest. The 10 states with the largest Asian alone-or-in-combination populations were *California* (5.6 million), *New York* (1.6 million), *Texas* (1.1 million), *New Jersey* (0.8 million), *Hawaii* (0.8 million), *Illinois* (0.7 million), *Washington* (0.6 million), *Florida* (0.6 million), *Virginia* (0.5 million), and *Pennsylvania* (0.4 million). Together, these 10 states represented nearly three-fourths of the entire Asian population in the United States.

Despite their educational attainment and portrayal as the "Model Minority", Asian Americans have trouble advancing beyond the Bamboo Ceiling in the workplace. Jane Hyun coined the term "bamboo ceiling" in her book, *Breaking the Bamboo Ceiling: Career Strategies for Asians.* According to Hyun, "bamboo ceiling" refers to the processes and barriers that serve to exclude Asians and American people of Asian descent from executive positions on the basis of subjective factors such as "lack of leadership potential" and "lack of communication skills" that cannot be explained by job performance or qualifications.

Based on publicly available government statistics, Asian Americans have the lowest chance of rising to management when compared with Blacks, Hispanics, and women, in spite of having the highest educational attainment. Asian American groups are often subject to "model minority" stereotypes, and viewed as quiet, hardworking, family-oriented, high achieving in math and science, passive, submissive, non-confrontational, and antisocial. In the workforce, some of these perceptions may seem positive in the short-term, but in the long-term they impede progression up corporate and academic ladders.

While Asian Americans are often viewed as a "model minority" group, many feel that they are an invisible or "forgotten minority" despite being one of the fastest growing groups in the country. For example, when reports were released about the lack of diversity in Silicon Valley, many narratives failed to state the fact that there is a burgeoning Asian American tech workforce. Even among Diversity and Inclusion efforts, there is a tendency to neglect Asian Americans in favor of women, African Americans, or Latinos.

The Indian Population

Not to be mistaken for Native (or indigenous) Americans, Asian-Indian migrants began arriving in the United States as early as 1820. Similar to early Chinese and Japanese immigrants, Indian arrivals in the 19th century were largely unskilled and uneducated farmers. Most came to work in agriculture in California. The restrictive Immigration Acts of 1917 and 1924, which effectively banned immigration from Asia, brought the already low levels of migration from India to a halt. As of 1960, there were only 12,000 Indian immigrants in the United States, representing less than 0.01% of the 9.7 million foreign-born population at the time.

The 1965 Immigration and Nationality Act, which removed country-of-origin-based quotas and created employment-based immigration channels, as well as subsequent legislation emphasizing highly skilled immigration, provided an entry pathway for a growing number of professionals and students from India. The Immigration Act of 1990, which further refined temporary skilled worker categories and increased the number of permanent work-based visas, contributed to a rapid increase in the size of the Indian-born population. In contrast to the initial wave, the majority of post-1965 arrivals from India were young, educated urban dwellers, with strong English language skills.

According to the Migration Policy Institute, individuals "from India are the second-largest immigrant group after Mexicans, accounting for almost 6 percent of the 43.3 million foreign-born population. In 2016, Indians were the top recipients of high-skilled H-1B temporary visas and were the second-largest group of international students in the United States. The U.S. is actually the third most popular destination for Indian migrants worldwide, after the United Arab Emirates and Pakistan, according to mid-2015 estimates by the United Nations Population Division. Other top destinations include Saudi Arabia (1,894,000), Kuwait (1,062,000), Oman (778,000), and the United Kingdom (777,000)."

The Migration Policy Institute (MPI) adds, "Compared with the overall foreign- and native-born populations, immigrants from India on average are significantly better educated, more likely to be employed in management positions, and have higher household incomes. In fiscal year (FY) 2015, nearly half of Indians who obtained lawful permanent residence in the United States (also known as receiving a green card) did so through employer sponsorship. The remainder qualified as immediate relatives of U.S. citizens or through other family-sponsored channels."

Further, a joint Duke University and UC Berkeley study revealed that Indian immigrants have founded more engineering and technology companies from 1995 to 2005 than immigrants from the UK, China, Taiwan, and Japan combined.

In spite of many educational and professional achievements, Asian Indians experience much discrimination due to anxiety about this immigrant group receiving highly-compensated, white-collar positions. Additionally, since the September 11, 2001 attacks, there have been scattered incidents of Indian Americans becoming mistaken targets for hate crimes. Some Americans mistakenly assume the Sikh turban indicates that the individual is a Muslim. According to a 2012 Pew Research Center report, 51% of Indian Americans consider themselves Hindus, 18% as Christians, 14% as Unaffiliated, 10% as Muslims, 5% as Sikh, and 2% as Jain.

It is important that Diversity and Inclusion practitioners distinguish Asian-Indian immigrants from the broader "Asian" category. D&I leaders must also employ structured approaches to exploring Indian culture in the workplace, as well as engage in open and consistent dialogue related to the challenges and expectations of immigrant employees. Once again, it is also necessary to dismantle myths in order to facilitate inclusion for Asian-Indian workers.

OTHER IMMIGRANT WORKER GROUPS

Around the world, there is a perception that there is an immigration crisis. From the U.K. and France, to Denmark and Turkey, some countries are restricting and monitoring immigrants for the sake of preserving the "culture" and thwarting terrorism.

While many acknowledge that the U.S. was founded as a nation of immigrants, throughout the centuries, discrimination against every immigrant group is well documented. Even today, America has a raging immigration debate that is being aggravated by politics. Like many European nations, at issue are perceptions of fairness and limited resources.

European Immigrants in America
Once the backbone of U.S. immigration, European migration to the United States has steadily declined since 1960, with a small uptick following the end of communism in the 1990s. The share of Europeans among the total U.S. foreign-born population plunged from 75% in 1960 to 11% in 2014, as immigration from Latin America and Asia surged to new prominence after the Immigration Act of 1965 abolished national-origin quotas that gave preference to European migration.

The motivations and demographic composition of immigrants have changed over the long history of European migration to the United States. The first wave of European immigrants, between the 16th and 18th centuries, largely consisted of English-speaking settlers from the British Isles seeking economic opportunity and religious freedom. Considering the high costs of crossing the Atlantic, Europeans arriving in this era were a mix of well-to-do individuals and indentured servants.

From the 1840s to 1850s, the second wave witnessed the arrival of immigrants from Ireland, Germany, and Scandinavia escaping famine, religious persecution, and political conflicts. Compared to first-wave Protestant settlers, the new arrivals were overwhelmingly Catholic, came from much poorer backgrounds, and were more likely to be young and unskilled. Following this boom, European migration to the United States mostly paused during the Civil War.

More than 20 million immigrants arrived in the third wave between 1880 and 1914. The new immigrants, primarily from Southern and Eastern Europe, were of different linguistic and religious backgrounds than earlier European arrivals. Most Southern European immigrants were motivated by economic opportunity in the United States, while Eastern Europeans (primarily Jewish individuals) sought protection from religious persecution. European immigration was slowed first by the outbreak of World War I in 1914, then by restrictive national-origin quotas established by the Immigration Act of 1924. The Immigration Act privileged individuals from Western and Northern Europe, and effectively halted immigration from Southern and Eastern Europe.

The most recent wave of European immigration followed the fall of the Iron Curtain in the early 1990s, when a substantial number of Eastern Europeans moved to the United States to reunite with family members or seek humanitarian protection. Between 1990 and 2010, the number of Eastern European immigrants increased significantly due to a sizeable inflow from the former Czechoslovakia, Soviet Union, and Yugoslavia territories.

Using data from the U.S. Census Bureau (the most recent 2014 American Community Survey [ACS] and pooled 2009-13 ACS data), the Department of Homeland Security's 2013 Yearbook of Immigration Statistics, and the World Bank's annual remittance data, the majority of European immigrants who have obtained lawful permanent residence in the United States (also known as receiving a green card) have done so as immediate relatives of U.S. citizens or through employment channels. Compared to the overall foreign and native-born populations, European immigrants on average were significantly older, more educated, and had higher household incomes, though they were less likely to participate in the labor force.

Figure 2 illustrates the age distribution of European immigrants in comparison to other immigrant groups and native-born American citizens.

Figure 2. Age Distribution by Origin, 2014

Age Group	All Immigrants	European Immigrants	Native Born
Under 18	6%	5%	26%
18 to 64	80%	65%	60%
65 and over	14%	31%	15%

Source: MPI tabulation of data from the U.S. Census Bureau, 2014 ACS. Numbers may not add up to 100 as they are rounded to the nearest whole number.

Black Immigrants in America

While the first white colonists (or permanent European settlers) arrived in 1607, the first black immigrants unwillingly came to Jamestown, Virginia as slaves in 1619. Slavery in the Americas triggered a revolution, civil war, and many rebellions before it was abolished in 1865. While slavery is documented as a common practice going back as far as the Book of Exodus in the Bible, the institution of slavery in America was an enduring system that still shows vestiges 400 years later.

In a controversial 2018 interview with TMZ, Rapper Kanye West said, "When you hear about slavery for 400 years. For 400 years?! That sounds like a choice." Social media backlash caused West to clarify his statement on Twitter, "Of course I know that slaves did not get shackled and put on a boat by free will," he wrote. "My point is for us to have stayed in that position even though the numbers were on our side means that we were mentally enslaved." Blacks did fight enslavement. They ran away, organized uprisings, and educated themselves. They also established relationships with whites who were instrumental in abolishing the institution of slavery. In fact, history is replete with examples of how whites and blacks worked together to enact social change in America.

Unlike slaves from other nations in prior eras, Africans did not return to their country of origin once slavery ended. And since arriving in America in 1619, these individuals have contributed to research, innovation, and productivity—although a majority of blacks did not receive acknowledgement or compensation for their intellectual contributions and their work. They unwittingly became part of a discriminatory, but profitable, economic system in which wealthy whites benefited from legal structures designed to advance their interests in everything from slavery and sharecropping to predatory lending and privatization of the prison industrial complex.

Today, the notion that blacks are lazy, intellectually inferior, and deserving of separate but unequal systems and services, runs counter to the reality that America was built from the contributions of both blacks and whites. Without either of these groups, America would be vastly different. Nevertheless, race is a powerful and debilitative social construct that affords privileges to some, but not others. It is also intentionally divisive so that some individuals are continually motivated to take action to preserve the benefits afforded to them because of race or ethnicity. In other words, whites are not the only individuals who are advantaged by America's social construct.

A recent Pew report found that America's current black immigrants emanate from two places—the Caribbean and Africa. The largest numbers of Caribbean-born immigrants originate from Jamaica and Haiti, respectively. Immigrants from Africa constitute a highly diverse and rapidly growing group in the United States. Nearly half of African immigrants are naturalized U.S. citizens, and 7 in 10 speak only English or speak it "very well". Just under three-quarters of African immigrants are Black; while roughly one-fifth are White. The largest numbers of African immigrants are found in California, New York, Texas, Maryland, and Virginia. The top countries of origin for African immigrants are Nigeria, Ethiopia, Egypt, Ghana, and Kenya.

There were 4.2 million black immigrants living in the U.S. in 2016, up from just 816,000 in 1980, according to a Pew Research Center analysis of U.S. Census Bureau data. Now, Black immigrants and their children make up roughly one-fifth (18%) of the overall black population in the U.S.

Black immigrant population in the U.S. rose to 4.2 million in 2016

Total foreign-born black population in the U.S., in thousands

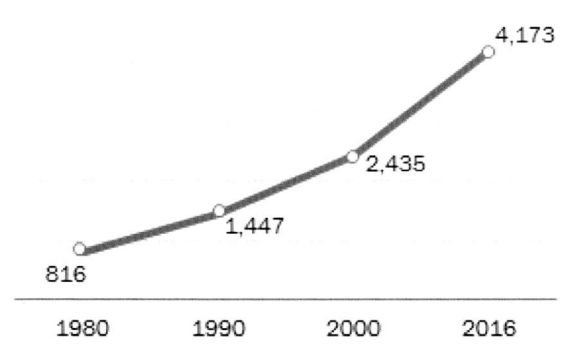

Year	Population
1980	816
1990	1,447
2000	2,435
2016	4,173

Note: In 2000 and later, foreign-born blacks include single-race blacks and multiracial blacks, regardless of Hispanic origin. Prior to 2000, blacks include only single-race blacks regardless of Hispanic origin since a multiracial option was not available.
Source: Pew Research Center tabulations of the 2016 American Community Survey (1% IPUMS) and the 1980, 1990 and 2000 censuses (5% IPUMS).

PEW RESEARCH CENTER

William H. Frey, a demographer and senior fellow with the Metropolitan Policy Program at the Brookings Institution, and author of "Diversity Explosion" asserted that black immigrants differed from U.S.-born blacks in important socioeconomic respects. Frey asserts that black immigrants tend to be older, more likely to have a higher education and a higher income, and are less likely to live in poverty. These findings have been substantiated by a 2016 Pew report entitled *Key Facts About Black Immigrants in the U.S.*

Not only are there differences in socioeconomic categories, it is a well-known fact that a shared complexion does not necessarily equate to a shared culture. In 2014, the story of the first-generation Ghanian-American student that was accepted by all eight Ivy League schools illustrated this point. The high school student was described as an individual that is "not a typical African-American kid" by several media outlets. Those five words read as a subtle nod to the lazy black American stereotype.

Some African immigrants have bought into that stereotype, which is reflected by the term "akata" a word that some Nigerians use to refer to black Americans. *Akata* translates into: wild animal or ghetto. White Americans echo this sentiment. A 2007 study in the American Journal of Education was detailed by the Washington Post, in which the study's authors noted that a quarter of Black students admitted to elite colleges were African immigrants—though they only represented 13% of America's college-age Black population. The study's authors provide several theories on why Black immigrants do better, including "to white observers, black immigrants seem to be more polite, less hostile, more solicitous and 'easier to get along with.' Native blacks are perceived in precisely the opposite fashion."

The Myth of Undocumented Workers
When addressing immigrants in the labor force, we must account for undocumented workers and their role in the workplace and marketplace.

Undocumented workers represent many nations around the world. Contrary to prevailing immigration myths, expired visa holders and victims of human trafficking make up a huge share of today's undocumented workers. In fact, individuals from China and India are among the fastest growing undocumented immigrant groups in the United States today. This increase is largely attributed to the expiration of visas.

There are also myths about immigrants taking resources away from taxpayers. While education and healthcare services may be impacted by large populations of illegal residents, state and local governments across America benefit from taxes paid by undocumented workers.

Several years ago, Forbes published an article entitled, *Addressing and Discrediting 7 Major Myths about Immigration* by Alvaro Vargas Llosa. Mr. Llosa reports that many Americans believe undocumented workers don't pay taxes. However, a 50-state analysis by the Institute on Taxation and Economic Policy released in April 2015 found that roughly 8.1 million of 11.4 million undocumented immigrants, who work, paid more than $11.8 billion in state and local taxes in 2012—even while they were living illegally in the U.S.

Mexico, China and India are top birthplaces for immigrants in the U.S.

Top five countries of birth for immigrants in the U.S. in 2015, in millions

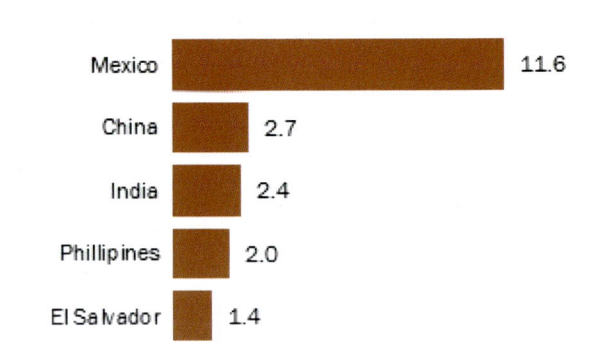

Country	Millions
Mexico	11.6
China	2.7
India	2.4
Phillipines	2.0
El Salvador	1.4

Note: China includes Taiwan and Hong Kong.
Source: Pew Research Center tabulations of 2015 American Community Survey (1% IPUMS).

PEW RESEARCH CENTER

The federal government also benefits from undocumented workers. According to Hunter Hallman, author of *How do Undocumented Immigrants Pay Federal Taxes? An Explainer*, "Since the Immigration Reform and Control Act of 1986, all employers are required to verify the work eligibility of all new hires by completing Form I-9, which mandates the employee provide a Social Security number and show documents to their employer to prove work authorization and identity." However, employers do not have a legal obligation to verify an employee's paperwork before hiring that person. Some workers use fake social security numbers, previously valid identification, or someone else's Social Security number. When the Internal Revenue Service (IRS) cannot match a person's name with their Social Security number, the federal government simply keeps the money.

Hallman's March 2018 article appeared in The Bipartisan Policy Center and reports that "the IRS estimates that undocumented immigrants pay over $9 billion in withheld payroll taxes annually." Hallman reminds readers that "Undocumented immigrants also help make the Social Security system more solvent, as they pay into the system but are ineligible to collect benefits upon retiring. In 2010, $12 billion more was collected from Social Security payroll taxes of undocumented workers than were paid out in benefits." These monies fund Social Security payments to retired U.S. citizens, whose life expectancy may reach an average of 90 years of age.

More than 11 million total undocumented immigrants toil in America's fields, construction sites, salons, and fast-food establishments. These workers have little ability to push back when employers disregard civil and human rights; including basic safeguards such as safe conditions and fair pay. The most commonly cited problem facing unauthorized immigrants is wage theft, an illegal practice in which employers withhold workers' pay.

In 2015, Forbes published an article by Art Carden, Economist, entitled, *Illegal Immigrants Don't Lower Our Wages or Take Our Jobs*. Carden attempts to dispel myths about undocumented workers by asserting, "The conventional wisdom says illegal immigrants take American jobs and lower American wages. That conventional wisdom is wrong. According to an April 2015 symposium on the effects of illegal immigrants in the Southern Economic Journal, illegal immigrants actually raise wages for documented/native workers. Meanwhile, rules preventing illegal immigrants from getting driver's licenses raise car insurance premiums and E-Verify requirements raise the cost of doing business and reduce employment".

Refugees in America

Each year, Americans welcome refugees to the U.S. Whether refugees come from Nepal, Sudan, Iraq, Burma, Somalia, Syria, or another part of the world, all refugees share a similar journey. Refugees, differ from other immigrants, in that they do not have the choice to remain in their home country. Refugees flee their country to save their lives. They run from war, genocide, and persecution—often losing or leaving behind beloved family members along the way.

Many refugees spend years and sometimes decades in substandard refugee camps. Less than 1% of all refugees get the chance to leave a camp and resettle in the U.S., Canada, Sweden, Australia, or another country which resettles refugees (Source: 2015 International Institute of St. Louis).

Globally, the support for refugees has changed dramatically given the public rhetoric that these individuals are a threat. The World Economic Forum reports that "more than 5 million Syrians have now found refuge in nearby countries, including more than 2.9 million in Turkey (now the largest refugee hosting country in the world) and large numbers in Lebanon, Jordan, Iraq and Egypt." Nevertheless, several U.S. governors have stated that they will no longer provide placement for Syrian refugees, arguing that they pose too great a risk to national security.

Diversity and Inclusion leaders must be aware of the intricate issues surrounding refugee workers, as well as distinguish between their needs and the needs of other immigrant groups.

A CLOSER LOOK AT THE LATINO POPULATION

As stated earlier, the Mexican-American War in 1846-1848 resulted in large Mexican territories being ceded to the U.S. In addition to land rich with oil (in Texas), filled with agricultural potential, bestowed with gold mines (in California), and accessible by water, the untold story is that America also acquired thousands of Mexican residents who already lived in these territories. By the turn of the century, however, America's immigration stance reflected a selective memory.

President Herbert Hoover was a moderately successful businessman who never held elected office. His campaign ran on the promise that he would create jobs for Americans by slashing immigration. Hoover introduced themes of efficiency in the business community and provided government support for standardization, efficiency and international trade. Nevertheless, as President, his domestic programs were overshadowed by the Great Depression from 1929 to 1933.

Hoover's tenure in the White House not only reflected economic struggle, but also racial resentment and xenophobia. One of Hoover's hallmark initiatives was the "Mexican repatriation" effort of 1929 to 1936, which resulted in 1.8 million Hispanic men, women, and children being illegally deported to Mexico. An estimated 60 percent of those deported were birthright citizens of the United States.

Hispanic Population Growth

U.S. Hispanic population, in millions

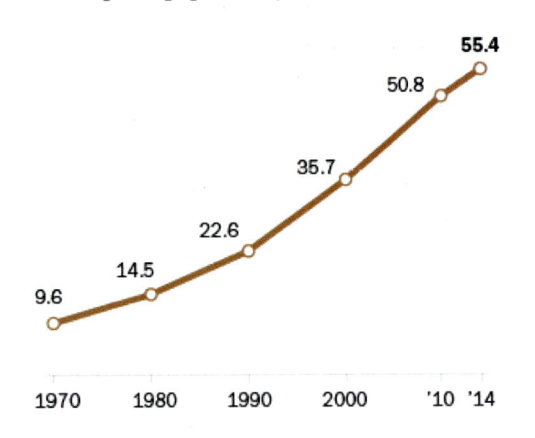

- 1970: 9.6
- 1980: 14.5
- 1990: 22.6
- 2000: 35.7
- '10: 50.8
- '14: 55.4

Note: 1990-2014 estimates are for July 1.
Source: 1970-1980 estimates based on the Decennial Censuses, see Passel & Cohn 2008. 1990-2014 estimates based on Intercensal population estimates and Vintage 2014.

PEW RESEARCH CENTER

Over the last 100 years, few racial or ethnic groups have had as great an impact on the demography of the United States as Latinos. In 1900, there were slightly more than 500,000 Latinos. As of 2017, the national Latino population is more than **58 million** and represents one of the most dynamic and diverse ethnic groups in the United States.

The most dramatic impact of the Latino population on the nation's demography has taken place over the last few decades. The number of Latinos in the United States has more than doubled between 1980 and 2000, accounting for 40% of the growth in the country's population during that period. In 2003, the U.S. Census Bureau designated Latinos as the nation's largest minority group. In California, a state with the world's 5th largest economy, Latinos are now the largest ethnic group, surpassing whites. This is an amazing event, considering that in 1980, the Latino population was nearly the same size as the Black population.

According to the U.S. Census Bureau, the Latino population is concentrated in eight states—California, Texas, Florida, Arizona, New Mexico, New York, New Jersey and Illinois. These states contain three-quarters (74%) of the nation's Latino population. However, because of the 2007-2008 economic recession, Latinos started moving to non-traditional states in larger numbers, such as Minnesota and Tennessee.

The Census Bureau projects that the Hispanic population will more than double, from 58.6 million in 2018 to 128.8 million by 2060. This growth is projected to be a natural increase, driven by American citizens giving birth to children. Nevertheless, President Trump's current immigration policy consisting of deporting/separating undocumented Hispanic males from their families and placing thousands of Hispanic children in foster care, may or may not have an impact on the size and growth of the Latino population.

The growth of the Latino population has led to a blurring of many boundaries—international (e.g., various countries of origin), identity (e.g., multi-layered), food (e.g., the rise in guacamole products/sales), sports (e.g., soccer), and language. The increased use of Spanish in foreign-language instruction, its entrance into mainstream popular culture (e.g., television and music), and the bilingual context in which many Latinos operate have also blurred language boundaries.

Hispanics accounted for more than half of total U.S. population growth last year

U.S. population increase, 2016 to 2017

	2017 population	Change, 2016-17	Share of total increase
Hispanic	58,603,060	1,132,773	51%
Asian	18,262,549	521,092	24%
Black	40,573,936	344,700	16%
White	197,959,872	-9,736	0%
Total	325,344,115	2,216,602	

Note: Estimates for 2017 are preliminary. White, black and Asian are single race, not Hispanic. Hispanics are of any race. American Indians/Alaska Natives, Native Hawaiians/Other Pacific Islanders and multi-race Americans not shown.
Source: Pew Research Center analysis of U.S. Census Bureau population estimates.

PEW RESEARCH CENTER

The experiences of various Latino groups in the United States have been quite different, and the blurring of locale and linguistic boundaries have not eliminated one important distinction. Mexicans and Puerto Ricans, two groups initially incorporated into the United States through warfare, are still viewed as "colonized groups". Similar to African Americans, Mexicans and Puerto Ricans have traditionally occupied a relatively low position in the nation's social and economic hierarchy. For example, during the Mexican Repatriation in the 1900's, Hispanic citizens were not compensated for their homes, land, and/or possessions. Fast forward to 2017 when Hurricane Maria devastated Puerto Rico, the government made many excuses for the lack of relief and/or aid. As a result, the island suffered a power outage that lasted for months, clean water and medical supplies were scarce, and Harvard University researchers estimated that more than 4,000 people died—not 64 as was previously reported. The effect of Hurricane Maria on Puerto Ricans has been compared to the devastation of Hurricane Katrina on African Americans.

Nevertheless, the great diversity challenge is to understand the rate and extent of the Latino population's integration into mainstream U.S. society. Diversity leaders, educators, policymakers, businesspeople, and others in the United States require knowledge about the Latino population and the groups within it to more effectively understand and serve the needs of the Hispanic community. This is particularly true given the fact that the Latino population has expanded geographically beyond its traditional hub areas into places that have historically had fewer Latinos.

The Difference Between Hispanic and Latino
Discriminatory terms should be avoided when referring to Latinos. For example, it is ethnically insensitive and illegal to blatantly refer to individuals from Latino descent as "Mexicans" (especially if they are **not** Mexican). Other inappropriate terms are "wetbacks", "border hoppers", "illegal immigrants", or "spics". It is also derogatory to call Latinos food names, such as "taco" or "nacho".

Similar to most words in the field of Diversity and Inclusion, many professionals use the terms "Latino" and "Hispanic" interchangeably. Dr. Robert Rodriguez, author of "*Latino Talent*", clarifies the difference between the words in Figure 3.

FIGURE 3. "LATINO OR HISPANIC?"
By Robert Rodriguez, Ph.D. ~ August 28, 2008

We Latinos are a highly diverse group. Because of the diversity that exists in our community, we tend to have different points of view on key topics. One such area of contention is the use of the terms Latino and Hispanic. There is a lot of history and strong feelings regarding these terms. In fact, some would argue a debate exists between those in the community that prefer Hispanic and those who prefer Latino. To fully comprehend this difference of opinion, it is best to look deeper into both terms.

Hispanic: Hispania was the name given by the ancient Romans in 200 BC to the whole Iberian Peninsula located in Western Europe. Upon the fall of the Roman Empire, Hispania was divided into two separate countries, one of which later became known as Spain. Because this area was called Hispania, it eventually became common to refer to people who could trace their lineage or cultural heritage back to Spain as *Hispanos*.

In 1960, the U.S. Census Bureau sought a term to refer to people of Spanish ancestry who were residing in the United States.

The Census Bureau had previously used the term Mexican but this confused those who were of Latin American descent but were not from Mexico. Because the Spanish had colonized parts of Latin America and other individuals around the world who could trace their lineage to Spain were called Hispanos, the Census Bureau coined the term *Hispanic* to refer to those of Spanish ancestry in the United States. Eventually, the Census Bureau expanded the use of the term to include those whose origin was Cuba, Central America, Mexico, Puerto Rico, the Spanish Caribbean and South America.

The key element of the term Hispanic is that it refers to residents within the United States regardless if they are U.S. citizens, permanent residents or temporary immigrants. This is important to remember because organizations often make the mistake of referring to individuals or programs focused outside of the United States as Hispanic. For example, some organizations mistakenly refer to someone who is born and raised in Mexico and working at a facility in the country of Mexico as being Hispanic. This is not the case since the individual does not reside in the United States. Similarly, some organizations mistakenly refer to efforts to build business and revenue in Latin America as Hispanic initiatives. Such efforts can only be correctly called Hispanic initiatives if the focus is on domestic efforts in the United States.

The use of Hispanic has been prevalent for a long time and is still quite popular in the names of several prominent organizations (such as the Hispanic Chamber of Commerce and the National Society of Hispanic MBAs). However, there is a growing trend against the use of the term Hispanic for a couple of reasons. First, some resent the fact that Hispanic is an English word that was created by English speakers. These individuals consider the term offensive because they see it as a word Anglos made up for Latinos. Second, others have difficulty with the term Hispanic because it conveys thoughts of the Spanish conquest of Latin America and Spanish colonialism.

Latino: Unlike Hispanic, the term Latino is an actual Spanish word and essentially refers to people with Latin American ancestry which includes the Spanish Caribbean, Central and South America as well as those from Spain. Unlike Hispanic, the term Latino also has gender connotations in that a male is a Latino and a female is a Latina. Latino also follows the usual conventions for Spanish words in that the masculine plural form Latinos refers to both males and females collectively. As ethnic pride has grown, so too has the popularity of the term Latino. Many prefer Latino because it more closely associates to the people and culture of Latin America as opposed to Spain. Others prefer it because it is a term that has come from within the community as opposed to one made up for them from outside the community.

Today, the terms Hispanic and Latino are often used interchangeably by organizations and by the members within the community. However, we should all remain aware that the debate over which term to use is more than a battle over names. The conflict involves a power struggle and the attempt by those who have been marginalized in the past to name themselves as opposed to allowing others to decide what labels will be used.

I personally prefer the term Latino and have found its use to be more "en vogue" by organizations. However I respect those who prefer to use the term Hispanic. Whichever term you prefer, I believe it is important for all of us to know the different meanings of these two words associated with this community.

Latinos in the Workforce

Latinos do not easily fit into the prevailing racial categories in the United States. Accordingly, one of their biggest challenges is how to manage the comfort level of others pertaining to their cultural identity. In the workplace, it is assumed that all Latinos are alike. Yet, the reality is that their race, national origin, language use, socioeconomic class, immigration status, and a number of other elements influence one's sense of Latino identity. Consequently, because of this group identity issue, some Hispanic employees may not readily identify themselves as Latino, or they may not participate in an employer's Latino inclusion efforts. Figure 4 illustrates the differences in Latino identity orientation.

FIGURE 4. LATINO IDENTITY ORIENTATION MODEL

Ferdman and Gallegos (2001) Latino/a Racial Identity Orientations Model (p. 49)

Orientation	Lens	Identify As/ Prefer	Latinos Are Seen	Whites Are Seen	Framing of Race
Latino-Integrated	Wide	Individuals in a group context	Positively	Complex	Dynamic, contextual, socially constructed
Latino-Identified (Racial/Raza)	Broad	Latinos	Very Positively	Distinct; could be barriers or allies	Latino/not Latino
Subgroup-Identified	Narrow	Own subgroup	My group OK, others maybe	Not central (could be barriers or blockers)	Not clear or central; secondary to nationality, ethnicity, culture
Latinos as Other	External	Not White	Generically, fuzzily	Negatively	White/not White
Undifferentiated/Denial	Closed	People	"Who are Latinos?"	Supposed color-blind (accept dominant norms)	Denial, irrelevant invisible
White-Identified	Tinted	Whites	Negatively	Very positively	White/Black, either/or, one-drop or "mejorar la raza" (i.e., improve the race)

Ferdman and Gallegos (2001) developed a theory about Latino Identity that: (1) ascertains how *Latino* is used as an umbrella term to identify similar looking cultural groups and people of mixed heritage and (2) suggests Latinos develop orientations or lenses based on experiences with social institutions including the family, education system, peer groups, and U.S. cultural racial constructs.

Ferdman and Gallegos explain the lenses as:

a) *Latino Integrated* – understands racial constructs and is able to challenge them;
b) *Latino Identified* – accepts the groups *Latino* and *White* and identifies with Latino;
c) *Subgroup Identified* – recognizes that there are multiple Latino groups and identifies with a regional subgroup (e.g., Cuban);
d) *Latino as Other* – identifies as a generic Latino due to a mixed heritage;
e) *Undifferentiated* – colorblind, adherent to the dominant culture, and tends to attribute failure to the individual rather than to racial constructs; and
f) *White Identified* – accepts the groups *Latino* and *White* and identifies with White.

The Bureau of Labor Statistics' report on *Labor Force Characteristics by Race and Ethnicity, 2016* made several notable findings:

- Hispanics accounted for 17 percent of total employment but were substantially overrepresented in several detailed occupational categories, including miscellaneous agricultural workers (53 percent); painters, construction and maintenance (51 percent); and maids and housekeeping cleaners (47 percent).

- By detailed ethnicity, the majority of Hispanics in the labor force were Mexican (61 percent). Central Americans—including Salvadorans and Other Central Americans (excluding Salvadorans)—made up another 10 percent. Nine percent of Hispanics were Puerto Rican, 7 percent were South American, and 4 percent were Cuban. An additional 9 percent were classified as Other Hispanics or Latinos, a category that includes two subcategories: Dominicans and Other Hispanics or Latinos (excluding Dominicans).

- Among adult men (ages 20 and older), Hispanics (80.5 percent) were more likely to participate in the labor force than any other group.

- Compared to Whites, Blacks and Asians who had more than a 90% high school completion rate in the labor force, only 74 percent of Hispanics in the labor force had completed high school and 20 percent of Hispanics in the labor force had a Bachelor's Degree or higher. Nevertheless, Blacks and Hispanics generally had lower earnings than Whites and Asians at nearly all educational attainment levels.

The Latino labor force is significantly more likely to be foreign born than the general population. According to BLS, in 2017, nearly half (47.9 percent) of the foreign-born labor force was Hispanic, and one-quarter (25.2 percent) was Asian. Hispanics and Asians made up much lower percentages of the native-born labor force, at 10.7 percent and 2.0 percent, respectively. About 16.5 percent of the foreign-born labor force was White and 9.4 percent was Black, compared with 72.3 percent and 12.2 percent, respectively, of the native-born labor force.

Compared to other foreign-born ethnic groups, Latinos were least likely to have advanced education. Low educational attainment, limited English language proficiency, and lack of work experience, training, and/or other skills contribute to decreased employment options for Latino immigrants. Although many Latinos enter the workforce at an early age, working in low-skilled jobs diminishes the opportunity to gain the kind of general work experience that brings about opportunities for better paying, lower-risk positions.

Further, the unemployment rate of foreign-born Latinos is more volatile or cyclical than that of the native born. It is a long-standing fact that Latinos typically have higher unemployment rates than Whites, but lower unemployment rates than African Americans. Nevertheless, unemployed Latinos experience a shorter duration of unemployment and are less likely to join the ranks of the long-term unemployed than are either their unemployed White or Black counterparts.

It's important for employers to follow the laws in respect to hiring immigrant workers. In the current political and economic environment, manufacturers and other employers who traditionally hire undocumented workers have been receiving "notices of inspection" from the U.S. Immigration and Customs Enforcement Office. These companies are being audited for their I-9 records. Not only are illegal immigrants being deported, but employers are facing jail time—resulting in job losses and company closures.

Additionally, there has been a trend among states to enact legislation that "cracks down" on illegal immigration. The reasoning behind the immigrant employment restrictions is that there would be more opportunities for American citizens if undocumented workers were not taking away jobs. However, the logic is flawed in that the immigrants' jobs are typically lower wage, higher risk, and entry-level positions—not the types of jobs that unemployed Americans are generally pursuing. Furthermore, other companies who may not hire undocumented workers, but who buy or sell to businesses that do hire illegal immigrants, have been adversely affected. Thus, the crackdowns have resulted in the loss of jobs in many places.

It is important for Diversity and Inclusion professionals to understand what the issues are pertaining to immigration, and to initiate and participate in discussions about how to introduce changes in the U.S. immigration process so that it can balance workforce and marketplace needs. The U.S. must have a temporary foreign worker program that extends legal immigration options to foreign workers in order to reduce the percentage of foreigners choosing undocumented means of coming to the U.S. Otherwise, illegal methods will always appear more attractive because in spite of all of the concentrated federal and state efforts, the risk of getting "caught" is still relatively low.

With the impending labor shortage and the continuous growth of the Hispanic population, this segment of human capital will become increasingly important to the enhanced competitiveness of America's workforce. One of the ways that Latinos can participate in the high-skill, high-wage labor market is to get enrolled in and complete postsecondary education programs. These programs should lead to certification, licensure, diploma, or an associate's/bachelor's/master's degree in growing fields, such as healthcare, technology, and self-employment.

In a Forbes article on *Examining the Growth of Hispanic Business Owners*, author Rohit Arora asserts that "there are more than four million Hispanic-owned businesses throughout the U.S., and their revenues have climbed to more than $660 billion, according to the U.S. Hispanic Chamber of Commerce. In fact, Hispanic entrepreneurs have been starting businesses at a pace 15 times the national average over the last decade." Arora adds, "As the Hispanic population and entrepreneurship grow, they will become increasingly more important to the U.S. economy. It is vital that they are able to obtain the funding, [contracts], and assistance to help build their enterprises."

Some Latinos are opting out of the workplace because of discriminatory practices in hiring, promotions, and work assignments. Nevertheless, organizations can still achieve inclusion goals by ensuring that Latino-owned enterprises are a prominent component of procurement and supply chain efforts. A working paper, entitled "*Hispanic Self-Employment: A Dynamic Analysis of Business Ownership*", advises organizations to offer technical assistance and support as "Latinos tend to have lower success rates with their new businesses and exit self-employment at a higher rate than Whites." This data presents another opportunity for supplier diversity and inclusive procurement development efforts to demonstrate success.

Pertaining to the labor market problems experienced by Hispanics, these employment issues are associated with many factors, not all of which are measurable. Some of the factors include a tendency to be employed in occupations with high levels of unemployment, lower average levels of schooling, greater concentration in the central cities of urban areas where job opportunities may be relatively limited, and the likelihood of discrimination in the workplace.

Diversity and Inclusion professionals must take proactive steps to prevent discrimination against Latino employees—whether it manifests itself through stereotyping the roles that Hispanics play within the organization, equal pay for equal work, or ensuring that Latinos have fair access to mentors, coaches, and other professional development opportunities.

Latin Culture
In addition to variances in the Latino Identity Orientation, Latin culture is very diverse. Figure 5 illustrates all of the different countries from which a Latino may originate.

The following provides an overview of Latin culture, but should not be used to stereotype all Hispanic Americans.

- **The needs of the group vs. the needs of the individual**
  In the Latino community, family or group needs take precedence over the needs of an individual. Hispanics tend to be brought up to be cooperative, whereas the Anglo culture typically encourages people to be more competitive and individualistic. When Hispanic individuals work in a group, not all are expected to do their equal share. It is not offensive if one group member is not working as hard, while in an Anglo group, each is expected to do his/her fair share. In education, sharing may mean helping another student during a test, which is considered cheating in an Anglo culture. In one class, a Hispanic student was reprimanded by a non-Hispanic instructor for copying from another student's test. Both students were stunned and offended, because to them, they were helping each other, not cheating.

FIGURE 5.

U.S. Hispanic Population By Country of Origin, 2010

Country	Population
Mexican	31,798,000
Puerto Rican	4,624,000
Cuban	1,786,000
Salvadoran	1,649,000
Dominican	1,415,000
Guatemalan	1,044,000
Colombian	909,000
Honduran	633,000
Ecuadorian	565,000
Peruvian	531,000

Source: The Pew Research Center/Pew Hispanic Center, "U.S. Hispanic Country-of-Origin Counts for Nation, Top 30 Metropolitan Areas," May 26, 2011, http://pewhispanic.org/reports/report.php?ReportID=142. Cited with permission.

- **Different perspectives about present and future**
  For most Hispanics, present time has more value than future time. For them, the time-dependent ways of the Anglo appears to be a misappropriation of the present. Therefore, it would be more appropriate to expect Hispanic employees and students to concentrate on short-term goals rather than longer-term targets. Additionally, it may not serve supervisors or instructors well to place excessive emphasis on fast-moving and closely timed activities. This creates a very tense environment for a professional/student who grew up in a relatively relaxed home atmosphere.

- **Communication Styles**
  The communication style of Hispanics is much more formal than that of Anglos. Hispanics tend to be very polite, which can be interpreted by Anglos as being subservient or servile. Respect is highly valued and shown by using formal titles. Additionally, Hispanics tend to show affection through touching; friends may kiss, and males may hug, shake hands, or pat each other on the back in public.

- **Children**
  Hispanics have a very special way with children, a way that appears to be too permissive. One hardly sees Hispanics spanking their children in public. When parents are annoyed, they tend to address their children with "usted" (you). They also playfully call their small children "papito" (little papa) or "mamita" (little mama). In addition, the older children of the family are expected to take care of the younger ones; nevertheless, the child is generally brought up to be very dependent on the parents, which affects the child's decision-making. In the traditional family, the child will have a strong sense of identity with his family, community, and ethnic group.

- **Adapting to the Environment Rather Than Controlling It**
  Hispanics try to adjust to the universe and may be relatively spiritual—with the majority belonging to the Catholic Church. However, that does not prevent them from believing in witchcraft and the "curadora" (or healing woman). Herbs play a significant role in healing and bringing good luck.

  The Hispanic employee/student, as a rule, thrives more in a cooperative environment than in a competitive one. The uniqueness of the individual is more important than individual accomplishment. The good of the whole is often more important than the individual's goals. There is also a tendency among Hispanic employees/students to credit his/her achievement to destiny, fate and other religious circumstances rather than ability.

- **About the Spanish Language**
  The Spanish language has a long history in the United States because many southwestern states were a part of Mexico, the U.S. acquired Puerto Rico, and Florida used to be a colony of Spain.

  Recently, the Spanish language has been revitalized in the U.S. by a new generation of Hispanics who are proud of their culture and heritage. In many parts of America, it is easy to find people who speak little to no English. This causes concern for some individuals who fear that the U.S. will become a nation split by language, similar to Canada. Others argue that the current boom in the use of Spanish is due almost entirely to new immigrants, and that their children will, for the most part, learn English. They point to 1990 census data, which indicates that by the third generation, two-thirds of Hispanic children speak English exclusively. Whether that number is going up or down will be difficult to determine since the Census Bureau did not track that information in its most recent census.

  What should be a concern is the growing number of Spanish-speaking Latinos who are "trapped" in economically disadvantaged neighborhoods throughout big cities and along the U.S.-Mexico border—although immigrant enclaves are common throughout American history. German and Polish enclaves were common throughout the Midwest. The Italians flourished in New York. However, those languages largely faded from use in the U.S. Few are predicting that will happen with Spanish. It is here to stay, although we will not know its ultimate impact for generations to come.

  Keep in mind, Spanish is spoken differently depending on the person's country of origin, how long the individual has been in the U.S., and whether the person lives in the South, Midwest, Northeast or West. Therefore, translating or interpreting the Spanish language should not be a one-size-fits-all process. As a best practice, it may be necessary to hire more than one interpreter/translator to serve customers, patients, or students.

CONCLUSION

The potential for Diversity and Inclusion leaders is clear: we must proactively involve all ethnic groups in our cultural competency and inclusion efforts. Not only will this demonstrate that our Diversity and Inclusion work extends beyond Black and White, but it will enable our organizations to tap into previously under-served demographic groups. To start, we can:

1. *Expand our definition of diversity to include nationality. Your organization may already employ individuals from 10 or 20 different nationalities and your D&I efforts can be viewed as more inclusive when whites can also embrace their German-, French-, Italian-, Jewish-, Irish-, and Polish-American heritage.*
2. *Be aware of intergroup conflicts between individuals from the same racial / ethnic category based on cultural differences, nationality, language barriers, or other unique characteristics.*
3. *Create opportunities for employees to learn about, and work in, different cultures.*
4. *Stay abreast of demographic and socioeconomic changes for employment purposes, as well as to refine multi-cultural marketing goals. Always remember, customers, students, patients, etc. always like to see people who look like them working for the organization with which they do business. Therefore, the broader the mix of employee representation, the better.*

References:

Immigrant Spirt. *Top ten most popular immigration countries.* Available at: http://www.immigrantspirit.com/top-ten-most-popular-immigration-countries/

Henley & Partners, 2018. *The Henley Passport Index.* Available at: https://www.henleyglobal.com/henley-passport-index/

Nash, Kieran, 2017. *The Difference Between an Expat and an Immigrant? Semantics.* BBC News. Available at: http://www.bbc.com/capital/story/20170119-who-should-be-called-an-expat

The Times of India, Feb. 24, 2018. *US Tightens H1-B Visa Rules, Indians to be Hit.* Available at: https://timesofindia.indiatimes.com/india/us-tightens-h-1b-visa-rules-indians-to-be-hit/articleshow/63050944.cms

Council of Economic Advisers, May 9, 2018. *CEA Report: Military Spouses in the Labor Market.* Available at: https://www.whitehouse.gov/briefings-statements/cea-report-military-spouses-labor-market/

Singer, Audrey, Mar. 15, 2012. *Immigrant Workers in the U.S. Labor Force.* Brookings Institute. Available at: https://www.brookings.edu/research/immigrant-workers-in-the-u-s-labor-force/

Lopez, Gustavo and Bialik, Kristen, May 3, 2017. *Key Findings About U.S. Immigrants.* Pew Research Center. Available at: http://www.pewresearch.org/fact-tank/2017/05/03/key-findings-about-u-s-immigrants/

Taylor, Paul, June 19, 2012. *The Rise of Asian Americans.* Pew Research Center. Available at: http://www.pewsocialtrends.org/2012/06/19/the-rise-of-asian-americans/

Hyun, Jane, 2006. *Breaking the Bamboo Ceiling: Career Strategies for Asians.* HarperCollins Publishers

Zong, Jie and Batalova, Jeanne, Aug. 31, 2017. *Indian Immigrants in the United States.* Migration Policy Institute. Available at: https://www.migrationpolicy.org/article/indian-immigrants-united-states

Duke University and U.C. Berkley, 2007. *America's New Immigrant Entrepreneurs.* Available at: http://people.ischool.berkeley.edu/~anno/Papers/Americas_new_immigrant_entrepreneurs_I.pdf

Bach, Natasha, May 2, 2018. *Kanye West Suggested Slavery Was 'a Choice.' Critics Are Decrying It as Self-Promotion Gone Way Too Far.* Fortune. Available at: http://fortune.com/2018/05/02/kanye-west-slavery-choice-tmz/

Anderson, Monica, 2015. *A Rising Share of the U.S. Black Population Is Foreign Born.* Washington, DC: Pew Research Center, April. Retrieved from: http://www.pewsocialtrends.org/2015/04/09/a-rising-share-of-the-u-s-Black-population-is-foreign-born/

Anderson, Monica and Lopez, Gustavo, Jan. 24, 2018. *Key facts about black immigrants in the U.S.* Pew Research Center. Available at: http://www.pewresearch.org/fact-tank/2018/01/24/key-facts-about-black-immigrants-in-the-u-s/

Fears, Darryl, March 6, 2007. *In Diversity Push, Top Universities Enrolling More Black Immigrants.* Washington Post. Available at: http://www.washingtonpost.com/wp-dyn/content/article/2007/03/05/AR2007030501296.html?noredirect=on

Hallman, Hunter, Mar. 28, 2018. *How do Undocumented Immigrants Pay Federal Taxes? An Explainer.* Bipartisan Policy Center. Available at: https://bipartisanpolicy.org/blog/how-do-undocumented-immigrants-pay-federal-taxes-an-explainer/

Llosa, Alvaro Vargas, May 29, 2013. *Addressing And Discrediting 7 Major Myths About Immigration.* Forbes. Available at: https://www.forbes.com/sites/realspin/2013/05/29/addressing-and-discrediting-7-major-myths-about-immigration/#54b9ca9a4a2c

Carden, Art, Aug. 28, 2015. *Illegal Immigrants Don't Lower Our Wages Or Take Our Jobs.* Forbes. Available at: https://www.forbes.com/sites/artcarden/2015/08/28/how-do-illegal-immigrants-affect-american-workers-the-answer-might-surprise-you/#76ec0747771a

Gutierrez, David G. *An Historic Overview of Latino Immigration and Demographic Transformation of the United States.* Washington, DC: Pew Hispanic Center, June 27, 2012

Henderson, Nia-Malika Henderson, 2014. *7 charts that explain the undocumented immigrant population.* Washington Post: The Fix, November. Retrieved from: https://www.washingtonpost.com/news/the-fix/wp/2014/11/21/7-charts-that-explain-the-undocumented-immigrant-population/

Passel, Jeffrey S., and Cohn, D'Vera, 2012. "Unauthorized Immigrants: 11.1 Million in 2011." Washington, D.C.: Pew Hispanic Center, December. Retrieved from: http://www.pewhispanic.org/2012/12/06/unauthorized-immigrants-11-1-million-in-2011/

Zong, Jie and Batalova, Jeanne, Dec. 2015. *European Immigrants in the United States.* Migration Policy Institute Spotlight.

Grandi, Filippo, 18 May 2017. *Syria has changed the way we respond to refugees. Here's how.* World Economic Forum. Available at: https://www.weforum.org/agenda/2017/05/syria-changed-our-response-to-refugees/

Florido, Adrian, Sept. 8, 2015. *Mass Deportation May Sound Unlikely, But It's Happened Before.* NPR. Available at: https://www.npr.org/sections/codeswitch/2015/09/08/437579834/mass-deportation-may-sound-unlikely-but-its-happened-before

Davis, Julie Hirschfeld, Apr. 2, 2018. *Trump's Immigration Tweets Followed by Policy Plans to Match.* The New York Times. Available at: https://www.nytimes.com/2018/04/02/us/politics/trump-immigration-mexico-daca.html

Krogstad, Jens Manuel, Aug. 3, 2017. *U.S. Hispanic Population Growth has Leveled Off.* Pew Research Center. Available at: http://www.pewresearch.org/fact-tank/2017/08/03/u-s-hispanic-population-growth-has-leveled-off/

Goodell, Jeff, May 30, 2018. *The Secret Buried in the Puerto Rican Death Toll.* Rolling Stone. Available at: https://www.rollingstone.com/politics/news/puerto-rico-hurricane-maria-death-toll-w520914

Ferdman, B.M., and Gallegos, P.I., 2001. *Racial identity development and Latinos in the United States.* New York: New York University Press.

The U.S. Department of Labor, Bureau of Labor Statistics. Oct. 2017. *Labor Force Characteristics by Race and Ethnicity, 2016.* Available at: https://www.bls.gov/opub/reports/race-and-ethnicity/2016/home.htm

Arora, Rohit, Oct. 22, 2016. *Examining The Growth Of Hispanic Business Owners.* Forbes. Available at: https://www.forbes.com/sites/rohitarora/2016/10/22/examining-the-growth-of-hispanic-business-owners/2/#4e47e8541f6f

Lofstrum, Magnus and Wang, Chunbei, May 8, 2006. *Hispanic Self-Employment: A Dynamic Analysis of Business Ownership.* Available at: https://papers.ssrn.com/sol3/papers.cfm?abstract_id=900377

Sample Test Questions:
IMMIGRANT GROUPS IN THE WORKPLACE

1. As a best practice, organizations that require Spanish language interpretation and/or translation services should:
   A. Communicate with a one-size-fits-all approach
   B. Hire more than one interpreter/translator
   C. Wait until the Latino population increases

2. All of the following are modern-day myths about Undocumented Workers EXCEPT:
   A. Expired visas contribute to the rise in undocumented workers
   B. Latino workers are the only undocumented immigrants
   C. The unsecure Mexican border increases illegal immigration

3. The difference between an immigrant and an expatriate is:
   A. Companies typically send expatriates to work abroad
   B. Immigrants do not pay any taxes but expatriates do
   C. There is no difference between expatriates and immigrants

4. An employer must submit this form in order to hire a foreign worker with an H1-B visa.
   A. EEO-1 Form
   B. Labor Condition Application
   C. Fair Trade Agreement

5. Mexican repatriation, where thousands of Hispanics were illegally deported to Mexico, was this businessman's campaign promise:
   A. President Hoover
   B. President Trump
   C. President Obama

6. In the Latino Orientation Identity Model, those who identify as Integrated Latinos frame race as:
   A. Latino / Not Latino
   B. White / Not White
   C. Socially Constructed

Sample Test Questions:

IMMIGRANT GROUPS IN THE WORKPLACE (cont'd)

7. **Today, this group of immigrants is more likely to be older, educated, and with a higher household income, but they are less likely to participate in the labor force:**
   A. Asian Immigrants
   B. European Immigrants
   C. African Immigrants

8. **The difference between the terms "Hispanic" and "Latino" is that Hispanic is a word that refers to:**
   A. Individuals with mixed heritage
   B. Individuals in Mexico
   C. Individuals in the U.S.

9. **The difference between a Passport and a Visa is that:**
   A. Countries provide Visas to foreigners
   B. Countries issue Visas to their own citizens
   C. Visas are always required for a green card

10. **This country is the second most popular destination for Immigrants:**
    A. The U.K.
    B. Russia
    C. Canada

11. **Intergroup conflicts do not exist between individuals within the same racial or ethnic category.**
    A. True
    B. False

12. **In the 1970's, European nations realized that the "brain drain" was a real problem.**
    A. True
    B. False

13. **Historically, U.S. legislation has been the key to restricting immigration from non-Western European countries.**
    A. True
    B. False

NAVIGATING THROUGH RELIGION & BELIEF SYSTEMS

> *How have we responded to the religious diversity that increasingly characterizes our neighborhoods, schools and places of work? Has it sunk into our awareness that the temple or mosque down the street is not just another church? Does it matter that our co-workers have radically different ideas of the sacred than we do? Does it bother us to hear about hate crimes directed at Muslims or Hindus?*

OVERALL OBJECTIVES AND COMPETENCIES

This competency is designed to help Diversity and Inclusion professionals identify the complexities associated with religion and non-religion at work; help supervisors and employees to steer through issues relative to sincerely held personal beliefs; and prevent discrimination by gaining a deeper understanding of worldviews, belief systems, and religious practices.

BACKGROUND AND CONTEXT

Text of the First Amendment to the U.S. Constitution says: "Congress shall make no law respecting an establishment of religion, or prohibiting the free exercise thereof; or abridging the freedom of speech, or of the press; or the right of the people peaceably to assemble, and to petition the Government for a redress of grievances." It guarantees the free exercise of religion. The Supreme Court has interpreted this as preventing the government from having any authority in religion. However, what is religion, and how does it affect our work?

Religion is the belief in and worship of a Higher Power. It entails a collection of cultural systems, beliefs, and worldviews that relate humanity to spirituality, and to moral values. Religion can be organized, such as attending worship services in a group, or unorganized, where an individual has firmly held beliefs outside of religious gatherings. A number of modern religious scholars have commented on the difficulty of defining religion. Moreover, there are peculiar difficulties associated with assigning a definition of religion that is too vague and general. Equally troubling is assigning a definition that is so narrowly defined that it is not "inclusive enough" to consider alternative forms of religious beliefs and practices that seem religious to most intelligent people. The key insight in arriving at a resolution to defining religion always begins in an experience that some individual has or that some group of people share. Hence, the concept of religion is personal.

Sometimes religion is used interchangeably with the terms faith or belief; but religion differs from private beliefs in that it has a public aspect. Most religions have organized behaviors, such as clerical hierarchies, congregations, places of worship, regular meetings or services, prayer, and scriptures. Practices may also include sermons, ways of dress, sacrifices, dances, symbols, meditations, festivals, arts, initiations, and other services.

FIGURE 1. RELIGIOUS SYMBOLS OF MAJOR WORLD RELIGIONS

Religious symbols from the top nine organized faiths of the world according to Major world religions. From left to right:

- *1st Row: Christian Cross, Jewish Star of David, Hindu Aumkar*
- *2nd Row: Islamic Star and crescent, Buddhist Wheel of Dharma, Shinto Torii*
- *3rd Row: Sikh Khanda, Bahá'í star, Jain Ahimsa Symbol*

The development of religion has taken different forms in different cultures. Some religions place an emphasis on belief, while others emphasize practice. Some religions focus on the subjective experience of the religious individual, while others consider the activities of the religious community to be most important. Some religions claim to be universal, believing their laws and cosmology to be binding for everyone, while others are intended to be practiced only by a closely defined or localized group.

In many places, religion has been associated with public institutions such as schools, hospitals, the family, government, and political hierarchies. Thus, as we consider the impact of diversity, it is important to go beyond the dimensions of race and ethnicity to the core of individual and group identities via religions, beliefs, convictions, and concerns.

Contact and tolerance between members of different religious groups often reduces prejudice and hostility, while education and information generally has a positive effect on attitudes between members of different religious groups. Presently, America remains one of the most religiously committed nations in the world, if commitment is measured in numbers professing belief in God and attending services at houses of worship. Nevertheless, the tension between religious groups has been exacerbated by 9/11, the War on Terror, and political elections.

Additionally, the United States has witnessed an unprecedented increase in the diversity of major religious traditions as millions of people migrate from countries in which Christians are only a small minority.

Some would venture to say that cultural interpretations, religious convictions, and the workplace are inextricably separate. However, it makes a difference how people think about questions of God, death, salvation, heaven, hell, good, evil, other religions, and the teachings in their own tradition. In a healthcare setting, many religious nuances can influence a doctor/patient relationship. Some of these issues pertain to treatment options (or the lack thereof), dietary restrictions, hygiene/cleanliness, quality of care, prayer, communication, and end-of-life rituals.

Conversely, religious traditions (e.g., the Pledge of Allegiance, invocation/prayer, songs, etc.) are incorporated during special occasions at K-12 schools, public meetings with elected officials, graduation ceremonies, and even sporting events. While Americans say they are tolerant and have respect for people whose religious traditions happen to be different from their own, they continue to speak as if their nation is or should be a Christian nation, founded on Christian principles, and characterized by public references to this tradition. This imbalanced approach can be both confusing and frustrating for religious minorities in the United States.

THE MAJOR RELIGIONS

Max Weber's influential writings about religion more than a century ago provide a helpful framework for thinking about the relationships among religious convictions, views of other religions, and ideas about purpose and destiny.

Weber understood that religion, among other things, provides people with a way of transforming an existence of apparent chaos into one having ultimate meaning. Religion renders existence meaningful by reinforcing the assumption that reality makes sense intellectually and intuitively. Weber realized that any religious system that provides meaning in this fashion, must also address the problem of evil. Answers and comfort must be provided in those instances that do not make sense and are not desirable. They may be explained as the work of an inscrutable God or the devil, in terms of fate, or a cycle of rebirths—but they must be explained. How they are explained, Weber argued, shapes what people value and how they believe they should live.

Although there are many religions that shape what people value and how they live, the four largest religious groups in the world are Christianity, Islam, Hinduism, and Buddhism. Judaism is not necessarily a major religion by number of believers, but it is recognized as having an influential role in the two largest religions, as well as other groups. Figure 2 illustrates the prevailing world religions.

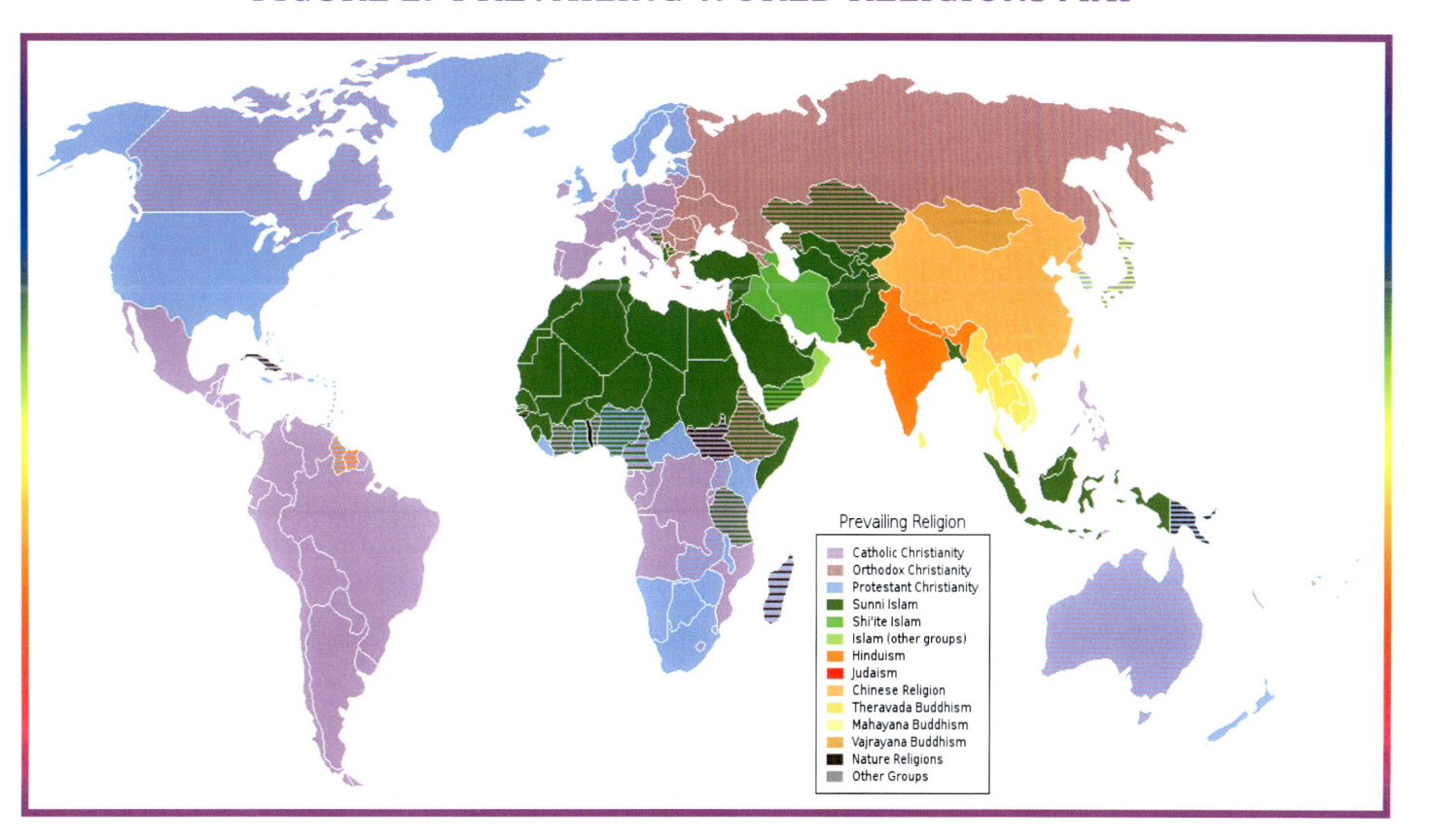

FIGURE 2. PREVAILING WORLD RELIGIONS MAP

As with all dimensions of diversity, there are some similarities between the religions as well as many differences. We will explore a few of the similarities and differences in this guide.

Christianity

Christianity is the world's largest religion, and its believers rely on faith—which is "being sure of what is hoped for and certain of what is not seen".

The foundation of Christianity is one's belief in Jesus Christ. Christians recognize Jesus as the Son of God, their Savior, and the Messiah. Christians read the Bible, which has 66 books divided into two time periods: the Old Testament, which is Before Christ (BC) and the New Testament, which starts with the birth of Christ, his life, and After Christ's Death (AD). Most of the Bible's books have similar stories or writings, authored from different perspectives. The Bible is the most read book in the world.

Christians typically worship on the Sabbath, which is generally Sunday. In accord with this practice, a Pastor (or similarly represented person) preaches and later in the week congregants meet for Bible Study, where the Pastor may teach. Additionally, Christians attend special services in celebration of certain holidays, which are almost universally recognized and secularized throughout the United States. For example, Christmas is the celebration of Jesus' birth, while Good Friday and Easter are the celebration of Jesus' death, burial, and resurrection.

Trinitarianism denotes those Christians who believe in the concept of the *Trinity*, which refers to the teaching that one God comprises three distinct, eternally co-existing persons: the *Father*, the *Son* (incarnate in Jesus Christ), and the *Holy Spirit*. Together, these three persons are sometimes called the Godhead.

In Christianity, water is used in the baptism ritual, which is the sacrament of regeneration and admission into the Christian community. In this manner, the person being baptized receives a new spiritual life. A baptism can be performed with the symbolic sprinkling of, or actual immersion in, water. After baptism, Christians await the second coming of Jesus, known to many as the rapture. Most Christians believe that human beings will experience divine judgment and will be rewarded with either eternal life or eternal damnation.

Reportedly, there are 38,000 Christian denominations; the main groups are Catholic, Orthodox, and Protestant. Among the major Protestant branches are Lutheran, Anglican, Baptist, Episcopal, Methodist, Pentecostal, Apostolic/Holiness, Evangelical, Church of God in Christ, and Presbyterian. Different denominations practice different things. For example, individuals in the Apostolic Church do not believe that women should wear make-up, jewelry, or clothing that is not modest (e.g., pants, skirts above the calf, or short sleeve shirts). Likewise, Catholics participate in Lent and Ash Wednesday services, whereas other Christian denominations may not recognize the tradition. Figure 3 demonstrates some of the major branches and movements within Protestantism.

FIGURE 3. MAJOR PROTESTANT BRANCHES

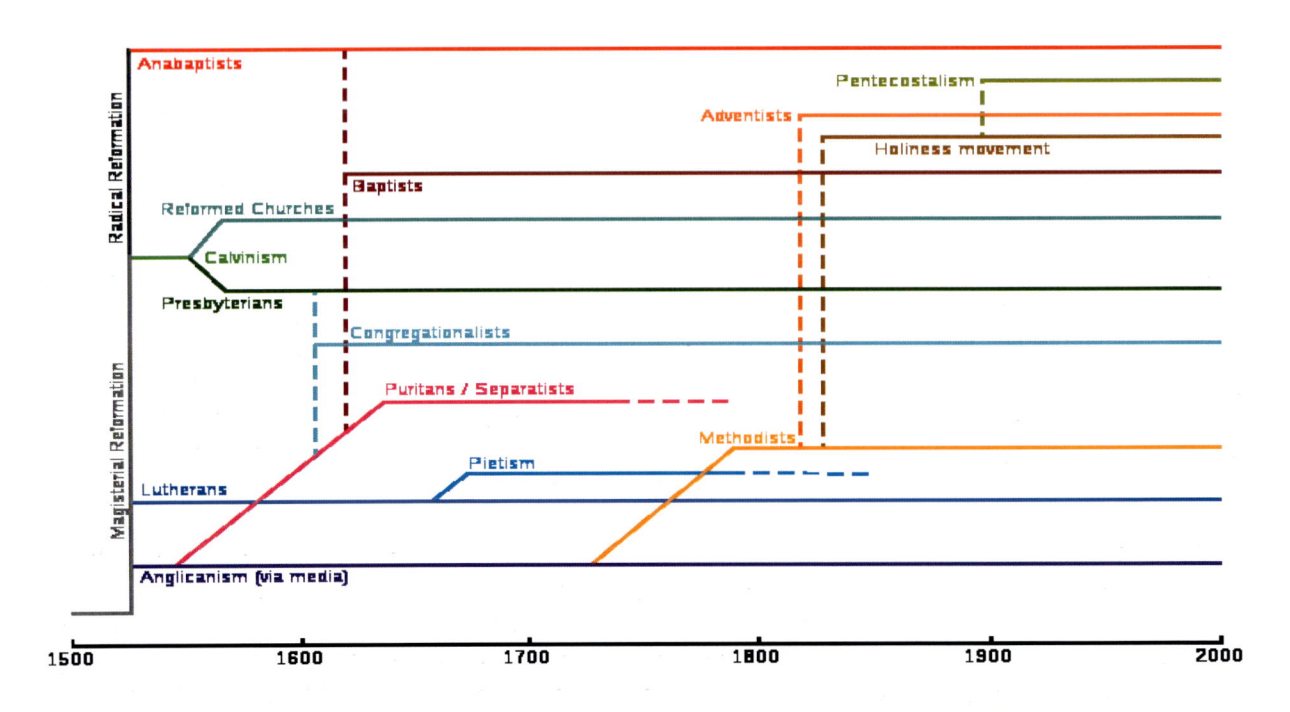

Judaism

Many of the customs, procedures, beliefs, and behavioral aspects of the Jewish religion date back hundreds and even thousands of years. As the world's oldest monotheistic religion, it includes those born Jewish, as well as converts to Judaism. The difference is that a Jewish birth represents an ethnicity, while Judaism embodies a belief system. Most Jewish individuals throughout history lived in small, closed communities. They did not mix with general society, except perhaps for work or mercantile purposes.

According to the Israel Central Bureau of Statistics, there were 14.3 million Jewish individuals worldwide in 2013, roughly 0.19% of the world's population at the time. According to the 2013 Pew Research Center's Religion and Public Life Project, the worldwide Jewish population could be larger if a broader definition (such as having a Jewish grandparent) or smaller if a tighter definition (such as an unbroken line of matrilineal Jewish descent) were imposed.

Nevertheless, the Jewish population is highly geographically concentrated—with the majority of Jewish people living in Israel (43%) and America (40%), as of 2013. Yet, the actual difference between the population sizes in Israel and America is less than 1 million. Smaller populations (less than 500,000) reside in France and Canada respectively, although these two countries contain a larger percentage of Jewish citizens than other countries around the world.

For Jewish individuals, the Sabbath is Saturday. Jewish people read the Torah, which is a sacred scroll (also, the first five books of Moses, known as the Pentateuch). During religious services, Jews recite the Kaddish, which is not a prayer per se; it extols the glory and name of God, but it does not ask for anything. The Kaddish is very similar to the Lord's Prayer that Christians recite.

Through the ages, education and wisdom were the means of gaining status in the Jewish community. As representatives of their congregations and instructors of the Jewish faith, the *rabbi* (which means "teacher") must attend rabbinical seminary and is ordained. Rabbi's are encouraged to marry, demonstrate the ability to lead, counsel, and manage. Jewish individuals do not direct their confessions to a rabbi as Catholics; instead, confession is directed to the party against whom a person has sinned.

Christians and Jews begin their relationship with several things in common: the Hebrew Scriptures (the Old Testament), the Ten Commandments, a Sabbath day, the importance of charitable giving, and similar versions of what is known as the golden rule. Jewish people agree that Jesus was a great man—a teacher, a prophet who traveled the land performing miraculous deeds, and a person who preached love and kindness. However, Jewish individuals generally do not believe that the Messiah has come, neither do they recognize Jesus as their savior nor as the Son of God. They believe that when the Messiah comes, world suffering will end.

In the Bible's New Testament, Jesus makes reference to the Pharisees and Sadducees. These were among the major Jewish movements in his day. A movement is similar to a Christian denomination. The main Jewish movements in the United States include the Orthodox, Conservative, and Reform movements. However, globally, it is difficult to estimate the size of these movements because they are not familiar or relevant to Jewish populations in many other countries. In Israel and elsewhere, distinctions are often made between Haredi or Ultra-Orthodox Jews, Modern Orthodox Jews, and less traditional forms of Judaism. This guide will focus on Judaism in the U.S. because there are specific laws that provide protection from discrimination, harassment, and retaliation in America.

Orthodox Judaism resists changes to its beliefs and practices. A central tenet of Orthodox Judaism is that the law of God was given to Moses on Mount Sinai and the Torah is divine. Thus, no law derived from the Torah should be tampered with, regardless of modern lifestyles, needs, or changes in society. Because of this, Orthodox rabbis believe that rulings of other U.S. Jewish groups are invalid.

There are many rules that govern the practice of Judaism. A person who practices Orthodox Judaism must learn these rules, which is no simple task, and keeping a given rule is not optional. Since Orthodox Jews traditionally do not travel by car on the Sabbath, their synagogues are generally located within walking distance of their home.

Conservative Judaism represents a mix of both traditional and more modern views. It accommodates the needs of Jewish life in contemporary society; but at the same time, accepts the divine inspiration of the law of the Torah. For example, it is okay to drive to the synagogue. It may be typical for men and boys to wear a kippah (skullcap) when in the synagogue, to wear a tallit (prayer shawl) when attending religious services, and to recite certain prayers in Hebrew and others in English. Girls participate in the bat mitzvah, while boys celebrate the bar mitzvah.

After the French Revolution and other political and social movements around the globe, Judaism experienced a reformation. Religious services began to be conducted in the local language instead of strictly in Hebrew; men and women were seated together, musical instruments provided accompaniment to the cantor and congregation, and restrictions on diet and on Sabbath activities were relaxed. The Reform movement originated in Germany and flourished in the United States. Reform Judaism places decisions regarding rituals and observances more on the individual, and accounts for modern lifestyles.

Food and dietary restrictions in accord with Jewish law is called kashrut, or kosher in English. Kashrut, derived from the Torah, involves rules regarding the ritual slaughter of animals, the separation of dairy and meat, preparation of food, and more. The whole concept of kashrut hinges not on health factors, as many people think, but on belief itself.

In Judaism, a day begins at sundown. Unlike Christmas and New Year's Day, Jewish holidays occur on different dates each year. The Jewish calendar, based on the lunar cycle, determine the Jewish holidays. Some Jewish holidays include:

- ***Hanukkah*** – A miraculous celebration where a light burned for 8 days after a military victory and temple rededication; signified by candles which are lit in a special candelabra, or *menorah* (this holiday is closely associated with Christmas)
- ***Rosh Hashanah*** – the Jewish New Year
- ***Yom Kippur*** – the Day of Atonement
- ***Passover*** - A festive celebration to remember the Jewish enslavement in Egypt, the ten plagues, and the story of the Exodus (this holiday is closely associated with Easter)

The rest of the world generally uses the Gregorian calendar, which is based on the solar cycle of 365 days. Although the calendars are synchronized, the typical lunar cycle has 29.5 days with a leap month. If there were no leap months, the Jewish calendar would be similar to the Muslim calendar.

A 2013 Pew Research Center Survey, entitled *A Portrait of Jewish Americans*, was the first comprehensive national study of the American Jewish population in a dozen years. The survey, which was based on interviews with 3,475 Jewish respondents, covered a wide range of topics, including population estimates, demographic characteristics, Jewish identity, religious beliefs and practices, intermarriage, child rearing, connections with Israel, and social and political views.

The survey found a significant rise in those who are not religious, marry outside the faith and are not raising their children in the Jewish faith—resulting in a rapid assimilation that is sweeping through every branch of Judaism except the Orthodox.

According to the report, the intermarriage rate reached a high of 58 percent for all Jewish Americans, and 71 percent for non-Orthodox individuals—a huge change from before 1970, when only 17 percent of the Jewish population married outside the faith. Two-thirds of Jewish individuals do not belong to a synagogue, one-fourth do not believe in God, and one-third had a Christmas tree in their home last year. In a surprising finding, 34 percent said you could still be Jewish if you believe that Jesus was the Messiah.

The percentage of "Jews of no religion" has grown with each successive generation, peaking with the millennials (those born after 1980), of whom 32 percent say they have no religion. This trend toward secularism is also happening in the American population in general, with increasing proportions of each generation claiming no religious affiliation.

Islam

A Muslim is someone who makes the declaration: "There is no god but God; and Muhammad is the Prophet of Allah". This affirmation, known as the Shahada—literally meaning "witness" or "testimony"—is all there is to being a Muslim. Anyone can become a Muslim, or claim to be a Muslim, simply by uttering these words. However, beyond the declaration is the struggle to live by the spirit and meaning of these words.

Islam is the world's second largest religion with a following of over one billion people called Muslims—one-fifth of humanity. In some nations, every citizen is born a Muslim. In fact, in *The Changing Global Religious Landscape*, the Pew Research Center estimates that babies born to Muslims will begin to outnumber Christian births by 2035.

The word "Islam" actually means "submission to God". Therefore, "a Muslim is one who strives to submit to God." There are five pillars of Islam, which are the foundation of Muslim life:

1. **Say the confession of faith.** A Muslim must confess, "There is no God but Allah and Mohammed is the prophet of God."
2. **Pray.** Muslims are supposed to pray five times a day: shortly before sunrise, mid-morning, noon, mid-afternoon, and after sunset.
3. **Give alms.** Muslims are to give about 2.5 percent of their wealth.
4. **Fast during Ramadan.** For one lunar month, from sunrise to sunset, Muslims are not to allow anything to pass down their throat. (Theoretically, a good Muslim would even spit out his or her saliva.) Then from sunset to sunrise, they are permitted to eat as little or as much as they want. This is their way of developing discipline and relating to the poor. (Travelers, young children and pregnant or nursing mothers do not need to keep the fast.)
5. **Make a pilgrimage to Mecca.** Every Muslim who is financially able is supposed to travel to the birthplace of Islam once in his or her lifetime.

Mohammed founded Islam in Mecca in 610 A.D. Mohammed is to Islam, what Jesus is to a Christian. During Mohammed's time, polytheism reigned. People were worshipping multiple gods. During one of Mohammed's trips as a trader, he had a vision from a being he perceived to be an angel who said, "There is only one God, and His name is Allah. Worship Him." This marked the beginning of the second largest monotheistic religion.

Since then, Islam has spread across the entire globe. Muslims can be found in North and South America as well as in Western Europe; but they are predominately found in Africa, the Middle East, and Asia. Their principal homeland lies in the area commonly referred to as the "10/40 Window" (between 10 degrees latitudinal north and 40 degrees latitudinal north ranging from the eastern side of North Africa to the western side of Asia). About 60% of Muslims are Asian. The regional breakdown of Muslims throughout the rest of the world is Arab, 22%; sub-Sahara African, 12%; and Eastern European, 5%. Those remaining are scattered throughout the world.

Just as Christians have the Bible, Muslims have the Quran. They believe God dictated the Quran to Mohammed through the angel Gabriel. Muslims are also told in the Quran to read three other holy books: the Torah (which are the first five books of the Old Testament), the Zabur (which are the Psalms of David), and the Injeel (the gospel of Christ).

Muslims around the world worship on Fridays in mosques. Mosques are buildings where men (and sometimes women, depending upon the country) pray to God. In a mosque, during prayer time, all Muslims face toward Mecca, the birthplace of Islam. Where men and women pray together, men are usually in the front and women in the back.

Many practices fall in the category of *adab*, or Islamic etiquette. This includes greeting others with "*as-salamu `alaykum*" ("peace be unto you"), saying *bismillah* ("in the name of God") before meals, and using only the right hand for eating and drinking.

Muslims are restricted in their diet. Prohibited foods include pork products, blood, carrion, and alcohol. All meat must come from an herbivorous animal slaughtered in the name of God by a Muslim, Jew, or Christian, with the exception of game that one has hunted or fished for oneself. Food permissible for Muslims is known as *halal* food.

The Islamic dress code promotes modesty and seeks to minimize vice and immorality in society. Obeying this dress code is a form of obedience to God. In Islam, both men and women are expected to dress simply, modestly, and with dignity. A man must always be covered in loose and unrevealing clothing from his navel to his knee. This is the absolute minimum covering required. He must never, for example, go out in public wearing a short bathing suit. When leaving the home, a Muslim woman must at least cover her hair and body in loose and unrevealing clothing, obscuring the details of her figure from the public; some also choose to cover their face and hands.

Other conditions for dress include:

1. *Female clothing must not resemble a man's clothing.*
2. *The design of the clothing must not resemble the clothing of non-believing women.*
3. *The design must not consist of bold designs which attract attention.*
4. *Clothing should not be worn for the sole purpose of gaining reputation or increasing one's status in society.*

The reason for this strictness is so that the woman is protected from the lustful gaze of men and exploitation from marketing to male lust. It is permissible for a man to catch the eye of a woman; however, it is haram (unlawful) for a man to look twice as this encourages lustful thoughts.

Although the two religions share similar terminology and even similar theology (monotheism, for instance), Islam is fundamentally different from Christianity. All Muslims believe Jesus was born of a virgin and that he was a great prophet—yet he was only a man. They believe he was sent by God to help people obey God. Muslims believe that Jesus was born miraculously; he healed the sick, and raised the dead. The Quran refers to Jesus as the breath of God, the spirit of God, the life of God, and the word of God. However, Muslims do not think Jesus died on the cross. They believe that right before he was to be killed, God took him up to heaven and someone else (probably Judas) replaced him on the cross. They trust that Jesus will return to the earth to usher in the final judgment from God and confirm that Islam is the true and final religion for all mankind.

Muslims have no guarantee of being saved. They believe that all their works will be accounted for and that on Judgment Day, if your bad works outweigh your good works, you are going to go to hell. However, if your good works outweigh your bad works, you will probably go to heaven. A third possibility is that you could go to hell and burn your sins off for a while and then be allowed into heaven. The only way Muslims can be guaranteed to go to heaven is through "jihad". Although it is often translated "holy war", *jihad* literally means, "exerting force for God". One could be in "jihad" by writing a book about Islam, or by sharing his faith to bring others to Islam, or by physically fighting for the cause of Islam. If a Muslim dies in *jihad*, he is guaranteed to go to heaven.

Islam varies greatly around the world. Although Muslims take pains to describe themselves as members of the brotherhood of "one religion", the Islam practiced in Indonesia is very different from the Islam practiced in Saudi Arabia, which is different from that in Kazakhstan, or Iran, or Morocco.

There are numerous sects within Islam, but Sunni Muslims and Shia Muslims comprise the two largest sects. Because data on the percentages of Sunni and Shia Muslims are rough estimates in many countries, this guide presents them as ranges. Sunnis make up 87-90% of the world's Muslims, whereas Shia Muslims make up 10-13% of the global population. Within these ranges, there may be a very slight increase in the percentage of Sunni Muslims and a very slight decline in the percentage of Shia Muslims, largely because of low fertility in Iran, where more than a third of the world's Shia Muslims live.

Muslims around the world have a tremendous misunderstanding of Christianity because their knowledge of Christianity comes from movies, music, television, and Rated-R films. Additionally, they believe that America is a Christian nation; accordingly, everything that comes out of America is Christian.

Many Muslims think Christians believe in three gods: God the Father, God the Son, and God the Mother (Mary). They believe that Christians and Jews have changed the Bible. Thus, although the Quran acknowledges the Gospel of Christ, the Torah of Moses, and the Psalms of David, the existing copies of the Bible cannot be trusted. Furthermore, because Western media created pornography, they equate Christianity with free sex, homosexuality, drugs, alcohol, rape, and divorce... all the "evils" of the West. This misconception confirms their belief that Islam is the true and final religion for all mankind.

Figure 4 compares the major monotheistic religions.

FIGURE 4. BASIC COMPARISON OF THE MAJOR MONOTHEISTIC FAITHS

Tenets	Islam	Judaism	Christianity
Adherents called	Muslims	Jews	Christians
Central Teacher/Leader	Mohammed	Moses	Jesus
Current adherents	1.3 billion	14 million	2 billion
Current size rank	2nd largest	12th largest	Largest
Major concentration	Middle East, Africa, Southeast Asia	Israel, North America, Europe	North and South America, Europe, rapid growth in Africa
Sacred text	Qur'an (Koran)	Torah	Bible (Old Testament & New Testament)
Other written authority	Hadith	Talmud, Midrash, Response	Church founders, church councils, papal decrees (Catholic only)
Religious law	Sharia	Halakhah	Canon Law, varies
Clergy	Imams	Rabbis	Priests, ministers, pastors, bishops
House of worship	Mosque	Synagogue	Church, chapel, cathedral
Main day of worship	Friday	Saturday	Sunday
Church and state	Integrated	Separate	Separate

Hinduism

A Hindu is an individual who accepts and lives by the religious guidance of the Vedic scriptures. The teachings of the Hindu tradition do not require that you have a religious affiliation to Hinduism in order to receive its inner teachings.

Hinduism is one of the oldest known polytheistic religions—its sacred writings date as far back as 1400 to 1500 B.C. While classified as an organized religion, Hinduism is also one of the most diverse and complex, having millions of gods. Hindus have a wide variety of core beliefs and exist in many different sects. Although it is the third largest religion in the world, Hinduism exists primarily in India and Nepal. Globalization, however, has resulted in millions of Indians migrating to other countries around the world for a better education and employment. This means that college campuses and workplaces are likely to have large populations of Hindus when there are corresponding numbers of Indian students and employees. Yet, everyone in India, or with Indian heritage, does not practice Hinduism.

Hinduism operates from the belief that there is only one supreme Absolute called "Brahman". However, it does not advocate the worship of any one particular deity. The gods and goddesses of Hinduism amount to thousands or even millions, all representing the many aspects of Brahman. Therefore, this faith is characterized by the multiplicity of deities. The fundamental Hindu deities include the Trinity of Brahma, Vishnu and Shiva—creator, preserver and destroyer respectively. Hindus also worship spirits, trees, animals, and planets.

There is no "one Hinduism", and so it lacks any unified system of beliefs and ideas. Hinduism is a conglomerate of diverse beliefs and traditions, in which the prominent themes include:

- *Dharma (ethics and duties)*
- *Samsara (rebirth)*
- *Karma (right action)*
- *Moksha (liberation from the cycle of Samsara)*

Hinduism also purports truth, honesty, non-violence, celibacy, cleanliness, contentment, prayers, austerity, perseverance, penance, and pious company.

The basic scriptures of Hinduism, which is collectively referred to as "Shastras", are essentially a collection of spiritual laws discovered by different saints and sages at different points in its long history. Two types of sacred writings comprise the Hindu scriptures: "Shruti" (heard) and "Smriti" (memorized). These writings were passed from generation to generation orally for centuries before they were finally written, mostly in the Sanskrit language. The major and most popular Hindu texts include the Bhagavad Gita, the Upanishads, and the epics of Ramayana and Mahabharata.

The religious tradition of Hinduism is solely responsible for the creation of such original concepts and practices as Yoga, Ayurveda, Vastu, Jyotish, Yajna, Puja, Tantra, Vedanta, and Karma.

Buddhism

Buddhism is the religion of approximately 300 million people around the world. The word comes from 'budhi', which means 'to awaken'. It originated about 2,500 years ago when Siddhartha Gotama, known as the Buddha, was himself awakened (or enlightened) at the age of 35.

Siddhartha Gotama was born into a royal family in Lumbini, now located in Nepal, in 563 BC. At the age of 29, he realized that wealth and luxury did not guarantee happiness, so he explored the different religious teachings and philosophies of the day in search of the key to human happiness. After 6 years of study and meditation, he finally found 'the middle path' and was enlightened. After enlightenment, the Buddha spent the rest of his life teaching the principles of Buddhism—called the Dharma or Truth—until his death at the age of 80. The Buddha was not a god, nor did he claim to be. He was a man who taught a path to enlightenment from his own experience.

To many, Buddhism goes beyond religion and is more of a philosophy or "way of life". Buddhism clarifies life's purpose, explains apparent injustice and inequality around the world, and provides a code of practice or way of life that leads to true happiness. One of the Buddhist teachings is that wealth does not guarantee happiness and wealth is impermanent. The people of every country suffer, whether rich or poor, but those who understand Buddhist teachings can find true happiness.

Buddhism is becoming popular in western countries for a number of reasons. Two of the most prominent reasons are: (1) Buddhism has answers to many of the problems in modern materialistic societies and (2) Buddhism includes a deep understanding of the human mind and natural therapies. Prominent psychologists around the world borrow from Buddhist principles discovering it to be both very advanced and effective.

Hence, Buddhists advocate for science because science is knowledge that translates into a system. It also depends on seeing and testing facts, as well as on general natural laws. The core of Buddhism fits into this definition, because the tenets of Buddhism can be tested and proven by anyone. Thus, Buddhism depends more on understanding than faith.

Buddhists sometimes pay respect to images of the Buddha—not in worship or to ask for favors. A statue of the Buddha, with hands rested gently in its lap, and a compassionate smile, reminds followers to strive to develop peace and love within themselves. Bowing to the statue is an expression of gratitude for the teaching.

Buddhism is also a belief system that is tolerant of other beliefs or religions. Thus, it is likely for someone in Japan, for example, to practice Buddhism and Shintoism. However, Buddhism goes further by providing a long-term purpose within our existence, through wisdom and true understanding. Therefore, Buddhists do not preach or proselytize; they will explain their beliefs if an explanation is sought.

The moral code within Buddhism is the precepts. The five main precepts are: not to take the life of anything living, not to take anything not freely given, to abstain from sexual misconduct and sensual overindulgence, to refrain from untrue speech, and to avoid intoxication, that is, losing mindfulness.

Karma is the law that every cause has an effect (i.e., our actions have consequences). This simple law explains a number of things: inequality in the world, why some are born disabled, why some are gifted, and why some live a short life. Karma underlines the importance of all individuals being responsible for their past and present actions. The karmic effects of one's actions are summed up by looking at: (1) the intention behind the action, (2) the effects of the action on oneself, and (3) the effect on others.

AGNOSTICS, ATHEISTS & THE NON-RELIGIOUS

Critics consider religion to be outdated, harmful to the individual (such as brainwashing of children, faith healing, circumcision), harmful to society (such as holy wars, terrorism, wasteful distribution of resources), an impediment to the progress of science, and immoral (such as blood sacrifice, and discrimination against gays and women).

The religiously unaffiliated population includes atheists, agnostics, and people who do not identify with any particular religion. However, many of the religiously unaffiliated do hold spiritual beliefs. For example, according to the Pew Research Center's October 2012 report *"'Nones' on the Rise,"* various surveys have found that belief in God or a higher power is shared by 7% of unaffiliated Chinese adults, 30% of unaffiliated French adults, and 68% of unaffiliated U.S. adults.

For this reason, there has been a change in the universal naming of the traditional calendar era. It used to be called BC for Before Christ and AD for After (Christ's) Death. Today, the name has been altered to "BCE" for Before Common Era and "CE" for Common Era. The two notations (CE/BCE and AD/BC) are numerically equivalent. Numerous universities, museums, historians, and book retailers around the world either dropped BC and AD entirely or are using it alongside the BCE/CE notation.

Some oppose the Common Era notation explicitly for religious reasons. Because the BC/AD notation is based on the traditional year of the conception or birth of Jesus of Nazareth, removing reference to him in era notation is offensive to some Christians. Non-religious critics have also expressed opposition. They assert that the use of identifiers that have common spellings is more ambiguous than the use of identifiers with divergent spellings. Both CE and BCE have in common the letters "CE", which is more likely to cause confusion.

In the popular sense, an agnostic is someone who neither believes nor disbelieves that there is a God. Agnostics prefer to leave the question of whether God exists open. They consider themselves "free thinkers". Agnosticism is criticized from a variety of standpoints. Some religious thinkers see agnosticism as a limitation of the mind's capacity to know reality other than materialism. Some atheists criticize the use of the term agnosticism as functionally indistinguishable from atheism.

Atheism is, in a broad sense, the rejection of belief in the existence of deities. The first individuals to identify themselves as "atheist" lived in the 18th century. The term *atheism* originated from the Greek (*atheos*), meaning "without god". The word was first used as a derogatory term applied to those who rejected the gods worshipped by the larger society. With the spread of free thought, skeptical inquiry, and the subsequent increase in religious criticism, application of the term narrowed in scope.

Atheists tend to be skeptical of supernatural claims, citing a lack of empirical evidence. Rationales for not believing in any deity include the problem of evil, inconsistent revelations, and non-belief. Other arguments for atheism range from the philosophical to the social to the historical. Although some atheists have adopted secular philosophies, there is no one ideology or set of behaviors to which all atheists adhere. Many atheists hold that atheism is a more prudent worldview than theism; therefore, the burden of proof lies not on the atheist to disprove the existence of God, but on the theist to provide a rationale for theism.

Since conceptions of atheism vary, determining how many atheists exist in the world today is no easy task. Growth in American atheism has been fueled by the partially successful attempts of the Discovery Institute to change U.S. science curriculum. The curriculum, which included creationist ideas, worked together to trigger noted atheist authors Sam Harris, Daniel C. Dennett, Richard Dawkins, Victor J. Stenger, and Christopher Hitchens to publish books that were best sellers in America and worldwide.

A 2010 survey found that those identifying themselves as atheists or agnostics were on average more knowledgeable about religion than followers of major faiths. It also found that Nonbelievers scored better on questions about tenets central to Protestant and Catholic faiths. Only Mormons and the Jewish faithful scored as well as atheists and agnostics.

"Atheism 3.0" is a movement within atheism that does not believe in the existence of God. However, it says that religion has been beneficial to both individuals and society, and that eliminating it is of lesser importance than other things that need to be done.

New Atheism is the name given to a movement among some early 21st-century atheist writers who have advocated the view that "religion should not simply be tolerated but should be countered, criticized, and exposed by rational argument wherever its influence arises". New atheists argue that recent scientific advancements demand a less accommodating attitude toward religion, superstition, and religious fanaticism than had traditionally been extended by many secularists.

Christians are the largest religious group in 2015

% of world population

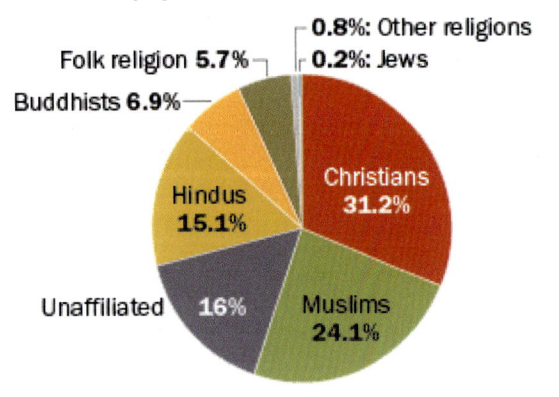

- Christians 31.2%
- Muslims 24.1%
- Unaffiliated 16%
- Hindus 15.1%
- Buddhists 6.9%
- Folk religion 5.7%
- Other religions 0.8%
- Jews 0.2%

Number of people in 2015, in billions

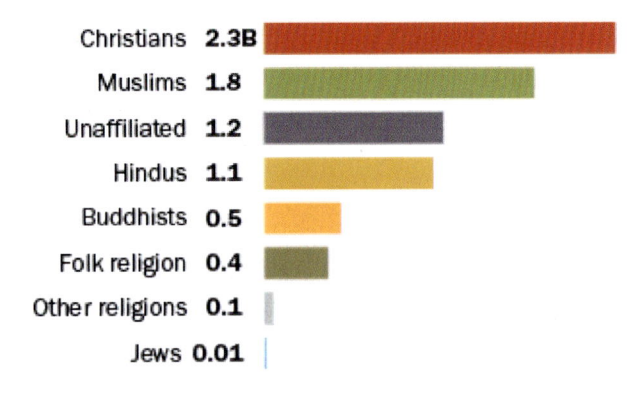

Religion	Billions
Christians	2.3B
Muslims	1.8
Unaffiliated	1.2
Hindus	1.1
Buddhists	0.5
Folk religion	0.4
Other religions	0.1
Jews	0.01

Source: Pew Research Center demographic projections.
See Methodology for details.
"The Changing Global Religious Landscape"

PEW RESEARCH CENTER

Another relatively new term is "non-religion". Non-religion is the absence of religion. It may be characterized as rejection, indifference, or hostility. According to the Pew Research Center 2017 report on *The Changing Global Religious Landscape*, the majority of the global non-religious population lives in Asia and the Pacific. However, "switching" from a religion to non-religion is expected to increase around the world over the next few years. In particular, 62% of Americans expect the share of non-religious individuals to increase by 2050 according to the Pew survey.

In stark contrast to previous generations, where most children visited a church at some point in their lives or where professionals invited co-workers to religious events, there is a growing percentage of individuals who have never been in a church, synagogue, or other house of worship. Notably, this will have an impact on the outlook and attitude of the next generation of religious and non-religious followers.

Nevertheless, people who are religiously active live more involved and connected lives, according to a Pew Research study released in December 2011. The study, titled "*The civic and community engagement of religiously active Americans*", painted a broad picture of religious Americans, and found that involvement in religious organizations usually go hand-in-hand with participation in civic organizations and a positive outlook on their community.

"There is something unique about religious and spiritually involved people that contribute to their trust, positive outlook, involvement, and engagement in the community," said Jim Jansen, senior fellow at Pew and the leader of the study.

Pew researchers asked Americans about their membership in 28 different kinds of organizations and clubs. The average person not involved with a religious organization participated in 2.11 groups. The average person involved in a religious organization participated in 5.11 groups. Additionally, 45% view their community as an excellent place to live, compared with 34% of those not active with religious groups. According to Jansen, that involvement and outlook contributes to the fact that religiously active Americans believe they can have a major impact on their community more than non-religious Americans can. The study, conducted by Pew Internet and American Life Project, also focused on American's use of technology. It was discover that religious Americans use technology slightly more than non-religious Americans. "Those who are active in religious groups seem to be joiners" said Jansen "and their use of technology may be tied to their desire to get involved in their community".

THE RELEVANCE OF RELIGION IN THE WORKPLACE

One recent poll found that American managers want a deeper sense of meaning and fulfillment on the job—even more than they want money and time off.

Once words like "virtue", "spirit", and "ethics" get through the corporate door, God is not far behind. Several years ago, best-sellers such as *Jesus, CEO* and *The Seven Habits of Highly Effective People* (one habit cultivates spirituality) began to line the oak-paneled bookshelves of America's top executives. Soon after, team building and conflict resolution programs began to sprout en masse. Seizing the moment, spiritual gurus such as Deepak Chopra and M. Scott Peck began advising corporate chieftains about how they could tie the new secular spirituality into their management techniques.

During this same time, some local government agencies responded with faith-based task forces, while employers created Interfaith Employee Resource Groups. Ideas generated from such groups were not only socially responsible, but they were also innovative, holistic, and improved productivity. Members of these employee resource groups also played a role in job satisfaction and retention efforts as they visited workers in hospitals and directed troubled employees to spiritual resources. They even said the vows on a co-worker's wedding day or delivered eulogies at funerals.

The late S. Truett Cathy, founder and former chief executive of Chick-fil-A Inc., hosted a hymn-filled prayer service on Monday mornings for those employees of the Atlanta Company who wanted to take part. On Sundays—when McDonald's and Burger King were doing a brisk business—Cathy closed his 1,000+ fast-food shops because he believed in keeping the Sabbath. For Cathy, it was not so difficult to negotiate the religious differences of his employees because, like so many of them, he too was an evangelical Christian. Cathy's beliefs literally paid off. According to Fox News, financial analysts say that Chick-fil-A is poised to become the third largest fast food company in America by 2020, trailing behind only McDonalds and Starbucks.

Nevertheless, some employers are very cautious when it comes to religion in the workplace. Not only do they want to avoid the appearance of mixing faith with business, they also want to preempt lawsuits.

Lawsuits should be prevented on both sides of the spectrum—whether the organization practices religious tenets or not. Therefore, it is important for supervisors, human resource personnel, and diversity practitioners to know the laws concerning religion and religious accommodations. Diversity leaders must not only know the laws in the U.S. but wherever the organization operates. For example, WWE hosted the 2018 Greatest Royal Rumble in Saudi Arabia. It was a sold-out crowd and the event was televised around the world. Nevertheless, since Saudi Arabia is a Muslim country, WWE female wrestlers could not attend or perform at the event. After the mega show, however, many in the Middle Eastern state expressed outrage because two "indecently exposed" females were featured in an advertisement at the event—prompting the Saudi government to issue an embarrassing apology.

Pertaining to religion and belief, Title VII of the Civil Rights Act of 1964 prohibits workplace discrimination based on religion, ethnicity, country of origin, race, or color. Such discrimination is prohibited in any aspect of employment, including recruitment, hiring, promotion, benefits, training, job duties, and termination. Additionally, an employer must provide a reasonable accommodation for religious practices unless doing so would result in an undue hardship.

Title VII prohibits retaliation against someone who complains about a discriminatory practice, files a charge, or assists in an investigation of discrimination in any way. Employers with 15 or more employees are required to comply with Title VII. Most unions and employment agencies are also covered.

> ## LAWSUIT
>
> Billy E. Hyatt claims he was fired from Pliant Corp., a division of Berry Plastics Corp. in northern Georgia near Dalton, after he refused to wear a sticker proclaiming that his factory had been accident-free for 666 days. That number is considered the "mark of the beast" in the Bible's Book of Revelation describing the apocalypse.
>
> Hyatt, who said he's a devout Christian, had worked for the north Georgia plastics company since June 2007. Like other employees, he wore stickers each day that proclaimed how long the factory had gone without an accident. But Hyatt grew nervous in early 2009 as the number of accident-free days crept into the 600s.
>
> As the company's safety calendar approached day 666, Hyatt said he approached a manager and explained that wearing it would force him "to accept the mark of the beast and to be condemned to hell." He said the manager assured him he wouldn't have to wear the number.
>
> When the day came on March 12, 2009, Hyatt sought a manager to discuss his request. He said he was told that his beliefs were "ridiculous" and that he should wear the sticker or serve a three-day suspension.
>
> Hyatt took the three-day suspension, but was fired at a human resources meeting several days later.

Religious discrimination involves treating a person (an applicant or employee) unfavorably because of his or her religious beliefs. The law protects not only people who belong to traditional, organized religions, such as Buddhism, Christianity, Hinduism, Islam, and Judaism, but others who have sincerely held religious, ethical, or moral beliefs. Keep in mind, individuals are protected even their beliefs run counter to mainstream culture. For example, a former U.S. Marine recently filed suit against Union Pacific Railroad after he was fired for his military-related upper-arm tattoo that was termed obscene and threatening. As the second discrimination lawsuit dealing with this issue, employers must remember that body piercings and tattoos could be considered a part of an individual's belief system. There have also been recent court cases alleging discrimination against employees who practice witchcraft, also known as wiccans.

Religious discrimination can also involve treating someone differently because that person is married to (or associated with) an individual of a particular religion or because of his or her connection with a religious organization or group.

The law forbids discrimination when it comes to any aspect of employment, including hiring, firing, pay, job assignments, promotions, layoffs, training, fringe benefits, and any other term or condition of employment.

It is also illegal to harass a person because of his or her religion. Harassment includes offensive remarks about a person's religious beliefs or practices. Although the law does not prohibit simple teasing, offhand comments, or isolated incidents that are not very serious, harassment is illegal when it is so frequent or severe that it creates a hostile or offensive work environment or when it results in an adverse employment decision (such as the victim being fired or demoted). The harasser can be the victim's supervisor, a supervisor in another area, a co-worker, or someone who is not an employee of the employer, such as a client or customer.

Title VII also prohibits workplace or job segregation based on religion (including religious garb and grooming practices), such as assigning an employee to a non-customer contact position because of actual or feared customer preferences. The law requires an employer to reasonably accommodate an employee's religious beliefs or practices, unless doing so would cause more than a minimal burden on the operations of the employer's business. This means an employer may be required to make reasonable adjustments to the work environment that will allow an employee to practice his or her religion.

> ### LAWSUIT
>
> A Michigan nursing home, Whitehall Healthcare, violated federal law when it fired an employee based on her religion and need for a religious accommodation. According to the EEOC's suit, Whitehall Healthcare terminated the discrimination victim, a Jehovah's Witness from Ann Arbor, from her job as a certified nursing assistant due to her need to have Wednesday's and Sunday's off to attend religious services.

Examples of some common religious accommodations include flexible scheduling, voluntary shift substitutions or swaps, job reassignments, or modifications to workplace policies or practices. Unless the accommodation would create an undue hardship on the operation of the business, an employer must reasonably accommodate an employee's religious beliefs or practices. This applies not only to schedule changes or leave for religious observances, but to such things as dress or grooming practices that an employee has for religious reasons. These might include, for example, dressing in religious attire, wearing particular head coverings (such as a Jewish yarmulke or a Muslim headscarf), or sporting certain hairstyles or facial hair (such as Rastafarian dreadlocks or Sikh uncut hair and beard). It also includes an employee's observance of a religious prohibition against wearing certain garments (such as pants or miniskirts).

> ### LAWSUIT
>
> Julie Holloway-Russell, who is Muslim, wore a *khimar* when she interviewed for the job of security guard. As required by her beliefs, the khimar is a religious garb that covers her hair, ears, and neck. However, when she reported to her first work assignment wearing her *khimar*, she was told to remove it. Holloway-Russell respectfully refused to do so because her religious beliefs mandated that she wear the religious head covering. She was fired in response to her request for religious accommodation. The EEOC charged that by failing to modify its dress code to allow Holloway-Russell to wear her *khimar* and instead terminating her, Imperial Security Inc. violated federal law. The Philadelphia-area security company settled the lawsuit for $50,000.

When an employee or applicant needs a dress or grooming accommodation for religious reasons, he should notify the employer that he needs such an accommodation. If the employer reasonably needs more information, the employer and the employee should engage in an interactive process to discuss the request. If the request would not pose an undue hardship, the employer must grant the accommodation.

An employer does not have to accommodate an employee's religious beliefs or practices if doing so would cause undue hardship to the employer. An accommodation may cause an undue hardship if it is costly, compromises workplace safety, decreases workplace efficiency, infringes on the rights of other employees, or requires other employees to do more than their share of potentially hazardous or burdensome work.

Also, an employee cannot be forced to participate (or not participate) in a religious activity as a condition of employment.

Since the attacks of September 11, 2001, the Equal Employment Opportunity Commission (EEOC) and state and local fair employment practices agencies have documented a significant increase in the number of charges alleging workplace discrimination based on religion and/or national origin. Individuals who are or are perceived to be Muslim, Arab, South Asian, or Sikh have filed many of the charges. These charges most commonly allege harassment and discharge.

The scenarios described below are based on charges EEOC has received over the past few years. The following questions and answers are meant to provide guidance on what constitutes illegal discrimination and positive steps you can take to promote inclusion in the workplace.

Hiring & Other Employment Decisions
Narinder, a South Asian man who wears a Sikh turban, applies for a position as a cashier at XYZ Discount Goods. XYZ fears Narinder's religious attire will make customers uncomfortable. What should XYZ do?

XYZ should not deny Narinder the job due to notions of customer preferences about religious attire. That would be unlawful. It would be the same as refusing to hire Narinder because he is a Sikh.

XYZ Discount Goods should consider proactive measures for preventing discrimination in hiring and other employment decisions. XYZ could remind its managers and employees that discrimination based on religion or national origin is not tolerated by the company in any aspect of employment, including hiring. XYZ could also adopt objective standards for selecting new employees. It is important to hire people based on their qualifications rather than on perceptions about their religion, race or national origin.

Harassment
Muhammad, who is Arab American, works for XYZ Motors, a large used car business. Muhammad meets with his manager and complains that Bill, one of his coworkers, regularly calls him names like "camel jockey," "the local terrorist," and "the ayatollah," and has intentionally embarrassed him in front of customers by claiming that he is incompetent. How should the supervisor respond?

Managers and supervisors who learn about objectionable workplace conduct based on religion or national origin are responsible for taking steps to correct the conduct by anyone under their control. Muhammad's manager should relay Muhammad's complaint to the appropriate manager if he does not supervise Bill. If XYZ Motors then determines that Bill has harassed Muhammad, it should take disciplinary action against Bill that is significant enough to ensure that the harassment does not continue.

Workplace harassment and its costs are often preventable. Clear and effective policies prohibiting ethnic and religious slurs, and related offensive conduct, are needed. Confidential complaint mechanisms for promptly reporting harassment are critical, and these policies should be written to encourage victims and witnesses to come forward. When harassment is reported, the focus should be on action to end the harassment and correct its effects on the complaining employee. Action should be taken promptly.

Religious Accommodations
Three of the 10 Muslim employees in XYZ's 30-person template design division approach their supervisor and ask that they be allowed to use a conference room in an adjacent building for prayer. Until making the request, those employees prayed at their work stations. What should XYZ do?

XYZ should work closely with the employees to find an appropriate accommodation that meets their religious needs without causing an undue hardship for XYZ. Whether a reasonable accommodation would impose undue hardship, and therefore not be required, depends on the particulars of the business and the requested accommodation.

When the room is needed for business purposes, XYZ can deny its use for personal religious purposes. However, allowing the employees to use the conference room for prayers likely would not impose an undue hardship on XYZ in many other circumstances.

Similarly, prayer often can be performed during breaks, so that providing sufficient time during work hours for prayer would not result in an undue hardship. If going to another building for prayer takes longer than the allotted break periods, the employees still can be accommodated if the nature of the template design division's work makes flexible scheduling feasible. XYZ can require employees to make up any work time missed for religious observance.

In evaluating undue hardship, XYZ should consider only whether it can accommodate the three employees who made the request. If XYZ can accommodate three employees, it should do so. Because individual religious practices vary among members of the same religion, XYZ should not deny the requested accommodation based on speculation that the other Muslim employees may seek the same accommodation. If other employees subsequently request the same accommodation and granting it to all of the requesters would cause undue hardship, XYZ can make an appropriate adjustment at that time. For example, if accommodating five employees would not cause an undue hardship but accommodating six would impose such hardship, the sixth request could be denied.

Like employees of other religions, Muslim employees may need accommodations such as time off for religious holidays or exceptions to dress and grooming codes.

Temporary Assignments
Susan is an experienced clerical worker who wears a hijab (head scarf) in conformance with her Muslim beliefs. XYZ Temps places Susan in a long-term assignment with one of its clients. The client contacts XYZ and requests that it notify Susan that she must remove her hijab while working at the front desk, or that XYZ assign another person to Susan's position. According to the client, Susan's religious attire violates its dress code and presents the "wrong image." Should XYZ comply with its client's request?

XYZ Temps may not comply with this client request without violating Title VII. The client would also violate Title VII if it made Susan remove her hijab or changed her duties to keep her out of public view. Therefore, XYZ should strongly advise against this course of action. Notions about customer preference—real or perceived—do not establish undue hardship. Therefore, the client should make an exception to its dress code to let Susan wear her hijab during front desk duty as a religious accommodation. If the client does not withdraw the request, XYZ should place Susan in another assignment at the same rate of pay and decline to assign another worker to the client.

Background Investigations
Anwar, who was born in Egypt, applies for a position as a security guard with XYZ Corp., which contracts to provide security services at government office buildings. Can XYZ require Muhammad to undergo a background investigation before he is hired?

XYZ may require Anwar to undergo the same pre-employment security checks that apply to other applicants for the same position. XYZ may not perform background investigations or other screening procedures in a discriminatory manner (e.g., no-one else is screened except Anwar).

In addition, XYZ may require a security clearance pursuant to a federal statute or Executive Order. Security clearance determinations for positions subject to national security requirements under a federal statute or an Executive Order are not subject to review under the equal employment opportunity statutes.

Dealing with Absences
An employee must first notify the employer of the conflict between his or her religious belief and an employment requirement. Without such notification, even if it is later determined that the absences were for religious purposes, an employer can legally discharge an employee for excessive absences from work.

Sabbath: Several religions observe the Sabbath as a day when followers cannot perform work. In recent years, Sabbath cases that have reached the courts have presented difficulties for employees seeking preferential treatment. Many employees asking to be excused from work on Saturday have been unsuccessful for a numbers of reasons. The courts have ruled that employers experience undue hardship when morale problems arise due to the resentment of fellow employees who have to work on Saturdays, or when the employer has to pay higher wages to fill an employee's vacancy.

Holy days: Employees have had more success in cases involving special leave to observe holy days or attend religious activities that were not regular and frequent. This is because the occasional religious observance does not fundamentally alter the employee's basic work schedule.

However, even a single absence can cause an employer undue hardship. In one case, a mechanical department could not perform repair and maintenance. The only employee with knowledge of certain machinery drawings took an unauthorized vacation to attend convocation at the Worldwide Church of God. The employer treated the employee as if he had quit; the employee alleged Title VII discrimination. The employer's action was upheld because there was no reasonable accommodation the employer could have made and continued business operations.

Conclusion
Religion is one of those things that can very quickly make work environments uncomfortable because many people can have very different opinions on the matter of religion and feel very passionately about their perspective. Therefore, issues involving religion in the workplace can be complex. Resolving these issues requires understanding the law and balancing the business's needs with an employee's desire to practice his or her religion.

Supervisors and senior leaders must understand that there are legal responsibilities pertaining to religion at work—even if the religious practices are unfamiliar or if the manager disagrees with the belief system. Beyond legal matters, employers must take great care to ensure the inclusion of different religious, as well as non-religious, groups. Further, even if a diversity leader personally practices a particular religion, doing one's job well depends on facilitating inclusion regardless of one's own personal beliefs. Diversity does not require comprising or changing who one is or what one may stand for, it simply creates room for different individuals to thrive and be included as unique people with different beliefs. Cultural competence, on the other hand, allows for tolerance and understanding without judgement or bias.

References:

Weber, Max. *The Protestant Ethic and the Spirit of Capitalism*. Oxford University Press: Oxford, England, UK (1905).

Jewish Virtual Library. *Vital Statistics: Latest Population Statistics for Israel* (2018). Available at: http://www.jewishvirtuallibrary.org/latest-population-statistics-for-israel

Pew Research Center. *A Portrait of Jewish Americans* (2013). Available at: http://www.pewforum.org/2013/10/01/jewish-american-beliefs-attitudes-culture-survey/

Pew Research Center. *The Changing Global Religious Landscape* (2017). Available at: http://www.pewforum.org/2017/04/05/the-changing-global-religious-landscape/

Pew Research Center. *"Nones" on the Rise* (2012). Available at: http://www.pewforum.org/2012/10/09/nones-on-the-rise/

Pew Research Center. *The civic and community engagement of religiously active Americans* (2011). Available at: http://www.pewinternet.org/2011/12/23/the-civic-and-community-engagement-of-religiously-active-americans/

Bartiromo, Michael. *Chick-fil-A to become nation's third-largest fast food restaurant by 2020, analysts say* (2018). Fox News. Available at: http://www.foxnews.com/food-drink/2018/04/03/chick-fil-to-become-nations-third-largest-fast-food-restaurant-by-2020-analysts-say.html

Cutts, Daniel. *'INDECENT SCENES' WWE news: Saudi Arabian government issue embarrassing apology for showing female stars during Greatest Royal Rumble*. The Sun. Available at: https://www.thesun.co.uk/sport/6173110/wwe-saudi-apology-female-greatest-royal-rumble/

U.S. Equal Opportunity Commission. *Religious Discrimination (Fact Sheet; Questions and Answers)*. Available at: https://www.eeoc.gov/laws/types/religion.cfm

Sample Test Questions:
NAVIGATING THROUGH RELIGION & BELIEF SYTEMS

1. **Food permissible for Muslims is known as:**
   A. Kosher
   B. Haram
   C. Halal

2. **According to the EEOC, religious discrimination involves treating a person:**
   A. As if they believe what you believe
   B. Unfavorably because of his/her religious beliefs
   C. The same as everyone else in the workplace

3. **Examples of common religious accommodations include all of the following EXCEPT:**
   A. Refusing time off
   B. Job reassignments
   C. Modifications to policies

4. **An employer does not have to accommodate an employee's religious beliefs or practices if doing so would:**
   A. Result in changes to employee schedules
   B. Result in an employee feeling uncomfortable
   C. Cause an undue hardship to the employer

5. **An agnostic is more similar to a(n) _____ than to other groups.**
   A. Muslim
   B. Hindu
   C. Atheist

6. **What can reduce prejudice and hostility between different religious and non-religious groups?**
   A. Ignoring religion in the workplace
   B. Increasing contact and tolerance
   C. Offering training about the top 3 religions

Sample Test Questions:

NAVIGATING THROUGH RELIGION & BELIEF SYSTEMS (cont'd)

7. **This group may believe in the Trinity:**
   A. Muslims
   B. Hindus
   C. Atheists

8. **This group may wear a head covering on a work day:**
   A. A Buddhist
   B. A Jewish Person
   C. A Hindu

9. **This group fasts during Ramadan.**
   A. African Americans
   B. Jehovah's Witnesses
   C. Muslims

10. **Rosh Hashanah is known as the:**
    A. Day of Atonement
    B. Passover
    C. Jewish New Year

11. **Customer preferences for an employee that does NOT have certain religious beliefs is considered an undue hardship and is allowable under the law.**
    A. True
    B. False

12. **The "Sabbath" is a day when certain individuals may request off due to religious needs.**
    A. True
    B. False

13. **Jehovah's Witnesses are the third largest religion in the world.**
    A. True
    B. False

LGBTQ+ INCLUSION

> *Discrimination against any qualified individuals based on characteristics unrelated to the job are not only detrimental to the victims but harmful to the larger workforce, customer, patient, and student populations that they represent. Yet, employment discrimination against lesbian, gay, bisexual, transgender, queer and other employees along the broad spectrum of sexual orientation and gender identity is pervasive.*
>
> *Because there is no global legislation prohibiting LGBTQ+ discrimination in the workplace, some individuals are free to harass, exclude, mistreat, and exhibit bias towards LGBTQ+ workers. It is currently legal in many countries to refuse to hire, demote, fire, or otherwise treat an LGBTQ+ employee unequally or unfairly based on their sexual orientation, gender identity, and/or gender expression. In the most extreme environments, LGBTQ+ individuals face harsh punishment including imprisonment, and even execution under certain laws.*
>
> *Beyond the threat to talent, organizations may sustain other losses by discriminating against and/or excluding LGBTQ+ individuals. In 2017, LGBTQ+ consumer buying power was over $917 billion. Moreover, LGBTQ+ consumers and high performing employment candidates can easily check a few websites to see if their prospective employers and vendors are LGBTQ+ friendly or if they would be better served to take their dollars and their talents elsewhere.*
>
> *With high rates of advanced degrees resulting in a Disposable Personal Income that surpasses the average straight consumer, the LGBTQ+ community can afford to be choosy about where it works and where it shops.*

OVERALL OBJECTIVES AND COMPETENCIES

The purpose of this competency is to build LGBTQ+ inclusive workplaces with policies that are discrimination- and harassment-free, as well as with practices that are fair. The LGBTQ+ workplace Inclusion competency provides Equity, Diversity, and Inclusion professionals with instruction about harmful myths and associated consequences related to the LGBTQ+ community.

BACKGROUND AND CONTEXT

The letters and symbol, LGBTQ+, is one sequence of frequently evolving initials adopted since the 1990s to describe those previously referred to as the "gay community." The current iteration of the acronym refers to Lesbian, Gay, Bisexual, Transgender, Queer, and related identities. There are many variations of this acronym, some of which are quite long and because there is often inconsistency in the acronyms, the simplified "LGBTQ+" describes many people who do not fit neatly into the heteronormative paradigm.

Heteronormativity is the theory that only those individuals who are assigned either boy or girl at birth, who grow up into gender roles that align with their assigned sex, and who go on to have opposite sex partners are normal, natural, and acceptable. Heteronormativity is the societal benchmark against which all other expressions of human sexuality or gender identity are assumed unnatural or unacceptable. It is important to note with regard to sexual orientation that there is no credible mainstream medical, psychiatric, or psychological body still recognizing same sex attraction as a pathology. Rather, lesbian, gay, and bisexual identities are natural and normal variations in human sexuality.

The American Psychological Association recognizes that prejudice against those who are gay, lesbian, or bisexual is harmful. *"Since 1975, the American Psychological Association has called on psychologists to take the lead in removing the stigma of mental illness that has long been associated with lesbian, gay and bisexual orientations. The discipline of psychology is concerned with the well-being of people and groups and therefore with threats to that well-being. The prejudice and discrimination that people who identify as lesbian, gay or bisexual regularly experience have been shown to have negative psychological effects."*

Variations in human sexual orientation, gender identity, and expression can be traced to ancient times. There are written and pictorial depictions of same sex coupling on ancient Mesopotamian, Egyptian, African, Roman, Greek, and Asian artifacts.

The first organization committed to advancing rights and protections for LGBTQ+ people in the Unites States was The Society for Human Rights founded by Henry Gerber in Chicago, IL in 1924. Since then, there has been ongoing back-and-forth tension between advancing LGBTQ+ rights and prohibiting them. In 1953, President Dwight D. Eisenhower issued an executive order prohibiting homosexuals from working for the federal government, claiming that they were a security risk; codifying discrimination against LGBTQ+ people into law.

The first lesbian organization of record was the San Francisco based, Daughters of Bilitis. They met in private homes in an effort to avoid police raids on clubs where lesbian women gathered. Various terms have been used to describe gay and bisexual men over the decades, most of which have fallen out of favor. For women, lesbian, gay and bisexual are among the words that have been used to describe same-sex couples. The word lesbian is derived from the name of the Greek island of Lesbos, home to the 6th-century BCE poet Sappho, who often proclaimed her love for girls. The term, "homosexual," is a clinical term rooted in the early diagnosis of homosexuality as a psychological pathology. The term "homosexual" gave way to "gay" and then "gay and lesbian."

One of the earliest mobilized gatherings of LGBTQ+ people in the Unites States was the Cooper Do-Nuts Uprising in Los Angeles in 1959. Although not commonly known as a 1960s gay protest, the Cooper Do-Nuts riot is considered the first gay uprising in modern history. A group of lesbians, drag queens and hustlers protested harassment by the LAPD at Cooper Do-Nuts, a gathering place for LGBTQ+ people in LA's "gay ghetto." Ten years later on June 28, 1969 outside of the Stonewall Inn in New York City, riots erupted again in response to a raid by the New York City Police Department. Undercover officers, who were posing as bar patrons, signaled to fellow Vice Squad officers outside, who stormed the Stonewall Inn late in the evening. As police officers awaited the arrival of patty wagons to transport the arrestees, local patrons and bystanders began gathering in the street. When officers aggressively threw one woman into a patrol wagon, the crowd became enraged. Several police officers were trapped inside the inn as spontaneous riots continued throughout the morning. The Stonewall Uprising is widely recognized as the beginning of the global gay civil rights movement.

In 2016, President Barrack Obama designated the Stonewall Inn as part of the Stonewall National Monument. The 44th U.S. President stated, *"I'm designating the Stonewall National Monument as the newest addition to America's National Park System. Stonewall will be our first national monument to tell the story of the struggle for LGBT rights. I believe our national parks should reflect the full story of our country, the richness and diversity and uniquely American spirit that has always defined us. That we are stronger together. That out of many, we are one."*

ASSIGNED SEX, SEXUAL ORIENTATION & GENDER IDENTITY/GENDER EXPRESSION

A person's assigned sex is their sex designation at the time of birth and is usually consigned by a physician based on a visual scan of a newborn's external genitalia. This is not always accurate as about one out of every 2,000 infants is born with Differences in Sex Development (DSD), many of which are not immediately evident at the time of birth. It is because of these variations in sexual development that a person's sex is referred to as "assigned sex" rather than "anatomical" or "biological" sex. It is also because of increased understanding about differences in gender and sex development that the binary gender construct of boy|girl, man|woman, male|female does not fit for many and is increasingly recognized as an inaccurate or incomplete understanding of gender.

In fact, the Spanish language is based on a binary gender construct, and many are now confounded by the term: Latinx (pronounced "La-teen-ex"). Tanisha Love Ramirez and Zeba Blay explain in a HuffPost articled entitled, *Why People are Using the Term Latinx*, "Latinx is the gender-neutral alternative to Latino, Latina and even Latin@. Used by scholars, activists and an increasing number of journalists, Latinx is quickly gaining popularity among the general public. It's part of a "linguistic revolution" that aims to move beyond gender binaries and is inclusive of the intersecting identities of Latin American descendants. In addition to men and women from all racial backgrounds, Latinx also makes room for people who are trans, queer, agender, non-binary, gender non-conforming or gender fluid."

The authors add, "In Spanish, the masculinized version of words is considered gender neutral. But that obviously doesn't work for some of us because I don't think it's appropriate to assign masculinity as gender neutral when it isn't," explains queer, non-binary femme writer Jack Qu'emi Gutiérrez in an interview with PRI. "The 'x,' in a lot of ways, is a way of rejecting the gendering of words to begin with, especially since Spanish is such a gendered language." Latinx is also, as pointed out by writer Gabe Gonzalez, a way to reclaim identity, a form of rebellion against "the language and legacy of European traditions that were imposed on the Americas." Latinx first began to emerge within queer communities on the internet in 2004, and saw a rise in popularity in late 2014, according to Complex." In the Equity and Inclusion space, the term Latinx is a silent nod to the intersectionality of diversity: one can be trans, Latino, a Millennial, and Catholic—or any combination of a variety of different dimensions.

Sexual orientation refers to an individual's primary attraction to another individual. Sexual orientation exists on a continuum with some people identifying as exclusively straight, some as exclusively gay or lesbian, and some with a similar attraction to both same sex and opposite sex partners.

Researchers who study human sexuality believe that sexual orientation can begin developing in early childhood, and may or may not change over the course of a person's lifetime. Human sexuality is complex and variations in human sexuality may be at least partially influenced by heredity as well as by social conditions. It is not as important to understand WHY variations in human sexuality exist as much as it is to understand that they DO exist and there is no need to assign any kind of anomaly or pathology to these variations. In the same way that we do not sit and wonder why certain people turned out to be straight, we need not wonder why some people turned out to be gay. A common misperception is that troubled family relationships cause people to be homosexual, but no scientifically sound research supports this myth.

In addition, sexual behavior is only one element of sexual orientation. Many individuals recognize their sexual orientation before ever having become sexually active. Primary attractions of the same sex have elements of physical amorousness, romantic attraction, and emotional and spiritual connection.

Gay and lesbian people can have sexual relationships with someone of the opposite sex for a variety of reasons, including the desire for a family with children and concerns of discrimination and religious ostracism. For instance, there are surprisingly high rates of unplanned pregnancies among lesbian youth as young lesbians attempt to convince themselves and others that they are straight. Some people feel pressured to "change" their sexuality, but trying to be something you are not can lead to stress, anxiety, and depression. Efforts to change a person's sexual orientation through programs called reparative or conversion therapy or transformational ministries typically cause more harm than help. Some states have outlawed these practices on anyone under age 18 and some states have gone so far as to penalize professionals practicing conversion therapies.

Some people may presume knowledge of another person's sexual orientation based upon stereotypes. These perceived characteristics include appearance, clothing, tone of voice, and accompaniment by, or their behavior with, other people. It can also include traditional gender norms such as grooming (e.g., a haircut or polished nails) or choice of colors (e.g., pink or blue). This perception of sexual orientation may affect how a person is treated.

The "**T**" stands for "transgender." Transgender is an umbrella term for those whose deepest sense of self does not align with the sex assigned to them at birth. A transgender person is transgender at the point they self-determine that they are transgender. No medical intervention of any kind, including hormone therapy, is required for a person to be transgender. Some people identify as gender fluid, gender non-conforming, or non-binary, meaning their innermost sense of self-does not fit completely into the traditional binary male and female construct.

Transgender people often face workplace discrimination at much higher rates than their counterparts who are cisgender (pronounced sis-gender, and refers to somebody whose deepest sense of self aligns with their assigned sex. It is the opposite of transgender.) Although some people recognize their sexual orientation as children, it is more common for lesbian, gay, and bisexual people to really accept their sexual orientation during adolescence. For transgender individuals, the recognition that their sense of self does not align with the gender labels assigned to them, often comes in early childhood.

Homophobia refers to an irrational fear, prejudice, or discrimination towards lesbian, gay and bisexual individuals. *Transphobia* is prejudice against transgender individuals. Homophobia and transphobia can take many forms, from name-calling and teasing to serious crimes like assault and murder. According to Figure 1, offenses against sexual orientation in America were slightly lower than for religion, making it the third largest group of hate crimes reported to the FBI in 2015. Together, race/ethnicity bias, religious bias, and sexual orientation bias account for more than 95% of the reported incidents.

FIGURE 1: FBI CRIME DATA

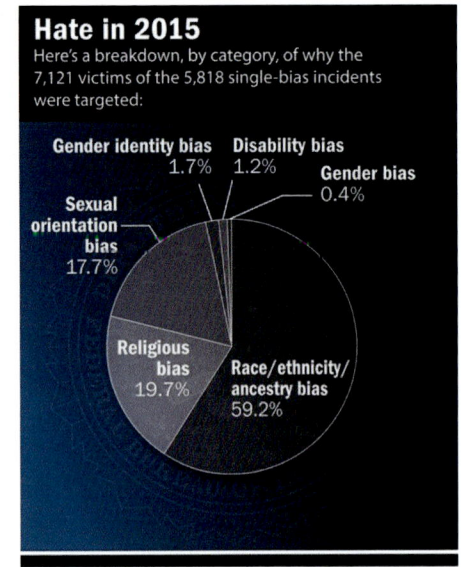

Hate in 2015
Here's a breakdown, by category, of why the 7,121 victims of the 5,818 single-bias incidents were targeted:

- Gender identity bias 1.7%
- Disability bias 1.2%
- Gender bias 0.4%
- Sexual orientation bias 17.7%
- Religious bias 19.7%
- Race/ethnicity/ancestry bias 59.2%

*From Hate Crime Statistics, 2015

The process of telling people about one's sexual orientation and/or gender identity is often referred to as coming out. "Coming out" is not a singular event but a lifelong process. The phrase "in the closet" is sometimes used to describe a person who is LGBTQ+ but who has not acknowledged it to friends and family members. It is up to each individual to choose when and to whom they might disclose their LGBTQ+ identity. "Outing" is a term that means that someone other than an LGBTQ+ person has told others about the LGBTQ+ person's identity. "Outing" can be a discriminatory practice.

The term "queer" is challenging for a lot of people, particularly the Baby Boomer and Generation X folks who grew up hearing the term "queer" used only as a slur. In the past decade, the term "queer" has been re-appropriated by many in the LGBTQ+ community, particularly among young people. Because many youth feel that even the identities of lesbian, gay, bisexual, and transgender are limiting, the term "queer" feels more affirming and authentic. In some intersectional communities where people face marginalization based on multiple identities, the term "queer" is sometimes a label of defiance. For instance, a less common acronym for LGBTQ+ people with intersectional identities is QTPOC which stands for Queer and Trans People of Color. Still, the term "queer" is a label best left to those who claim it for their own identity.

What is the plus sign at the end about? Quite literally, the terms used to describe the LGBTQ+ community are changing almost daily. There are many terms that are common among some people within the community today that even a year ago were hardly used. For instance the term, "pansexual" or "pan" refers to those who are attracted to and romantically drawn to others regardless of assigned sex or gender identity. Sometimes those who fall in love with transgender people refer to themselves as pan. The term 2-S or Two-Spirit is a term that some Native American individuals in the LGBTQ+ community use to self-identify. It is a term that has its roots in Native beliefs and is not attached to any binary gender construct or post-colonial heteronormative patriarchal labels. Because there are so many identities that do not fit into the other labels, the [+] means that there is much more to the story of sexual orientation and gender identity than can be reflected by a few letters.

The Gay and Lesbian Alliance Against Defamation (GLAAD) produces a media reference guide and revises it frequently with the most contemporary terminology related to the LGBTQ+ community. The Tenth Edition of the guide may be found at https://www.glaad.org/reference and it offers a comprehensive glossary of terms.

What Are Allies?
Allies are typically straight and cisgender individuals who work to end oppression in their private and professional lives through support of, and advocacy for, the oppressed population. In the context of this guide, Allies are "straight identified individuals who are supportive advocates for the LGBTQ+ Community through their activism, involvement or their nature to speak out against oppression and inequality". Allies can help the LGBTQ+ community by advocating that LGBTQ+ individuals be entitled to the same rights as any other person regardless of their sexual orientation or gender identity.

LGBTQ+ WORKPLACE ISSUES IN AMERICA

The number of LGBTQ+ employees who are "out" in the workplace has grown significantly over the last decade. Historically, being open about one's sexual orientation in the workplace was not an option due to fear of being treated differently, viewed negatively, passed over for promotion, or worse, losing employment. An example of this omission is Leonard P. Matlovich, a United States Air Force Technical Sergeant, who was a Vietnam War veteran and recipient of the Purple Heart and the Bronze Star medals. In March 1975, after years of exemplary service, Matlovich informed his commanding officer that he was a homosexual. Despite his perfect military record, tours of duty in Vietnam, and high-performance evaluations, Matlovich was found unfit for military service and he was discharged solely for being a homosexual.

The movie, *The Imitation Game*, was based on the true story of Alan Turing. In World War II Turing played a pivotal role in cracking intercepted coded messages that enabled the Allies to defeat the Nazis in many crucial engagements, including the Battle of the Atlantic. It has been estimated that this work shortened the war in Europe by as many as two to four years. A few years later, during an investigation of a burglary of his home it was discovered that Turing was gay. At that time, homosexual acts were illegal in the United Kingdom. Turning was tried and found guilty of gross indecency under Section 11 of the Criminal Law Amendment Act of 1885. At the sentencing, Turing was provided the option of prison or probation on condition that he agree to hormonal therapy. Turing chose to submit to the hormonal therapy, which negatively impacted his health. He lost his security clearance and was barred from working for the British Government. On 8 June 1954, Turning was found dead and after an inquest, it was discovered he had committed suicide. These cases and many others have encouraged LGBTQ+ employees not to disclose their sexuality in the workplace.

Today, many large companies provide equal rights and benefits to their lesbian, gay, bisexual and transgender employees, as measured by the Human Rights Campaign (HRC) through the Corporate Equality Index. When the Human Rights Campaign's Corporate Equality Index was first utilized in 2002, thirteen companies were rated 100 percent. By 2014, more than 734 large companies participated in the Corporate Equality Index, and 304 employers received a 100% rating. Additionally, each year, corporations send thousands of employees to the Out & Equal Regional Summit, a conference that intends to create a more inclusive work environment for lesbian, gay, bisexual and transgender employees.

The Williams Institute asserts that widespread adoption of private workplace policies may be motivated by good business sense. Its conclusion is based on a set of studies which show that LGBTQ+ employees who have come out at work report lower levels of anxiety, less conflict between work and personal life, greater job satisfaction, higher levels of satisfaction with their co-workers, more self-esteem, and better physical health. On the other hand, those who hide their sexual orientation for fear of unequal treatment or harassment, experience discomfort and inconvenience around asking for time off when their partner is ill or bringing their partner along to work functions. They also feel the constant pressure of being "on guard". In addition, they may experience subtle or overt harassment in the form of jokes and innuendos, homophobic comments, and threats of being forced out of the closet. These individuals fear reporting harassment or not being taken seriously. They also worry about being accused of oversensitivity, lacking a sense of humor, or "bringing it on themselves".

According to the Human Rights Campaign 2016 Corporate Equality Index (CEI), hundreds of U.S.-based multinational companies are not only promoting LGBTQ+ friendly workplace policies in the United States, but are helping to advance the cause of LGBTQ+ equality around the globe. For example, 511 out of 851 companies participating in the 2016 CEI offered transgender workers at least one health care plan that has transgender-inclusive coverage. That's a 150 percent increase since 2012, when the CEI first included trans-inclusive health care as a requisite for companies to receive a perfect score. Gender identity is now part of non-discrimination policies at 75 percent of Fortune 500 companies, up from just 3 percent in 2002. More than 330 major employers have adopted supportive inclusion guidelines for transgender workers who are transitioning.

LGBTQ+ employees who are open in the workplace are on the rise. Personalities such as Tim Cook, CEO of Apple; Tammy Baldwin, Wisconsin U.S. Senator; Anderson Cooper, CNN News Anchor; and Laverne Cox, Actress, prove that this demographic of employees are becoming common in predominate positions. Organizations will assumedly experience a culture change as LGBTQ+ employees choose to be open in the workplace. Diversity and Inclusion professionals will play an important role in proactively helping organizations with this change.

Employment Non-Discrimination Act (ENDA)
The United States is one of the few developed nations in the world that does not have specific legislation prohibiting LGBTQ+ employment discrimination.

The *Employment Non-Discrimination Act (ENDA)* is a proposed bill in the United States Congress that would prohibit discrimination against employees based on sexual orientation or gender identity by civilian, nonreligious employers with at least 15 employees. The bill is closely modeled after existing civil rights laws, including Title VII of the Civil Rights Act of 1964 and the Americans with Disabilities Act.

Religious organizations are provided with a special exception to this protection, similar to the other tenets of the Civil Rights Act. Non-profit membership-only clubs (except labor unions) are likewise not bound to this rule. Presently, the U.S. Senate passed ENDA, but the U.S. House has not.

America's ban on gays and lesbians serving openly in the military has officially ended. Since 1993, the "Don't Ask, Don't Tell" policy had allowed gays to serve in the military so long as they kept their sexual orientation quiet. More than 13,000 service members were discharged in the 18 years following this Congressional mandate. The policy came to an official end at 12:01AM on September 20, 2011 via The Don't Ask, Don't Tell Repeal Act of 2010, which did not replace the policy with any other nondiscrimination guidelines.

Nevertheless, the presidential election of 2016 resulted in some reversals of hard-won rights for LGBTQ+ individuals in the United States. In August 2017, President Donald J. Trump announced a prohibition on transgender persons serving in the United States military and required the discharge of existing transgender service members. Judge Colleen Kollar-Kotelly blocked provisions of the memorandum concerning the enlistment and retention of transgender military service members, holding that the plaintiffs "*have established that they will be injured by these directives, due both to the inherent inequality they impose, and the risk of discharge and denial of accession that they engender.*"

In March 2018, BBC News reported that "President Trump signed a memorandum that bans some transgender people from U.S. military service but rolls back the blanket ban he ordered in 2017. The new directive adopts recommendations from Defense Secretary Jim Mattis that "transgender persons who require or have undergone gender transition" cannot serve. The new memorandum says that transgender individuals with a history of gender dysphoria are barred from military service "except under certain limited circumstances". The Department of Defense (DoD) had submitted a report to the president which said allowing those with a history of gender dysphoria to serve entailed "substantial risks" and could, by exempting them from existing physical, mental and sex-based standards, "undermine readiness... and impose an unreasonable burden on the military"."

The Defense of Marriage Act

The Defense of Marriage Act (DOMA) was signed into law by U.S. President Bill Clinton on September 21, 1996, whereby the federal government defined marriage as a legal union between one man and one woman. Under the law, no state (or other political subdivision within the U.S.) was required to recognize a same-sex marriage performed in another state. This law affected everything from taxation, to Visa requests, to child custody decisions.

DOMA resulted in a slew of lawsuits—one of which led to its demise. On November 9, 2010, Edith Windsor filed a lawsuit against the federal government for refusing to recognize her marriage to her partner of 44 years, Thea Spyer. When Thea passed away in 2009, Edith was forced to pay more than $363,000 in federal estate taxes that she would not have had to pay if the government had recognized her marriage to Thea. The lawsuit was filed in New York's District Court and claimed Section 3 violated the equal protection guarantee of the U.S. Constitution.

United States v. Windsor is a landmark case in which the United States Supreme Court held that restricting U.S. federal interpretation of "marriage" and "spouse" to apply only to heterosexual unions is unconstitutional under the Due Process Clause of the Fifth Amendment. In response to this June 2013 Supreme Court decision, the U.S. Department of the Treasury and the Internal Revenue Service (IRS) ruled that same-sex couples, legally married in jurisdictions that recognize their marriages, will be treated as married for federal tax purposes. The ruling applies regardless of whether the couple lives in a jurisdiction that recognizes same-sex marriage or a jurisdiction that does not recognize same-sex marriage. The IRS ruling applies to all federal tax provisions where marriage is a factor, including filing status, claiming personal and dependent exemptions, taking the standard deduction, employee benefits, contributing to an IRA, as well as claiming the earned income tax credit or child tax credit.

Recent U.S. Developments

A Bathroom Bill restricts or defines access to public restrooms based on one's gender assigned at birth. The National Center for Transgender Equality reports that "since the beginning of 2018, 10 states have introduced 21 anti-trans bills, and 2 states are considering anti-trans ballot initiatives." However, many of these state initiatives have failed or have since become inactive.

Indeed, the U.S. in general is becoming increasingly hostile toward the LGBTQ+ community. It is important, however, that the public's short-term sentiment does not reflect the composition and culture of the workplace. Employers in states with Bathroom Bills can proactively introduce unisex or family restrooms for employees and customers. Unlike voters, organizations must consider the long-term effects of their actions. Diversity and Inclusion means that organizations are not simply meeting the minimum requirements of the law, they are doing what is good for business. Serving as a plaintiff or a defendant in a discrimination lawsuit should not be any organization's priority in today's highly competitive business environment.

Yet, in June 2018, Fox News reported that "the U.S. Supreme Court ruled in favor of a Colorado baker who declined to make a wedding cake for a same-sex ceremony. The case – *Masterpiece Cakeshop, Ltd v. Colorado Civil Rights Commission* – asked the high court to balance the religious rights of the baker against the couple's right to equal treatment under the law. The Supreme Court ruled 7-2 in favor of Masterpiece Cakeshop."

"The laws and the Constitution can, and in some instances must, protect gay persons and gay couples in the exercise of their civil rights, but religious and philosophical objections to gay marriage are protected views and in some instances protected forms of expression," the Court said in its decision. "While it is unexceptional that Colorado law can protect gay persons in acquiring products and services on the same terms and conditions as are offered to other members of the public, the law must be applied in a manner that is neutral toward religion." Fox News added, "In its decision, the Supreme Court did not decide whether a business has the right to refuse to serve gay and lesbian people outright."

In the United States, same-sex marriage has been legal nationwide since June 26, 2015, after the United States Supreme Court ruled in *Obergefell v. Hodges* that state-level bans on same-sex marriage were unconstitutional. The court ruled that the denial of marriage licenses to same-sex couples and the refusal to recognize those marriages performed in other jurisdictions violated the Due Process and the Equal Protection clauses of the Fourteenth Amendment of the United States Constitution. This ruling overturned a precedent, *Baker v. Nelson*.

Recent activities by EEOC, including the filing of lawsuits on behalf of transgender employees, the filing of amicus briefs related to coverage of sexual orientation and transgender status, and the issuance of federal sector decisions in these areas, have triggered increased interest about protections for lesbian, gay, bisexual, transgender, and queer (LGBTQ+) individuals under federal employment-discrimination laws.

While Title VII of the Civil Rights Act of 1964 does not explicitly include sexual orientation or gender identity in its list of protected bases, the EEOC, consistent with case law from the Supreme Court and other courts, interprets the statute's sex discrimination provision as prohibiting discrimination against employees on the basis of sexual orientation and gender identity. Further, in January 2013, the EEOC began tracking information on charges filed alleging discrimination related to gender identity and/or sexual orientation.

Since the most recent election, many individuals and states have become emboldened in their homophobic and transphobic positioning. Several states have placed bans on same sex adoptions, made it legal to refuse services to LGBTQ+ people, and places bans on rights and protections for LGBTQ+ people. These policies and the myth-fueled rhetoric that has given them traction have resulted in increased harassment of and violence against LGBTQ+ people.

California taxpayers have taken a stand against prejudiced government policies with a ban on state-funded or state-sponsored travel to other states with discriminatory legislation. A 2017 California law requires that the attorney general track state laws that discriminate on the basis of sexual orientation, gender identity or gender expression. Nine states have been identified as having discriminatory legislation and are currently banned, including Oklahoma, Alabama, Kentucky, Kansas, Mississippi, North Carolina, South Dakota, Tennessee, and Texas.

INTERNATIONAL LGBTQ+ CONSIDERATIONS

European Union (EU) legislation protects lesbians, gays, and bisexuals (LGB) against discrimination in the workplace. Introduced in November 2000, the legislation came in the form of Council Directive 2000/78/EC and is generally known as the Framework Directive. As with all Council Directives, member states are required to transpose the provisions of the Directive into their individual domestic laws.

Member States of the Union were under an obligation to translate the minimum standards defined in the Directive into their national legal systems by December 2, 2003, and May 1, 2004 for accession countries. For example, discrimination on the grounds of sexual orientation in employment has been illegal in the UK since 2003. The Employment Equality (Sexual Orientation) Regulations of 2003 mean that lesbians, gay men, and bisexuals can take legal action if they are the victim of harassment or discrimination at work. Similarly, countries preparing to join the European Union in the future, such as Turkey, are equally obliged to transpose the Directive into national law prior to their accession.

The introduction of this Directive represents an important step forward in the struggle for equal rights for the LGB people in the EU member states. In the first instance, national laws had to change. Furthermore, in the process of changing laws, legislators, employers, trade unions, and other relevant stakeholders had to engage, some for the first time, with the workplace issues relevant to LGB people. By initiating this debate in the workplace, it contributed to the broader project of changing societal attitudes toward LGB people.

The Directive applies to both the public and private sectors and to all types of working arrangements, including agency, contract, self-employed and temporary. Protection against discrimination is provided for in relation to:

- Access to employment and self-employment, and opportunities for promotion
- Access to all levels of vocational guidance and training, including work experience
- Employment and working conditions, including dismissals and pay
- Membership of trade unions and professional bodies and access to the benefits they provide

According to EU legislation, there are three ways in which discrimination in the workplace is practiced: *direct discrimination, indirect discrimination*, and *harassment.* An example of direct discrimination would be when an employer denies promotion opportunities to an employee, whom he knows to be well qualified, because he has discovered that the employee is gay and lives with his boyfriend.

Should Society Accept Homosexuality?

	No	Yes
N. America		
Canada	14	80
U.S.	33	60
Europe		
Spain	11	88
Germany	11	87
Czech Rep.	16	80
France	22	77
Britain	18	76
Italy	18	74
Greece	40	53
Poland	46	42
Russia	74	16
Middle East		
Israel	47	40
Lebanon	80	18
Turkey	78	9
Palest. ter.	93	4
Egypt	95	3
Jordan	97	3
Tunisia	94	2
Asia/Pacific		
Australia	18	79
Philippines	26	73
Japan	36	54
S. Korea	59	39
China	57	21
Malaysia	86	9
Indonesia	93	3
Pakistan	87	2
Latin America		
Argentina	21	74
Chile	24	68
Mexico	30	61
Brazil	36	60
Venezuela	42	51
Bolivia	49	43
El Salvador	62	34
Africa		
S. Africa	61	32
Kenya	90	8
Uganda	96	4
Ghana	96	3
Senegal	96	3
Nigeria	98	1

PEW RESEARCH CENTER Q27.

Indirect discrimination occurs when a person is placed at a disadvantage when, for example, a condition that applies to everyone presents more difficulties for LGB people, e.g., bringing a partner to company functions. One way to think of the difference between direct and indirect discrimination is to think of the former as being intentional and the latter as being unintentional. Becoming aware of unintentional discriminatory practices, and amending them in line with the principle of equal treatment, is a legal requirement for employers.

Harassment is behavior that creates a hostile or offensive environment for the person being hassled. It might take the form of being ignored or excluded, physically or verbally abused, outed as gay, or made the subject of jokes and offensive remarks.

It is also discriminatory to issue instructions to discriminate based on sexual orientation. This would apply in the case of an employer issuing instructions to a recruitment agency in relation to the type of candidate sought for a particular position. If someone believes that they have been discriminated against, they are entitled to bring a case in which they present the facts that are deemed to constitute discrimination. The onus is on the entity accused of discrimination to disprove the case. This "shift" in the burden of proof to the employer is an important aspect of EU legislation.

Figure 2 illustrates a 2013 Pew Research Center Survey in which there are huge variances by region on the broader question of whether homosexuality should be accepted or rejected by society.

For example, LGBTQ+ rights in Russia face legal and social challenges as well as discrimination not experienced by non-LGBTQ+ people. Same-sex relations between consenting adults in private was decriminalized in 1993. Currently, there are no laws prohibiting discrimination on the basis of sexual orientation, gender identity, or gender expression. Households headed by same-sex couples are ineligible for the legal protections available to opposite-sex couples. Nevertheless, homosexuality was declassified as a mental illness in 1999 and transsexuals have been able to change their legal gender since 1997.

In 2013, Russia received criticism from around the world for enacting a law that bans the distribution of "propaganda of non-traditional sexual relations" to minors. This effectively makes it illegal to suggest that gay relationships are equal to heterosexual relationships or to distribute material on gay rights. Currently, gay marriage is not legal in Russia.

LGBTQ+ people in Brazil enjoy the same legal protections available to non-LGBTQ+ people, with gay marriage available nationwide since May 2013. According to the Guinness World Records, the São Paulo Gay Pride Parade is the world's largest LGBTQ+ Pride celebration; it had more than 4 million participants in 2009. Brazil had more than 60,000 same-sex households, according to the Brazilian Census of 2010 (IBGE). Additionally, the South American country has 300 active LGBTQ+ organizations.

The Declaration of Montreal on Lesbian, Gay, Bisexual, and Transgender Human Rights is a document adopted in Montreal, Quebec, Canada, on July 29, 2006, by the International Conference on LGBT Human Rights, which was formed as part of the first World Out Games. The Declaration outlines a number of rights and freedoms pertaining to LGBT people that are proposed to be universally guaranteed. It encompasses all aspects of Human Rights, from the guarantee of fundamental freedoms to the prevention of discrimination against LGBT people in healthcare, education, and immigration. The Declaration also addresses various issues that impinge on the global promotion of LGBT rights. Intended as a starting point in listing the demands of the international LGBT movement, it will ultimately be submitted to the United Nations, which currently does not recognize LGBT rights as human rights.

Montreal's Declaration calls for the development of programs to promote fair chances in employment and business for LGBT people in order for their economic independence to be insured. Canadian governments are asked to lead by example in eliminating such discrimination and in promoting the equality and safety of LGBT people in public sector workplaces. When operating globally, however, employers should be aware of the particular laws governing each region, as the laws may have an effect on recruitment, professional development, retention, and inclusion.

Homosexuality is illegal in India, as well as in most African and/or Islamic countries. Nigeria, the most populous country in Africa, recently passed a bill that calls for a 14-year sentence for anyone convicted of homosexuality. The bill also calls for a 10-year sentence for anyone who aids or "abets" same-sex unions. Nations such as Britain have threatened to withhold foreign aid from Nigeria in response to the discriminatory legislation.

In Dubai, sexual relations outside of a traditional heterosexual marriage are a crime. Punishments include jail time, fines, deportation, and the death penalty. LGBTQ+ people may face forced hormone treatments; chemical castration is also an option. The laws, some of which were introduced by the British during the colonial period, are still vigorously enforced.

In 2009, a Ugandan lawmaker introduced a proposal calling for the execution of people convicted of homosexuality. The proposal sparked an international outcry and threats from some European countries to cut aid to the nation, which relies on millions of dollars from foreign countries. Ugandan government spokesperson Fred Opolot said the proposal was the opinion of a sole lawmaker and did not reflect the government view. On 20 December 2013, the Uganda Anti-Homosexuality Act, 2014 was passed with life in prison substituted for the death penalty. However, on 1 August 2014, the Constitutional Court of Uganda ruled the act invalid on procedural grounds. The legislation was eventually shelved, but regularly pops up in parliament and remains a simmering issue.

AFFIRMING TRANSGENDER EMPLOYEES

Several actions need to occur if an employee notifies management or human resources that they plan to undergo medical treatment to more closely align their anatomy with their sense of self. What has historically been referred to as gender reassignment therapy, is now commonly referred to as gender affirmation or gender confirmation surgery. Workplace policies and practices that are culturally competent provide guidance for management and work teams in order to ensure an easier transition and allow for workplace continuity.

Keep in mind, no medical intervention is required for a transgender person to identify as transgender. All that is necessary is for a transgender person to feel a deep sense of self that does not align with their assigned sex. Requiring medical proof of transgender identity or suggesting that a person is not truly transgender unless they are postoperative is an oversimplified and alienating view of transgender identity. Some individuals live fully as the gender that corresponds with their sense of self without ever undergoing any medical interventions.

It is entirely up to each transgender person to determine when, and to what extent, workplace contacts will be informed that they intend to transition. Because gender affirmation processes may include both physical interventions and behavioral health treatment, any information related to gender affirmation should be considered protected medical information under the Health Insurance Portability and Accountability Act of 1996.

The National Transgender Law Center provides a model transgender policy and guidelines that say, in part:

> "Employees who transition on the job can expect the support of management and human resources staff. HR will work with each transitioning employee individually to ensure a successful workplace transition."
>
> Insert specific guidelines appropriate to your organizational structure here, making sure they address:
>
> - Who is charged with helping a transitioning employee manage his/her workplace transition,
> - What a transitioning employee can expect from management,
> - What management's expectations are for staff, transitioning employees, and any existing lesbian, gay, bisexual, transgender, and queer (LGBTQ+) employee resource group in facilitating a successful workplace transition, and
> - What the general procedure is for implementing transition-related workplace changes, such as adjusting personnel and administrative records, and developing an individualized communication plan to share the news with coworkers and clients.

The National Transgender Law Center also provides a model transition plan that employers can reference.

Organizations benefit from offering regularly occurring required training related to sexual orientation, gender identity and gender expression. By offering this level of visibility and setting expectations with regard to equitable treatment, if and when employees transition in the workplace, the workforce will already have some understanding of transgender issues.

Transition plans may include the following:

- Best practices for managers and colleagues about transgender issues.
- Information for the transitioning employee related to leave requests for medical and legal needs.
- Materials related to the Family Medical Leave Act (FMLA) and the Health Insurance Portability and Accountability Act (HIPAA).
- The process by which employees can change their names and gender markers legally for workplace purposes.
- A communication plan to inform co-workers, clients, and others.
- Information about restroom access.
- How to handle any harassment, hostile reactions or unwanted media interest.

Undergoing the gender transition process may simultaneously feel very liberating and extremely frightening for the individual involved. There may be a loss of familial relationships or other valued community connections. Alternatively, significant others could unexpectedly react positively to the transition. Employers who can help employees through the process of transitioning are on the leading edge of talent acquisition in a global market vying for the best talent.

Harassment Policies
Voyeuristic, intrusive, and personal questions, or clandestine discussions, about transgender colleagues may be offensive to trans individuals. Progressive workplaces will make it clear that no harassment, bullying, or victimization of any kind will be tolerated-- such behavior is unacceptable. Communicate this to staff and/or students, and ensure they know that disciplinary measures will be enforced if this directive is ignored.

All employees and/or students share responsibility for challenging inappropriate behavior, promoting equality, and ensuring that there is no discrimination or harassment towards transgender workers or students. Check in periodically with the transgender employee/student to ensure that they are not experiencing harassment or discrimination.

Time Off
Managers should promote flexibility for time off wherever possible to enable staff to undergo gender affirmation processes. Discuss workload allocation, or other accommodations, with the trans employee before any absence from work and upon return. Time off for medical or legal obligations should not trigger discipline for excessive time off.

Name Change, Records and Confidentiality
Current personnel records and all other documents for transgender staff should refer to the new name. In a small number of cases, it may be necessary for some records (e.g., pension and insurance) to retain a reference to the sex of the employee at birth. Access to such records, and other personnel file information, should be restricted to staff on a need to know basis. No formal name change process is necessary for the following:

- Workstation name placards.
- Names input into global e-mail contact lists.
- Name and pronoun usage in the workplace. Management, colleagues, and others should refer to the transgender employee by the name and pronoun that corresponds to their identity, not their birth record.

- Payroll and tax records require that an individual's name correspond with their social security identification. Typically this requires acquisition of a new driver's license wherever possible, then a new social security card, and in some cases, re-issuance of a birth certificate. These requirements and provisions vary by state.
- Continuity is important. For those individuals requiring background check clearance for positions, provision of all previous names is a likely requirement for employment. This information is protected by law.

Making Practical Arrangements
The most appropriate practice with regard to privacy spaces for transgender employees is to allow employees to attend restrooms, locker rooms, etc. that correspond to their gender identity. Single stall restrooms that are accessible to all genders are preferable.

Recruitment
It should not be expected that applicants and interviewees for employment will disclose their transgender status. Some people consider it a very private matter and others have experienced prejudice and discomfort as a result of previous disclosures. If the applicant does choose to disclose, this should not be a reason for selecting another candidate.

Regarding references, if giving a reference for someone moving to a new job, the referee should use the name used by the transgender employee and not refer to a former name or gender identity.

BEST EMPLOYMENT PRACTICES FOR LGBTQ+ WORKERS

In establishing an inclusive culture for all employees, there are some best practices that employers can undertake to ensure that LGBTQ+ diversity is good for business.

1) *Build a culture of respect*
    a. Provide leadership at all levels: (1) senior executives should issue public statements in support of LGBTQ+ employees (expressly state support of LGBTQ+ employees vs. making a generalized statement like "we support all people"); (2) designate LGBTQ+ role models within the organization; (3) launch corporate diversity and inclusion efforts for LGBTQ+ employees/customers/students; and (4) seek to win equality awards.
    b. Explicitly invite and include same-sex partners to the organization's social events

2) *Support the establishment of LGBTQ+ employee resource groups*

3) *Tackle workplace bullying and harassment*
    a. Ensure the policy covers harassment on the grounds of sexual orientation, gender identity, and gender expression
    b. Establish a mechanism to report problems and effectively resolve complaints

4) *Publicize, implement, and monitor equality policies that your organization adopts*

5) *Provide training and awareness-raising to all employees*

6) *Review employment policies*
   a. Provide benefits for same-sex partners, wherever possible
   b. Choose providers (pension, life and health insurance companies) that are committed to equal treatment
   c. Ensure equal compensation for LGBTQ+ employees
   d. Recruit, select and promote fairly

7) *Be proactive. Routinely assess the organization's shifting needs, as well as changing legislation. Identify potential issues before they become problems. If necessary, develop more than one possible solution.*

Support for LGBTQ+ Efforts
As the largest civil rights organization working to achieve equality for lesbian, gay, bisexual, and transgender Americans, the Human Rights Campaign (HRC) represents a force of more than 1.5 million members and supporters. Founded in 1980, the Human Rights Campaign advocates on behalf of LGBTQ+ Americans, mobilizes grassroots campaigns in diverse communities, invests strategically to elect fair-minded individuals to office, and educates the public about LGBTQ+ issues. HRC provides research, education, and outreach for many groups who are establishing a business case for LGBTQ+, seeking training, or are forming LGBTA/LGBTQ Employee Resource Groups.

Out & Equal Workplace Advocates is the world's largest nonprofit organization specifically dedicated to creating safe and equitable workplaces for lesbian, gay, bisexual and transgender people. Out & Equal has created numerous programs to advance its mission; including the first Global Summit in London, the annual Out & Equal Workplace Summit, the LGBTQ+ Executive Forum and Leadership Celebration, bimonthly Town Call seminars, Regional Affiliate networks across the United States, and the world's largest LGBTQ+ Employee Resource Group Registry.

Additionally, there are workplace resources for how allies can create a more inclusive work environment, such as the Out & Equal publication, *Allies at Work*, by David M. Hall. The book details the importance of LGBT allies in shaping workplace climates, the business case for developing a strong ally program at work, and the cultural competencies required to understand the closet. *Allies at Work* serves an important mission of helping to establish an open dialogue that engages new and old allies in support of workplace equality for all people.

MARKETING TO THE LGBTQ+ COMMUNITY

LGBTQ+ marketing is the act of promoting products and/or services directly to LGBTQ+ consumers, either with dedicated or general advertising; through sponsorships of LGBTQ+ organizations and events; or through the targeted use of technology. The LGBTQ+ market comprises a group of customers who buy goods and services from a broad range of companies across industry segments and in many countries around the globe.

The Human Rights Campaign Corporate Equality Index lets candidates know whether companies will be open and affirming, but its Buying for Workplace Equality tool is available as an app so that consumers need only look at their phone to know where to shop for LGBTQ+ equality.

As with most disciplines within the Diversity and Inclusion industry, marketing to the gay and lesbian community faces statistical obstacles. Few credible peer-reviewed estimates of the gay and lesbian marketplace have been published. In particular, the common use of nonrandom "convenience surveys" of attendees at gay resorts or subscribers to gay or lesbian newspapers have resulted in some unreliable statistical estimates of gay buying power. Thus, the exact number of gays and lesbians in a given market is generally unknown. However, some national governments have started to publish data that includes sexual orientation demographics from census results. For example, in the 2000 U.S. Census, two questions were asked that allowed same-sex partners to provide responses. Based on that data, the Census Bureau reported that there were more than 658,000 same-sex couples heading households in the United States. From 2000 to the present, American Community Survey has collected data about same-sex couples.

The preponderance of peer-reviewed studies of populations in Canada, the U.S., the U.K., Australia, Sweden, and the Netherlands show that gay males have lower average incomes than heterosexual males, while lesbians have higher average earnings than heterosexual females. Nevertheless, compared to heterosexual couples, gay and lesbian households tend to have more disposable income since same sex partners are more likely to be college-educated and have dual incomes with no kids.

While over 15 years old in the United States, LGBTQ+ marketing is a relatively new phenomenon in other countries such as Australia and Europe, including Belgium and the Netherlands. Many brands that have previously ignored this segment of society now aggressively target LGBTQ+ customers.

Businesses and the LGBTQ+ community have not co-existed without controversy. Organizations like Target and Chick-fil-A were the subjects of negative publicity for months because of the actions or comments of senior level leaders. Coors Brewing Company was the subject of a boycott by the LGBTQ+ community starting in 1973. The boycott was actually initiated by labor unions to protest the company's antagonistic practices. The LGBTQ+ community eventually joined to protest Coors' hiring policies because polygraph tests were often required, during which the prospective employee was asked about his/her sexual orientation. Coors ignored the boycott for several years, but made some concessions in 1978. In 1995, Coors began several countermeasures, including dropping the questions regarding homosexuality and extending domestic partner benefits to its LGBTQ+ employees. The company also hired an LGBTQ+ marketing representative, and began advertising in The Advocate and at events such as Denver's PrideFest.

Although global attitudes toward LGBTQ+ individuals have become more accepting over the years, there are still millions of people around the world who believe that homosexuality is wrong or sinful. Some people may not have a problem with homosexuality per se. However, they are offended by gay sex in public restrooms or gay couples raising children.

Muslims and Conservative Christian groups often boycott large corporations that endorse homosexual behavior. Even to non-religious folks, the gay affiliation may be enough to turn the consumer onto the competing brand. Therefore, marketing to the LGBTQ+ community is not without peril.

Nevertheless, there are many business advantages to targeting the LGBTQ+ market. According to proponents, it is important for a company to take a stand by endorsing gay rights. In order to do this, a company should not apply the same creative approach that it uses in the mainstream media.

Marketing needs to use a gay-oriented creative approach, one that depicts a same-sex couple in a manner that traditionally was used to depict a heterosexual couple (e.g., a commercial depicting a same-sex couple enjoying an anniversary dinner). Additionally, the organization must exemplify commitment, regardless of how the public perceives its strategic business decisions.

References:

J. Nelson and C. Mitchell, *'LGBT Economy Is America's Future,' 2018* [Online] Available: https://www.advocate.com/commentary/2018/1/02/lgbt-economy-americas-future. [Accessed 31-January-2018]

Human Rights Campaign Corporate Equality Index [Online] Available: http://www.hrc.org/campaigns/corporate-equality-index [Accessed 31-January-2018]

Human Rights Campaign Buyer's Guide [Online] Available: http://www.hrc.org/apps/buyersguide/ [Accessed 2-February-2018]

American Psychological Association. (2008). *Answers to your questions: For a better understanding of sexual orientation and homosexuality*. Washington, DC: Author. [Retrieved from www.apa.org/topics/sorientation.pdf.]

The White House of President Barrack Obama. (2016). *President Obama Designates Stonewall National Monument*. Available: https://obamawhitehouse.archives.gov/blog/2016/06/24/president-obama-designates-stonewall-national-monument

T. L. Ramirez and Z. Blay, *Why People Are Using The Term 'Latinx'*, 2017 (Online) Available: https://www.huffingtonpost.com/entry/why-people-are-using-the-term-latinx_us_57753328e4b0cc0fa136a159

Morten Tyldum, Director. *The Imitation Game*, 2014 movie. Black Bear Pictures. Run time: 114 minutes
The Williams Institute, Economic Impact Reports (Online) Available: https://williamsinstitute.law.ucla.edu/

Ariane de Vogue, 2017. *Judge blocks enforcement of Trump's transgender military ban.* CNN Politics. Available: https://www.cnn.com/2017/10/30/politics/judge-blocks-trump-transgender-military-ban/index.html

BBC News, 2018. *Trump Signs New Transgender Military Ban.* (Online) Available: http://www.bbc.com/news/world-us-canada-43525549

Kaitlyn Schallhorn, 2018. *Supreme Court decides Colorado gay wedding cake case: A timeline of events.* Fox News (Online) Available: http://www.foxnews.com/us/2018/06/04/supreme-court-decides-colorado-gay-wedding-cake-case-timeline-events.html

National Center for Transgender Equality. *Take Action Against Anti-Trans Legislation Now* (Online) Available: https://transequality.org/action-center

Ryan W. Miller, 2018. *California bans travel to another state based on its 'discriminatory' LGBT adoption law.* USA Today. Available: https://www.usatoday.com/story/news/nation/2018/06/02/california-bans-travel-oklahoma-due-discriminatory-lgbt-law/666320002/

Pew Research Center, 2013. *The Global Divide on Homosexuality* (Online) Available: http://www.pewglobal.org/2013/06/04/the-global-divide-on-homosexuality/

National Transgender Law Center. *Model Transgender Employment Policy* (Online) Available: https://transgenderlawcenter.org/resources/employment/modelpolicy

David M. Hall, 2009. *Allies at Work: Creating a Lesbian, Gay, Bisexual and Transgender Inclusive Work Environment.* California: Out & Equal Workplace Advocates.

Sample Test Questions:
LGBTQ+ INCLUSION

1. The Framework Directive prohibits LGBT employment discrimination in Canada.
   A. True
   B. False

2. Although this was not the first uprising among LGBTQ+ people, _____ is widely recognized as the beginning of the gay civil rights movement.
   A. Cooper Do-Nuts Riots
   B. Stonewall Riots
   C. Los Angeles Riots

3. The plus sign (+) that often appears at the end of Lesbian Gay Bisexual and Transgender (LGBTQ) stands for "and ___":
   A. Positive relationships with same-sex and opposite sex individuals
   B. Allies who support the LGBTQ community around the world
   C. Other identities that don't fit the heteronormative paradigm

4. The Corporate Equality Index, which measures LGBTQ+ employment fairness, was developed by:
   A. The Human Rights Campaign
   B. Out and Equal
   C. Gay Straight Alliance

5. "In the closet" is a metaphor that is used to describe individuals who have not:
   A. Participated in the gay rights movement
   B. Disclosed their sexual orientation
   C. Had gender affirmation surgery

6. The DOMA-related lawsuit that resulted in equal tax treatment for same-sex couples is:
   A. Dragovich vs. US Department of Treasury
   B. Golinski vs. Office of Personnel Management
   C. Windsor vs. United States

7. Someone whose perception of their own gender identity that does not conform to the sex they were assigned at birth may identify as:
   A. Transgender
   B. Cisgender
   C. Pansexual

Sample Test Questions:
LGBTQ+ INCLUSION (cont'd)

8. What is the primary reason why sexual orientation, gender identity, and gender expression in the workplace are strategic business opportunities?
   A. Harassment prevention
   B. Competitive advantage
   C. Affirmative Action law

9. Same-sex relations are illegal in this country:
   A. Brazil
   B. India
   C. Russia

10. Best practices for accommodating an employee who undergoes gender affirmation surgery while employed, entails an employer:
    A. Being flexible in providing work assignments, time off, restroom facilities, and privacy
    B. Changing policies regarding restroom use, harassment, and employee terminations
    C. Lobbying insurance companies to pay for sex change operations and hormone treatments

11. Which country intends to use their LGBTQ+ anti-discrimination policies as a framework for change in the United Nations?
    A. Britain
    B. France
    C. Canada

12. Compared to heterosexual couples, gay and lesbian households tend to have more disposable income because they are:
    A. More likely to be recruited and retained in senior level positions.
    B. Less likely to be discriminated against in developed nations where the pay is higher.
    C. More likely to be college-educated and have dual incomes with no kids.

13. Which of the following is NOT true pertaining to best practices for LGBTQ+ workers?
    A. Employers should explicitly invite same-sex partners to social events
    B. LGBTQ+ efforts should be separate from traditional diversity and inclusion work
    C. Companies must ensure equal compensation for LGBTQ+ employees

MEASURING THE IMPACT OF DIVERSITY & INCLUSION

> **CAUTION!**
>
> Quantifying performance and measuring results are no longer the sole domain of for-profit enterprises. Today, many nonprofit organizations, educational institutions, and government agencies also find themselves on the hot seat—not with stockholders but with donors, students and citizens who expect similar levels of accountability to show how their money was spent and what that spending achieved. Nevertheless, there has been little agreement on a set of hard-and-fast metrics to measure performance in this realm called Diversity and Inclusion.
>
> The success of Diversity and Inclusion initiatives is measured not by the number of activities performed, but by quantifiable results and sustainable achievements engendered over time. To realize true success, seek first to understand that which is being measured, then clearly communicate your vision for reaching organizational goals. Next, realize that bottom-line impact is going to differ depending on whether you are a for-profit, nonprofit, educational institution, or government agency.

OVERALL OBJECTIVES AND COMPETENCIES

The purpose of this competency is to evaluate Diversity and Inclusion efforts by assessing the achievement of annual plan goals, identifying areas for improvement, and directing future progress. Leaders will also have the tools to calculate the quantifiable benefits or return on investment from D&I work.

BACKGROUND AND CONTEXT

There are two primary conversations paramount among Diversity and Inclusion professionals—one focuses on accountability and the other focuses on performance, particularly impact. For years, many practitioners have been disappointed with the inability to demonstrate measurable impact through Diversity and Inclusion. There are two points to make here: accountability should be addressed in the evaluation process and impact should be demonstrated with progressive illustrations, examples, and empirical evidence.

Point #1: You need a Strategic Diversity & Inclusion Plan
The successful evaluation process begins with a formal, written Diversity and Inclusion plan. If you already have a plan, then you are well on your way to demonstrating measurable outcomes.

Conversely, if you do not have a plan, it will be difficult to demonstrate that you made an intentional and strategic impact. The establishment of desired outcomes, activities, and indicators should take place during the strategic Diversity planning stages.

*Think of the desired **outcomes** as what you ultimately want your Diversity and Inclusion effort to accomplish; **activities** as what you will do to get there; and **indicators** as the gauge of whether, and to what degree, you are making progress.*

Outcomes should be consistent with what could reasonably and realistically be accomplished and not overly idealistic. Reasonable and realistic does not mean limiting your effort or the expanse of the outcomes. A properly designed Diversity plan is clearly defined, with measurable outcomes, which translates into benefits for the business and its stakeholders. The plan should also indicate who is responsible for which tasks.

Outcomes provide a foundation for *all* subsequent program implementation and evaluation activities, and each of the outcomes will need to be evaluated. While you and your internal Inclusion partners will undoubtedly seek to obtain a vision that is much bigger and beyond the scope of the Office of Diversity & Inclusion, focus your outcomes on what can realistically be accomplished within a designated timeframe (e.g., 6 months or 1 year).

Activities are the interventions that your Diversity and Inclusion effort will provide in order to facilitate or bolster the intended outcomes. Programs can be created for many different activities to achieve desired outcomes. For purposes of this course of study, activities will be classified as any type of direct service or information provided to employees, students, customers, patients, constituents, or other stakeholders, that will facilitate an outcome.

Indicators act as the gauge of whether, and to what degree, your Diversity and Inclusion effort is making progress. The progress needs to be examined in two distinct ways:

1. The quantity and quality of the **program activities you are delivering** (commonly referred to as process indicators), and

2. The quantity and quality of the **outcomes that your program is achieving** (commonly referred to as outcome indicators).

Therefore, indicators must be developed to measure both types of progress. *Process indicators* help track the progress that your Diversity and Inclusion effort is making as you work toward achieving the desired outcomes. Process indicators often provide important feedback to senior leadership long before you can expect to see evidence that outcomes are being achieved. *Outcome indicators* provide the most compelling evidence that the Diversity and Inclusion effort is making a difference in the lives of employees, students, customers, constituents, or other stakeholders.

Now that an understanding of what outcomes, activities and indicators entail, the question becomes, what is the best way to develop them for your particular organization? That brings us to our next point.

Point #2: Plan your evaluation strategy based on where you fit on the Diversity Development Continuum

The problem with most evaluations is that some people assume that their organization's evaluation results should yield the same outcomes as other organizations that are more or less mature in their Diversity and Inclusion journey. Since organizations are at different stages on the Diversity development continuum, it is necessary to determine where your organization is situated before developing a comprehensive evaluation strategy.

Figure 1 illustrates the various stages on the Diversity development continuum. Essentially, this tool determines the organization's competency in the realm of Diversity and Inclusion. Each stage of the continuum will use different measurement tools to assess the impact of Diversity on business operations or the organization's climate. As the organization progresses through the continuum and the Diversity and Inclusion efforts grow more complex, the evaluation methods should also become more elaborate to reflect bottom-line impact. Nevertheless, evaluation data should not be so intricate that it is confusing to the average person. However, it should reflect standard business measurement practices.

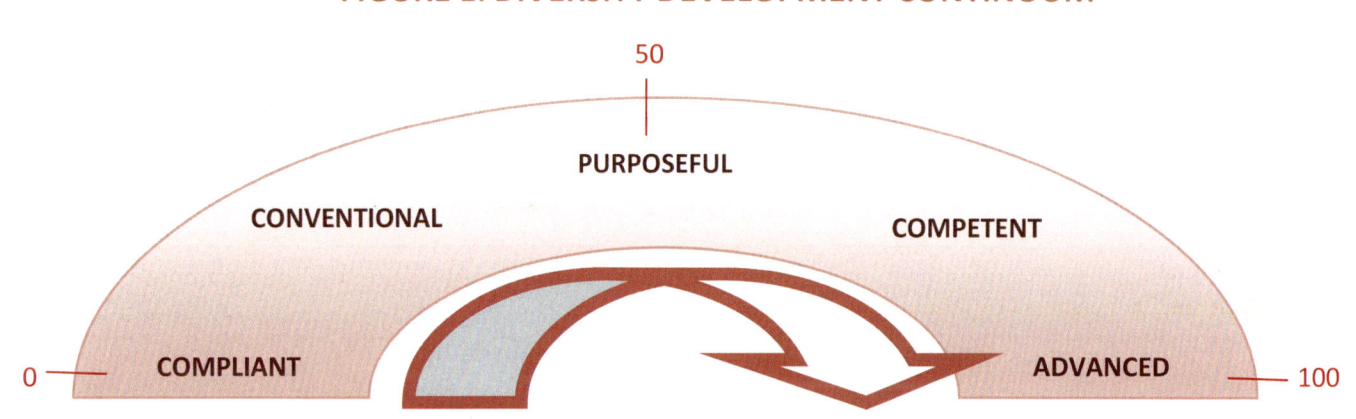

FIGURE 1. DIVERSITY DEVELOPMENT CONTINUUM

THE COMPLIANT ORGANIZATION

In the Compliant mode, an organization is doing the minimum to ensure compliance with the law. This type of activity does not register on the Diversity continuum because the organization is not attaining Diversity or Inclusion. The organization is ensuring compliance with Equal Employment Opportunity law (or applicable national/state/local legislation), which is a separate, although related, matter.

Thus, the goal for compliant organizations is to move beyond compliance toward conventionalism. In order to satisfy this goal, the organization's readiness must be assessed. To this end, a model (see Figure 2) is provided as a guide. This model can be incorporated into a more comprehensive assessment tool included in an online survey sent to your employees or used during a focus group meeting.

FIGURE 2. ASSESSING YOUR ORGANIZATION'S READINESS FOR DIVERSITY & INCLUSIVENESS

ONE	TWO	THREE	FOUR	FIVE	SIX
Level of Commitment to Diversity & Inclusion	Training & Professional Development	Operations & Internal Support Systems	Performance Management & Accountability	Marketing & Communications	Community Relationships & Philanthropy

1. **Level of Commitment to Diversity & Inclusion**
   - What is driving your need for Diversity and Inclusion?
   - Do you have a formal Diversity plan? Is it integrated into your organizational Strategic Plan?
   - Is there a dedicated professional responsible for Diversity and Inclusion (e.g., a Chief Diversity Officer, Director of Diversity, etc.)? Does he or she have decision-making authority and a budget?
   - Is there visible senior management support for D&I goals? Are there executive sponsors for key Diversity initiatives?

2. **Training & Professional Development**
   - Have you conducted a formal assessment to determine what type of Diversity and Inclusion training would best suit employees?
   - What other professional development programs would benefit from a Diversity and Inclusion component (i.e., coaching, mentoring, consultation, etc.)?
   - Do New Hire Orientations indicate your Diversity & Inclusion values?
   - Is Diversity management a required competency for new supervisors or promotions?

3. **Operations & Internal Support Systems**
   - How could a Diversity Council or Employee Resource Group best support organizational objectives?
   - How should business units/departments integrate Diversity and Inclusion goals (e.g., customer service unit strives to increase diverse client retention by 0.05%)?
   - Are field offices involved in Diversity planning and Inclusion efforts?

4. **Performance Management & Accountability**
   - Have employee policies been updated and distributed to workers and managers? Are existing policies enforced?
   - Are Diversity and Inclusion goals (e.g., recruiting, retention, training, etc.) incorporated into managers' performance evaluations and bonus requirements?
   - Are there managers who receive more discrimination/harassment complaints than others? What interventions are available to remediate behavior?

5. **Marketing & Communications**
    - What are the projected demographics for your customer, student, patient, or constituent base in the next 10 years? Are you currently marketing to these audiences?
    - How has the industry changed? What has your organization done to adjust to these changes?
    - Are your marketing and communications materials available in other languages?
    - Are corporate visual images consistent with your Diversity and Inclusion values (e.g., your website, social media, printed materials, etc.)?
    - If you operate in other countries, are social media and online marketers knowledgeable about the cultural nuances in each region?

6. **Community Relationships & Philanthropy**
    - What diverse community-based organizations can help you reach your target audience for employees, customers, students, board members, etc.?
    - Do you have a supplier Diversity program?
    - Do you sponsor or financially support diverse organizations and events?

In the compliant mode, the evaluation of success is measured by moving beyond legal compliance toward deriving organizational value from serving different groups better than competitors. In "valuing" Diversity, most evaluation data will be qualitative or "soft" data. A good strategy for gathering data might be to start by defining Diversity, locating a consultant to help with Diversity training, or designing and distributing an employee survey.

THE CONVENTIONAL ORGANIZATION
In the Conventional mode, an organization truly begins its Diversity and Inclusion journey. This is where an employer may hold a mandatory Diversity training session on how to value differences. In this mode, the company is looking for ways to deal with issues that have surfaced. When discriminatory behavior is detected, sometimes only involving one or two people, a training date, time, and location is set, and a consultant is hired by HR. Employee feedback will generally be negative, reflecting resistance to change. However, the goal for conventional organizations is to keep the momentum going; don't stop with one mandatory training session for all employees.

In this mode, evaluation criteria may be based on how many people attended the session and whether the training laid the foundation to help solve "the problem". To inculcate the conventional mentality into the company, it may be advantageous to conduct a cultural climate audit before and after the training. Some organizations may even create a Diversity plan in this phase.

It is important to note that in this stage, the strategic Diversity and Inclusion plan should be simple. This means that the plan may be one-page and the goals are very easy to accomplish. *Simple.* Not only will this approach give employees and senior leadership confidence toward the change management process, it will increase buy-in for future D&I efforts. In this phase, employees resist Diversity because it is HR-led; therefore, it is important to utilize communication to keep senior executives engaged and excited about D&I's potential so that they can eventually play a key role in leading it to the next stage.

These small, incremental steps are necessary to ensure that everyone is on board, in the right seat, at the right time. Achieving Diversity is a journey, while Inclusion is a process. Initial resistance is normal, and it will be significantly less than a whirlwind campaign with a lot of conflict, minimal support, and few results.

THE PURPOSEFUL ORGANIZATION

In the Purposeful mode, an organization understands that it needs to do more than hold an annual Diversity training session. In this phase, the organization may develop a business case for Diversity, create a multifaceted Diversity plan, and/or design a recruitment strategy for diverse employees. Hence, the company recognizes that there is a genuine purpose for Diversity and Inclusion efforts. This stage is transformative because it is where senior leadership typically buys-into Diversity and Inclusion. At this juncture, a senior executive calls for D&I versus HR initiating it. A higher level of employee support for D&I is evident when a senior executive launches the effort.

In this mode, "how to value" Diversity training sessions are no longer presented unless one is facilitating a new hire orientation. During this stage of the continuum, training should focus on Diversity and Inclusion skills—communication, customer service, team building, conflict resolution, management, etc. If the organization is an educational institution or non-profit, training could focus on researching different demographic groups in an effort to attract new students, constituents, donors, or volunteers. Concurrently, training for the Information Technology (IT) department could revolve around working with employees and/or customers from different generational groups. For a corporation, ensuring that the sales and marketing team is culturally competent with different groups will go a long way in appealing to, or generating new revenue from, diverse sources. Essentially, all Diversity and Inclusion training in this stage should focus on skills that employees can take back to the job and apply immediately.

In this mode, the Diversity plan should be revised to reflect growth. With the initial goals accomplished, what is next? At this point, it may be necessary to comb through the organizational plan and map out a strategy to link Diversity and Inclusion efforts to specific organizational goals. Again, do not go overboard in setting goals, keep it simple! Everything at this point should have a purpose.

Begin preparing managers for the next stage, **Competence**. To assist in achieving competence, keep managers engaged in the process. Ideas include:

- Identifying what the organization rewards and ensuring that supervisors are rewarding behaviors that align with D&I values.
- Empowering managers with tools to address bullying, harassment, and other unprofessional behavior.
- Holding leadership retreats that are not focused on Diversity, but includes a Diversity and Inclusion component.
- Publicly acknowledging managers who are making an effort in hiring, developing, and promoting personnel who are diverse.
- Providing coaching, and follow-up, for supervisors who are challenged by the demands of Diversity and Inclusion.
- Utilizing a pre-determined schedule to regularly update managers about D&I successes.

In the Purposeful stage, your efforts can be evaluated by whether you accomplished Diversity and Inclusion goals, which should be linked to business objectives. You can also measure how the culture has changed, and what impact the changes have had on customers, students, patients, volunteers, donors, etc. Are there reportable increases? Are there more compliments from external stakeholders? Is there greater employee satisfaction?

Evaluation data at this point will be considerably "soft". The data does not get entirely "hard" or quantitative until after this phase. Nevertheless, there should be adequate documentation of your processes, progress, and outcomes. This documentation should include **at least** one annual report. The Office of Diversity and Inclusion can also prepare a monthly, quarterly, or semi-annual report.

THE COMPETENT ORGANIZATION

What makes an organization competent is the integration of D&I practices into everyday business operations, and its focus on setting Diversity and Inclusion goals that are more intricate. Thus, instead of the D&I leader being solely responsible for equity and inclusion, responsibility for goal-setting and achievement spreads throughout the enterprise. For example, pay increases and bonuses for managers may be linked to achieving departmental Diversity and Inclusion objectives. Intercultural curriculum and co-curriculum may be developed. Several employee resource groups may be formed and trained. A supplier Diversity program for Tier 1 and Tier 2 vendors may be rolled out, with training for procurement officers/corporate buyers, traditional vendors, or diverse suppliers. Alternatively, the organization may apply the research from the previous phase to a marketing campaign targeting a diverse segment.

There is a saying that goes, "that which gets measured, gets done". The same could be said in the converse: "That which gets done, gets measured". However, not all activities need be measured, unless they are deemed important and are tied to the overall success of the organization's core business. This will engender a competitive advantage. Too many organizations spend time trumpeting the success of activities that yield no measurable impact or benefit to their strategic goals or customer needs. As a result, they experience the absence of key stakeholder support, employee resistance to change, and shareholder distrust.

Practitioners must approach Diversity and Inclusion management in the same manner as other business objectives measured by tangible and specific results. This will also help reinforce the business case established in the previous phase.

In a Society for Human Resources Management (SHRM) Study on Workplace Diversity, *How Can the Results of Our Diversity Initiative Be Measured?*, it was suggested that measurement is done by a "comparative process that includes both baseline data detailing the starting conditions and clear objectives against which change can be measured". Therefore, as a rule, **never start a change process without collecting baseline data**.

The measurement process requires that you clearly define a starting point for change and collect two to three months of baseline data before "transforming" anything. This process anchors the change and enables your organization to measure the impact of the change over time. Determining a starting point also ensures that evaluation is a forethought, rather than an afterthought. When evaluation is an afterthought, the D&I leader performs a lot of work and then asks, "How can I measure D&I's impact"? However, there were never any intentional targets set, or data collected throughout the process to ascertain whether the impact is net positive, negative or neutral.

There are a number of sources from which baseline data can be gathered, such as:

- *Collecting existing organizational data.* Information from various internal departments (e.g., human resources) can be used in your measurement process. For example, existing staff satisfaction survey results can tell you a lot about what is on the minds of your rank-and-file employees that may not surface in face-to-face interviews. Look for patterns or recurrent themes in groups such as women or underrepresented ethnic groups.

You can also initiate inquiries into policies and processes. For example, determine the impact of turnover among diverse groups, as well as the cost to hire and replace people who have left your organization within a short amount of time. Is there an inordinate amount of absenteeism within a particular group or department? What about an increase in EEO complaints in mono-cultural or less diverse divisions or teams? Is there a disparity in the levels of dissatisfaction of employees according to ethnicity, job classification, and gender? How often does the organization "innovate", and what has been the customer response to new products/services?

- *Facilitating focus groups.* Convene small groups of 6-10 employees, customers, or students to talk about the perceptions, challenges, values, and expectations of your organization. To ensure constructive discussions, these meetings must be led by skilled facilitators who can guide meaningful group conversations while important anecdotal information is being captured.

Once baseline data has been gathered, work with your business partners to identify, monitor, and measure the key metrics. From a Human Capital perspective, employing more diverse individuals is not the goal, engaging more diverse perspectives that lead to breakthrough thinking is the goal. From a marketing perspective, more multicultural marketing is not the goal, deeper penetration into new and emerging markets is the goal. From a Procurement perspective, collecting more small business qualification surveys is not the goal, awarding more contracts to diverse suppliers is the goal. Look for tangible measures, and be specific and intentional from the onset. Make sure the metrics clearly support business goals and note past criticisms.

In addition to collecting the baseline data, you want to:

- **Establish a Clear Aim**

Establish a clear improvement aim or target. Such a target should: (a) be realistic yet ambitious (e.g., do not expect 100 percent completion), (b) be linked to organizational objectives, and (c) avoid confusion, especially with percentages (e.g., say reduce turnover from 65 percent to 25 percent, rather than 'improve turnover by 62 percent').

- **Consistently Collect Data**

The ability to establish consistent channels for collecting measurement data on a regular basis is a crucial part of the change process. These channels may exist in current data systems; however, you may need to collect the data manually. Often it is easier to rely on manual collection for quick and direct feedback on the success of the intervention. This means relying on small samples collected over short periods of time to measure progress.

- **Chart Your Progress**

Over time, your organization will collect both pre-change (baseline) and post-change data, and the data should be shared with stakeholders within your organization. The most effective tool for sharing this information is charting your progress over time using simple line graphs. These powerful visual aids should follow one simple axiom: one graph, one message.

- **Ask Questions**

The most important step in the process is to ask questions. For example, what is the information telling me about change in my organization? If the Diversity initiative was unsuccessful, why did it fail? If the intervention worked, what contributed to the effectiveness of this effort? How can we make improvements? If change is successful, the information you have collected may affirm which intervention(s) had the most success in meeting your goals.

To set good goals, use the SMART model: Specific, Measurable, Achievable, Relevant, and Time Bound. Working closely with internal business partners will allow you to set goals that meet these criteria. The next step is to establish who will do what, when it will be done, and what are the rewards and consequences. Serious attention must be paid to monitoring each step of the implementation process. As always, everything done in each step of the process should be documented.

FIGURE 3. ENSURING ORGANIZATIONAL COMPETENCY	
Method	Activities
Establish corporate-wide goals	• Review strategic plan • Interview senior executives • Document and confirm objectives and goals • Review bonus goals for all senior level executives
Pinpoint departmental goals	• Review departmental plans • Interview department managers • Document and confirm objectives and goals • Review bonus goals for each manager • Confirm alignment with senior management goals. If not aligned, review with Senior leadership and seek alignment
Ascertain supporting initiatives	• Review departmental level projects • Discuss program specifics with the project manager
Select appropriate interventions	• Assess current organizational projects and proposals • Identify high impact, high visibility projects that can be influenced by D&I
Identify business partners	• Interview department managers • Identify D&I champions • Assess D&I skills and capabilities • Select business partner(s) with unique perspectives
Review and understand departmental jargon	• Discuss with the department manager • Review past projects • Identify the most successful projects • Isolate the key areas of focus and reporting • Use the language of the department, not HR or D&I • Align language and terminology with specific bonus goals for managers and senior leadership
Develop key metrics	• Link interventions with corporate strategic targets • Connect goals with departmental objectives • Align projected outcomes with bonus goals • Design SMART (Specific, measurable, achievable, realistic and time bound) goals • Monitor team generated goals

By helping departments and managers achieve key goals, D&I efforts present a win-win for everyone. This builds enthusiasm, teamwork, engagement, and Inclusion. Accordingly, the outcomes will also contribute to the accomplishment of key organizational goals.

THE ADVANCED ORGANIZATION

As we progress up the Diversity development continuum, you will note that Diversity and Inclusion efforts become more involved. Hence, the evaluation of business impact becomes more complex as well.

In the final phase—Advanced—there is a specific expectation for results and a push toward integrating Diversity and Inclusion into corporate growth strategies and everyday business operations. The Advanced phase deals with tangible and intentional outcomes. Here, the Diversity and Inclusion expert can fully demonstrate that D&I can be evaluated according to commonly accepted business principles—that is, quantitative hard-core metrics. Moreover, because of programs like the Institute for Diversity Certification, D&I practitioners will speak on one accord versus everyone using different standards. Thus, success will no longer be an anomaly; it will be the expected norm.

The advanced phase involves:

- Solving a business problem that threatens sustainability (e.g., how to increase foot traffic in malls),
- Coordinating interventions across systems (e.g., connecting D&I across a university system, on the federal/state level, or other multi-state initiative)
- Enhancing product/service offerings (e.g., introducing a scalable 'customization' feature to an existing product/service),
- Venturing into new markets (e.g., developing a new app that traverses different ages, genders, races, nationalities, etc.),
- Facilitating simultaneous cultural developments (e.g., translating your website into 23 different languages while building an international call center),
- Achieving other inherently complex feats.

The advanced phase allows for revolutionary ideas and enterprise-wide transformations. At a university, the D&I office may lead an initiative to establish a sister campus in Dubai. At a corporation, the D&I office and African American Employee Resource Group may lead a delegation consisting of business, government, nonprofit and academic leaders to an African country to discuss international business opportunities. At a nonprofit, the D&I office may lead an effort to expand international services, as well as publicity and fundraising. At a state government agency, supplier diversity efforts may result in robust economic development. At any of these entities, the D&I office may establish a job rotation program that allows American personnel to gain work experience overseas, and international employees to gain experience working in the Americas.

International business strategies are the way of the future. Not only has the Internet expanded global opportunities, but the proliferation of Asian, African, and Latino middle class families has facilitated emerging markets overseas with unmet or under-served needs. Thus, a global focus allows organizations to seize more financial opportunities through Diversity and Inclusion. A state government agency may have an interest in attracting foreign businesses to the state in order to create jobs, stimulate foreign investment, or model best practices. Likewise, a hospital may want people to come from outside of the local area for specialized treatment at the facility. Finally, a multinational organization may want to ensure that it has a diverse, global supply chain. Each of these strategies presents opportunities for the Office of Diversity and Inclusion to capitalize on increased economic activity in partnership with other business units within the organization.

If you remember one thing in this phase, remember this: **do the math, or the math will do you.** In other words, operating a fully functional diversity and inclusion effort is expensive. If you don't demonstrate a positive benefit, a negative value proposition will *not* work in your favor.

Diversity words should not be used to show positive benefits. In order to speak the language of the CEO, President, Executive Director, Secretary, or other senior leaders, the savvy Diversity and Inclusion professional must speak the language of the Corporate Suite (C-Suite)—*revenue generation or cost savings*. Keep in mind, whether you work at a for-profit, educational institution, nonprofit, or government agency, **every executive has some level of concern for finance**. Accordingly, in the advanced phase, D&I professionals are more fluent and transparent in business dealings, and they are more comfortable talking about money and/or operating in other nations. Therefore, we will reference D&I outcomes in financial terms (i.e., the language of executives).

This is fairly new for the D&I industry, and it is the next generation of Diversity thought leadership. In our capacity as experts in the field, we will use words such as "asset", "calculate", "measure", "return on investment", "value", and "bottom line". Each of these terms must be used in order to establish and maintain the importance of Diversity and Inclusion to organizations.

Value implies usefulness or something of worth. It can also denote principles or character. In transferring values (i.e., passion for Diversity and Inclusion) to an organization, and creating *more* value, it is important to move beyond warm and fuzzy (soft) data toward cold, hard facts.

Andres Tapia, Senior Partner at Korn Ferry, was the 2011 keynote breakfast speaker at the annual Forum on Workplace Inclusion in Minnesota. He spoke on the topic, "*Diversity 1.0 is Tired, Spent, and Obsolete: It's Time to Invent the Next Generation of Diversity Work*". Mr. Tapia's presentation centered on retiring Diversity and Inclusion tenets that do not work. He proposed adapting a new Diversity and Inclusion platform that is strategic, successful, and sustainable. Otherwise, if D&I practitioners resist moving past Diversity 1.0, they eventually succumb to the math.

Life generally requires movement, transition, or advancement because time and change are constant. Moving or progressing requires change, the same thing that we are asking others to do, and change is not easy; however, change is necessary. Over time, what makes people feel good—valuing one another (the beginning of the Diversity development continuum)—is not perceived as valuable to the company. That is why, at this level, organizations need the Office of Diversity and Inclusion to produce a tangible bottom line impact.

It is important to remember that bottom line impact differs from organization to organization. For example, the American Red Cross counts volunteers and donations, not profits; and government organizations, like the IRS, may have a service-oriented bottom line. Still all employers, whether for-profit or not-for-profit, depend on their ability to get the best possible return on dollars invested. Thus, it is necessary to understand how your organization makes money and its long-term goals. Additionally, you will have to know how to operationalize key terms such as:

- *Bottom Line:* The final outcome of a process, showing a gain or loss; the most important fundamental aspect of a situation
- *Return on Investment:* A form of cost-benefit analysis that measures the costs of a program (i.e., the investment) versus the financial return realized by that program
- *Measurement:* A collection of quantitative data; allowing for comparison against accepted standards

In the field of Diversity and Inclusion, *impact* can be defined as the quantifiable change, or potential change, in one or more key areas:

- *Economic* (including sales, donations, enrollments, and other factors that affect finances)
- *Environmental* (such as the organizational climate or culture)
- *Professional* (including hiring, training, advancement, and retention)
- *Legal* (such as the number of complaints or lawsuits filed)

Essentially, there are four components involved in measuring impact.

1. **Combining** quantitative and qualitative data to get deeper insights.

2. **Customizing** the metrics to reflect what is important in the organization's culture, its business results, and industry.

3. **Collaborating** in both traditional and nontraditional ways to acquire information, allow for innovation, and activate integration throughout the organization.

4. **Communicating** both expectations and accomplishments in a predetermined format on a predetermined schedule.

Impact focuses on corporate benefits in terms of:

- *Knowledge gained and how that knowledge is applied.*
- *Behavior or attitude changes.*
- *Practice or situation changes.*
- *Results of those behavior, attitude, practice, or situation changes.*

Impact can be positive or negative. Sometimes, when it comes to Diversity and Inclusion, as is the nature of most people, it is easier to remember the negative impacts than the positive impacts. Nevertheless, almost every organization has experienced unsuccessful projects—programs that go astray, cost too much or that fail to deliver on promises. Critics of the projects suggest that failure could have been avoided if:

1. The project was based on legitimate need from the beginning
2. Adequate planning was in place at the outset
3. Data was collected throughout the project to ensure it was on track
4. Greater emphasis was placed on accountability

Calculating impact has been difficult because, in the Diversity industry as a whole, activity has been confused with impact. Unlike other departments and business units that have a definitive career path and expectation for results, the Office of Diversity and Inclusion often has two problems:
(1) Some organizations hire or promote practitioners without prior experience or formal education in the field of Diversity and Inclusion (2) Some individuals have experience and/or the education, but they are used to "winging it" (e.g., no definition of Diversity, no strategic Diversity plan, no annual evaluation, etc.). In either case, there may be a lot of activity (i.e., travel, events, meetings, training sessions, etc.), but none of these endeavors have real bottom-line impact.

Figure 4 compares and contrasts activity to impact.

FIGURE 4. D&I ACTIVITY VS. IMPACT	
Activity	**Impact**
• Organizing cultural events throughout the year	• Creating a formal Diversity plan with regular interventions and evaluation criteria
• Revising Policies, such as Paid Time Off (PTO)	• Soliciting input and feedback from Supervisors about how the new policies will affect operations and management practices
• Mandatory Diversity Training for all employees	• Providing Diversity & Inclusion Training by Business Unit to demonstrate the link to day-to-day tasks & responsibilities
• Hiring a Diversity Coordinator	• Creating a Succession Plan for the Office of Diversity
• Participating in a Supplier Diversity Fair	• Following up to ensure that those small businesses are added to your list of vendors and that they get contracts
• Recruiting Diverse Candidates	• Training supervisors "how to" model inclusion and manage diverse teams

As figure 4 indicates, some organizations spend thousands of dollars recruiting diverse candidates to no avail. How could a greater impact be created? Before spending money recruiting diverse candidates, find out whether the organization is inclusive in policies, practices, and communications. A simple way to determine the level of inclusiveness at the organization is to ask current employees. Don't just ask the women or the people of color, ask everyone. If or when they make suggestions, vet the ideas. If the ideas are viable, implement them. Not only will this build an inclusive workplace, but it will also stimulate innovation, creativity, and engagement.

When Eli Lilly, a Fortune 500 pharmaceutical giant, conducted its first employee survey more than 20 years ago, senior management was surprised at the Diversity of its workforce. This led to the creation of many work-life programs. Ultimately, Eli Lilly became an award winning, best place to work for talented scientists and health care professionals. Today Eli Lilly does not consider Diversity to be an add-on to their business, nor is it vulnerable to changes in strategic direction. The organization's commitment to Diversity and Inclusion is embedded in the way the company operates. The success of Diversity and Inclusion in an organization as vast as Eli Lilly is the result of it being attached to as many key business metrics, goals, and targeted wins as possible.

Understanding and communicating the essence of true organizational impact, or the business benefits, is key. Diversity representatives often report things like attendance figures, what people like about an event, the number of meetings held, business units served, and/or a new award, as impact. While some of this information provides context, at this stage, none of it indicates impact.

Impact can be indicated by demonstrating changes in sales, productivity, the ability to recruit and retain high quality talent or attract exceptional students, and any other bottom line data point. Similarly, these items are factors that can be incorporated in your business case for Diversity. Other data that signifies impact includes savings from diverse suppliers, favorable publicity, product development, decreases in EEO Complaints/Lawsuits, and other statistics. Additionally, buying patterns, trends, and demographics are changing, thus requiring an adjustment to the organizational strategy for Diversity.

Ralph V. Gilles is a Haitian-American automobile designer. He formerly served as the President and CEO of the SRT Brand and Senior Vice President of Design at Chrysler Group LLC until he was promoted to Head of Design for Fiat/Chrysler. Mr. Gilles served as the executive sponsor of the Chrysler African American Network (CAAN) and is a leading player in The Chrysler Global Diversity Council. Mr. Gilles was responsible for re-designing the Chrysler 300 luxury sedan, which won the most new car awards in history and resulted in over one million vehicles sold around the world. This example of Diversity in Chrysler's senior leadership has led to innovations in product development, efficiencies, and increased sales and publicity—impacting employees, customers, and shareholders.

You can also indicate impact with soft data. However, care must be taken not to base your entire case for Diversity and Inclusion on soft data. In the industry, we have been doing this for years and it has led critics to assume that Diversity does not work. A better strategy is to utilize both soft and hard data to validate impact.

An example of hard data is a quantifiable measure of the turnover rate; an example of soft data is employee satisfaction. Soft data can be converted into hard data, if there is enough statistical evidence to support it. For example, a Sears metric demonstrated that employee attitudes (soft data) were linked directly to customer retention. Sears found that a 0.05% rate of employee dissatisfaction equaled a 1.3% rate of customer dissatisfaction, which translated into a 0.05% revenue loss or $200 million in lost sales. In this instance, it is clear that soft data, quantified in numerical terms, can be valued information for determining the impact on the bottom line.

FIGURE 5. MAKING PROFIT AND LOSS (P&L) SENSE

Strategy + Analysis + Performance = Profit
- Strategic Planning
- Financial Control
- Cycle Time Reduction
- Focused Products
- Continual Improvement
- Motivated Staff
- Training
- Investment

PROFIT

BREAKEVEN

LOSS
- Bad Debts
- Skills Shortages
- Competition
- Rising Costs
- Inefficiencies
- Quality Issues
- Cheap Imports
- Dissatisfied Customers
- Waste (Wrong First Time)

THE P&L BATTLEGROUND

Business performance is determined by many factors other than the level of sales. Even though, the importance of this element should not be underestimated. Figure 5 illustrates the impact that everyday actions, other than sales, will have on business performance and on an organization's profitability. The successful Diversity and HR professional will understand the relationship between the items listed and their short term and long term impact on the organization.

Dr. Edward Hubbard, author and Diversity pioneer, developed a revolutionary process to measure Diversity's impact: the Diversity Scorecard. He describes this process as a balanced, carefully selected set of objectives and measures derived from the organization's strategy that link to the Diversity strategy. According to Dr. Hubbard, professional credibility in the field of diversity and inclusion hinges on one's ability to connect meaningful interventions to the organization's overall strategy.

The measures selected for the Diversity scorecard represent a tool for Diversity leaders to use in communicating Diversity's outcomes and performance drivers by which the organization will achieve its mission and strategic objectives. Executives, managers, employees, and other stakeholders (e.g., board members) can use the Diversity scorecard to determine how their work made an impact as well.

Because each organization's strategy is different (i.e., reflecting distinctions in the industry, types of products/services offered, targeted customers, etc.), key Diversity scorecard perspectives will also vary. Nonetheless, the basic objectives and measures of a Diversity scorecard will generally view the organization's performance from six broad perspectives.

Financial Impact → Diverse Customer/Community Partnerships → Workforce Profile → Workplace Climate/Culture → Diversity Leadership Commitment → Learning & Growth

FIGURE 6. SAMPLE SCORECARD

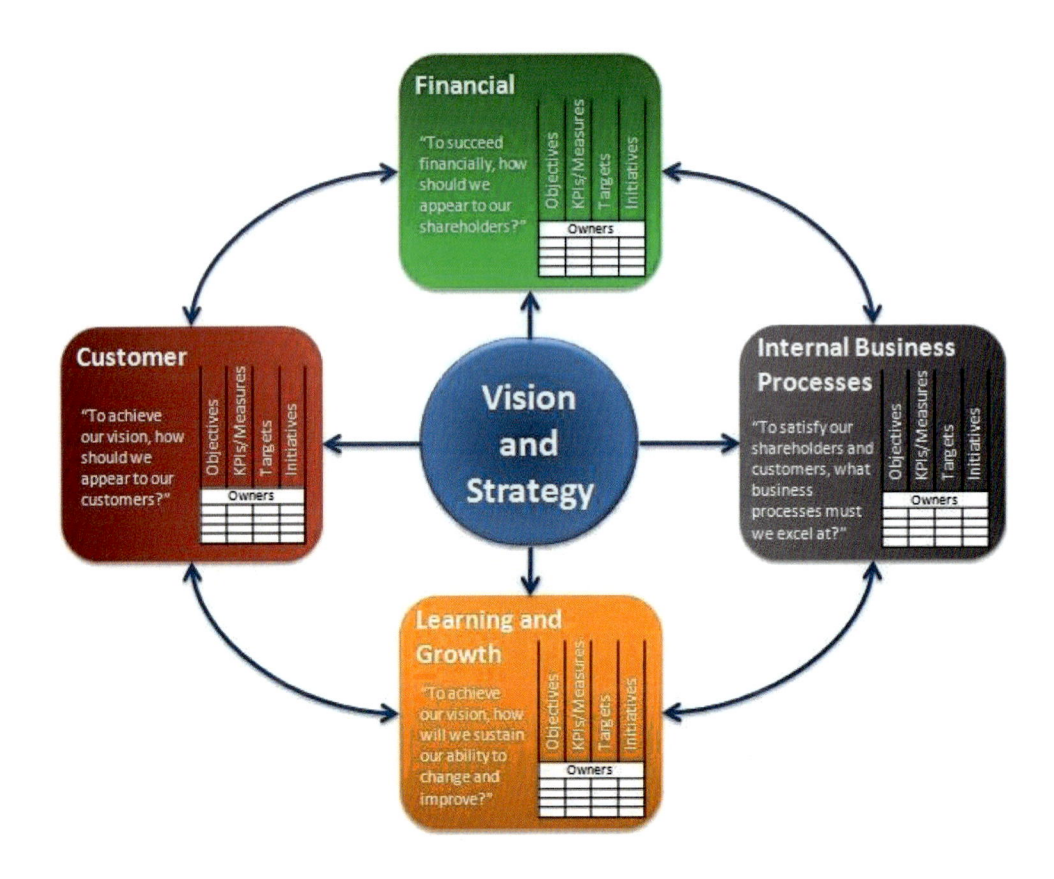

Source: adapted from Kaplan and Norton, 1996

In addition to demonstrating impact through our scorecards, we must also show value.

Value is not defined as a single number. Rather, its definition is composed of a variety of data points. Thus, value must be balanced with qualitative and quantitative data, as well as financial and anecdotal perspectives. This data is sometimes reflected as the Diversity Return on Investment (DROI). Dr. Hubbard asserts, *"A lot of organizations will say they have Diversity measures in place. However, when you check them, you see that they are activity counts. They'll look around and say they've established a council or had a celebration on a particular day. And while those are important, senior leaders don't always see these things as bottom-line outcomes. They're not looking at how the Diversity process increased market penetrations in key ethnic markets or how it added customers."*

As stated throughout this guide, the DROI pertains to financial impacts—how Diversity and Inclusion helps to make money or save it. Calculating the DROI enables Diversity practitioners to demonstrate impact in a way that senior executives value and understand. To calculate the Diversity Return on Investment (DROI), use the steps in Figure 7.

FIGURE 7: HOW TO CALCULATE THE DROI

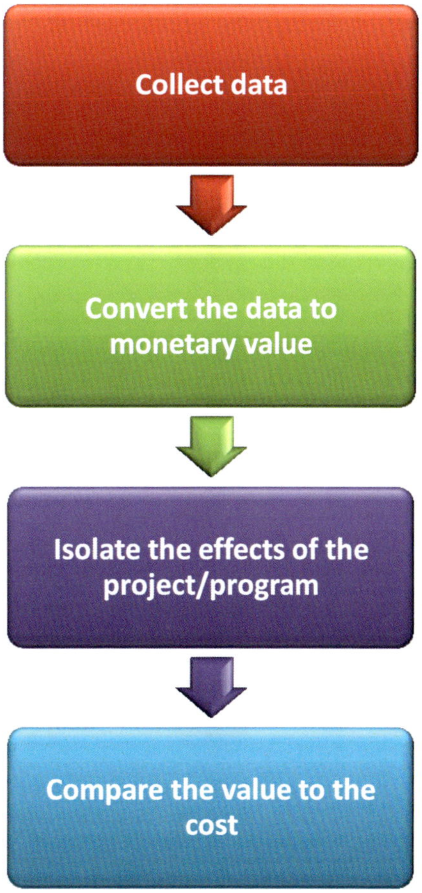

1. Collect data
2. Convert the data to monetary value
3. Isolate the effects of the project/program
4. Compare the value to the cost

Dr. Hubbard adds, *"Getting a handle on ROI means identifying units of measure for the interventions and activities that have a measurable impact on performance. We must consistently apply measurement sciences, track our interventions, and publish them as DROI studies such that they can be used as best practices."*

When calculating the DROI, the benefit or return of an investment is divided by the cost of the investment. The result is expressed as a percentage or a ratio.

FIGURE 8: A SIMPLE DROI FORMULA

$$DROI = \frac{(\text{Gain from Investment} - \text{Cost of Investment})}{\text{Cost of Investment}}$$

CONCLUSION

Essentially, there are four (4) components involved in measuring D&I's impact.

1. *Know what you want to measure; then figure out how to track and calculate impacts over time.*
2. *Regularly assess where you are on the Diversity Development Continuum. Combine quantitative and qualitative data to get deeper insights into how D&I impacted the organization.*
3. *Customize the metrics to reflect what is important to the organization's culture, the business results, and the industry.*
4. *Communicate expectations and accomplishments in a predetermined format on a predetermined schedule.*
5. *Remember to report overall program outcomes, not just individual events or activities.*

Going forward, do as much research on measurement, evaluation, and Diversity return on investment as possible. Dr. Edward Hubbard is a formidable expert in Diversity measurement. He has written almost a dozen books relating to Diversity ROI and impact. In *Diversity Training ROI: How to Measure the Return on Investment of Diversity Training Initiatives,* there is a step-by-step guide to developing a customized measurement plan for your organization. You can purchase Dr. Hubbard's books online, at the SHRM bookstore, or request his book at your local library. As the movement for Diversity measurement evolves, additional reliable resources will be created.

Measuring impact is not a haphazard activity. It encompasses a strategic approach. It takes time and effort to demonstrate the positive effects derived from Equity, Inclusion, interconnectivity, and innovation. The problem is not that we cannot measure the impact of D&I to satisfy our stakeholders. The real issue is that we need to adjust ***how*** we measure and communicate Diversity and Inclusion's impact. Finally, how and what we measure must adjust continuously as the organization progresses through the Diversity Development Continuum. Keep in mind, the purpose of Diversity and Inclusion is to continually advance Equity, Diversity, and Inclusion from one stage to the next.

References:

SHRM Study on Workplace Diversity, 1999. *How Can the Results of Our Diversity Initiative Be Measured?* (pp.27-29)

Jayne, M. E., & Dipboye, R. L. *Leveraging diversity to improve business performance: Research findings and recommendations for organizations.* Human Resource Management, 43, 4, 409-424. 2004.

Kaplan, Robert S., and David P. Norton. *The Balanced Scorecard: Translating Strategy into Action.* Boston: Harvard Business School Press, 1996.

Hubbard, Edward E. *The diversity scorecard: Evaluating the impact of diversity on organizational performance.* Burlington, MA: Elsevier Butterworth. 2004 (first edition: 2003)

Hubbard, Edward E. *Diversity Return on Investment Fundamentals.* Global Insights Publishing. 2015

Hubbard, Edward E. *Diversity Training ROI: How to Measure the Return on Investment of Diversity Training Initiatives.* Global Insights Publishing. 2010

Hubbard, Edward E. *The Power of Diversity ROI Measurement Alignment — Part 2.* Diversity Executive Blog, December 14, 2012. Available at http://blog.diversity-executive.com/2012/12/14/the-power-of-diversity-roi-measurement-alignment-%E2%80%94-part-2/

Sample Test Questions:
MEASURING THE IMPACT OF DIVERSITY & INCLUSION

1. **An organization should evaluate its Diversity and Inclusion efforts based on:**
   A. Financial metrics, namely the Diversity Return on Investment (DROI)
   B. Where the organization is on the Diversity Development Continuum
   C. Whether the organization accomplished its strategic plan goals

2. **In compliant mode, an organization is doing the bare minimum, which is:**
   A. Holding mandatory Diversity training
   B. Recruiting veterans with disabilities
   C. Ensuring compliance with the law

3. **The final outcome of a process, showing a gain or loss, is the:**
   A. Bottom line
   B. Return on Investment
   C. Cost-benefit analysis

4. **A collection of quantitative data that allows for comparison against accepted standards is called:**
   A. Evaluation
   B. An Asset
   C. Measurement

5. **In the field of Diversity and Inclusion, impact can be defined as the quantifiable change in economics, professionals, legal or:**
   A. Social
   B. Planning
   C. Environment

6. **Which of the following areas are NOT included in a Diversity and Inclusion scorecard?**
   A. Customer spending habits
   B. Productivity
   C. Organizational culture

Sample Test Questions:
MEASURING THE IMPACT OF DIVERSITY & INCLUSION (cont'd)

7. Calculating impact has been difficult because, in the Diversity industry as a whole, we have:
   A. Linked Diversity efforts with organizational goals
   B. Been ineffective with Affirmative Action programs
   C. Confused Diversity and Inclusion activities with impact

8. This evaluation and management process provides a carefully balanced view of corporate strategies and Diversity performance.
   A. Strategic Diversity Plan
   B. The Balanced Scorecard
   C. Cultural Climate Analysis

9. The third step in calculating the Diversity Return on Investment is:
   A. Isolate the effects of the program
   B. Collect baseline data from HR
   C. Compare the value to the cost

10. The Diversity thought leader who wrote books on the Diversity Scorecard process and the Diversity Return on Investment is:
    A. Elsie Cross
    B. Dr. Roosevelt Thomas
    C. Dr. Edward Hubbard

11. Diversity is valuable to international business strategies, which is the way of the future.
    A. True
    B. False

12. Competence is the second level of the Diversity Development Continuum.
    A. True
    B. False

13. Indicators act as the gauge of whether, and to what degree, your Diversity and Inclusion effort is making progress.
    A. True
    B. False

ANSWER KEY

CDP ANSWER KEY

The Role of a Diversity Practitioner

1. B
2. B
3. A
4. C
5. C
6. C
7. B
8. C
9. B
10. A
11. C
12. C
13. B
14. A

The Business Case for Diversity & Inclusion

1. C
2. B
3. C
4. A
5. C
6. A
7. C
8. B
9. A
10. A
11. C
12. A
13. B
14. A
15. B

EEO Laws in the U.S. & Abroad

1. A
2. B
3. C
4. C
5. A
6. A
7. A
8. B
9. A
10. B
11. A
12. C
13. C
14. A
15. C

Harassment Around the World

1. C
2. B
3. C
4. B
5. C
6. B
7. C
8. B
9. C
10. A
11. A
12. A
13. B

Diversity Recruiting & Retention

1. A
2. C
3. B
4. A
5. B
6. B
7. C
8. C
9. A
10. A
11. C
12. B
13. B

Reinventing Diversity Training

1. C
2. C
3. C
4. A
5. B
6. A
7. B
8. B
9. A
10. B
11. B
12. B
13. C

CDP ANSWER KEY

Handling Difficult Conversations
1. B
2. C
3. A
4. C
5. A
6. B
7. C
8. C
9. C
10. B
11. A
12. B
13. A

Resource Groups & Diversity Councils
1. B
2. C
3. A
4. B
5. A
6. C
7. A
8. C
9. C
10. B
11. A
12. B
13. A

Empowering Women in the Workplace
1. A
2. B
3. A
4. C
5. C
6. B
7. B
8. A
9. A
10. C
11. B
12. A
13. A

Disability & Special Needs Accommodations
1. C
2. C
3. A
4. A
5. B
6. B
7. A
8. B
9. B
10. A
11. B
12. A
13. A

Generational Intelligence
1. B
2. A
3. A
4. C
5. C
6. B
7. C
8. A
9. A
10. C
11. B
12. B
13. A

Designing Programs for Veterans
1. C
2. C
3. B
4. A
5. C
6. A
7. C
8. B
9. A
10. B
11. C
12. B

CDP ANSWER KEY

Immigrant Groups in the Workplace

1. B
2. A
3. A
4. B
5. A
6. C
7. B
8. C
9. A
10. B
11. B
12. B
13. A

Navigating Through Religion & Belief Systems

1. C
2. B
3. A
4. C
5. C
6. B
7. B
8. B
9. C
10. C
11. B
12. A
13. B

LGBTQ+ Inclusion

1. B
2. B
3. C
4. A
5. B
6. C
7. A
8. B
9. B
10. A
11. C
12. C
13. B

Measuring the Impact of Diversity and Inclusion

1. B
2. C
3. A
4. C
5. C
6. A
7. C
8. B
9. A
10. C
11. A
12. B
13. A

References

Ashford, Jose B. & LeCroy, Craig W. "Human Behavior in the Social Environment: A Multidimensional Perspective", 4th Edition. Belmont, CA. Cengage Learning, 2009

Bennett, Janet M. "Cultural Marginality: Identity Issues in Intercultural Training," in R. Michael Paige, ed. Education for the Intercultural Experience. Milton J. Bennett and Janet M. Bennett, 2000

Bennett, Milton J. "Towards a Developmental Model of Intercultural Sensitivity" in R. Michael Paige, ed. Education for the Intercultural Experience. Yarmouth, ME: Intercultural Press, 1993

Bennett, M. J. (1993). Towards ethnorelativism: A developmental model of intercultural sensitivity (revised). In R. M. Paige (Ed.), Education for the Intercultural Experience. Yarmouth, Me: Intercultural Press.

Bertrand, Marianne & Mullainathan, Sendhil. "Are Emily and Greg More Employable Than Lakisha and Jamal? A Field Experiment in Labor Market Discrimination". *American Economic Review* 94 (4): 991–1013.) September 2004.

Buchanan, D. & Boddy, D. "The Expertise of the Change Agent: Public performance and backstage activity". Prentice Hall. 1992

Butrica, Barbara B.; Iams, Howard M.; and Smith, Karen E. "The Changing Impact of Social Security on Retirement Income in the United States", Social Security Bulletin, Vol. 65 No. 3, 2003/2004

Cabot, L. "Professional development for IT leaders". *Education Quarterly. 1*:54-56. 2006.

Canterucci, Jim: "Are You a Change Leader?" Available at http://www.corpchange.com/archives/article_archives/a19_are_you_a_change_leader/a19_are_you_a_change_leader.htm

Day, H. R. "Race relations training in the military". In D. Landis & R. Brislin (Eds.), Handbook of Intercultural Training, Vol. II: Issues in training methodology (pp. 241-289). New York: Pergamon Press. 1983.

Devine, P. G., & Monteith, M. J. "The role of discrepancy-associated affect in prejudice reduction". In D. Mackie & D. Hamilton (Eds.), Affect, cognition, and stereotyping: Interactive processes in group perception (pp. 137-166), San Diego, CA.: Harcourt, Brace, & Jananovich. 1993.

Digh, P. "Creating a new balance sheet: The need for better diversity metrics". November 2001. Retrieved April 13, 2005, from www.centeronline.org/knowledge/whitepaper.cfm?ID=813&ContentProfileID=122197&Action=searching_.

Dittman, M. "Generational differences at work." Monitor on Psychology. 2005. Retrieved on 11/15/2007 http://www.apa.org/monitor/jun05/generational.html

Dong Olson, Valerie. "Generational Diversity: Implications For Healthcare Leaders". *Journal of Business & Economics Research –Volume 6, Number 1.* November 2008

Dugas, Christine. "Gender Pay Gap Persists", USA Today, October 24, 2012. Retrieved from http://www.usatoday.com/story/money/personalfinance/2012/10/24/gender-pay-gap/1652511/

Durose, Matthew R.; Schmitt, Erica L.; and Langan, Patrick A. "Contacts Between Police and the Public: Findings from the 2002 National Survey. U.S. Department of Justice", (Bureau of Justice Statistics), April 2005.

Gates, S. "Measuring more than efficiency: The new role of human capital metrics." 2004. Retrieved April 13, 2005, from www.conference-board.org.

Goldsmith, Marshall. "4 Tips for Efficient Succession Planning", Harvard Business Review Blog. May 2009. Available at http://blogs.hbr.org/goldsmith/2009/05/change_succession_planning_to.html

Greenberg, Josh. "Increasing Employee Retention Through Employee Engagement", Ezine Articles. 2004. Available at http://ezinearticles.com/?Increasing-Employee-Retention-Through-Employee-Engagement&id=10575

Hansen, Fay. "Diversity's Business Case Doesn't Add Up", p. 28-32, Workforce Management Magazine, April 2003

Hubbard, Edward E. "The diversity scorecard: Evaluating the impact of diversity on organizational performance". Burlington, MA: Elsevier Butterworth. 2004.

Hubbard, Edward E. "The Power of Diversity ROI Measurement Alignment — Part 2". Diversity Executive Blog, December 14, 2012. Available at http://blog.diversity-executive.com/2012/12/14/the-power-of-diversity-roi-measurement-alignment-%E2%80%94-part-2/

Jayne, M. E., & Dipboye, R. L. "Leveraging diversity to improve business performance: Research findings and recommendations for organizations". Human Resource Management, 43, 4, 409-424. 2004.

Kanter, Rosabeth Moss: "The Enduring Skills of Change Leaders." In Leader to Leader, Nr. 13 Summer 1999. Available at http://www.pfdf.org/leaderbooks/l2l/summer99/kanter.html

Kirkpatrick, D. "The Human Resources Program Evaluation Model, *Evaluating Training Programs*", 1994.

Kupperschmidt, B. "Addressing multigenerational conflict: Mutual respect and carefronting as strategy". *Online Journal of Issues in Nursing,11*(2):4. 2006.

Lamb, Robert, Boyden. "Competitive strategic management," Englewood Cliffs, NJ: Prentice-Hall, 1984

Leibman, M., Bruer, R., & Maki, B. "Succession management: The next generation of succession planning". *Human Resource Planning, 19*. 1996.

Manzoni, Jean-Francois, Strebel, Paul, and Barsoux, Jean-Louis. "Why Diversity Can Backfire on Company Boards" The Wall Street Journal, January 25, 2010

Miles, Stephen A. "Succession Planning: How To Do It Right", Forbes.com, July 2009. Available at http://www.forbes.com/2009/07/31/succession-planning-right-leadership-governance-ceos.html.

Munnell, Alicia H., and Annika Sundén. "Coming Up Short: The Challenge of 401(k) Plans." Washington, DC: Brookings Institution Press, 2004

Noble, S., Schewe, C., & Kuhr, M. "Preferences in health care service and treatment: A generational perspective". *Science Direct, 57*(9):1033-1041. 2004.

Norris, Donald M., Joelle, M.C. *"Winning with Diversity – A Practical Handbook for Creating Inclusive Meetings, Events and Organizations,"* Fignole Lofton, 1995.

Ogunjimi, A. "What are the benefits of diversity councils?" Ehow. November 2010. Available at: What Are the Benefits of Diversity Councils? | eHow.com http://www.ehow.com/about_7549534_benefits-diversity-councils.html#ixzz1McSJMvLv

Jney, Angie. "How to Measure Diversity Training". e-How. 2011. Available at: How to Measure Diversity Training | eHow.co.uk http://www.ehow.co.uk/how_8320277_measure-diversity-training.html#ixzz1M9EePOFI

Ostrower, Francie. "Nonprofit Governance in the United States", The Urban Institute, 2007

Puckett, C. "Administering Social Security: Challenges Yesterday and Today". Social Security Bulletin, Vol. 70, No. 3, 2010

Raines, C. *"Connecting Generations: The Sourcebook."* Crisp Publication. 2003.

Recklies, Dagmar. "What Makes a Good Change Agent?", October 2001. Available at http://www.themanager.org/Strategy/change_agent.htm

Sherman, R. "Leading a multigenerational nursing workforce: Issues, challenges and strategies". *Online Journal of Issues in Nursing,* 11(2):3. 2006.

Smola, K. & Sutton, C. "Generational differences: revisiting generational work values for the new millennium". *Journal of Organizational Behavior.* 23(4):363-382. 2002.

Stachura, Jim & Murphy, M. "Multicultural Marketing: Why One Size Doesn't Fit All", 2005. Available at: http://www.marketingprofs.com/articles/2005/1652/multicultural-marketing-why-one-size-doesnt-fit-all#ixzz1MBa4J0WC Available at: http://www.marketingprofs.com/articles/2005/1652/multicultural-marketing-why-one-size-doesnt-fit-all#ixzz1MBZcONBO

Stanley, K. "Age to age: Insight into managing a multigenerational staff". *Journal of Medical Practice Management,* 22(5):269-75. 2007.

Schwarz, R. "Why managing generational differences is important." Retrieved on 5/10/08 http://www.marsvenusatwork.com/generations/htm

Sokou, Katerina. "The surprising reason we need more women in the global workforce." July 2, 2013. Available at: http://www.washingtonpost.com/blogs/wonkblog/wp/2013/07/02/the-surprising-reason-we-need-more-women-in-the-global-workforce/

Vaughn, B.E. "Diversity Pioneers In The History Of Diversity Education", Ezine Articles, 2008. Available at: http://EzineArticles.com/988500

Vaughn, B. E. "Heuristic model of managing emotions in race relations training". In E. Davis-Russell (Ed.), Multicultural Education, Research, Intervention, & Training (pp. 296-318). San Francisco, CA.: Jossey-Bass. 2002.

Whalen, Charles & Barbara. "The History of Affirmative Action Policies; Americans for Fair Chance", The Longest Debate, page 116, Seven Locks Press 1985

Wildman, Stephanie M.; Armstong, Margalynne; Davis, Adrienne D.; Grillo, Trina. "Privilege Revealed: How Invisible Preference Undermines America". New York: NYU Press. 1996.
Wiseman, M. & Yčas, M. "The Canadian Safety Net for the Elderly", Social Security Bulletin, Vol. 68 No. 2, 2008

Diversity/The Bottom Line Beyond HR, "Creating A Culturally Diverse Organization: 10 Keys to Success", The Kaleel Jamison Consulting Group.

"How Can the Results of Our Diversity Initiative Be Measured?" *Workplace Diversity- A Product of the SHRM Diversity Initiative,* 1999.

FREQUENTLY UTILIZED REFERENCES

- www.wikipedia.org
- www.eeoc.gov
- www.dol.gov
- www.ssa.gov
- www.census.gov
- www.ehow.com
- www.shrm.org
- www.diversityinc.com
- www.hbr.org